CHICAGO AND COOK COUNTY SOURCES

A Genealogical and Historical Guide

By *Loretto Dennis Szucs*

Ancestry Publishing

P.O. Box 476
Salt Lake City, UT 84110

Library of Congress Catalog Card Number 86-072002
ISBN Number 0-916489-12-4 (Hardbound)
ISBN Number 0-916489-17-5 (Paperback)

First Printing 1986
10 9 8 7 6 5 4 3

Printed in the United States of America

Contents

Introduction

N
o history can be written or genealogy compiled without a precise knowledge of available resources. Yet, the sheer magnitude of Chicago and Cook County records, and the complications of bureaucratic barriers, present such formidable challenges that a complete knowledge of sources is almost impossible without the benefit of many years of experience or a very comprehensive guide. Without one or both of these, any research project can be quite overwhelming. This book has been especially designed as a guide to the abundant Chicago and Cook County family and local history sources.

There are several obstacles hindering research in the Chicago/Cook County area. Foremost among the county's problems is its great size. The density of its population is multiplied hundreds of times over by the volume of records created by millions of people. Management of these records is no easy task. In fact, the Illinois state-wide Historical Records Needs Survey Assessment *Final Report* (1982) singled out this area as having the most critical records problem in Illinois. No archival program for historical records existed, and no records management system was in place. The fact that Cook County has "Home Rule" tends to confuse further those accustomed to research policies of other Illinois counties. It has been frequently stated that Cook County is a "state unto itself."

The 1980 census counted 5.1 million residents in Cook County, which means that roughly half the citizens of Illinois live in that metropolitan area. Since 1871, there are records of 7,237,802 live births; 3,785,893 marriages; and 4,120,916 deaths in Cook County. Records of delayed births, still births, coroner's death records, and miscellaneous other vitals give the County Clerk the responsibility of caring for nearly 40 million records. This number would be substantially inflated if it were not for the Great Chicago Fire which destroyed all previous vital statistic recordings. On a typical day, one thousand requests are processed by the Office of the County Clerk, giving it the distinction of being the world's busiest vital statistics office. A description of the types of records kept, available indices, location of records, and access policies as presented in this guide can save wasted time, expense, and frustration.

Chicago and its 116 incorporated suburbs comprise the major portion of Cook County, and are divided into over 1.5 million parcels of real estate. Those figures grow as large acreages of farmlands are subdivided for residential and other uses. Recorded deeds and tract books hold treasures of information, but tracing property history and locating documents are not as easy as in less populated areas. Because of the great number of property transactions in Cook County, the grantor-grantee indexing system is not practical. The description of the records, the record-keeping system, and a step-by-step guide to tracing real estate property given in this volume can eliminate much of the confusion associated with these records.

The Circuit Court of Cook County is the largest trial court in the world. Court files kept over the years now number over 75 million and are expanding at a rate of over 5 million a year. Court documents are so numerous that they are stored in nine storage locations. Unbiased history, recorded in its original form, is hidden away in this mass of case files. The types of available records, some examples of interesting cases, the research potential they hold, and their locations and procedures for accessing files are presented in the section on Court Records.

As an industrial center, a transportation center, and for a long time America's fastest growing city, Chicago drew millions. But it was only a temporary residence for many, and some moved so frequently that their presence in the area is difficult to document. Finding records for this transient segment of the population is often the most difficult of research problems, and it becomes necessary to go beyond the commonly used vital, court, and census records. The reader will find the alternative sources suggested in this volume most helpful.

The Chicago area was first settled predominantly by New Englanders and New Yorkers. German and Irish came in great numbers from the mid to late nineteenth century, and Italians, Russian Jews, and Poles flooded into the area early in this century. A migration of blacks from the south, Mexicans, and Asians added substantially to the ethnic diversity in later years. At different times in its history, Chicago has been the largest Lithuanian city, the second largest Bohemian city, the second largest Ukrainian city, and the third largest Swedish, Irish, Polish, and Jewish city in the world. Knowing the unique record collections that exist for each of the ethnic groups can mean the difference between success or failure in research attempts. Presenting the many available yet harder to find ethnic sources is one of the primary goals of this work.

Church records are acceptable supplements to civil vital records and are considered primary sources. These documents fill gaps where official county records are missing, and they often include important facts not found in other sources. Finding the records of religious congregations in the Chicago metropolitan area is especially difficult because of the great number of churches and synagogues supported by the enormous population for over 150 years. Population, geography, and ethnic differences make searching for religious records problem enough; but over the years some institutions closed, consolidated, and moved as neighborhoods changed. An especially large section of this book is devoted to information on church and religious records which, though more difficult to locate, are valuable sources.

The havoc wrought by the Chicago fire which began in Mrs. O'Leary's barn on 8 October 1871 continues to threaten the success of research projects previous to that date. Many primary sources disappeared and critical documents were destroyed. It wouldn't be honest to say that every pre-fire case is solvable, but an educated approach and some idea of alternative sources is critical. The checklist of existing and often little known pre-fire sources included in this guide can offer new possibilities for that very challenging time period. The same sense of determination that rebuilt Chicago after the fire of 1871 may be equally necessary for reconstructing a family or local history.

There is an abundance of rich sources for local and family history in Cook County. If researchers are thwarted by problems which are a result of a massive population in one respect, they are compensated at least in part by the fact that the size of the city and county has created sources not available in less-populated areas. Besides the original records held by governmental agencies, Cook County has excellent research centers such as the Newberry Library, the National Archives—Chicago Branch, the Chicago Historical Society, the Municipal Reference Library, and the Chicago Public Library.

There are literally hundreds of archives, libraries, churches, cemeteries, and other potential research centers in Cook County, but unless one has worked regularly in this area, important resources can be easily overlooked. Changes in community, town, street names, ward boundaries, and even court jurisdictions can complicate or even block research progress. Locating record sources and knowing where to find answers to changed names and jurisdictions can eliminate hours of wasted time.

This book is the result of a prolonged and careful survey of available sources. Further, it is an outgrowth of the experiences of the author who had the privilege of working with many others who willingly shared their knowledge and expertise. Doing genealogical research for so many individuals with Cook County ancestry, working for inheritance researchers, writing for genealogical journals, and becoming fascinated with the rich history of Cook County contributed to the compilation of this much needed guide. The project evolved from a pamphlet which was compiled as a handout for a seminar given at the Illinois State Genealogical Conference in 1981. Until that time there were no such guides available for doing Cook County research.

The contributing authors have greatly enhanced the value of this volume by sharing their expertise. Their first-hand experience with the records they describe provides another important dimension to Chicago and Cook County research.

Although *Chicago and Cook County Sources* is intended as a research guide, no attempt has been made to give instructions for doing genealogical research. There are a host of how-to books available in libraries and bookstores which provide information necessary for getting started. Special effort was made to address the unique problems in Cook County research. Greatest attention was given to the collections of interest to genealogists and historians, while others appear only in the form of an address list. The mere mention of the existence of a source is sometimes enough to trigger an investigation, and for this reason they were included. In most sections, records are thoroughly described. The less commonly known sources and those which are unique to the area are dicussed with an explanation of what they are, why they were created, and how to use them.

To catalog all of the sources available for Cook County genealogical and historical research would take more than a lifetime. It is hoped that the information provided here will acquaint genealogists, historians, journalists, students, and teachers with the wealth of documentation that exists in this area, and will help facilitate research. Better than all the handed-down history in the world is the experience of being personally involved in research and reconstructing the lives and times of those who are long dead.

ACKNOWLEDGEMENTS

This kind of a project, with its widely divergent sources, required the assistance of many. Every effort was made to be accurate and up to date with the information presented here. Custodians of almost all the collections mentioned were consulted and many generous people have provided guidance.

From the outset, my husband, Bob, played a vital role by providing technical assistance with a new and often user-unfriendly computer.

He and our daughters, Juliana, Diana, Patricia, and Laura, showed remarkable patience waiting for a book they thought would never end.

I am deeply indebted to the contributing authors, Peter Bunce, Brian Donovan, Linda Lamberty, Sandra Luebking, Ron Otto, Herbert Post, Diane Schweitzer, and Patricia Szucs.

Father Charles Banet, President of Saint Joseph's College; Peter Bunce of the National Archives—Chicago Branch; Brian Donovan, President of the Northwest Suburban Council of Genealogists; Linda Lamberty, Professional Genealogist; Sandra Luebking, First Vice President of the Illinois State Genealogical Society; Jayare Roberts of The Library of the Church of Jesus Christ of Latter-day Saints, Salt Lake City; Ralph Schneider of the Chicago Public Library; David Thackery of the Newberry Library; Lowell M. Volkel, Senior Archivist of the Illinois State Archives; David Weber, formerly of the National Archives—Chicago Branch; Bob Welsh of Ancestry; and my daughter Tricia all gave invaluable encouragement, suggestions, and editorial assistance throughout the project. There isn't any way I could have ever accomplished this work without them.

Others who helped significantly in this work were: June Barekman of the Chicago Genealogical Society who shared so much of her knowledge and materials on Cook County; Doris Bowers, Past President of the Illinois State Genealogical Society was responsible for the publication of the pamphlet which was the basis for this expanded publication; Noel Barton of the Genealogical Society of Utah contributed information and made important suggestions regarding the format of the book.

For information on the Vital Records section I wish to thank Stanley Kusper, County Clerk. Michael Fish, Director, Bureau of Vital Statistics, and James Romberg, Deputy Director-Vital Records went out of their way to help in providing important information and editorial suggestions.

For the section on court records, I appreciate the assistance offered by Sam Fink, Attorney at Law. Additionally, valuable assistance was given by Robert Williams, Supervisor, Law Division of the Circuit Court, and Anthony Girolami, Associate Clerk of the Probate Division.

Kenneth Grenier, Land Survey Officer, Chicago Title and Trust provided much needed help with the section on land records. John Sullivan provided expert help in emergency situations with the computer.

At the Chicago Historical Society, Janice McNeil, Librarian; Archie Motley, Curator of Archives and Manuscripts; and Larry Viskochil, Curator of Prints and Photographs graciously verifed the information regarding the Society.

Shirley J. Burton, Thomas Kruski, and Kenneth Shanks of the National Archives—Chicago Branch Staff went out of their way to extend help in several phases of the project.

Others who provided generous help in the project were: Sheila Aszling, President of the Chicago Genealogical Society; Stanley Balzekas, President of Balzekas Museum of Lithuanian Culture; Edmund J. Brophy, Research Consultant; Dr. Dominic Candeloro, Governors State University; Elaine Shemoney-Evans, IRAD Co-Ordinator; Morgan M. Finley, Clerk of Cook County Circuit Court; John Gambro, O.P., Fenwick High School; Tom Kane of The Printer's Quill; Mary Lambertino of The Charlie Club; Carol Schiffman, President of Genealogy Unlimited; Peggy Tuck Sinko, formerly Curator at The Newberry Library; James Walsh, Administrator, Office of The Medical Examiner; and Edmund B. Zygmunt, President, Landex Research.

CHAPTER 1

Chicago and Cook County Facts

CHICAGO FACTS

Town of Chicago incorporated .... 12 August 1833
Population 350
City of Chicago incorporated .... 4 March 1837
Population 4,170
1980 Chicago Population 3,005,072
1980 Six-County Metropolitan Area Population 7,103,624

Geography
Area (square miles) 228.126
Length (miles) 25.0
Breadth (miles) 15.0
Lake front (miles of shoreline) 29.0
City block (average size) .... 330'x 660'or 5 acres

100 numbers equal one block
Eight city blocks, or 800 numbers equal one mile.
Five city blocks, or 500 numbers equal one kilometer.
North and south street numbers are divided by Madison Street.
East and west streets are divided by State Street.
Even numbered buildings are on the north and the west sides of the street.
Uneven numbered buildings are on the south and the east sides of the street.
Lake Michigan is always on the east.

THE CHICAGO WATER TOWER

The Chicago Water Tower has played a major role in the city's history since it was constructed during the years 1867-69. Built in an architectural style called "castellated Gothic," the water tower is made

Figure 1. *The Chicago Water Works and Tower—1870*
(courtesy The Chicago Historical Society)

of rough-faced yellow limestone from quarries near Joliet. It was designed by William W. Boyington. After the Great Chicago Fire of 1871, the water tower was one of the few buildings to survive without being burned. It came to symbolize the city's ability to overcome calamity. The tower has remained as one of the city's best known landmarks and was officially designated as such by the Chicago City Council in 1971. The adaptive redesign of the water tower as a visitor information center has been coordinated by the Chicago Convention and Tourism Bureau.

CHICAGO CONVENTION AND TOURISM BUREAU, INC.
McCormick Place-on-the-Lake
Chicago, IL 60616
(312-225-5000)

COOK COUNTY FACTS

Created . . . . 15 January 1831
    Named after Daniel P. Cook; Member of Congress and first Attorney of the State of Illinois
Area . . . . 956 square miles
Suburban cities and municipalities . . . . 444 square miles
Unincorporated areas . . . . 285 square miles
Incorporated cities and villagse 126
1980 Cook County population . . . . 5.1 million

Two Chicago buildings constitute the seat of Cook County government. The Richard J. Daley Center (formerly called the Civic Center) towers above the old County Courthouse, sometimes known as the County Building. Together they house the courts, the elective county offices, and many county and city departments. Notable is the famous Picasso sculpture in the courtyard of the Daley Center. Construction of the County Building, with its classic pillars, was begun in 1906 and completed in 1907. Daley Center construction was started in 1963 and completed in 1966.

Cook County is the only home-rule county in the state of Illinois and the only county with a directly elected executive officer. It is governed by an elected president and board of commissioners, ten from the city of Chicago and five from suburban Cook County.

Cook County may exercise all powers as a local government unless preempted by the state or limited by the Constitution, as long as its ordinances do not conflict with ordinances of municipalities within the county. It carries out state policy, enforces law, prosecutes offenders, keeps records including vital statistics, issues marriage licenses, conducts elections, assesses property, and collects and distributes taxes for all taxing bodies within the county.

A CHRONOLOGY OF CHICAGO AND COOK COUNTY HISTORY

1673 Father Marquette and Louis Joliet are the first known Europeans to explore the region.

1696 Father Pierre Pinet establishes the short-lived Mission of the Guardian Angels.

1779 Jean Baptiste Point DuSable builds a trading post and establishes a permanent settlement on the Chicago River near the current location of the Tribune Tower.

1795 Indian Tribes give the U.S. government land at the mouth of the "Chikago River" as part of the Treaty of Greenville.

1803 Captain John Whistler and Lieutenant James S. Swearingen, U.S.A., with a company of United States regular infantry, build and establish the first Fort Dearborn.

1804 John Kinzie and his family, the first American civilians, settle in Chicago. First white child born in Chicago, Ellen Marion Kinzie, daughter of John and Eleanor Kinzie.

1810 First doctor arrives in Chicago, John Cooper, surgeon's mate, U.S.A., detailed for duty at Fort Dearborn. Illinois Pottawatomies begin hostilities against the whites. Attention of government drawn to scheme of canal connecting Lake Michigan with Mississippi River.

1812 (15 August) Fort Dearborn massacre. 16 August, Indians burn Fort Dearborn.

1816 Fort Dearborn rebuilt, Indian agency and warehouse reestablished and John Kinzie and family return to Chicago to live.

1817 Schooners *Baltimore* and *Hercules* establish routes between Chicago and Mackinac.

1818 Illinois admitted to the Union as a state. First large sailing vessel, the United States revenue cutter *Fairplay*, enters the Chicago River.

1822 First baptism in Chicago, Alexander Beaubien baptized by Rev. Stephen D. Badin.

1823 Illinois and Michigan Canal bill passed by legislature. First marriage is celebrated in Chicago, that of Dr. Alexander Wolcott and Miss Ellen Marion Kinzie.

1825 New York's Erie Canal is completed, providing immigrants and manufactured goods a greater access to Chicago via the Great Lakes.

1826 First gubernatorial and congressional elections held in Chicago.

1827 First company of state militia organized. First slaughterhouse built on north branch by Archibald Clybourne.

1828 Fort Dearborn regarrisoned by United States troops. John Kinzie, first settler, died at Fort Dearborn.

1829 First ferry established, near present site of Lake Street bridge. "Wolf Tavern," Chicago's first hotel, built by James Kinzie and Archibald Caldwell, at the "forks" of the Chicago River.

1830 Chicago's population is about 50. Chicago first surveyed and platted. First bridge built across Chicago River (south branch) near Randolph Street crossing.

1831 Cook County created and Chicago designated as the county seat. First county election held. First county roads established, the present State Street and Archer Avenue, and Madison Street and Ogden Avenue. First lighthouse constructed.

1832 First frame building, Robert A. Kinzie's store, on the West Side. First drug store established by Philo Carpenter. Black Hawk war broke out and four companies of volunteers are organized in Chicago and go to the front. First cholera epidemic in Chicago brought by United States troops on steamer *Sheldon Thompson*.

1833 Village or town of Chicago incorporated (350 inhabitants). First issue of first Chicago newspaper, the *Chicago Democrat*, a weekly, by John Calhoun. First Roman Catholic priest to establish a permanent parish. Rev. John Mary Ireneus St. Cyr arrived in Chicago and established St. Mary's parish. First Presbyterian church organized by Rev. Jeremiah Porter, chaplain U.S.A. First Baptist church erected. First appropriation for harbor commenced. First fire marshall, Benjamin Jones, appointed, then known as "fire warden." First shipment from port of Chicago by Newberry and Dole on Schooner *Napoleon*. First Tremont house built.

1834 First authorized town loan. First Protestant Episcopal church, St. James, established by Rev. Isaac W. Hallam. First mail coach route established by Dr. John T. Temple between Chicago and Detroit. First drawbridge erected over Chicago River, at Dearborn Street. First vessels navigate Chicago River, Steamer *Michigan* in June and Schooner *Illinois* in July. First divorce suit and murder trial.

1835 First bank established in Chicago known as the Chicago Branch of the Illinois State Bank. Opening of United States land office: great land craze. First board of health organized. Volunteer fire department organized. First courthouse erected, corner Clark and Randolph Streets. After the Indians' defeat in the Black Hawk War of 1832, and because of the treaties of 1833 and 1835, the Potawatomis and other Indian tribes begin leaving for lands promised to them west of the Mississippi River.

1836 First spadeful of earth thrown out in digging Illinois and Michigan Canal, 4 July. First sailing vessel, *Clarissa,* launched May, 1836. First house built from architectural designs, for William B. Ogden. First Chicago railroad chartered, Galena and Chicago Union Railroad. First water mains laid, two miles of wooden pipe.

1837 City of Chicago created. First city election held and William B. Ogden becomes the Chicago's first mayor. First census taken, population 4,107. First great financial panic. First theater opened.

1838 First steam fire engine bought by Chicago. First Chicago steamer, the *James Allen* built. First invoice of wheat, exported from Chicago.

1839 First great fire in Chicago. A steamship line between Chicago and Buffalo, New York makes the round trip in sixteen days.

1840 Reorganization and permanent establishment of free public schools.

1841 Office of city marshal created.

1843 First book compiled, printed, bound, and issued in Chicago (1843 Chicago Directory).

1844 First university (St. Mary's of the Lake), established.

1845 Cook County Court established. First permanent school (Dearborn School) building erected. First power printing press brought to Chicago by "Long John Wentworth" and used by him in printing the *Chicago Democrat.*

1847 First county hospital opened in "Tippecanoe Hall." First law school opened. McCormick, inventor of the reaper, starts making farm implements.

1848 Illinois and Michigan Canal opens. First United States Court opens. Chicago and Galena Union Railroad is built. First telegram received in Chicago (from Milwaukee). First smallpox epidemic and first vaccination. Chicago Board of Trade was founded.

1849 Third cholera epidemic. Bank panic. Great storm and flood; over $100,000 damage to vessels, wharfs, etc. Chicago's second big fire—twenty buildings destroyed.

1850 Chicago's population is 29,963. Fifty percent are foreign immigrants. City first lighted by gas. First opera performed in city. Stephen A. Douglas delivered his great speech in Chicago.

1851 Chicago, Rock Island, and Pacific and the Chicago, Milwaukee, and St. Paul railroads organized.

1852 City waterworks operated for first time. First through train from the east enters Chicago over the Michigan Southern Railroad, 20 February. First railroad wreck, passenger trains on Michigan Central and Michigan Southern railroads collide at Grand Crossing; eighteen killed. Office of superintendent of schools created. Northwestern University founded.

1853 First labor strike. A horse-drawn omnibus service becomes the city's first form of mass transit.

1854 Cholera epidemic claimed nearly 1,500 lives.

1855 "Beer riot." Main line of Illinois Central Railroad completed, and with ten major lines, Chicago has become a prominent railroad center. Police department created. Direct drainage into river inaugurated. The city began raising level of streets up to twelve feet to fill in swampy areas and improve drainage.

1856 First steam tugs in river. First suburban trains. First high school opened. First sewers laid. First iron bridge built at Rush Street.

1857 Destructive fire; twenty-three lives lost, and $500,000 in property loss. Great financial panic.

1858 First street car run in State Street. Paid fire department organized.

1859 Street car franchises granted by state legislature. The first horse-drawn railway went into operation.

1860 Chicago's population is 112,172. Loss of steamer *Lady Elgin* results in 203 deaths.

1861 Outbreak of Civil War and establishment of Camp Douglas at current location of 31st and King Drive is used as a prison for Confederate soldiers until the Civil War's conclusion in 1865.

1862 First internal revenue collector appointed.

1863 City limits extended to take in Bridgeport.

1864 Work commenced on first lake tunnel.

1865 First lake crib placed. Union Stockyards were established to consolidate all slaughterhouses into one area. Fire alarm telegraph inaugurated.

1867 Lake tunnel completed, new waterworks building and tower erected. A sanitary water system was installed.

1870 Chicago's population is 298,977.

1871 The Great Chicago Fire of 8-10 October destroys an area nearly five miles long and one mile wide. About 300 people die and almost 100,000 are left homeless. A newspaper reports that Catherine O'Leary and her cow were responsible for starting the fire, but no evidence is found to support that accusation. Loss of property amounts to $280,000,000. City reincorporated under general law.

1872 Ordinance outlawing wooden buildings in downtown area.

1873 United States Subtreasury established. Second serious financial panic. As a symbol of Chicago's growth after the Great Fire, an Inter-State Industrial Exposition is held.

1877 Savings bank crash. Chicago's first telephones are installed.

1880 Chicago's population is 503,185. George Pullman built his car shop and the town of Pullman.

1882 Cable cars first operated by Chicago City Railway Company.

1883 Courthouse and city hall completed.

1885 The nine-story Home Insurance Building is erected. Its skeletal construction of iron and steel beams leads the way to future.

1886 Anarchists riots in the Haymarket.

1889 Sanitary district of Chicago created. Jane Addams and Ellen Gates Starr open Hull House to aid immigrants.

1890 Chicago's population is 1,099,850. The city has 2,048 miles of streets, but only 629 miles are paved. About half are paved with wooden blocks.

1892 First elevated road built. Ground broken for Drainage Canal. University of Chicago founded. Electric streetcars (trolleys) and a steam-powered, elevated railway system (the "El") begin widespread service. The "El" system is converted to electric power in 1897. Telephone lines connect Chicago to New York and Boston.

1893 World's Columbian Exposition held. Mayor Carter H. Harrison, Sr. assassinated.

1894 Third financial panic. Pullman car plant strike led to a railroad strike.

1897 Chicago Loop encircled by new "El" lines.

1898 Union Elevated Loop built.

1899 Drainage canal opened. Corner stone of new federal building laid, "Chicago Day," 9 October, by President William McKinley. The number of automobiles rises this year from three to over 300. By 1901, an eight mph speed limit is established.

1900 Chicago's population is 1,698,575. Chicago Sanitary and Ship Canal opened; flow of Chicago River reversed so that sewage no longer flows into Lake Michigan.

1903 Chicago Centennial celebration; Iroquois Theater fire with loss of 575 (or 603) lives.

1906 Municipal Court of Chicago established doing away with old justice court system.

1907 New Cook County Courthouse (County Building) completed at a total cost of $5,000,000. New street railway ordinances passed and work of rebuilding lines begun.

1908 William H. Taft nominated for President at the National Republican Convention held in Coliseum. City Hall razed in order to build a new structure.

1909 The Chicago Plan was originated by Daniel Burnham and streets were renumbered.

1910 Chicago's population is 2,185,283.

1911 Present day City Hall and County Building was completed. Carter H. Harrison, Jr. elected mayor for a fifth term.

1914 A freight subway system beneath the Loop relieves traffic congestion by transporting merchandise, coal, and garbage through sixty-two miles of tunnels.

1915 The excursion steamer *Eastland* overturned in the Chicago River killing 812 people.

1916 Municipal Pier, later called Navy Pier, is completed for passenger and freight vessels.

1917 Motor coaches (buses) begin operations in the city.

1919 A violent race riot leaves fifteen whites and twenty-three blacks dead.

1920 Chicago's population is 2,701,705. The Michigan Avenue Bridge was completed.

1924 Despite prohibition, there were at least fifteen breweries and 20,000 retail alcoholic beverage outlets operating illegally in Chicago.

1927 Chicago's first municipal airport, later called Midway Airport, opens.

1929 Gangsters machine-gun seven of Al Capone's enemies in the St. Valentine's Day Massacre.

1930 Chicago's population is 3,376,438.

1932 Due to the nationwide depression, more than 750,000 Chicagoans (nearly one-quarter of the city's population) are out of work. Only fifty-one of the city's 228 banks are still open.

1933 The Century of Progress Exposition ran successfully for two years.

1940 Chicago's population is 3,396,808.

1942 The world's first controlled atomic reaction is achieved at the University of Chicago.

1943 Chicago's first passenger subway was opened beneath State Street.

1950 Chicago's population reaches all-time high of 3,620,962. The population of the entire six-county metropolitan area is 5,177,868.

1953 Chicago becomes the world's steel capital.

1955 Richard J. Daley is elected mayor. He serves six consecutive terms until his death in 1975. O'Hare Airport opens and goes on to become the world's busiest airport.

1956 The Congress Expressway, later called the Eisenhower Expressway, is the first high-speed automobile route to open in the city.

1959 St. Lawrence Seaway opens.

1960 Chicago's population is 3,550,404.

1968 Riots and fires occur in parts of Chicago's West Side following news of the assassination of Dr. Martin Luther King, Jr.

1970 Chicago's population is 3,369,357.

1971 The Union Stockyards close.

1974 The world's tallest building, the 110-story Sears Tower is erected.

1979 Jane M. Byrne is elected Chicago's first woman mayor.

1980 Chicago's population is 3,005,072. The population of the entire six-county metropolitan area is 7,102,328.

Further details about the people and events highlighted in this chronology and about ethnic groups, politics, industry, labor, and architecture can be found in the bibliography.

CHICAGO FIRE AND PRE-FIRE SOURCE CHECKLIST

The Great Chicago Fire of 1871 began Sunday, 8 October, in a barn behind the Patrick O'Leary home at 137 (now 558 West) De Koven Street. Although the actual cause of the fire is unknown, over a dozen theories have been advanced, the most common being that Mrs. O'Leary's cow kicked over a lighted lantern.

At that time, Chicago, a city built almost entirely of wood, was experiencing a severe draught. During the week preceding the Great Fire, there had been many serious fires. The Great Fire that began the following evening quickly spread north and east from the O'Leary barn, ironically sparing their home but rapidly destroying houses, fences, sidewalks, and other structures—almost entirely constructed of dry, resinous pine.

The fire spread rapidly, at a rate of about six miles an hour or fifteen feet a minute. The wind carried flaming debris which ignited new fires as they settled in new spots.

Although the fire had begun west of the south branch of the Chicago River, most of the damage was concentrated east of the river's North and South branches. The burned area—4 3/4 miles long and averaging a mile wide—covered 3.32 square miles or 2,124 acres, including the entire central business district. Lost were 17,450 buildings and much of the city's industrial capacity. About 98,500 people were left homeless by the conflagration. There is no record—not even a partial list—of people killed. It is estimated that at least 300 people lost their lives. The Chicago Fire Academy now stands on the site of the O'Leary home.

The preceding information is published with other details of the fire in a booklet entitled: "The Great Chicago Fire, October 8-10, 1871" which is available for sale from the Chicago Historical Society, Clark at North Avenue, Chicago, IL 60614. The booklet also includes a map of "Burnt District" and a bibliography of books on the Chicago Fire.

A CHECKLIST OF PRE-FIRE SOURCES
☐Archives and Manuscript Collections
   Some history survives only in the form of original manuscripts housed in special archives collections.

Figure 2. *Chicago—10 October 1871 (courtesy The Chicago Historical Society)*

Figure 3. *Map showing the Burnt District (courtesy The Chicago Historical Society*

☐ Cemetery records
☐ Census records
☐ Church records
☐ City directories
☐ Court records
Probate and divorce records which, though filed after the fire, may contain vital statistics and other dates of events previous to the fire. Land disputes were frequent and resulting lawsuits often provide pre-fire deeds, testimony, and other important information.
☐ Death certificates
☐ Fraternal organization records
These often provide pre-fire birth-dates and residences.
☐ Genealogical societies
Many have collected and indexed records from various public and private sources. These records often include documented proof of dates, places, and relationships.
☐ Historical societies
☐ Illinois State Archives
☐ Land and property records
Particularly those at Chicago Title and Trust Company and documents which were rerecorded as part of the "Burnt Record Series." (See section on Land Records.)
☐ Military records
☐ Newspapers
☐ Occupational records
☐ Published histories and biographies
☐ School records
☐ Vital records (indexed from Chicago newspapers)

ILLINOIS STATE ARCHIVES—CHICAGO RECORDS ACCESSION

In April 1984 the Illinois State Archives accessioned 584 bound volumes and 1,075 cubic feet of loose papers from the office of the Chicago city clerk. Included in the accession are records generated by Chicago city government as well as by several towns and villages which were annexed by it around the turn of the century. A significant portion of the accession predates the Great Fire of 1871; because these records were previously believed to have been destroyed, they are of particular value. Most of the loose records consist of Chicago City Council Proceedings Files, 1833-1942. The records are the council's working papers which in summary form appear in the minutes. They include such records as committee reports, orders, assessment rolls, appointments, official oaths and bonds, ordinances and resolutions, poll books and tally sheets, licenses, officials' reports, contracts and specifications, communications, and citizens' petitions and remonstrances. The remaining loose records consist of council or trustees' proceedings from the various annexed towns and villages.

BIBLIOGRAPHY

Abbot, Edith. *The Tenements of Chicago, 1908-1935.* Chicago: University of Chicago Press, 1936. A documented study of this serious urban problem.

Addams, Jane. *Twenty Years at Hull House.* New York: Macmillan, 1910.

Ahern, Michael Loftus. *Political History of Chicago.* Chicago, 1886. Contains biographical notes on several individuals who were prominent in politics.

Allswang, John Myers. *The Political Behavior of Chicago's Ethnic Groups 1918-1932.* New York: Arno, 1980.

Andreas, Alfred T. *History of Chicago.* 3 Vols. Chicago: A. T. Andreas, 1884-86. One of the most often cited of the nineteenth century histories of Chicago.

_____. *History of Cook County, Illinois.* Chicago: A. T. Andreas, 1884. The South Suburban Genealogical and Historical Society added an every-name index to this volume and sponsored its reprinting by Unigraphic Press in 1976.

Andrews, Wayne. *Battle for Chicago.* New York: Harcourt, Brace and Company, 1963.

Angle, Paul M., ed. *The Great Chicago Fire, Described in Seven Letters by Men and Women Who Experienced its Horrors.* Chicago, 1946.

Asbury, Herbert. *Gem of the Prairie.* Garden City: Garden City Publishing Co., 1942.

Bach, Ira J. *Chicago on Foot.* Chicago: Follett Publishing Company, 1977.

Barton, Elmer. *A Business Tour of Chicago, Depicting Fifty Years of Progress.* Chicago, 1887.

Beadle, Muriel. *The Fortnightly of Chicago: The City and Its Women, 1873-1973.* Chicago: Henry Regnery Co., 1973.

Beijbom, Ulf. *Swedes in Chicago: A Demographic and Social Study of the 1846-1880 Immigration.* Stockholm, 1971.

Bennett, Fremont O. *Politics and Politicians of Chicago, Cook County and Illinois.* Chicago, 1886. A detailed narrative with lists of officials and excerpts from documents.

Birmingham, George A. *From Dublin to Chicago: Some Notes on a Tour of America.* New York, 1914.

Bishop, Glenn A. and Gilbert, Paul T. *Chicago's Accomplishments and Leaders.* Chicago: Bishop Publishing Company, 1932.

Blanchard, Rufus. *Discovery and Conquests of the North-West with the History of Chicago.* Wheaton, Illinois, 1881. A long history of Chicago with a substantial amount of primary material. Some of the information was compiled from original records and part was solicited by Blanchard from early volumes which carried the history another two decades. The two versions are different, making it necessary to consult both editions.

Bronstein, Don. *Chicago, I Will.* Text by Tony Weitzel. Cleveland, 1967. Photographic essay.

Bross, William. *History of Chicago.* Chicago, 1876.

Burg, David F. *Chicago's White City of 1893.* Lexington, 1976.

Burns, Walter N. *The One Way Ride: The Red Trail of Chicago Gangland from Prohibition to Jake Lingle.* New York, 1931.

Butt, Ernest. *Chicago Then and Now.* Chicago, 1933.

Campbell, Edna F., Smith, Fanny R., and Jones, Clarence F. *Our City—Chicago.* New York, 1930.

Chamberlain, Everett. *Chicago and Its Suburbs.* Chicago, 1874.

Chapin, Louella. *Round About Chicago.* Chicago, 1907.

Chatfield-Taylor, Hobart C. *Chicago.* Boston, 1917.

Chicago, Department of Development and Planning. *Historic City: The Settlement of Chicago.* Chicago, 1976. A survey of the settlement and growth of the city with emphasis on the ethnic groups that made the city, with a set of fold-out maps.

The Chicago Fact Book Consortium. *Local Community Fact Book Chicago Metropolitan Area.* Chicago: 1984. A convenient compilation of a variety of information on local communities within the metropolitan area embracing the entire nine county Chicago-Gary-Kenosha Standard Consolidated Statistical Area. Data presented for 131 incorporated communities of 10,000 or more population in the area as for seventy-seven community areas within the city of Chicago inclues brief histories of each community and statistical tables based on the 1970 and 1980 censuses.

Chicago and Northwestern Railway Company. *Yesterday and Today: A History.* Chicago, 1905. A study of the role played by the railroad in the development of Chicago and the West.

Chicago Association of Commerce, eds. *Chicago. The Great Central Market.* Chicago, 1923.

Chicago Bureau of Statistics and Municipal Library. *The Chicago City Manual.* Containing a list of the executive and other city officers, with descriptions of their duties; lists of the aldermen and of the committees of the city council; and the rules regulating that body and many other matters relating to the city government, or that are of municipal concern. Chicago, 1908.

Chicago Evening Post. *The Book of Chicago*. 1911.
Chicago Herald. *Illustrated History of Chicago*. Chicago, 1887.
Chicago Historical Society. *Documents*. History of Communties, Chicago. 6 vols. Chicago, 1925-1930. The documents consist of oral histories, excerpts from newspapers, pamphlets, and scrapbooks regarding Rogers Park, West Rogers Park, Uptown, Ravenswood, North Center, Hamlin Park, Lake View, Lower (Near) North Side, Near South Side, Armour Square, Douglas, Oakland, Grand Boulevard, Washington Park, Woodlawn, Grand Crossing, West Englewood, Bridgeport, Canaryville (Fuller Park), Riverdale, East Side.
Chicago History. (Published quarterly by the Chicago Historical Society).
Chicago Plan Commission. *Forty-four Cities in the City of Chicago*. Chicago, 1942.
Chicago's First Half Century: The City as It was Fifty Years Ago and As It Is Today. Chicago, 1883.
City of Chicago, Department of Development and Planning. *Historic City: The Settlement of Chicago*. Chicago, 1976.
Cleaver, Charles. *Early Chicago Reminiscences*. Chicago, 1882.
Colbert, Elias. *Chicago: Historical and Statistical Sketch of the Garden City*. Chicago, 1868.
_____, and Chamberlain, Everett. *Chicago and the Great Conflagration*. Chicago, 1871. First-hand account of the great fire.
Cook, Frederick F. *Bygone Days in Chicago: Recollections of the Garden City of the Sixties*. Chicago: A. C. McClurg and Co., 1910.
Coyne, F. E. *In Reminiscence: Highlights of Men and Elements in the Life of Chicago*. Chicago, 1941. Colorful study containing a number of interesting anecdotes.
Cressey, Paul Frederick. "The Succession of Cultural Groups in the City of Chicago." Ph.D. Diss., University of Chicago, 1930.
Cromie, Robert. *The Great Chicago Fire*. New York: McGraw-Hill, 1958.
_____. *A Short History of Chicago*. San Francisco: Lexikos, 1984.
Currey, Josiah S. *Chicago: Its History and Its Builders: A Century of Marvelous Growth*. Chicago, 1912.
_____. *Manufacturing and Wholesale Industries of Chicago*. 3 vol. Chicago, 1918. Sketches of many businessmen and businesses.
Cutler, Irving. *Chicago: Metropolis of the Mid-Continent*. Dubuque, Iowa: Kendall/Hunt Publishing Company, 1976.
Davis, Allen F. *Spearheads for Reform: The Social Settlements and the Progressive Movement, 1890-1914*. New York, 1967. A descriptive, detailed study of the founding and work of the various settlement houses in the nation with major emphasis on Chicago.
Dedmon, Emmett. *Fabulous Chicago*. Chicago: Random House, 1953. A popular history of the city.

Drake, St. Clair, and Cayton, Horace. *Black Metropolis: A Study of Negro Life in a Northern City.* New York, 1935.

Drury, John. *Old Chicago Houses.* Chicago, 1941.

Duis, Perry. *Chicago: Creating New Traditions.* Chicago: Chicago Historical Society, 1976.

Duncan, Otis D., and Duncan, Beverly. *The Negro Population of Chicago: A Study of Residential Succession.* Chicago, 1957. Well-documented work dealing with the growth and mobility of blacks in Chicago.

Farr, Finis. *Chicago: A Personal History of America's Most American City.* New Rochelle, N.Y.: Arlington House, 1973.

Ffrench, Charles, ed. *Biographical History of the American Irish in Chicago.* Chicago, 1897.

Flinn, John Joseph. *History of the Chicago Police.* New York, 1973.

Furer, Howard B., ed. *Chicago: A Chronological and Documentary History, 1784-1970.* Dobbs Ferry, N.Y.: Oceana Publications, Inc., 1974.

Gale, Edwin O. *Reminiscences of Early Chicago.* Chicago: F. H. Revell Company, 1902.

Gates, Paul. *The Illinois-Central Railroad and Its Colonization Work.* Cambridge, 1934. A detailed study of the influence of this railroad in the development of Chicago.

German Press Club of Chicago. *Prominent Citizens and Industries of Chicago.* Chicago, 1901.

Gilbert, Frank. *Centennial History of the City of Chicago: Its Men and Institutions.* Chicago, 1905.

Gilbert, Paul T., and Bryson, Charles L. *Chicago and Its Makers.* Chicago, 1929.

Gosnell, Harold F. *Negro Politicians: The Rise of Negro Politics in Chicago.* Chicago, 1935.

Greene, Victor. *For God and Country: The Rise of Polish and Lithuanian Ethnic Consciousness in America, 1860-1970.* Madison, 1975.

Grossman, Ron. *Guide to Chicago Neighborhoods.* Piscataway, N.J.: New Century Publishers, Inc., 1981.

Gutstein, Morris A. *A Priceless Heritage: The Epic Growth of Nineteenth Century Chicago Jewry.* New York: Block Publishing Co., 1953.

Guyer, Isaac D. *History of Chicago: Its Commerical and Manufacturing Interests—with Sketches of Manufacturers and Men Who Have Most Contributed to Its Prosperity.* Chicago, 1862.

Hamilton, Henry R. *The Epic of Chicago.* 1932.

Hansen, Harry. *The Chicago.* New York, 1942. A detailed study of the Chicago River, its influence and importance in the growth of Chicago.

Harper, William H., ed. *Chicago: A History and Forecast.* Chicago, 1921.

Hayes, Dorsha. *Chicago, Crossroads of American Enterprise.* New York: J. Messner, 1944.

Heimovics, Rachel Baron. *Chicago Jewish Sourcebook.* Chicago: 1981.

Hletka, Peter. "The Slovaks of Chicago." *Slovakia* XIX, 42 (October 1969): 32-63.

Hirsch, Arnold R. *Making the Second Ghetto: Race and Housing in Chicago 1940 to 1960.* Cambridge: Cambridge University Press, 1983.

Hoffman, Charles Fenno. *A Winter in the West: Letters Descriptive of Chicago and Vicinity in 1833-34.* Chicago, 1882.

Hofmeister, Rudolph A. *The Germans in Chicago.* Urbana: University of Illinois Press, 1976.

Holli, Melvin G., and Jones, Peter d'A. *Ethnic Chicago.* Grand Rapids: William Eerdmans, 1984.

Holt, Glen E., and Pacyga, Dominic A. *Chicago: A Historical Guide to the Neighborhoods, the Loop and South Side.* Chicago: Chicago Historical Society, 1979.

Hoyt, Homer. *One Hundred Years of Land Values in Chicago, 1830-1933.* Chicago, 1933.

Hull House Residents. *Hull House Maps and Papers.* New York, 1895. Invaluable collection of records and documents of the first and most important Chicago Settlement House.

Hurlbut, Henry Higgins. *Chicago Antiquities.* Chicago, 1881.

Illinois State Archives. *For the Record. . .Newsletter of the Illinois State Archives.* Vol. 6, No. 2 (Winter 1984); Vol. 7, No. 2 (Winter 1985); and Vol. 8, No. 2 (Winter 1986).

Inglehart, Babette, ed. *Walking With Women Through Chicago History.* Chicago: Salsedo Press, 1981.

Jewell, Frank. *Annotated Bibliography of Chicago History.* Chicago: Chicago Historical Society, 1979. A comprehensive work and a most valuable source for locating hundreds of history titles by subject: general studies, city planning, architecture, transporation, government, economics and business, labor, social statistics, social life and customs, social conditions, religion, racial and ethnic groups, neighborhoods, education, communication, religion, politics, disasters, etc.

Johnson, Charles B. *Growth of Cook County.* 2 Vols. Chicago: Board of Commissioners of Cook County, Illinois, 1960.

Johnston, W. Wesley. *Researcher's Guide to the Pre-Fire Records of Chicago and Cook County.* Springfield, Ill.: The Author, 1982.

Kinze, Juliette A. *Wau-Bun.* Chicago: Rand McNally Company, 1901.

Kirkland, Joseph. *The Story of Chicago.* 3 Vols. Chicago: Dibble Publishing Company, 1892-1894.

Koenig, Harry C., ed. *A History of the Parishes of the Archdiocese of Chicago.* 2 Vols. Chicago: Archdiocese of Chicago, 1980.

Kogan, Herman and Rick. *Yesterday's Chicago.* Miami: E. A. Seeman, 1976. Text and numerous photographs.

_____, and Wendt, Lloyd. *Chicago: A Pictorial History.* New York: Bonanza Books, 1958.

Lane, George A. *Chicago Churches and Synagogues: An Architectural Pilgrimage.* Chicago: Loyola University Press, 1981.

Lepawsky, Albert. *Home Rule for Metropolitan Chicago.* Chicago, 1932.

Lewis, Lloyd, and Smith, Henry J. *Chicago, the History of Its Reputation.* New York: Harcourt Brace, 1929.

Lindberg, Richard. *Chicago Ragtime: Another Look at Chicago 1880-1920.* South Bend: Icarius Press, 1985.

Longstreet, Stephen. *Chicago, 1860-1919.* New York: David McKay Co., 1973. Mason, Edward G., ed. *Early Chicago and Illinois.* Chicago, 1890.

Mayer, Harold M. *Chicago: City of Decisions.* Chicago, 1955.

_____, and Wade, Richard C. *Chicago, Growth of a Metropolis.* Chicago: The University of Chicago Press, 1969. A narrative of Chicago's growth to 1969. It is recognized as one of the most important books on Chicago. It was one of the first books to use photographs and other images as a principal source of information. There are nearly 1,000 photographs and fifty maps. It is available at many Chicago bookstores.

McCarthy, Kathleen D. *Noblesse Oblige: Charity and Cultural Philanthropy in Chicago, 1849-1929.* Chicago: University of Chicago Press, 1982.

McClure, James B., ed. *Stories and Sketches of Chicago: An Interesting, Entertaining, and Instructive Sketch History of the Wonderful City "By the Sea."* Chicago, 1890.

McIlvaine, Mabel. *Reminiscenses of Chicago During the Civil War.* New York: Citadel, 1967.

McIntosh, Arthur T. *Chicago.* 1921. A popular history of Chicago, laden with anecdotal material.

Meites, Hyman, ed. *History of the Jews of Chicago.* Chicago. 1924. Divided into three main sections: narrative account of the Jewish community; accomplishments in the arts, professions, politics, labor, finance, industry, and athletics; major Jewish organizations and institutions. All sections have biographical sketches interspersed.

Moses, John, and Kirkland, Joseph. *History of Chicago.* 2 Vols. Chicago, 1895.

Nelli, Humbert S. *The Italians in Chicago, 1880-1930.* New York: Oxford University Press, 1970.

Nelson, Otto M. "The Chicago Relief and Aid Society, 1850-1874" *Journal of the Illinois State Historical Society* LIX, 1 (Spring 1966): 48-66.

Pacyga, Dominic A. and Skerrett, Ellen. *Chicago: City of Neighborhoods, Histories and Tours.* Chicago: Loyola University Press, 1986. The history and present of Chicago neighborhoods are explored in a volume which is enhanced with numerous photographs and maps.

Palickar, Stephen J. "The Slovaks of Chicago." *Illinois Catholic Historical Review* IV, 2 (October 1921): 180-96.

Palmer, Vivien M. *Social Backgrounds of Chicago's Local Communities.* Chicago, 1930.

Pasley, Fred D. *Al Capone: The Biography of a Self-Made Man.* New York: Ives Washburn, 1930.

Phillips, George S. *Chicago and Her Churches.* 3 Vols. New York: Knopf, 1937, 1940, 1957. This massive study is probably the best single work on Chicago churches.

Pierce, Bessie L. *A History of Chicago.* 3 vols. New York: Knopf, 1937, 1940, 1957. This massive study is probably the best single work on the history of Chicago.

Poles of Chicago, 1837-1937. Chicago: Polish Pageant, Inc., 1937.

Proba, Daniel. *Czech and Slovak Leaders in Metropolitan Chicago.* Chicago, 1934.

Putnam, James Williams. *The Illinois and Michigan Canal: A Study in Economic History.* Chicago: University of Chicago Press, 1918.

Quaife, Milo M. *Checagou: From Indian Wigwam to Modern City, 1673-1835.* Chicago, 1935.

_____. *Chicago and the Old Northwest, 1673-1835: A Study of the Evolution of the Northwestern Frontier, together with a History of Fort Dearborn.* Chicago, 1913.

_____. *Chicago's Highways Old and New: From Indian Trails to Motor Road.* Chicago: D. F. Keller and Company, 1923.

Randall, Frank A. *History of the Development of Building Construction in Chicago.* Urbana, Illinois, 1949.

Reichman, John J., ed. *Czechoslovaks in Chicago.* Chicago, 1937.

Riley, Elmer. *The Development of Chicago and Vicinity As A Manufacturing Center Prior to 1880.* Chicago: McElroy Publishing Co., 1911.

Rilery, Thomas James. *The Higher Life of Chicago.* Chicago, 1905.

Robb, Frederick H., ed. *The Negro in Chicago, 1779-1929.* 2 vols. Chicago, 1927-1929.

Schiavo, Giovanni E. *The Italians in Chicago: A Study in Americanization.* Chicago, 1928.

Seeger, Eugene. *Chicago, the Wonder City.* Chicago, 1893.

Sentinel Publishing Company. *The Sentinel's History of Chicago Jewry, 1911-1916.* Chicago: Sentinel Publishing Company, 1961.

Shackleton, Robert. *The Book of Chicago*. Philadelphia, 1920.
Skogan, Wesley G. *Chicago Since 1840: A Time Series Data Handbook*. Urbana, 1976.
Siegel, Arthur, ed. *Chicago's Famous Buildings*. Chicago, 1965.
Sinclair, Upton. *The Jungle*. New York. 1906. Devastating classic of the Chicago meat packing industry.
Smith, Henry J. *Chicago's Great Century, 1833-1933*. Chicago, 1933.
Solomon, Ezra and Bilbija, Zarko G. *Metropolitan Chicago: An Economic Analysis*. Glencoe, Illinois, 1959.
Spear, Allan H. *Black Chicago: The Making of a Negro Ghetto, 1890-1920*. Chicago, 1967.
Strand, Algot E., comp. *A History of the Norwegians of Illinois*. Chicago, ca 1905. A long narrative of Norwegian settlement in Illinois includes many references to Chicago. In addition, there is an entire section on Chicago. Essays treat Norwegian churches, organizations, industry, and leading citizens.
Thorn, W. & Co. *Chicago in 1860: A Glance at Its Business Houses*. Chicago, 1860.
Thrasher, Frederic M. *The Gang*. Chicago: University of Chicago Press, 1927 Chicago's gangland.
Townsend, Andrew J. *The Germans of Chicago*. Chicago, 1932. University of Chicago Center of Urban Studies. Mid-Chicago Economic Development Study. 3 Vols. Chicago: Mayor's Committee for Economic and Cultural Development, 1966.
Vanderbosh, Amry. *The Dutch Communities of Chicago*. Chicago, 1927.
Waterman, A. N. *Historical Review of Chicago and Cook County and Selected Biography*. 3 Vols. Chicago: The Lewis Publishing Co., 1908.
Wrigley, Kathryn, ed. *Directory of Illinois Oral History Resources*. Springfield, Ill.: Sangamon State University, 1981.
Writer's Program. Illinois. *Selected Bibliography: Illinois, Chicago and Its Environs*. Chicago, 1937.
Zorbaugh, Harvey W. *The Gold Coast and the Slum*. Chicago, 1929.

CHAPTER 2

Adoption Records

A lthough it is not the purpose of this work to serve as a comprehensive guide to adoption research, it is sometimes necessary in the course of genealogical or historical research to have some knowledge of adoption laws, records, and agencies. Information in this section is intended to provide some jurisdictional background, an address list of some important agencies, and a selected bibliography of potentially helpful guides.

The Circuit Court has jurisdiction over adoption proceedings in Illinois. Adoption records in Cook County are impounded by the Clerk of the Court and the files may be opened for examination only on the specific order of the Court. (See Court Records Chapter for additional information.)

On 3 June 1985, all files, dockets, and other papers concerning adoptions which were formerly part of the records of the Superior Court of Cook County, the County Court of Cook County and the Family Court of Cook County were transferred to the County Division of the Circuit Court of Cook County (8th Floor of the Daley Center) by Special Order 85-208. At that time, all ledger entries pertaining to adoptions in the former courts were obliterated from all indexes in other court divisions, and information on files must now be secured from the County Division.

There is one helpful guide to older records. Orphan Court Ledgers were transcribed by June B. Barekman and published in the *Chicago Genealogist* II, No. 1, (September 1969) to IX, No. 4, (Summer 1977). Included in Barekman's work are names of adopting parents, name of child, general number, and filing date. The entries begin in 1871 and end in 1899.

For more recent adoptions, new legislation offers a glimmer of hope for those seeking adoption information. The Illinois Legislature passed bills in 1985 (House Bills 0765 and 1853) which allow for an official registry to help consenting adult adopted children and their biological parents find each other. The registry is maintained by the Illinois Department of Public Health. Adoption records remain confidential unless both a birth parent and an adoptee who has reached age 21 registered with the state, and if both consented to the exchange of information. The bills require that background information regarding medical history, excluding any identifying information, be given to all adoptive parents at the time of adoption.

There are several adoption support groups in the Chicago area which meet regularly, offer suggestions, and exchange information. One such group is Adoption Triangle, P.O. Box 96, South Holland, IL 60473.

Since an unspecified year previous to 1935, adoptees' birth certificates have been amended (Illinois Annotated Statutes, Chapter III-1/2, Sec. 73-17(4) Supp. 1972). This section was amended in August of 1971 to permit the use of a false birthplace on amended birth certificates.

Searching in Illinois by Beckstead and Kozub is a reference guide to public and private records, listing addresses for state and independent agencies, maternity homes, hospitals, orphanages, cemeteries, colleges and universities, libraries and governmental agencies. Each list is broken down by Illinois counties.

BIBLIOGRAPHY

Askin, Jayne. *Search: A Handbook for Adoptees and Birthparents.* New York, N.Y.: Harper & Row, 1982.

Beckstead, Gayle and Mary Lou Kozub. *Searching in Illinois.* Costa Mesa, Calif.: ISC Publications, 1984.

Niles, Reg. *Adoption Agencies, Orphanages and Maternity Homes.* Garden City, N.Y.: Phileas Deigh Corporation, 1981.

Rillera, Mary Jo. *The Adoption Search Book.* Huntington Beach, Calif.: Triadoption Publications, 1981.

ADDRESSES

ADOPTION INFORMATION CENTER, 201 North Wells St., Chicago, IL, 60602. (Toll-free Hotline 800-572-2390).

ADOPTION RESEARCH FORUM, P.O. Box 2517, Chicago, IL 60690.

ALLIANCE FOR ADOPTION REUNIONS, 63 West 540 Lake Drive, Clarendon Hills, IL 60514.

ALMA CHAPTER (ADOPTEES LIBERTY MOVEMENT ASSOC.), P.O. Box 59345, Chicago, IL 60659.

CATHOLIC CHARITIES OF CHICAGO, 126 N. DesPlaines St., Chicago, IL 60606 (312-236-5172).

CHILDREN'S HOME AND AID SOCIETY OF ILLINOIS, 1122 N. Dearborn St, Chicago, IL 60610 (312-944-3313).
CONCERNED UNITED BIRTHPARENTS, 156 W. Burton, Chicago, IL 60610.
THE CRADLE SOCIETY, 2049 Ridge Ave., Evanston, IL 60204 (312-475-5800).
ILLINOIS DEPARTMENT OF CHILDREN AND FAMILY SERVICES, 510 North Dearborn St., Suite 400, Chicago, IL 60601 (312-793-6800).
JEWISH CHILDREN'S BUREAU, 1 So. Franklin, Chicago, IL 60606.
EDWARD E. KELLEY, (Consultant-Adoption, Missing Heirs and Missing Persons), 574 Babcock, Elmhurst, IL 60126.
LUTHERAN SOCIAL SERVICES OF ILLINOIS, CHICAGO METROPOLITAN SERVICES, 4840 W. Byron, Chicago, IL 60641 (312-282-7800).
SEARCH RESEARCH, P.O. Box 48, Chicago Ridge, IL 60415.
TRUTHSEEKERS IN ADOPTION, P.O. Box 286, Roscoe, IL 61073.
YESTERDAY'S CHILDREN, P.O. Box 1554, Evanston, IL 60204.

CHAPTER 3

Architectural and House History Sources

Most buildings have rich histories which may be reconstructed by using the many collections of materials which are available for research in the Chicago area. A project is enhanced by tackling it as though collecting biographical information on a long-deceased ancestor. A building can take on a distinct personality as discoveries give it identity and a place in the history of the community. The following guide is offered for doing research in property and building records.

1. Begin research by investigating printed sources which are available on architectural records in this area. The bibliography at the end of this chapter and the chapter on Land/Property Records includes some of the standard and most helpful works. An especially well detailed, step-by-step handbook for architectural research in the Cook County area is: *Architectural Records in Chicago* by Kathleen Roy Cummings.

2. It is possible that research has already been done on the building of interest. It may have been designated as a landmark or included in a landmark district. Buildings which have been placed on the National Register of Historic Places have been researched and copies of nomination forms for Chicago buildings are on file at the Burnham Library of the Art Institute and at the Commission on Chicago Historical and Architectural Landmarks. Surveys of historic buildings and neighborhoods may have been conducted by local preservation groups. Consult the city's Commission on Chicago Architectural and Historical Landmarks, the Landmarks Preservation Council of Illinois, or a local commission to determine if a building has been included in a survey. The Chicago Historical Society has a wealth of information on buildings, and local community historical societies should not be overlooked for their potential.

Figure 4. *Chicago's oldest house—The Clarke House*

3. Determine the location of the property in question. A legal description of the address will be needed and details for obtaining these are provided in the Land Records chapter. Title insurance policies, mortgage papers, deeds, Torrens Certificates, and probate records are also means of obtaining legal descriptions. If you are the owner of the property in question, The Permanent Index Number can be found on your tax bill. Keep in mind that nineteenth-century buildings in Chicago may have undergone a street numbering change since the building was constructed.

4. The Department of Inspectional Services issues permits to construct, add to, alter, or wreck buildings in the city of Chicago. Permit applications accompanied by plans, specifications, lot surveys, and house number certificates are filed with:

> Department of Inspectional Services
> Room 800, City Hall
> 121 North LaSalle Street
> Chicago, IL 60602

Applications, permits, and supporting documents are microfilmed soon after permit issuance and placed on file in the:

> Department of Inspectional Services
> Records Section, Room 903
> City Hall, 121 North LaSalle
> Chicago, IL 60602 (312-744-3452)

Viewing of permit records is restricted and researchers must write or call for an appointment. Unfortunately, these records are by no means complete and are particularly spotty for the years 1880-1900. Take along proof of ownership to look at the property.

5. Construction dates can be estimated from tax assessment records. You'll need your tax index number for this. (If you do not know your number, call the Cook County Maps Department at 312-443-6253.) You can look at the complete history of the assessments for your property by going to the Assessor's Vault on Floor 3 1/2 of the County Building (118 North Clark Street). A substantial increase in the assessment for a property often reflects construction of a building.

6. Atlases of the city published for fire insurance companies indicate a building's original and later outlines, its height, and the materials used. These maps can be used to estimate construction dates. If you trace your lot back through preceding editions of these atlases until the outline of your house no longer appears on the site, you will

have some idea of the time period in which it was built. The Chicago Historical Society Library has a large collection of fire atlases.

7. Old issues of newspapers and periodicals sometimes contain reports of building permits issued. These can give you the architect's name if you weren't able to find it on the building permit application. Architectural magazines, construction trade publications, and real estate journals also published information about construction undertaken.

8. If your house was designed by a well-known architect, there's a chance you will find some biographical information about him, including other buildings he designed. The Burnham Library at the Art Institute has a card catalog on locally prominent architects, and biographical directories of architects are useful for those who were nationally prominent.

9. Early city directories can also be helpful in tracking down the earlier residents of your house. (See Directories chapter for additional information.)

10. A number of books on community history can be helpful in relating a house to a neighborhood. (See the bibliographies in the History and Community/Neighborhood/Suburbs chapters.)

11. Don't overlook the possibility that the property of interest may have been involved in a local or federal court case. Property line disputes, insurance lawsuits, and a multitude of other reasons have created many court records which usually include detailed building and property descriptions. The courts were flooded with lawsuits against fire insurance companies after the Chicago Fire of 1871. The testimony provided in many of these cases yields unique first-hand accounts.

12. If a building permit record cannot be found, it could be for one of the following reasons: (a) the house was built before permits were issued in 1872 or between 1872 and 1891 when records are not available for inspection; (b) The house was built without a permit; (c) The records have been misfiled or lost; (d) The property was not located within the Chicago city limits as they existed at the time of construction; or (e) Some permit applications issued in 1923 were lost in a fire.

BIBLIOGRAPHY

The Art Institute of Chicago. *The Plan of Chicago: 1909-1979*. Chicago: 1979.

Bach, Ira.*Chicago's Famous Buildings*. 3rd. ed., Chicago: University of Chicago Press, 1980.

Block, Jean F. *Hyde Park Houses: An Informal History, 1856-1910*. Chicago: University of Chicago Press, 1978.

Condit, Carl W. *The Chicago School of Architecture: A History of Commercial and Public Building in the Chicago Area, 1875-1925*. Chicago: University of Chicago Press, 1964.

Cummings, Kathleen Roy. *Architectural Records in Chicago*. Chicago: The Burnham Library of Architecture, The Art Institute of Chicago, 1981.

Drury, John. *Old Chicago Houses*. Chicago: University of Chicago Press, 1941.

Randall, Frank Alfred. *History of the Development of Building Construction in Chicago*. Urbana, Ill.: University of Illinois Press, 1949.

Sharp, Ed. *The Old House Handbook for Chicago and Suburbs*. Chicago: Chicago Review Press, 1979.

Tallmadge, Thomas Eddy. *Architecture in Old Chicago*. Chicago: University of Chicago Press, 1975.

ADDRESSES

The Art Institute of Chicago
Burnham Library of Architecture
Michigan Avenue at Adams Street
Chicago, IL 60603 (312-443-3666)
Note: Membership in the Art Institute is required to use the Library.

Chicago Historical Society
Clark Street at North Avenue
Chicago, IL 60614 (312-642-4600)

Chicago Architecture Foundation
Glessner House
1800 South Prairie Avenue
Chicago, IL 60616 (312-326-1393)

CHAPTER 4

Collected Biographies

A biographical sketch found in a county, city, ethnic, or neighborhood history is often the beginning of a rewarding research project. *Who's Who* publications, occupational collections, and obituaries offer additional sources to search for personal information. Biographies, which are usually based on the testimony of the subject of the sketch generally include information which would be difficult, if not impossible to obtain elsewhere. These printed sources are a means of learning a person's birth, parentage, spouse, children, occupation, military service, prior residence, and political and religious affiliation. They are especially valuable in the study of immigrants and their descendants if they specify the town of foreign origin.

Because they usually deal with prominent persons, many researchers fail to look at biographies, assuming that their ancestor was not prominent enough for inclusion. It is worth considering, however, that other family members may have been included; and since their origins are the same, the source is equally valuable. Important clues on migrational patterns, ethnic communities, religious affiliation, and occupation can be gleaned from a biographical sketch of a member of a group to which an ancestor belonged. These clues may then provide a starting place to look for records of the less prominent members of a particular group. An example of this approach is the case of an Irish servant girl. Family tradition preserved the fact that a grandmother had been employed by a prominent Chicago citizen who happened to have come from her own hometown in Ireland. While the name of the town was not remembered nor could it be found in ordinary channels of research, a biographical sketch of her employer divulged the exact town where the research could be continued.

Some of the disadvantages of biographical works are immediately obvious. First, a person had to be living and prominent at the time a publication was going into print. The popularity of the biographical sketch in histories was greatest around the turn of the century, and so a search for people of that time period will often be most productive. Genealogists continually emphasize the importance of facts, documentation, and accuracy. For this reason these secondary or here-say accounts must be judged with some degree of skepticism. Biographical sketches are noted for being "richly embroidered" so that they portray the subject in saintly light. One must examine the motives of the publisher when considering the accuracy of the material. Much biographical information was included in special local histories which were usually produced on a subscription basis. To be included in one of these publications, the "leading citizen" could be anyone who had the desire and the money to pay for the subscription. Despite the rather exaggerated nature of the sketches, they are generally accurate when it comes to religious, political, or fraternal affiliation as well as former residences. Basic information regarding the family is usually fairly reliable and will at least provide an outline which a researcher should verify elsewhere. These accounts should never be accepted as totally accurate even though the subject may have provided the basis for the article. Consider the father who was so displeased with a son's activities that he disinherited him and refused to even acknowledge his existence when submitting data for inclusion in a biographical publication.

The following extraction is a typical example of a biographical sketch which was found in Charles Ffrench's *Biographical History of the American Irish in Chicago* (Chicago: American Biographical Publishing, 1897):

FRANCIS T. MURPHY

This great Western metropolis contains a great many able men who have made the law the profession of their lives. That all should be equally successful in such a career, would be an impossibility; the prizes in life's battle are few and far between, and the fortunate must be gifted with qualifications of a diverse character, exceptional legal ability, good judgement, ready perception, and also personal charm of manner or power of intellect sufficient to dominate and control their fellowmen. Among the representative lawyers of the west, there are but a few who possess these necessary characteristics in a higher degree than the subject of the present sketch, the big, genial-natured, open-hearted young lawyer, Francis T. Murphy.

He was born in this city, where he was destined to make himself so well known, January 25th, 1863, his father, Thomas Murphy being a native of County Meath, Ireland, and his mother from West Meath. It is from his father unquestionably that Francis T. inherits his perserverance and energy, for Thomas Murphy left the dear old land as a mere boy of twelve, traveled all alone to the far country beyond the seas, where he possessed neither kith nor kin, friend nor acquaintance, and when the big ocean journey was finished, set off once more across the continent to Chicago, determined to seek a living and possible fortune in the boundless West. In this city he fought his way, married, and in 1894 died at the comparatively premature age of fifty-seven.

Mr. Murphy was married April 11th, 1893, in Chicago, to Mary V. Halpin, the daughter of one of Chicago's best known citizens. A man of intensely social nature, the chief delight of Frank Murphy—as he is generally known—is to be surrounded with his friends and to dispense the historical hospitality. For fast horses he admits a decided partiality, and is fortunate of several that can show a good pace.

For persons who lived in the Chicago metropolitan area, there is a considerable amount of biographical material which should be consulted. The size and diversity of the urban population generated an abundance of materials to draw from. Besides the many well-known standards such as A.T. Andreas' *History of Cook County Ilinois* (1884); and his three volume *History of Chicago* (1884-1886), there were those which focused on particular ethnic groups and occupations as well. In addition, books of this nature were also published which covered ethnic, political, and social groups for the entire state of Illinois, the entries for Chicago citizens frequently forming the largest portion of the biographical section. Many biographical sketches are buried in illusive volumes which contain partial or no indexes. It should be noted that many of the indexes in biographical histories have only partial indexes and a page by page search may be necessary to be thorough. There is no single reference available for this area which will include all the biographical sources, but there are some important indexes and collections which are worthy of mention and they are the most logical starting places for a biographical search.

THE NEWBERRY LIBRARY'S CHICAGO AND COOK COUNTY BIOGRAPHY AND INDUSTRY FILE

The following description of the Newberry Index has been extracted from an article by David Thackery as it appeared in *Origins* (A Newsletter of the Local and Family History Section and the Family and Community History Center at The Newberry Library) Volume 1, No.3, April 1985.

For the last several years the Newberry's Local and Family History section has been compiling a card index to all the biographical sketches appearing in a number of selected Chicago and County—as well as Illinois—collective biographies and mug books published before 1930. In all, seventeen titles, some of them in two or three editions, have been indexed in this fashion. The project is ongoing and will ultimately index twenty-five titles. Historical sketches of industries are also included in this file, but the bulk of the entries (totaling over six thousand at present) refer to individuals.

The diversity of Chicago is well reflected in the titles that have been indexed. On the one hand, WASP "big wigs" are well represented by such titles as David Ward Wood's *Chicago and Its Distinguished Citizens* (Chicago: M. George & Co., 1881), while its ethnic communities are represented by sketches taken from such books as Charles Ffrench's *Biographical History of the American Irish in Chicago* (Chicago: American Biographical Publishing, 1897), *Chicago und Sein Deutschthum* (Cleveland: German-American Biographical Pub. Co., 1902) and A. E. Strand's *History of the Norwegians of Illinois* (Chicago: John Anderson, 1905).

Books representing particular occupations include the *History of Chicago and Souvenir of the Liquor Interest* (Chicago: Belgravia, 1891) and Charles H. Taylor's *History of the Board of Trade of the City of Chicago* (Chicago: Robert O. Law, 1917), as well as John Joseph Flinn's *History of the Chicago Police* (originally published in 1887). Cutting across occupational lines are the sketches contained in the three volumes of *Memorials of Deceased Companions of the Commandery of the State of Illinois* (1901, 1912, 1923), consisting of obituaries for the Civil War officers belonging to this veterans' group.

The file itself is located with the card catalogues at at the Newberry Library. Correspondents may ask Local and Family History staff to consult the file as long as such requests are limited to no more than three per letter. Library patrons are free to consult the file in person.

THE CHICAGO HISTORICAL SOCIETY LIBRARY

The main card catalog of the Chicago Historical Society Library is an important source for locating biographical material on individuals who have resided in the Chicago metropolitan area. Although it is by no means an all-inclusive index to the printed collection, a surprising number of citizens are represented in the card catalog. As one might expect, the majority of the entries are for prominent citizens, but some cards refer to the "Clippings File" or provide citations for obituaries for less famous individuals. Card catalog entries for war deaths can provide further information by referring to the newspaper cited on the card.

An especially valuable source for biographical information is: Herbert, Miranda C. and McNeil, B. eds. *Biography and Genealogy Master Index*. Detroit: Gale Research Company. A consolidated index to more than 3,200,000 biographical sketches in over 350 current and retrospective biographical dictionaries.

CHAPTER 5

Cemetery Records

by Brian Scott Donovan

Cemetery and other death records are often the logical starting point for the researcher who applies good genealogical procedure: working from the present to the past. Besides being more numerous than at any other time in an individual's life, records generated at death generally contain more references to important events in a person's life as well as serving to identify family relationships. It is important to check all of these sources carefully for the different information contained within them.

With over 200 cemeteries in Cook County, determining where a burial occurred is the first priority. There is no single source that lists all the burials in Cook County, though most comprehensive records of burials are contained in the Certificates of Death available from the county clerk, Bureau of Vital Statistics, 118 North Clark Street, Chicago, Illinois 60602 (See chapter on Vital Records). The destruction of all vital records in the Great Chicago Fire makes it necessary to check other sources for deaths which occurred prior to 8 October 1871. Additionally, unknown death dates, and deaths which could have taken place outside Cook County tend to make searching county created vital records impractical or too expensive. In these instances there are some alternatives.

ROLLS OF HONOR

The burial places of deceased veterans are listed in the following publications. The first roll covers deceased veterans from the Revolution to World War I: Lewis, E. R., comp. *The Roll of Honor*. Chicago: The Honorable Board of Cook County, Illinois, 1922.

Under each cemetery the following information is given for each veteran: name, rank, company, U.S. regiment, state organization or vessel, date of death, number of grave, number of lot, block, and section. Besides listing the burials in Cook County, burials in state, but outside Cook County, burials outside of the state and county, and unknown burial places are listed. However, neither the cemeteries nor the veterans buried therein are listed in alphabetical order. This problem was resolved with the recent publication of the following index:

Index to the Roll of Honor, Cook County, Illinois. Salt Lake City, Ut: Markam Publications, 1986.

The second roll covers burials prior to 1 July 1955, therefore it not only includes veterans of World War II and Korea, but veterans given in the previous volume and those who died in the intervening years.

Honor Roll, Cook County, Illinois. Springfield, Ill.: Illinois Veterans' Commission, 1956.

The veterans are arranged alphabetically under each cemetery, and the following information is given for each veteran: name, war, rank, branch, unit of organization, date of death, grave number, lot number, block, section, and head stone. The above roll is part of a twelve-volume set covering all the counties of Illinois. The first three volumes cover Cook County. Cemeteries whose names begin with the letters *A-J* are in the first volume, *K-O* are in the second volume, *P-Z* and unknown places of burial are in the third volume. This source is unindexed.

CAMP DOUGLAS PRISONERS

Five thousand Confederate soldiers who died while being held as prisoners of war at Camp Douglas were buried at Oakwoods Cemetery, which is therefore often referred to as Confederate Mound Cemetery. Two sources that list soldiers buried there are:

Ingmire, Frances Terry. *Confederate P.O.W.s: Soldiers and Sailors Who Died in Federal Prisons and Military Hospitals in the North.* Nacogdoches, Tex.: distributed by Ericson Books, 1984.
Pompey, Sherman Lee. *Burial Lists of the Confederate Federal Infantry.* Kingsbury, Calif.: Pacific Specialties, 1972.

EARLY CEMETERIES

Of the original dozen cemeteries in Chicago, not a single one remained by the late 1870s. Due to health considerations, were closed and the bodies removed to cemeteries outside the city. It was not until the annexation of 1889 that any cemetery land was again within the city limits. John Kenzie, the first white settler of Chicago, was buried four times; first on his property, then the city cemetery followed by the North Side Cemetery (in what is now the south end of Lincoln Park), before he was finally laid to rest in Graceland Cemetery.

The records of removals of bodies from early city cemeteries can now be found in the Calvary, Graceland, Rose Hill, Oak Woods, Wunder, and Hebrew Benevolent cemeteries which were opened in the late

1850s and early 1860s outside the then city limits of Chicago. The following sources give a good history of early development of cemeteries in Chicago:

Denmark, B. "Early Chicago Cemeteries." Reference Report, Chicago Historical Society, 3 March 1971.

Lowes, Helen H. "Early Cemeteries in Chicago." *Illinois State Genealogical Society Quarterly* 1, No.4, (Winter 1969).

POTTERS FIELD

Since January 1980, Homewood Memorial Gardens has had the contract with Cook County to bury the indigent and the unclaimed bodies in its Garden of the Good Samaritan section. From 1970 through 1980, Archer Woods Cemetery, now Mount Glenwood West Cemetery had the contract with Cook County.

From 1910 through November 1970 Oak Forest, which later became Cook County Cemetery had the responsibility for county burials. Records of burials in all three cemeteries have been maintained. In the case of Cook County Cemetery, which is no longer used for interments, the records are maintained by the Medical Records Department of Oak Forest Hospital, 159th and Cicero Avenue, Oak Forest, IL 60452 (312-687-7200).

TRANSCRIPTIONS

Transcriptions from cemetery monuments are very useful sources of information, but relying on the work of others has its limitations. The variety of information inscribed varies from dates of birth and death, place of birth and death (especially where far removed from place of burial), maiden name, parents' names, spouse's name, siblings, relationships, occupations, military service, biographical information, fraternal symbols, photographs, or signatures. The lack of uniformity in this information makes an orderly compilation of inscriptions difficult and details may be lost in the transcription. Family relationships, especially between in-laws, may be lost in the alphabetization of transcriptions. Additionally, everyone memorialized on a stone is not necessarily buried in the plot. The best transcriptions include not only the monumental inscriptions, but will also include a cross-reference to cemetery records or obituaries when the compilers have had access to them. Following is a list of the known transcriptions for Cook County:

"Arlington Heights, Wheeling Township Cemetery, 1840." *Chicago Genealogist.* (July 1968).

Barekman, June B. "Mt. Olive Cemetery, Jefferson Township, Cook County, Illinois," *Chicago Genealogist* XI, No. 1, (Fall 1978): 15-17.

Bodett, Tom. "Reading of the Gravestones of St. Mary's Cemetery, Located on River Road, on the Grounds of Maryville Academy, Des Plaines, IL." Reading done 10 July 1985.

Golay, Myrna, and Huff, Joan. "Elk Grove Cemetery, Early 1840s-1976." 1976.

Koss, David, and Melnick, Louis D., and Melnick, Michael A. "Inscriptions from Cady Cemetery, Palatine Township, Cook County, Illinois". *Newsletter of the North Suburban Genealogical Society* II, No. 2 (March 1977): 10-12.

Jacyna, Sister Josephine. "Partial List of St. Henry's Catholic Cemetery at Devon near Damen Avenue, Chicago IL." Holograph. Salt Lake City: s.n., 1977. Available from the Genealogical Department of the Church of Jesus Christ of Latter-day Saints, microfilm 1,036,723, item 6.

Jensen, Mary Ann, and Gifford, John and Mary Ellen. *St. Patrick's Cemetery of Lemont, Illinois*. South Holland, Ill.: South Suburban Genealogical and Historical Society, 1978.

Kruse, Adeline. "Sutherland Cemetery, Palatine Township, Cook Co., Illinois." *News from the Northwest* VII, No. 1 (Sept.-Oct. 1986).

Leonard, Craig and Debbie. "Tombstone Inscriptions from St. John's Cemetery, West Lake Street, Northbrook, Illinois," Summer, 1975.

Lundberg, Gertrude W. *Some German Name Cemeteries, Cook County, Illinois*. Homewood, Ill.: Root & Tree Publications, 1967. The above transcription includes the following cemeteries: Immanuel German Lutheran, Glenview; St. Paul's Lutheran, Skokie; Old Immanuel Lutheran, Des Plaines; St. John's Lutheran, Northfield Township, Lutheran Home and Service for the Aged.

_____. "St. John's Lutheran Church Cemetery, Mt. Prospect, Illinois, Cook County," Homewood, Ill.: Root and Tree Publications, 1970.

_____. "Glenview Area Burial Places, Northfield Township, Cook County, Illinois," *Chicago Genealogist* VII, No.1, (Fall 1974): 5-12. This article includes a transcription of St. John's Lutheran Church Cemetery, first recorded in 1966, and revised to 1973.

_____. *Cook County Tombstones, Cemetery ©3. St. John's Lutheran, Elk Grove Township*. Homewood, Ill.: Root and Tree Publications, 1970.

Mc Harg, Christopher G. "Tombstone Inscriptions, Arlington Heights Wheeling Township Cemetery, Cook County, Illinois," 1976.

Santroch, Gail, ed. *A Transcription of Wunder's Cemetery, Chicago, Illinois*. Chicago: Chicago Genealogical Society, 1985.

Scheskie, Debra Lynn and James. "Inscriptions from the Cemetery Located on Rand Road at Seegers Road, Des Plaines, Illinois, Affiliated with Emanuel Lutheran Church, Des Plaines, Illinois," *Chicago Genealogist* X, No.4, (Summer 1978): 139-144.

Scheskie, James , Beverly, Debra and Susan. "St. Joseph's Cemetery at Lake and Gross Point Roads. Wilmette, Illinois." June 1974.

Other cemeteries transcribed and indexed by Gertrude Lundberg are:

Arlington Heights Cemetery (#4), Wheeling Township
Sacred Heart Cemetery, Northbrook, Northfield Township
St. Joseph's Catholic Cemetery, Wilmette, New Trier Township
St. John's Lutheran Cemetery, Elk Grove Township
St. Peter's Lutheran Cemetery (#2), Wheeling Township
St. Peter's United Chuch of Christ Cemetery (#13), Skokie, Niles Township

The South Suburban Genealogical and Historical Society has transcribed and indexed the following cemeteries:

Bloom Presbyterian Cemetery, Bloom Township
Oak Glen Cemetery, Lansing
Oakland Memory Lanes Cemetery, Lansing
Old Thornton Township Cemetery
St. James Cemetery, Bloom Township
St. Patrick's Cemetery, Lemont
Trinity Lutheran Church Cemetery, Tinley Park, Bremen Township
Zion Lutheran Cemetery, Tinley Park, Bremen Township

The cemeteries listed here are in booklet form and for sale from the South Suburban Genealogical & Historical Society, P.O. Box 96, South Holland, IL 60473.

"Arlington Heights Wheeling Township Cemetery, 1840-July 1968" is a transcript which includes a history taken from the minute books and transcriptions by Joan Allen. Allen's work and an article which appeared in the *Arlington Heights Herald*, 3 September 1948 with transcriptions by Dr. Bruce T. Best are available in the pamphlet file of the Arlington Memorial Library.

"Records from the First Record Book of Graceland Cemetery, 1860-1866, Chicago, Illinois" is a typescript of 114 leaves, is indexed (1945), and available from the Genealogical Department of the Church of Jesus Christ of Latter-day Saints, microfilm 843,587, item 5.

TRANSCRIPTIONS IN PROGRESS

Currently, the Chicago Genealogical Society is transcribing St. Henry's Cemetery and the Jewish Genealogical Society of Illinois is transcribing Hebrew Benevolent Society Cemetery. For further information on any of these cemeteries, send limited queries with a self-addressed, stamped envelope to Brian Scott Donovan, 241 Ridge Avenue, Evanston, IL 60202.

The following organizations maintain lists of cemetery surveying and transcribing projects in progress and completed for Cook County, Illinois:

The Association for Gravestone Studies
46 Plymouth Road
Needham, MA 02192

The Illinois State Genealogical Society
Cemetery Committee
P.O. Box 157
Lincoln, IL 62656

Cemetery Project Committee
Chicago Genealogical Society
P.O. Box 1160
Chicago, IL 60690

The following booklets are useful for cemetery transcribing information:

Jones, Mary Ellen. *Photographing Tombstones: Equipment and Techniques.* Technical Leaflet No. 92. Nashville: American Association for State and Local History, 1977.

Newman, John J. *Cemetery Transcribing: Preparations and Procedures.* Technical Leaflet No. 9. Nashville; American Association for State and Local History, 1971.

Paddock, Shirley, and Angelos, Christine Walsh. *Symbols in Stone.* Northbrook , Ill.: The Printing Post, Inc., 1982.

DEATH INDICES

When the date of death is unknown, the decedent had a very common or easily misspelled name, or for any other reason you are having trouble obtaining a death certificate, these indices may prove very useful in obtaining the correct death record from the Bureau of Vital Statistics. There are two death indices available through the Branch Genealogical Libraries of the Genealogical Department of the Church of Jesus Christ of Latter-day Saints.

The first, as a series of microfilms (1,295,943; 1,295, 949; and 1,295,971-1,295,796) covers the period 1871 to 1933 and includes the following information: name, place of death, date, and register number. The inclusion of addresses is very useful in highlighting possible relationships between decedents and for use with city directories. However, this index only covers deaths occurring in Chicago or where burials occurred in Chicago during the period burial permits were the same as certificates of death.

The second as a series of microfiche (6,016,533 fiche 0001-0070) covers only the period 1871 to 1916, but covers all of Cook County. Information includes individual's name, death date, age at death, death place (restricted to Chicago or Cook County— does not give addresses outside of Chicago), and the identification number (equivalent to register number above).

NEWSPAPERS

Death notices and obituaries are a particularly useful source for determining the place of interment for the period prior to the Great Chicago Fire of 1871. Families and friends paid for death notices to notify others of these events. Look for additional death notices placed by fraternal organizations. Because obituaries were news stories, they may or may not contain information concerning funeral services or burials. For a while the *Chicago Tribune* ran an "Official Death Record" taken from the county clerk's records and the *New World* ran a list of burials in Catholic cemeteries. These lists were usually more comprehensive than the death notices, but they also tended to run after the burial had occurred. Accidental, violent, or otherwise news worthy deaths may appear in other sections of the newspaper besides the obituary section. Death notices were often scattered throughout early newspapers as fillers and so it is important to make a thorough search.

The following sources are useful in locating death notices and obituaries. Sam Fink's Index (BGL microfilm 1,321,939) indexes death notices and obituaries in ten newspapers between 1833 and 1889. The Chicago Genealogical Society published seven volumes of vital records from Chicago newspapers covering the period from 1833 to 1848. Also check the clipping file and card catalog at the Chicago Historical Society.

ADJACENT COUNTIES

While this guide is to genealogical research in Cook County, burials occur sufficiently regularly in adjacent counties to justify mentioning them here. Cemeteries in adjacent counties were included in the following list if they were contained in a list of frequently called telephone numbers distributed by the Wilbur Vault Company to funeral directors. This was used as an indication of the frequency with which these cemeteries may be used for burial of late Cook County residences.

Following is a list of sources concerning burials and cemeteries in adjacent counties:

The Cemetery Committee, Lake Co. (IL) Genealogical Society. *A Guide to Cemetery Names and Locations in Lake County, Illinois*. Waukegan, Ill.: Sir Speedy, 1980.

Price, Clarence and Florence. *Lombard Cemetery Records.* Lombard, Ill.: DuPage County Genealogical Society.

Thomas, Nancy Roeser, ed. *Genealogical Sources: Du Page County, Illinois.* Lombard, Ill.: DuPage County Genealogical Society.

The Kane County, Illinois Master Every Name Index includes fortyseven cemeteries. Contact the Kane County Genealogical Society, P.O. Box 504, Geneva, IL 60134.

CHAPTER 6

Census Records

FEDERAL POPULATION CENSUS

I t is generally acknowledged that the Federal Population Census is the most popular information source available to the American genealogist. U.S. population censuses were taken in 1790 and every tenth year thereafter. The Census schedules for 1790 through 1910 are open to the public and available on microfilm with the exception of 1890 schedules which were almost entirely destroyed by fire. Addresses of archives and libraries having census collections can be found at the end of this section.

Federal Census Schedules for Chicago and Cook County are available on the following microfilm publications:

NATIONAL ARCHIVES

YEAR	U.S. CENSUS SCHEDULES	MICROFILM NUMBER
1820	Chicago (As part of Clark County, IL)	M33,12
1830	Chicago (As part of Putnam County, IL)	M19,24
1840	Chicago and all of Cook County, IL	M704, 57
1850	Cook County including city of Chicago	M432, 102 & 103
1860	Cook County including city of Chicago	M653, 164-170
1870	Cook County including city of Chicago	M593, 198-213
1880	Cook County including city of Chicago	T9, 184-202
1890	Not available	
1900	Cook County including city of Chicago	T623, 244-295
1910	Cook County including city of Chicago	T624, 237-283

1920 + The schedules from 1920 on are confidential by law for 72 years. Many individuals do not have birth certificates and, for this reason, may use transcripts of population census records to qualify for social security or retirement benefits, obtain passports, prove citizenship or relationships, or satisfy other situations where a birth certificate may be needed. The Bureau of the Census releases information only to the person, his or her heirs, or a legal representative. Census transcripts cannot be furnished for use in tracing missing persons. The Bureau maintains files from 1900 through 1980 for transcription purposes. These files are administered by the Personal Census Services. Transcripts may be ordered by completing form BC-600. For applications and help in completing them write or call: Personal Census Service Branch, Bureau of the Census, 1600 N. Walnut Street, Pittsburg, KS 66762, Telephone: 316-231-7100. In the Chicago area call 312-353-0980 for general information.

WHERE TO FIND U.S. POPULATION CENSUS RECORDS

The National Archives-Chicago Branch
7358 South Pulaski Road
Chicago, IL 60629
(312-581-7816)

The Chicago Branch of the Archives has all of the Federal Population Census on microfilm for all available states from 1790 to 1910, including the Soundex and most other indexes which are helpful for locating individuals within the actual census schedules.

The Newberry Library
60 West Walton
Chicago, IL 60610
(312-943-9090)

The Newberry has microfilms of all extant U.S. Population Census schedules for Illinois up to and including 1910. It also has the 1880 and 1900 Soundex reels for Illinois, but does not have the 1910 Miracode index. A detailed set of maps serves as a finding aid for locating Chicago addresses. See explanation with description of the appropriate year. The Newberry also has some census schedules for certain other counties and states.

The Chicago Public Library
Social Sciences and History Division, 12th Floor
425 North Michigan Avenue
Chicago, IL 60611
(312-269-2830)

The Chicago Public Library has only the U.S. Population Census Schedules for Chicago and Cook County from 1850 to 1910 inclusive. CPL does not have the Soundex or Miracode or other indexes, but does have some ward and enumeration district maps to assist in locating street addresses.

The Chicago Historical Society
Clark Street at North Avenue
Chicago, IL 60614
(312-642-4600)

The Chicago Historical Society has the Federal Census Schedules of 1840-80 and 1900 for Chicago and Cook County. Indexes for those schedules are not available at the Society Library. The 1810 and 1820 census schedules for Illinois were published in *Collections of the Illinois State Historical Library*, Vols. XXIV and XXVI, respectively. Volume XXIV also contains the 1818 Illinois Territory census schedules. The CHS Library and The Newberry have copies of the publication.

For those outside of the Chicago area, there are other branches of the National Archives and some large libraries in the country such as the Allen County Public Library (900 Webster Street, Ft. Wayne, Indiana 46802) which have complete collections of census schedules for the entire United States.

The Illinois State Archives (Archives Building, Springfield, IL 62956) has all available Illinois census. The State Archives does not participate in interlibrary loan, but can provide paper printouts or typed transcriptions.

Illinois census films may be borrowed through the standard interlibrary loan process from the Illinois State Library (Centennial Building, Springfield, IL 62756). Microfilms may also be borrowed from: Microfilm Rental Program, Box 2490, Hyattsville, MD 20784. These may be borrowed through public or university libraries, genealogical or historical societies, or through some educational institutions. Ask your local librarian for order forms.

Films for the 1790-1910 Census may be borrowed directly or purchased from: American Genealogical Lending Library, Box 244, Bountiful, UT 84010 (801-298-5358).

In some instances a poor microfilm copy of a particular census will not be legible nor will it provide a good paper copy. Experience has proved that it is worth investigating the possibility of getting a better copy from another library, or the National Archives in Washington since microfilm quality will often differ from copy to copy.

INDEXES AND FINDING AIDS

The Illinois State Archives has an index covering state and federal census records for Illinois from 1810-1855. The 1860 Census Index is segregated from the 1810-1855 Census Index, and Cook County is interfiled with other counties within that index. The Archives will do a limited amount of research in reply to mail requests. Please ask only for one or two specific items at a time, designate the specific census to be searched, provide the complete name of the person to be searched, and do not submit a second request until you have received an answer to your first request.

1830 U.S. Census Index

Jackson, Ronald Vern, David Schaefermeyer and Gary Ronald Teeples. *Illinois 1830 Census Index.* Bountiful, Ut.: Accelerated Indexing Systems, Inc. 1976.

1840 U.S. Census Indexes

Smith, Marjorie. "Index to the 1840 Federal Census of Cook County" *Chicago Genealogist* 2, No.1 (1970): 14-19; J 2, No.2 (1970): 39-42; 2, No.3 (1970), 80-83: 2, No.4 (1970): 75-78.

Jackson, Ronald Vern and Gary Ronald Teeples. *Illinois 1840 Census Index.* Bountiful, Ut.: Accelerated Indexing Systems, Inc. 1977.

1850 U.S. Census Indexes

The 1850 Index at the State Archives included with the "Name Index 1810-1855" includes every name (including children) on a separate card. This is particularly helpful when parents' names are unknown. Printed indexes contain only names of heads of families.

Barekman, June B., Gertrude Lundberg and Bernice C. Richard. *Surname Index to the 1850 Federal Census of Chicago, Cook County Illinois.* Chicago: June B. Barekman Genealogical Services and Publications, 1976.

Daughters of the American Revolution-Dewalt Mechle Chapter. *Old Settlers of Chicago 1850-70.* Chicago: by the editors. 1956. (Transcription of census records for Southwest Chicago and Cook County including the communities of Worth, Beverly Hills, Morgan Park, Brainerd, Chicago Ridge, Blue Island, Evergreen Park, Oak Lawn, Roseland, Mt. Greenwood, and Washington Heights, but not all communities are covered for all of the census years.

Lundberg, Gertrude. *1850 Census of Cook County Illinois Outside of Chicago.* Chicago: Chicago Genealogical Society. 1985. The above two publications are available from the Chicago Genealogical Society, P.O. Box 1160, Chicago, IL 60690.

Jackson, Ronald Vern and Gary Ronald Teeples. *Illinois 1850 Census Index.* Bountiful, Ut.: Accelerated Indexing Systems, Inc. 1976.

The South Suburban Genealogical and Historical Society has indexed the 1850 Census for the townships of Bloom, Bremen, Lemont, Palos, Rich, Thornton and Worth in quarterly publications of *Where the Trails Cross* (1970-74). For further information write to the Society at P.O. Box 96, South Holland, IL 60473.

Adams, James N. comp. "Illinois Place Names." (*Occasional Publications,* No.54. Illinois State Historical Society, Springfield, Ill., 1968).

Parker, J. Carlyle. *City, County, Town and Township Index to the 1850 Federal Census Schedules.* Detroit, Mich.: Gale Research Company, 1979. A helpful source for locating townships and some towns which are no longer in existence.

1860 U.S. Census Index

All of the 1860 Federal Census for Cook County, Illinois, was transcribed and indexed by Bernice C. Richard of the Chicago Genealogical Society. The original card index has been integrated into the Census Index at the Illinois State Archives. Microfilm copies are available for purchase from the Illinois State Archives, Springfield, IL 62756.

The National Archives-Chicago Branch and The Newberry Library also have microfilm copies of this 1860 Census Index for Cook County. Contrary to other published information, The Newberry Library does not have a state-wide index for the 1860 Census for Illinois.

Roll numbers for the 1860 Cook County Index are as follows:
124-27 Begins UNKNOWN, John and ends CATHANES, John
124-28 Begins CATHAINE, Sister Mary and ends FAUBEL, G.W.
124-29 Begins FEAKES,Thos. and ends GRIFFIN, Margaret
124-30 Begins GRIFFIN, Mary and ends LARKIN, Michael
124-31 Begins LARKIN, Patrick and ends MUNROE, Kenneth
124-32 Begins MUNROE, Fred and ends RYAN, James.
124-33 Begins RYAN, Jas. and ends TURNER, Henry
124-34 Begins TURNER,Henry and ends ZWING, M.

Note: It has been discovered that surnames beginning with the letters HA are missing from the microfilm copies of the 1860 Cook County Index.

The South Suburban Genealogical and Historical Society has indexed the 1860 Census for the townships of Lemont, Orland, Palos, Thornton, and Worth in quarterly publications of *Where the Trails Cross.* (1973-79)

1870 U.S. CENSUS INDEXES AND FINDING TOOLS

There is no complete 1870 census index available for Chicago or Cook County at this time. However, there are some finding aids which will minimize searching through the heavily populated area.

The geographical arrangement of the census schedules makes finding aids vital when searching for urban residents. Historian Keith Schlesinger devised a system to locate individuals overlooked by Soundex and other indexing processes. Schlesinger gleaned addresses from city directories,which he found both accurate and accessible, then plotted them on maps of census enumeration districts, which normally followed the boundaries of voting precincts in most cities. By narrowing the search for the nonindexed individual to one or two enumeration districts, this scheme permits the historian to escape the confinement of the Soundex. The technique is described by Keith Schlesinger and Peggy Tuck Sinko in "Urban Finding Aid for Manuscript Census Searches," *National Genealogical Society Quarterly* 69 (Sept. 1981): 171-80.

The Illinois State Archives has a surname (only) index for 1870. However, each ward is indexed separately which makes it difficult to use.

The 1871 Edwards Census Directory for Chicago complements the use of the 1870 ward index at the State Archives since each entry provides ward numbers as well as street addresses. Additionally, this unique directory lists the occupation of the head of house; number of males; number of females; and total number in residence at the address. The birthplace of the head of house is also stated. The directory, correctly titled *The Chicago Census Report and Statistical Review* is essentially an alphabetically arranged city directory with the addition of statistical information. It was compiled from a canvassing which was requested by the mayor, city council, business firms, and capitalists of Chicago who were not satisfied with the results of the 1870 federal census.

The Newberry Library 1870 Chicago Census Finding Aid

The staff at the Newberry has developed a specialized finding aid for the 1870 census for the city of Chicago. The census enumerators' routes have been plotted on a city map so that a specific address can be located by approximate enumeration date. Addresses may be determined by consulting an 1870 or 1871 city directory for the individual or household being sought in the census schedules. The maps are available at the Local and Family History section at The Newberry. The staff will answer correspondence or telephone requests but must place a limit of three addresses at a time.

1870 Indexes for Southern Cook County Townships

The South Suburban Genealogical and Historical Society has indexed the 1870 Census for the townships of Bremen, Calumet, Orland, and Palos in quarterly publications (1982-84) of *Where the Trails Cross*.

1880 U.S. Census Index

Although 1880 census indexes have not been compiled specifically for Chicago and Cook County, the 1880 Soundex (index) to the Federal Census for Illinois is a significant aid for locating individuals or households in the census schedules. Unfortunately, the 1880 Soundex is only a partial index which includes only households where children ten years of age or younger were in residence. This partial index was compiled in the 1930s under the auspices of the Work Projects Administration (WPA) to determine how many then living would be eligible for benefits under the Social Security Act which was then being considered. Often names were misspelled or completely omitted in transcription from the original census schedules. Another limitation of the 1880 Illinois Soundex microfilm publication is the omission of over 1,000 cards for the last names beginning with the letter *O*. The section for the letter was transcribed, however, from the original Soundex cards and has been published separately in book form by Nancy Gibb Frederick, 1208 Maple Avenue, Evanston, IL 60101. Copies of Frederick's index are available at the National Archives-Chicago Branch, the Newberry Library, and at several other area libraries. The original 1880 Soundex cards for Illinois are now housed at the Northwestern Memorial Hospital Group Archives, 516 West 36th Street, Chicago, IL 60609.

The 1880 Soundex for Illinois is available at the National Archives-Chicago Branch and at the Newberry Library. Although several area libraries have the actual census schedules for 1880 Chicago and Cook County, they do not have the Soundex Index in their collections.

The Illinois State Archives has the Soundex indexes for 1880 and the Illinois State Library makes it available through the interlibrary loan service.

The Newberry Library 1880 Chicago Census Finding Aid

The staff at The Newberry has developed a system to locate people omitted by the Soundex by using enumeration descriptions, ward, and precinct maps. Street addresses for individuals sought in the census schedules should first be determined by consulting an 1880 Chicago Directory. Addresses then become the key to locating individuals or households in exact enumeration districts within the census schedules. The 1880 finding aids are available at the Local and Family History section of the Newberry Library. The staff will answer correspondence but must place a limit of three addresses at a time.

1900 U.S. Census Index

Although there are no special 1900 Census indexes for Chicago or Cook County, the 1900 Soundex (index) for Illinois is probably the most complete of any of the census indexes. Because the 1900 Soundex is so reliable, it is often the suggested starting point to begin census and other genealogical and historical projects. Individual Soundex cards provide the name of the head of household (or persons of different surnames in the household), race, month and year of birth, age, birthplaces of parents, occupation, citizenship status, place of residence by state and county, civil division, city name, house number, and street number. The cards also list the volume number, enumeration district and both page and line numbers of the original schedules from which the information was taken.

The Newberry Library 1900 Chicago Finding Aid

The staff at the Newberry Library has created a 1900 Chicago census finding aid by using the same system described in the 1880 Chicago Census Finding Aid Section.

The Chicago Public Library Social Science and History Division has a set of maps to locate households or individuals by address in the 1900 census in Chicago.

The National Archives-Chicago Branch and the Newberry Library are the only places in the Chicago area which have the 1900 Soundex index for Illinois. Additionally, the Chicago Branch has an Enumeration District Finding Aid for the 1900 Census for Chicago which was developed by former staff member, David S. Weber. Even though the 1900 Soundex is the most complete index, occasionally there were transcription omissions or misspellings which necessitate the use of the maps as finding aids.

The Illinois State Archives has the Soundex for the 1900 federal census, and the Illinois State Library makes it available on interlibrary loan.

1900 U.S. Census Schedules for Cook County National Archives Microfilm Reel Numbers:

T623-244 = Ward 1
T623-245 = Wards 1 & 2
T623-246 = Wards 2 & 3
T623-247 = Wards 3 & 4
T623-248 = Wards 4 & 5
T623-249 = Wards 5 & 6
T623-250 = Ward 6
T623-251 = Wards 6 & 7
T623-252 = Wards 7 & 8
T623-253 = Wards 8 & 9
T623-254 = Wards 9 & 10
T623-255 = Ward 10
T623-256 = Ward 10
T623-257 = Wards 10 & 11
T623-258 = Wards 11 & 12
T623-259 = Ward 12
T623-260 = Wards 12 & 13
T623-261 = Wards 13 & 14

T623-262 = Ward 14
T623-263 = Wards 14 & 15
T623-264 = Ward 15
T623-265 = Wards 15 & 16
T623-266 = Ward 16
T623-267 = Wards 16 & 17
T623-268 = Wards 17, 18 & 19
T623-269 = Ward 19
T623-270 = Wards 19,20 and 21
T623-271 = Wards 21 & 22
T623-272 = Wards 22 & 23
T623-273 = Wards 23 & 24dd,
T623-274 = Wards 24 & 25
T623-275 = Ward 25
T623-276 = Wards 25 & 26
T623-277 = Wards 26 & 27
T623-278 = Wards 27 & 28
T623-279 = Wards 27 & 28

T623-280 = Wards 28 & 29		T623-286 = Ward 32
T623-281 = Wards 29		T623-287 = Wards 32 & 33
T623-282 = Ward 30		T623-288 = Wards 33 & 34
T623-283 = Wards 30-31		T623-289 = Ward 34
T623-284 = Ward 31		T623-290 = Ward 34
T623-285 = Wards 31 & 32		T623-291 = Wards 34 & 35

T263-292 = Townships of Cook County, including Calumet, Schaumburg, Elk Grove, Evanston, and others.

T263-293 = Hanover, Lemont, Leydon, New Trier, and others.

T263-294 = Northfield, Orland, Palatine, Palos, Proviso, Thornton, Rich, and others.

1910 U.S. Census Index

The 1910 Soundex/Miracode for Illinois should be the quickest approach for locating persons in Chicago or Cook County census schedules, however, it is especially notable for its omissions. Experience has proven that many individuals who were actually enumerated in the census were missed in the transcription to the Miracode cards or that names were misspelled in the original census in such a way as to be thrown into the wrong Soundex code. Street addresses are not provided on Miracode cards as they are in previous census years so it is not always as easy to identify individuals of common names by the index alone. In spite of the omission factor, the Soundex/Miracode is the best starting place to locate persons in the 1910 Census. The National Archives-Chicago Branch is the only place in the Chicago area having a copy of the 1910 Miracode for Illinois.

1910 Index to City Streets and Enumeration Districts

An index to city streets and census enumeration districts for thirty-nine cities in the 1910 Federal Population Census is reproduced on fifty sheets of microfiche. Chicago is one of the cities which is indexed in this fashion. The Federation of Genealogical Societies sponsored a NARS Gift Fund which has made the 1910 Street Index available at the National Archives branches. Entries in the index give a list of Chicago streets and house numbers (new and pre-1909) numbering and the appropriate enumeration district needed to locate individuals in the census. Named streets, arranged alphabetically, are listed first, followed by numerical streets. Immediately preceding the index portion of each volume is a table listing the enumeration districts covered in that volume with a cross reference to the corresponding volume of the original population schedules. The Chicago Street Index is contained on Microfiche Publication M-1283:

Fiche:
  6 A Street thru Curtis Street
  7 Curtis thru Ingraham Avenue
  8 Institute Place thru Ogden Avenue
  9 Ogden Avenue thru Wabash Avenue
  10 Wabash Avenue thru 38th Place East
  11 38th Place East thru 87th Street West
  12 87th Street West thru 138th Street East

Presently, the National Archives-Chicago Branch is the only archive or library in the Chicago area that has this street index. The Newberry Library and the Chicago Public Library have the 1910 map finding aids that operate on the same principles as do the 1880 and 1900 census finding aid.

The Illinois State Archives has the 1910 Miracode (index) for Illinois and the Illinois State Library makes this index available through inter-library loan service.

Mortality Schedules

Mortality schedules list deaths for the twelve months prior to the census (1 June through 31 May 1849, 1859, 1869, 1879). They provide the deceased person's name, sex, age, color, marital status, place of birth, month in which the death occurred, profession or occupation, cause of death, and number of days ill.

The 1850 Mortality Schedule for Illinois is integrated into the Census Index at the Illinois State Archives, Springfield, IL 62756. Additionally, Lowell M. Volkel has published *Illinois Mortality Schedule 1850* in three volumes. Volume I covers Adams through Iroquois counties (including Cook County).

The 1860 Mortality Schedule for Illinois is not included in the Census Index at the Illinois Archives. However, it has been indexed and is available in book form. Lowell M. Volkel has published *Illinois Mortality Schedule 1860* in five volumes. Volume I covers Adams through Effingham counties (including Cook County). Although no specific addresses were given for those who died in Chicago in the original schedules, decedents were enumerated by wards.

An index for the 1870 Mortality Schedule for Illinois is in progress, although, the schedules for all counties beginning with the letters *A* through *Ka* are missing. That, of course, includes Cook County. Other Illinois counties have been indexed by Lowell M. Volkel.

The Newberry Library has mortality schedules for Illinois 1850-1880 on seven reels of microfilm. (Call # = Microfilm 118).

AGRICULTURE SCHEDULES

Agricultural schedules, though primarily useful in statistical studies, do help to fill gaps when land and tax records are missing or incomplete, distinguish between men with the same name, and document land holdings, movement, and economic changes.

The originals for these special schedules for Illinois are at the Illinois State Archives. Additionally, the State Archives has microfilmed the Agriculture Schedules. These records are not indexed.

Illinois State Archives numbers for Cook County Agricultural Schedules are: 1850−31-1; 1860−31-5; 1870−31-45; 1880−31-65.

The Newberry Library has Agriculture Schedules on microfilm (unindexed) for Illinois:

1850 Cook County is included on Microfilm 111, Reel 1.
1860 Cook County is included on Microfilm 112, Reel 2.
1870 (1865) Cook County is included on Microfilm 113, Reel 4.
1880 Cook County is included on Microfilm 116, Reel 4.

MANUFACTURES' SCHEDULES

Manufactures' Schedules tabulated the owner's name, the establishment location, the number of employees, kind and quality of machinery, capital invested, articles manufactured, annual production, and general remarks on the business and the demand for the products.

The Illinois State Archives has microfilm copies of Manufactures Schedules (unindexed) for Illinois.

Numbers for Cook County are: 1850−31-97; 1860−31-60; 1870−31-60; 1880−31-54.

Newberry Library has 1880 Manufactures' Schedules on six reels of microfilm. (Cook County is Call # Microfilm 114, Reel #1).

ILLINOIS STATE CENSUSES

Censuses of the Territory and State of Illinois were taken in the years 1810, 1818, 1820, 1825, 1830, 1835, 1840, 1845, 1855, and 1865. Only a transcript of a portion of the 1810 census has been found. The records of most of the 1818 supplementary census, of the 1825 and 1830, and most of the 1835 and 1840 censuses are missing from the State archives. The 1855 census has been integrated into the Census Index at the Illinois State Archives. The archives staff will search this index for two specifically named individuals, including both first and last names, for one census year in a designated county location. The state censuses listed only the heads of families by names. Other family members were represented only by numerical totals in various age categories. The 1865 census is unindexed.

1934 CHICAGO CENSUS

Upon recommendation to the city council, an ordinance was passed 12 December 1933, providing for the taking of a census of the city of Chicago. From discussions, it was made clear that the facts and data of the 1930 federal census were considerably out of date for the planning of the needed public works and services. This project would require the services of over 2,800 men and women out of work to take over the task of supervision and enumeration. Furthermore, these workers were to be recruited from the ranks of unemployed clerks and semi-professionals not otherwise provided for in the usual line of Civil Works Administration projects. The laws of the State of Illinois empower the city council to provide for the taking of a census. Accordingly, an ordinance was drawn up authorizing a census of the population of the city of Chicago to be taken in January, 1934 using workers to be employed by the Civil Works Administration for Illinois. The ordinance provided for an official body designated as the Chicago Census Commission to be composed of seven members to organize and supervise the taking of census. Mayor Edward J. Kelly was the Chairman and Charles S. Newcomb served as Director of the special census. The task of enumerating the population of the second largest city in the United States with only a few weeks for preparation was a tremendous undertaking, but according to *Census Data of the City of Chicago, 1934* edited by Charles S. Newcomb and Richard O. Lang (Chicago: the University of Chicago Press) the census was completed. It is believed that all that survives of the 1934 Census of the city of Chicago is the statistical data which is published in the Newcomb and Lang report. Attempts to locate the original manuscripts have been unsuccessful, and the Municipal Library has no record of their existence.

BIBLIOGRAPHY

Eakle, Arlene and Johni Cerny. *The Source: A Guidebook of American Genealogy.* Salt Lake City, Ut.: Ancestry Inc., 1984. A comprehensive chapter on census records, availability and use.

Kirkham, E. Kay. *A Handy Guide to Record Searching in the Larger Cities of the United States.* Logan, Ut.: Everton, 1974. Includes 1850-1855, and 1878 Ward Maps of Chicago.

U.S. National Archives. National Archives Trust Fund Board, *Federal Population Censuses, 1790-1890.* Washington, D.C., 1979.

_____. National Archives and Record Service, *1900 Federal Population Census.* Washington, D.C., 1978.

_____. National Archives Trust Fund Board, *The 1910 Federal Population Census.* Washington, D.C., 1982.

The preceding three items are catalogs which provide census roll numbers and prices for microfilm copies. Catalogs are available for purchase from the Publications Sales Branch (NEPS), National Archives and Records Administration, Washington, DC 20408.

U.S. Department of Commerce. Department of Commerce, Bureau of the Census, *Twenty Censuses—Population and Housing Questions 1790-1980.* Washington, D.C., 1978.

_____. Department of Commerce, Bureau of the Census. *Age Search Information.* Washington, D.C., 1979.

Note: Indexes which were compiled by Lowell Volkel have been published and are available from Ye Olde Genealogie Shoppe, Indianapolis, IN 46239. (317-862-3330).

CHAPTER 7

Chicago Communities and Neighborhoods

Linda Stone Lamberty and Loretto Dennis Szucs

I t has been said that the soul of Chicago is reflected in its old neighborhoods. To know Chicago, you have to go beyond Michigan Avenue and the Loop to discover Logan Square, Bridgeport, Beverly, Kenwood, Hyde Park, Greektown, Wicker Park, and the many other official and unofficial communities where Chicago thrives.

Anyone who looks at a city history will immediately realize that only a small fraction of the population gains municipal recognition. A citizen prominent enough to be found in a major printed source is inevitably the same individual who will be easily found in every other source. For most Chicagoans, a more manageable and productive search area is the neighborhood or community. Usually, the neighborhood will have its own library where a researcher can expect to find more information on that immediate area, including local histories, sometimes still in manuscript form, and even neighborhood newspapers. Community newspapers allowed a great deal of space for local events and personalities ignored by the big city papers. Neighborhood historical societies and museums are often goldmines of information, but are sometimes more difficult to access since they are not always listed in the phone book, are operated by volunteers, and are often open for only a few hours each week. The local library is often the key to locating community historical collections.

In recent years a variety of excellent publications have become available which focus on neighborhoods. Enhanced with charming photographs, most of these histories provide an indepth study of the community and provide bibliographies which become research tools in themselves. A bibliography of general works which explore some of the many Chicago neighborhoods follows the list of communities.

A breakdown of Chicago communities into seventy-five areas was accomplished through the work of the Social Science Research Committee of the University of Chicago more than fifty years ago. This breakdown was based on the following criteria: (1) the settlement, growth and history of the area; (2) local identification with the area; (3) the local trade area; (4) distribution of membership of local institutions; and (5) natural and artificial barriers such as the Chicago River and its branches, railroad lines, local transportation systems, and parks and boulevards. Requirements of the U.S. Bureau of the Census also figured in the final determination of boundaries. Two additional community areas have been designated since 1960, bringing the total of official Chicago communities to seventy-seven.

Those official neighborhoods and other well-known districts are listed here together with works focusing on respective areas. Every effort has been made to be complete, but further research could produce additional names. Historical societies serve some neighborhoods or groups of neighborhoods and some of these resources are included in the enumeration. Special Collections at the Cultural Center of the Chicago Public Library has an extensive neighborhood collection, including books, manuscripts, photographs, scrapbooks, and pamphlets. The City of Chicago Municipal Reference Library maintains a newspaper clipping file featuring Chicago's seventy-seven official neighborhoods, and the Chicago Historical Society has a wealth of material catalogued by community, neighborhood and/or town name. Frank Jewel's "Annotated Bibliography of Chicago History" lists many works focusing on the neighborhood and can be found in the Chicago Historical Society Library.

ALBANY PARK (14) Centered at the intersection of Lawrence and Kimball avenues on the northwest side of Chicago, Albany Park lies about eight miles from the Loop. The northwest section was settled by Bohemians during the 1870s and 1880s and developed as a part of Mayfair.

ANDERSONVILLE – Uptown

ANNEXED AREA (O'HARE) (76) In June 1942 the federal government chose Orchard Place, a strip of land eighteen miles northwest of downtown Chicago, as the site for a huge Douglas Aircraft Company plant and airfield, completed within eighteen months. The site had been orchard land before being donated for use as a railroad station. The plant became the largest of its kind in the country, and the Chicago Orchard Airport became O'Hare International Airport, thus explaining the ORD baggage symbol recognized by air travelers. In earlier years, Higgins Road was a thin connection between the distant airfield and the city, spawning the city council's need to secure its legal hold on O'Hare by continually encroaching upon surrounding land. Nine hundred acres were annexed in March 1958, and what had once been a small residential area (of less than 800 inhabitants) in the midst of forest preserves was by the end of the 1970s a community of homes, condominiums and apartments accomodating more than 6,000 people.

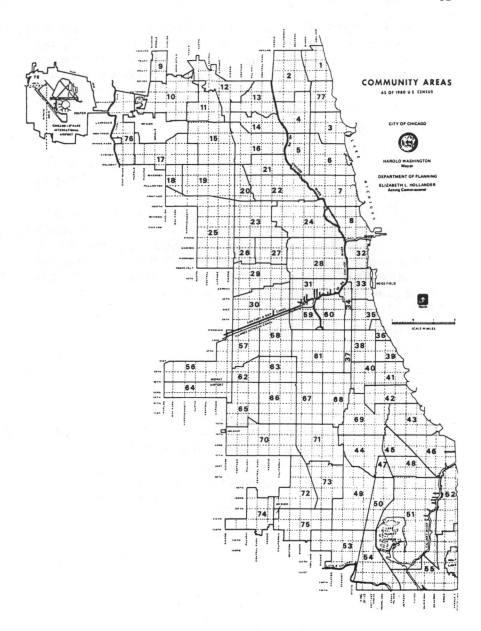

COMMUNITY AREAS
AS OF 1980 U.S. CENSUS

CITY OF CHICAGO

HAROLD WASHINGTON
Mayor

DEPARTMENT OF PLANNING
ELIZABETH L. HOLLANDER
Acting Commissioner

Figure 5.

ARCHER HEIGHTS (57) Once called the Archer Road district for Archer Avenue, this southwestern community is bounded by the Stevenson Expressway on the north, the Belt Line Railroad on the south and west, and the Santa Fe Railroad on the east. It was under the jurisdictions of Lake and Cicero townships until the district was annexed to Chicago in 1889.

ARGYLE PARK—Uptown

ARMOUR SQUARE (34) Named for Armour Square Park, the area is located about two miles south of Chicago's heart and comprised of land from surrounding Near South Side, Bridgeport, and Douglas communities.

ASHBURN (70) Between 1865 and its annexation to Chicago in 1889, Ashburn existed under the jurisdiction of the Town of Lake. A subdivision was opened between Crawford and Central Park avenues from 79th to 85th streets shortly before the World's Fair in 1893 by the real estate firm of Clark and Marsdon. Clarksdale, as it became known, was also the name of the Wabash Railroad shop located at the intersection of 83rd Street and Central Park Avenue.

ASHBURN ESTATES—Ashburn

ASHLAND—Near West Side

AUBURN GRESHAM (71) Settled during the 1850s by German and Dutch farmers, the community area developed from several settlements located on Chicago's far South Side. Cummorn is the name once given to a perimeter of land surrounding Ten Mile House tavern and post office at what is now the intersection of 79th Street and Vincennes Avenue, once a major thoroughfare into Chicago from the south .

AUSTIN (25) Austin began to develop in the 1840s with the construction of the Lake Street Plank Road and the Galena and Chicago Union Railroad. The whole area became part of Cicero Township at its organization in 1857, including Sand Ridge and territory south of it, and incorporation ten years later. All of the present community of Austin having been forced within Chicago city limits in 1889, (the only built-up section then being the original village of Austin bounded by Cicero Avenue, Augusta, Washington, and Austin boulevards), the resulting spurt of residential growth within the first three years finally brought the neighborhood to maturity by 1930.

AVALON HIGHLANDS—Chatham

AVALON PARK (45) Located about ten miles south of the Loop, Avalon Park forms part of a triangle completed by the communities of Burnside and Calumet Heights. Avalon Park was undeveloped swampland until the early 20th century, its first settlers being railroad workers who settled on the northern edge near Grand Crossing.

AVONDALE (21) One of the northwest side communities that grew with the development of Milwaukee Avenue and the railroads.

BACK OF THE YARDS—New City

BELMONT CENTRAL—Portage Park, Dunning, Belmont Cragin

BELMONT CRAGIN (19) Largely a prairie and woodland area, Belmont Cragin was settled around Whiskey Point (presently Armitage and Grand Crossing avenues. In later years it was incorporated into Jefferson Park.

BELMONT GARDENS—Avondale, Logan Square

BELMONT HEIGHTS—Dunning

BELMONT TERRACE—Dunning

BEVERLY (72) Located east of Western Avenue from 87th Street to 107th Street, Beverly Hills sits on the Blue Island ridge some thirty to forty feet above the rest of the city. This ridge was, with marshland below it to the east, the site of several Indian trails; one being the Vincennes Trail linking Fort Dearborn and later Chicago to Blue Island. Due to the appearance given it from the city by mists hanging above its trees, the whole elevation of land of which Beverly Hills is a part was originally called Blue Island, and then North Blue Island until the early 1870s. In 1844, Thomas Morgan bought almost 3,000 acres from John Blackstone and established a home, called Upwood after his father's home in England, at about 92nd Street and Pleasant Avenue. That name seems to have been confined to the area immediately surrounding his house. Railroad service in the 1850s encouraged development of the entire area, including Morgan Park to the south and Washington Heights to the east, whose histories are closely tied to that of Beverly. In 1890 the section of Beverly north of 95th Street, once called Longwood, was annexed to Chicago. A month later Washington Heights, including the area east of Western Avenue between 95th and 107th streets, was annexed and in 1914 a third section of Beverly west of Western Avenue and South of 99th Street was annexed to the city. Presently containing the largest designated historic district in the country, Beverly residents fondly call their neighborhood "a village in the city."

BEVERLY VIEW—Ashburn

BEVERLY WOODS—Morgan Park

BIG OAKS—Norwood Park

BLUE ISLAND—Beverly (also see gazeteer)

BOWMANVILLE–Lincoln Square

BRIDGEPORT (60) The development of Bridgeport was largely due to the construction of Archer Road and the Illinois and Michigan Canal. Early settlers were mainly Irish and German. When the canal was completed in 1848, boats stopped at a station near Ashland Avenue and the canal. The settlement along the South Fork of the Chicago River expanded on both sides of the water. This stopping place, located in what is now McKinley Park, was called Bridgeport, as was the settlement along the South Fork. Irish laborers who had worked on the construction of the canal settled here and to the northeast. The latter settlement, centering at Archer Avenue and Mary Street, was also named Bridgeport. In 1853 the Chicago city limits were extended south to 31st Street and west to Halsted Street, thereby bringing the northeastern portion of future Bridgeport within the city. In 1863 the remainder of the territory included in present Bridgeport became part of the city when the city limits were extended west to Western Avenue and south to 39th Street. In 1864-1865, the Union Stock Yards and Packingtown were established south and west of Pershing Road in New City, giving new impetus to the neighboring area of Bridgeport.

BRIGHTON PARK (58) Settled in the early years of the city, this southwestern community took its name from a race track built in the 1850s by "Long John" Wentworth where McKinley Park is today. Attention to the area was first attracted in the 1830s by the creation of the Illinois and Michigan Canal and Archer Avenue. When Cicero was organized in 1857, it assumed the land north of Pershing Road. When in 1889 Brighton Park was annexed to Chicago, it included that area presently situated north of Pershing Road to the Stevenson Expressway, and land to the south of Pershing Road became part of the Town of Lake.

BROOKLINE–Greater Grand Crossing

BRYN MAWR–South Shore

BUCK TOWN–Lincoln Square

BUDLONG WOODS–Lincoln Square

BURNSIDE (47) Burnside was originally a marshy swamp area south of early Chicago. It became part of the Village of Hyde Park and was annexed to Chicago in 1889.

BUSH–South Chicago

CABRINI-GREEN–Near North Side

CALUMET HEIGHTS (48) A South Side Chicago community, Calumet Heights is situated on the old Stony Island ridge just over ten miles south of today's loop. During the 1850s and 1860s the area's only attraction consisted of the two major roads passing through it. Settlers were drawn by the opening of the Calumet and Chicago Canal and Dock Company in the late 1870s. Calumet Heights was annexed to Chicago as part of Hyde Park in 1889.

CANALPORT—McKinley Park

CANARYVILLE—Fuller Park

CANFIELD—Edison Park

CENTRAL PARK—West Garfield Park

CHICAGO JUNCTION—Englewood

CHICAGO LAWN (66) Located southwest of the Loop, Chicago Lawn is comprised of the early communities of Marquette Manor (east of California Avenue, north of Marquette Road) and Chicago Lawn (originally west of Kedzie Avenue, north of Marquette Road). Under the jurisdiction of the Town of Lake until after 1865, Blue Island Road (now Western Avenue) was the only avenue into the area at that time.

CHATHAM (44) Settled by Italian stonemasons in the 1880s and 1890s, marshy Avalon Highlands was the first residential community in today's Chatham, nine miles south of the Loop. From 87th to 93rd streets between South Park Avenue and the Illinois Central tracks, Dauphin Park subdivision was laid out in 1889 after Chatham was annexed to Chicago as part of Hyde Park Village and Lake Township.

CHINATOWN—Armour Square

CHRYSLER VILLAGE—Clearing

CLARK—Jefferson Park

CLARKDALE—Ashburn

CLEARING (64) A newer Chicago community on the city's far southwest side, Clearing was home to only a few Dutch and German farmers before the turn of the century. The "Silk Stocking Boulevard" east of Central Avenue on 63rd Place attracted Italians, Poles and Lithuanians after 1905. Annexed to Chicago in 1889 as part of Lake Township and incorporated as a village in 1891, Clearing presently extends along 59th and 65th streets between the Belt Railroad and Harlem Avenue, including a smaller section south of 65th to 67th Street from Cicero Avenue east to the tracks. Present boundaries were established by several annexations before 1924.

CLEAVERVILLE—Oakland

COLEHOUR—East Side

CORNELL—Greater Grand Crossing

COTTAGE GROVE HEIGHTS—Pullman

CRAWFORD—North and South Lawndale

CRESTLINE—Ashburh

CROSSING—Washington Heights

CUMMORN—Auburn Gresham

DAUPHIN PARK—Chatham

DEARBORN HOMES—Douglas

DEATH CORNER—Near North Side

DONEGAN STATION—Englewood

DOUGLAS (35) One of the city's oldest communities, Douglas was named for Senator Stephen A. Douglas, whose tomb is located at the east end of 35th Street. In separate acts, the Illinois legislature in 1853 first annexed the area north of 31st Street to Chicago and ten years later added the remainder.

DREXEL ESTATE, DREXEL PARK—West Englewood

DUMMY JUNCTION—Washington Heights

DUNNING (17) Apparently as a result of the Indian Treaty of 1833, white settlers began farming this area. Arriving after the Civil War and settling on a large farm, Andrew Dunning later became a land developer and platted the area around Irving Park Road and Nashville Avenue in Jefferson Township. While this became the center of the settlement named for him, a significant factor in the development of the community became its proximity to the County Infirmary and Insane Asylum, now Chicago State Hospital built in 1868. The city erected a depot near the hospital in 1882 and a settlement of primarily Swedes, Germans, and native Americans grew around it. As part of the Town of Jefferson, portions of Dunning were annexed to Chicago in 1889.

DUTCHMAN'S POINT—Edison Park

EAST GARFIELD PARK (27) Residential growth in the region including East Garfield Park was slow due to the lack of transportation. Annexation of what is presently East Garfield Park to the city of Chicago brought some public improvements in 1869, but access to the area was still poor enough to limit its growth until shortly before 1900.

EAST SIDE (52) Surrounded by the Calumet River on the north and west and by Lake Michigan and the Illinois-Indiana state line on the east, East Side is nearly an island. Originally part of the Village of Hyde Park, this community accompanied Hyde Park's addition to the city in 1889.

EDEN GREEN—Riverdale

EDGEBROOK—Forest Glen

EDGEWATER (77) Until recently considered part of Uptown, in 1980 Edgewater was officially designated by the Chicago Department of Planning as divided from Uptown by Foster Avenue. A homestead called Seven Mile House (its distance from Chicago's City Hall), constructed in 1848 at what is today Ridge and Clark streets, functioned as a tavern, inn, and local meeting place. Edgewater was annexed to Chicago with the city of Lake View in 1889.

EDGEWATER GLEN—Edgewater

EDISON PARK (9) Edison Park, jutting up from the northwest corner of the city, shares its beginnings with the village of Niles, presently to its north and east. The 1834 arrival and subsequent settlement by German families is responsible for its being called "Dutchman's Point." An abortive attempt at land development came when the Illinois and Wisconsin Railroad laid tracks and established the station of Canfield from 1853 to 1857. Another effort was made after the Chicago Fire in 1871, but it was after annexation to the city with the Town of Jefferson in 1889 that development really stepped up.

ELECTRIC SUBURB (THE ELECTRIC SUBURB)—Edison Park

ELSDON—Gage Park

ENGLEWOOD (68) In the 1840s Englewood was only a stop on the Michigan City stage road which had been built atop the ridge now defined by Vincennes Avenue. Located seven miles south of Chicago's Loop, Englewood's earliest settlers were German and Irish farmers and railroad workers who settled around Junction Avenue, now 63rd Street. The Michigan, Southern, and Northern Indiana Railway built through this area in 1852. Later, the Rock Island and Wabash Railroads were built. The depot at 62nd Street was called Chicago Junction, but was officially changed to Englewood late in 1868. Between 1852 and 1856 eight significant railway lines were laid through this area which had polled less than 200 voters. The junction of railroads spurred growth and Junction Grove surrounding it became a part of the Town of Lake in 1865. Englewood was annexed to Chicago with the Town of Lake in 1889 and experienced even further growth as a result of the Columbian Exposition of 1893.

ENGLEWOOD ON THE HILL—West Englewood

EPIC—Edgewater

FERNWOOD—Washington Heights

FIFTH CITY—East Garfield Park

FISHTOWN—Near North Side

FORD CITY VILLAGE—West Lawn

FOREST GLEN (12) About fourteen miles from downtown Chicago, Forest Glen on the northern edge of the city is surrounded by forest preserves, parks, and cemeteries. Peterson serves as a main street for the community which contains the prestigious neighborhoods of Edgebrook and Sauganash. Between 1828 and 1836 what is now Forest Glen was in great part known as Billy Caldwell's Reserve. Its first urban settlement taking place in the 1880s, most of Forest Glen was annexed to the city in 1889 as part of the Town of Jefferson. Growth in earnest did not begin until the mid-1920s.

FORESTVILLE—Hyde Park

FORRESTVILLE—Grand Boulevard

FREE DISTRICT OF LAKE MICHIGAN—Near North Side

FULLER PARK (37) Hemmed in between railroad tracks, Fuller Park is a long strip of land running two miles from Pershing Road on the north to Garfield Boulevard on the south. First Irish, followed by Austrian and German railroad and stockyard workers were among the first settlers to live in Fuller Park. From 1871 to 1895 the community matured, having been annexed to Chicago in 1889 with the Town of Lake. During the 1950s the Dan Ryan Expressway was built through the heart of Fuller Park and resulted in a population displacement from which the community has not recovered.

GAGE PARK (63) First settled in the 1840s and 1850s by Germans, Gage Park was named for politician George W. Gage, one of the original members of the South Park Commission which was organized to institute a system of parks and boulevards for the South Side. The Town of Lake, including all of Gage Park, was organized in 1865. A small railroad community called Elsdon grew up at 51st and Kedzie after the Grand Trunk Railroad entered Chicago via the area in 1880.

GANO—West Pullman

GARFIELD RIDGE (56) Located on the city's far southwest side, Garfield Ridge is bounded on the north and west by the Chicago city limits, on the east by the Belt Railway and on the south by 59th Street. At the end of the Archer Avenue streetcar line, it was known as Archer Limits as late as the 1920s. Sleepy Hollow between Cicero Avenue and the beltline tracks and from the Sanitary and Ship Canal to 47th Street was the area's earliest settlement. Primarily on land annexed to the city after 1900, the Garfield Ridge community is one of the newer in Chicago. Only a small strip annexed in 1889 dates back to the Town of Lake. The old village of Clearing, today Midway Airport, was annexed in 1915 and the remaining residential areas had been annexed by 1921.

GARYLAND—Irving Park

GLADSTONE PARK—Jefferson Park, Forest Glen, Portage Park

GOLD COAST—Near North Side

GOLDEN GATE—Riverdale

GOOSE ISLAND—West Town

GRAND BOULEVARD (38) About four miles south of the Loop, Grand Boulevard was originally part of the Town of Hyde Park, formed in 1861. The area known as Forrestville was served by School District No. 7, formed in 1873. The South Park Commission's Boulevard System Plan, begun on Grand Boulevard in 1874, inspired impressive building and beautification which attracted the general sight-seeing populace to the avenue.

GREATER GRAND CROSSING (69) Located approximately nine miles from the Loop, and made up of several neighborhoods in one, Grand Crossing exists as a result of the tragic collision between trains of the Illinois Central and the Michigan Southern Railroads. Occurring in 1853 where 75th Street intersects South Chicago Avenue, the incident made clear the need for various safety precautions.

GREEKTOWN—Near West Side

GRESHAM—Auburn Gresham

GROVE (THE GROVE)—Auburn Gresham and Englewood

GROVELAND PARK—Douglas

HAMILTON PARK—Englewood, Greater Grand Crossing

HARDSCRABBLE—Bridgeport

HEART OF CHICAGO—Lower West Side

HEGEWISCH (55) In the southeastern corner of the city, Hegewisch is isolated from nearby Chicago communities by stretches of landfill and vacant, undeveloped land. In 1867 it became part of Hyde Park Township, but there was little settlement before the 1880s when development at Calumet Harbor and along the Calumet River occurred as new railroads laced the area. Inspired by the town of Pullman, Adolph Hegewisch fostered the concept of a similar community. Hegewisch joined Chicago with the annexation of Hyde Park in 1889.

HERMOSA (20) During the 1870s and 1880s in Jefferson Township, the Hermosa community began as a suburban development. Though subdivision took place during the 1870s, the first actual settlement did not occur until the 1880s. Kelvyn Grove, named for the eighth Lord Kelvyn, was settled by Scotch immigrants; Germans and Scandinavians following to the northwest. At Jefferson Township's annexation to Chicago in 1889, the communities were collectively named Hermosa by request of the city.

HOLLYWOOD PARK—North Park

HOPE—Roseland

HORSE THIEF HOLLOW—Morgan Park

HUMBOLT PARK (23) When the Chicago city limits were extended to North Avenue and Pulaski Road in 1869, most of Humbolt Park became part of the city. Including Pacific Junction and Simon's Subdivision, the present community (named for the park outside its eastern border) came fully into the city with the annexation of the Town of Jefferson in 1889.

HYDE PARK (41) Hyde Park, auspiciously named for the communities in London and New York, was developed by Paul Cornell, a lawyer from New York who purchased 300 acres of uninhabited land in 1853 with the intention of building a suburb. In 1856 he convinced the Illinois Central Railroad to create a station at the intersection of 53rd Street, then called Oak, and Lake Park Avenue. Incorporated in 1861, the Town of Hyde Park from 39th to 63rd streets between State Street and the Lake included the settlements of Oakland, Egandale, Forestville, Kenwood, and South Park, later adding the territory south to 138th Street. The Village of Hyde Park was incorporated in 1872 and Hyde Park Township was annexed to Chicago in 1889. The opening of the University of Chicago in Hyde Park in 1892 and construction for the Columbian Exposition of 1893 contributed to the rapid growth of the area.

ICKES PRAIRIE HOMES—Near South Side, Douglas

IDA S. WELLS/DARROW HOMES—Douglas, Oakland

IRONDALE—South Deering

IRVING PARK (16) The early railroad stations of Montrose, Garyland, and Irving Park were the beginnings of Irving Park on the city's northwest side. Originally called Irvington, the Village of Irving Park was named for Washington Irving. The first settlement was in 1869, and good transportation attracted more settlers to the area after the Chicago Fire of 1871. Montrose, at the junction of the Chicago, Milwaukee, and St. Paul and the Chicago and North Western railroads, was later renamed Mayfair. Including Garyland (in the southwest) and Irving Park, the three communities were annexed to Chicago as part of Jefferson Township in 1889.

IRVING WOODS—Dunning

IRVINGTON—Irving Park

ISLAND (THE)—Austin

JEFFERSON PARK (11) Jefferson Park was first settled in the 1830s by John Kinzie Clark. More settlers were attracted to the area in 1844 by the construction of the Northwestern Plank Road, providing farmers an important link to the city, where Milwaukee Avenue exists today. The name Jefferson was adopted by the post office, built in 1845 and originally named Monroe, when a prior community of the same name was found to exist. In 1850 local farmers organized the Township of Jefferson; originally extending from North to Devon avenues between Harlem and Western, it was centered at Milwaukee and Lawrence avenues. In 1872 the Village of Jefferson was incorporated and the community was annexed to Chicago as part of Jefferson Township in 1889.

JUNCTION (THE JUNCTION)—Englewood

JUNCTION GROVE—Englewood

KELVYN GROVE (PARK)—Hermosa

KENNEDY PARK—Morgan Park

KENSINGTON—West Pullman

KENWOOD (39) This community received its name from the estate of the first settler, Dr. John A. Kennicott, who named it for his mother's birthplace in Scotland. Used for the Illinois Central Railroad station at 47th Street three years later, the name eventually spread to the entire area. Another settler, Dr. William B. Egan, built his sprawling estate, Egandale, between 47th and 55th streets from Woodlawn to Cottage Grove Avenue, but was forced to sell half of it in 1863. The area became part of Hyde Park Township in 1861 and was incorporated into the city of Chicago as part of it in 1889.

KILBOURN PARK—Portage Park, Irving Park

LAKE FOREST OF THE SOUTH SIDE—Kenwood

LAKE MEADOWS—Douglas

LAKEWOOD-BALMORAL—Edgewater

LAKE VIEW (6) The Lake View community, once a part of the City of Lake View, was first settled in 1836 by Conrad Sulzer and his wife in what is now its north section. Immigrants from Germany, Luxembourg and Sweden, mostly farmers, were to follow. The wooden Lake View

House Hotel, on the Lake Michigan shore just south of what is now Irving Park Road, stood three stories high at the center of a wealthy, mainly summer residential community. In 1857 Lake View Township was organized and was incorporated in 1865. The city of Lake View was incorporated in 1887, extending from the lake to Western Avenue between Fullerton and Devon avenues, and was annexed to Chicago in 1889.

LAWNDALE—North Lawndale and South Lawndale

LE CLAIRE COURTS—Garfield Ridge

LINCOLN PARK (7) Lincoln Park takes its name from the well-known city park on its eastern border. A small U.S. Army post built in the 1820s stood where forest and stretches of grassland had been made dangerous by pockets of quicksand. As of 1830 the trustees of the Illinois and Michigan Canal held deed to most of the area's southern two-thirds. At the incorporation of Chicago in 1837, the city limits included a small piece of the community's southeast side, used for a smallpox hospital and the city cemetery. After the improvement of Green Bay Road (now Clark Street) in the 1830s, the land became more attractive to farmers and speculators. The community expanded to the north with the annexation of the city of Lake View in 1889.

LINCOLN SQUARE (4) Formerly part or all of the five separate communities of Bowmanville, Budlong Woods, Ravenswood, Summerdale, and Winnemac, Lincoln Square was first settled in the 1830s. Its connection to Chicago and Waukegan, then Little Fort, was Little Fort Road which is now Lincoln Avenue. In an area dubbed Roe's Hill after Hiram Roe, proprietor of a local tavern, a cemetery was laid out on land purchased in 1859. The name was later adulterated and Rosehill Cemetery in northeast Lincoln Square stands as one of the city's most historic.

LITHUANIAN PLAZA—Chicago Lawn

LITTLE HELL—Near North Side

LITTLE ITALY—Near West Side

LITTLE SICILY—Near North Side

LITTLE VILLAGE—South Lawndale

LOGAN SQUARE (22) Named for Illinois politician and Civil War General John A. Logan, Logan Square is a sizeable neighborhood. Though few families lived north of North Avenue early in the 1860s, gradual development began along Milwaukee Avenue when the city limits were extended in 1863 to Western and Fullerton avenues. Directly north of that, the northeast corner of the present community was annexed in 1869, and the following year saw the construction of the

Chicago and North Western Railroad's Maplewood station which gave its name to the area surrounding it.

LONGWOOD/LONGWOOD MANOR–Beverly

LOOP (32) Built over the site of the original Chicago settlement, the Loop is the heart of the city's business district. Described by a ring of elevated railroad tracks running along Wells, Van Buren, Wabash, and Lake streets, consolidated in 1897 as the Union Loop, the area bounded on the south by Roosevelt Road and otherwise hemmed in by the Chicago River and Lake Michigan is still Chicago's most important retail district.

LOWER WEST SIDE (31) Once a region of swamp and small farms called the southwest side, today's Lower West Side was the eastern end of a portage connecting the DesPlaines River with Lake Michigan. When the city was incorporated in 1837 it included the northeastern third of this area. Owned by either John Welsh or the Illinois and Michigan Canal Commission, land there increased in value and was sold and claimed by 1845. With the exception of truck farmers, little settlement was taking place; but industrial development began along the South Branch of the Chicago River when construction on the canal came to a close in 1848. The remainder of the Lower West Side was annexed to Chicago in 1853.

MCKINLEY PARK (59) About four miles southwest of downtown Chicago, McKinley Park was settled in the 1840s largely by farmers from New England. An attempt had been made earlier to settle Canalport around Ashland and Damen avenues, but it was soon vacated. The Irish who had worked on the canal before its completion in 1848 afterward settled in the vicinity of Archer and Ashland avenues, now called Bridgeport. Platted in 1840, Brighton, in the vicinity of Western Avenue and 35th Street, was incorporated in 1851 and took its name from the race track located at the present site of Mc Kinley Park. The park, laid out in 1901 and named for the recently assassinated president, lent its name to the community, most of which was brought into the city limits when they were extended to Pershing Road and Western Avenue in 1863.

MAPLEWOOD–Logan Square

MARQUETTE PARK–Chicago Lawn

MARYNOOK–Chatham, Avalon Park

MAYFAIR–Irving Park

MILLGATE–South Chicago

MONROE–Jefferson

MONTCLARE (18) On the western border of the city about nine miles from the Loop, Montclare was first settled in 1836 by William E. Sayre. The road he and other farmers used to get into the city follows the course of the present Grand Avenue. A right-of-way over the Sayre farm granted to the Chicago and Pacific Railroad Company led to the establishment there of Sayre Station, renamed Montclare in 1873 for a community in New Jersey. Annexed as part of the Town of Jefferson in 1889, Montclare is primarily residential.

MONTROSE—Irving Park

MORGAN PARK (75) Morgan Park sits south alongside Beverly thirty to forty feet above the Chicago plain, having received its name from an early settler, Thomas Morgan. Once referred to as North Blue Island, the community had several names over the years. Criminals taking advantage of the densely wooded ridge hid in ravines such as the spot that is now 108th Street and Longwood Drive, then known as Horse Thief Hollow. The area from 91st Street (now Beverly) to 115th Street (now Morgan Park) was first owned by John Blackstone who sold most of it to Thomas Morgan in 1844.

In 1874 the Village of Washington Heights was incorporated, including the area east of Western Avenue between 95th and 107th streets, and in 1882 Morgan Park (south of Washington Heights) was incorporated as a village. The names Washington Heights and Morgan Park having been used almost interchangeably, the Village of Washington Heights and land north of it were annexed to Chicago in 1890 and 1891. Almost a quarter century later in 1914, a Morgan Park of larger proportions than exists today was annexed to the city. The area between 99th and 107th streets from Vincennes to California avenues having been adopted by Beverly, Morgan Park's boundaries today are 107th to 115th streets between Halsted Street and California Avenue and 115th Street to 119th Street from Ashland Avenue to the Baltimore and Ohio Railroad tracks near Rockwell.

MOUNT GREENWOOD (74) The land just west of the ridge along 111th Street was once abundant with oaks, hickory, aspen, and other trees. When George Waite surveyed this area (now Morgan Park) in 1877, he found it ideally suited for cemetery use. Calling it Mount Greenwood for its endowment of foliage, he obtained a charter from the State in 1879 to develop eighty acres, with an option for eighty more. Now adjacent to and home to several cemeteries, Mount Greenwood grew in response to funeral traffic that was captively drawn to the area. Morgan Park to the east being dry, restaurants and saloons around 111th Street and Sacramento Avenue provided refreshment and relaxation to funeral observers before their long journies home. Early settlers included Dutch and German truck farmers. Incorporated as a village in 1907, Mount Greenwood was annexed to the city in 1927.

NEAR NORTH SIDE (8) The earliest manufacturers of Chicago built along the north bank of the Chicago River in what is the heart of the Near North Side. The entire community was part of the City of Chicago when it was incorporated in 1837. Due to difficulties involved in crossing the river during the 1840s, most of the city's development took place south and west of it. Grand Bridges constructed over the river at Rush Street in 1856 and at Erie Street and Grand Avenue in 1857 provided the North Side with needed access to the rest of the city. In 1882 Potter Palmer bought land on what became North Lake Shore Drive, building an impressive mansion there. Over the next ten years, Chicago society deserted its other upper class neighborhoods for the Near North Side, and the city's "Gold Coast" was born.

NEAR SOUTH SIDE (33) Between 1836 and 1848 German, Irish and Scandinavian laborers came to the Near South Side to work on the Illinois and Michigan Canal. These first residents stayed to work along the South Branch of the Chicago River in the lumber district. Due to the predominance of Irish in the community, their crude conglomeration of homes was called the Patch.

NEAR WEST SIDE (28) Wolf Point Tavern was standing as early as 1828 at the convergance of the North and South Branches of the Chicago River. The city limits were extended to Wood Street and Cermak Road when Chicago incorporated in 1837, and developing industry fostered an Irish settlment of wooden cottages along the river. Railroads brought rapid growth in the 1850s, and the Near West Side was the port of entry for immigrants to Chicago for over a hundred years. A real estate development begun along Western Avenue in 1864 by Samuel A. Walker, being named Ashland for Henry Clay's mansion, remained a fashionable residential area until the 1890s.

NEW CITY (61) In recent years called Back of the Yards, the name New City applied to a more affluent residential section south of 47th Street and was part of the Town of Lake when it incorporated in 1865. The Union Stock Yards opened Christmas Day of the same year, replacing eight separate livestock centers across the city, and remained of primary significance in the area before beginning its decline after 1920 and closing in 1952. The Town of Lake was annexed to Chicago in 1889.

NOBLE SQUARE—West Town

NORTH BLUE ISLAND—Beverly and Morgan Park

NORTH CENTER (5) North Center, fittingly centered in the North Side, lies about seven miles northwest of Chicago's Loop. Due to limited accessibility from the city, the area was not developed until after the Chicago Fire of 1871. Today the community is comprised of parcels from the old townships of Lake View and Jefferson, both annexed to Chicago in 1889.

NORTH END—Beverly

NORTH LAWNDALE (29) North Lawndale was originally included in the township of Cicero, organized in 1857, and was intersected by the Southwestern Plank Road, which is today Ogden Avenue. The small, unincorporated village of Crawford developed in 1863 as a result of the newly laid Chicago, Burlington, and Quincy Railroad tracks. Named for landowner Peter Crawford whose home had been built on Ogden Avenue, Crawford's German, Dutch, and native American inhabitants witnessed its gradual emergence as a residential suburb of the city.

NORTH MARYFAIR—North Park, Albany Park

NORTH PARK (13) Part of the newly-organized Jefferson Township, the village of North Park was settled in the 1850s. Platted in 1855, it developed into a market town. Originally settled by German and Swedish farmers, the opening of the Bohemian National Cemetery in 1877 drew in a Czechoslovakian which dissipated around the turn of the century. North Park was annexed to Chicago in 1889 as part of the Town of Jefferson.

NORTH TOWN—West Ridge

NORWOOD PARK (10) The Norwood Park community was first settled by the Mark Noble family, settlers from Chicago, in 1833. In 1868 the Norwood Land and Building Association was formed by a group of Chicagoans and plans were laid out for a village of arched and curving streets around an unusual circular avenue. The community's name was taken from Henry Ward Beecher's popular novel, *Norwood* (1867), about life in a New England country town during the Civil War period. Norwood Park was incorporated as a village shortly after Norwood Park Township incorporated in 1874, and in 1893 the village voted to join Chicago.

O'HARE—Annexed Area

OAKLAND (36) In 1851 a soap factory and lard rendering works was established between 37th and 39th streets by Charles Clearver. For his workers he created a company town of wooden houss, places to worship, govern and buy goods, and for himself an elaborate estate called Oakwood Hall at Oakland Boulevard and Ellis Avenue. An outgrowth of the Cleaverville settlement, Oakland is presently located between

35th and 43rd streets from Lake Michigan to Vincennes and Cottage Grove avenues; it fully joined Chicago in 1889 with the annexation of Hyde Park Township.

OAKWOOD HALL—Oakland

OLD NORWOOD—Norwood Park

OLD TOWN—Near North Side

OLD TOWN TRIANGLE—Lincoln Park

OLD WICKER PARK—Logan Square, Humbolt Park

ORIOLE PARK—Norwood Park

ORCHARD PLACE—Annexed Area

PACIFIC JUNCTION—Humbolt Park

PACKINGTOWN—Bridgeport

PARK MANOR—Greater Grand Crossing

PARKSIDE—South Shore

PARK WEST—Lincoln Park

PARKVIEW—Ashburn

PATCH—Near South Side

PENNYTOWN—Avalon Park

PETERSON PARK—West Ridge

PILSEN—Near West Side

PORTAGE PARK (15) At the time of the settlement of Chicago, Portage Park was a west grassland intersected by two parallel ridges which are today Cicero and Narragansett avenues. Popular portage routes between the Chicago and DesPlaines rivers, these ridges and the trail which is today Irving Park Road were used by Indians and explorers in the early days. While the Indian Treaty of 1816 attracted some settlers to the area, it was not until the end of the Blackhawk War in the mid-1830s that real settlement began to take place. By the 1840s the area's main access to the city was the recently constructed Northwest Plank Road, now Milwaukee Avenue. The town of Jefferson was organized in 1850 at Dickenson Tavern at the present intersection of Milwaukee and Belle Plaine avenues. Most of what is now Portage Park became part of Chicago in 1889 with the annexation of Jefferson. The community's present western boundary was established in 1924 with the annexation of the town of Norwood Park.

PRAIRIE SHORES—Douglas

PRINCETON PARK—Roseland

PULASKI PARK—North Park

PULLMAN (50) George M. Pullman was a pioneer with his planned model industrial town. A railroad car manufacturer, Pullman, chose 3,500 acres of undeveloped land from 103rd to 115th streets on the western shore of Lake Calumet for his Pullman Palace Car Company shops. Owned and operated by the company and served by an Illinois Central depot at 111th Street, the self-sufficient complex of plants, public facilities, and homes had incepted in 1880, and in 1889 the employee-residents voted against the wishes of George Pullman in favor of the annexation of Hyde Park to Chicago. A showplace to the outside world, the undercurrent of unrest among the captive employee/tenant community became apparent with the 1894 strike of Pullman workers. Spreading through the American Railway Union, the strike had historic consequences. A result was the Illinois Supreme Court ruling that the charter of the company did not authorize it to own or manage a town. Though residents were then allowed to own homes in Pullman, the loss of company support forced the neighborhood to decline.

RANCH TRIANGLE—Lincoln Park

RAVENSWOOD—Lincoln Square

RAVENSWOOD GARDENS—Lincoln Square

RAVENSWOOD MANOR—Albany Park

RIDGE (THE RIDGE)—Rogers Park and Beverly

RIDGELAWN—Edison Park

RIDGEVILLE—West Ridge

RIVERDALE (54) At the far south city limits, Riverdale is bounded by the community of Pullman on the north, the Calumet Expressway (I94) on the east, 138th street to the south and the suburb of Riverdale on the southwest. George Dolton was the first settler, arriving with his family in 1836, followed by German and Dutch farmers during the 1840s and 1850s. In 1867 Riverdale became part of Hyde Park which was annexed to Chicago in 1889.

ROE'S HILL—Lincoln Square

ROGERS PARK (1) At the northeast city limits about ten miles from the Chicago Loop, Rogers Park is one of Chicago's most densely populated areas. Phillip Rogers, an Irishman, was the first white settler in the area and built a cabin at the present intersection of Ridge and Lunt avenues in 1839. Scotch, Irish, German, and English farmers settled later along "the Ridge" on the community's western boundary. In 1893 Rogers Park was formally annexed to Chicago.

ROGERS RIDGE—Rogers Park

ROSEHILL—Lincoln Square

ROSELAND (49) This was a Dutch settlement on the Thornton Ridge Road, west of Pullman and south of Chicago. Roseland was settled as a farm district in 1848. First called Hope (1861), and later changed to Rosela (1870s), the community was in Lake Township, but territory east of State Street became part of the newly incorporated Village of Hyde Park in 1867. When Lake and Hyde Park townships were annexed in 1889, all of Roseland came into the city limits.

ROSENEATH—Edison Park

SANDS (THE SANDS)—Near North Side

SAUGANASH—Forest Glen

SAYRE—Montclare

SCHORSCH FOREST VIEW—O'Hare (Annexed Area)

SCHORSCH VILLAGE—Dunning

SHEFFIELD NEIGHBORS—Lincoln Park

SHELDON HEIGHTS

SIMON'S SUBDIVISION—Humbolt Park

SIX CORNERS—Portage Park

SLEEPY HOLLOW—Garfield Ridge

SOUTH CHICAGO (46) Though settlement had taken place as early as the 1830s, the real catalyst for growth came to south Chicago in 1869 when the federal government appropriated money for the improvement of Calumet Harbor. Industries located near the mouth of the river and workers' houses sprang up nearby; the business center having developed at 92nd and Commercial Avenue. South Chicago joined the city with the annexation of Hyde Park in 1889.

SOUTH COMMONS—Douglas

SOUTH DEERING (51) By about 1850 eight railroads had laid tracks through what is now South Deering. The major part of the district was uninhabited until the 1860s, and much of it remains so today. With Congressional appropriation for Calumet Harbor, a channel was cut to connect the Calumet River with Lake Michigan. Docks and artificial harbors were put into operation shortly afterward andland was bought and subdivided for workers. The area was once known as Irondale.

SOUTH LAWNDALE (30) Though closely associated with North Lawndale, South Lawndale's growth was more greatly affected by the Illinois and Michigan Canal, now the Stevenson Expressway, on its southern bounder. To the east between Western Avenue and Pulaski Road,

South Lawndale became a part of Chicago in 1869, and in 1889 the territory west of Pulaski Road was annexed.

SOUTH LYNN—West Englewood

SOUTH PARK—Hyde Park

SOUTH SHORE (43) A swampy, sparsely populated land south of Chicago when it was incorporated in 1837, this area's only inhabitants were a few German truck farmers. The South Kenwood Station of the Illinois Central Railroad was built at 71st Street and Jeffrey Boulevard in 1881, and by 1889 the small settlement of Bryn Mawr had grown up nearby. Bryn Mawr eventually included the territory from 71st to 73rd streets between Cregier and Paxton avenues, and the community of Parkside to the northwest lay from 67th to 71st streets west to Dorchester.

SOUTH SIDE—Grand Boulevard, Washington Park, Woodlawn, Greater Grand Crossing.

SOUTHWORKS—South Chicago

STATEWAY GARDENS—Douglas

STICKNEY—Clearing

STONEY ISLAND PARK—Avalon Park

STREETERVILLE—Near North Side

SUMMERDALE—Lincoln Square

TOWERTOWN—Near North Side

TRACEY—Beverly

UKRAINIAN VILLAGE—West Town

UNION RIDGE—Norwood Park

UNION STOCK YARDS—New City

UPTOWN (3) Several old communities, once comprising the northern part of the township and later part of the city of Lake View, are included in the Uptown of today. With the construction of Marine Hospital, some building took place in the southeast corner in the 1860s, being the exception in an area that was predominantly undeveloped wilderness. Uptown experienced comparatively heavy growth in the 1870s and 1880s and the German population was joined by a growing number of Swedes. In 1889, when the City of Lake View annexed to Chicago, Uptown came into the city limits.

UPWOOD—Beverly and Morgan Park

THE VALLEY—Near West Side

VILLA (THE) – Irving Park

VILLAGE IN THE CITY (THE VILLAGE IN THE CITY) – Beverly

VIT TUM PARK – Garfield Ridge

WALDEN – Beverly

WASHINGTON HEIGHTS (73) On Chicago's southwest side east of Vincennes Avenue between 89th and 107th streets, Washington Heights today is only a portion of its former size. The high ground from whence came its name drifted into Beverly, but the community still contains some of the old Fernwood and Brainerd settlements. In the 1830s the first homes were built and more settlers arrived between 1840 and the Civil War. A transient population of Irish and German railroad workers lived near the vicinity of 103rd and Vincennes, known as The Crossing for the juncture of the Rock Island and the Pittsburg, Cincinnati and St. Louis railroads. The Blue Island Land and Building Company bought and developed land in 1869 and built the "dummy line" (no longer in existance) to the Rock Island tracks, spurring growth around the new station known as Dummy Junction. The village was incorporated in 1874 and annexed to Chicago in 1890 and 1891, eventually having lost territory west of Vincennes Avenue to Beverly Hills.

WASHINGTON PARK (40) Washington Park is centered about seven miles south of the Chicago Loop. Development began in the Lake Township territory north of 55th Street/Garfield Boulevard and west of State Street. East of State Street was the Village of Hyde Park. Irish and German workers for the Rock Island Railroad yards settled north of 51st Street in 1856. After 1880 Washington Park developed rapidly due to its parks, its racetrack, and the appeal of Grand Boulevard, annexing to Chicago in 1889.

WENTWORTH GARDENS – Armour Square

WEST CHESTERFIELD – Chatham, Roseland

WEST ELSDON (62) A residential community, West Elsdon on the southwest side of the city parallelled adjacent communities in that its development was greatly influenced by the railroads. This area was part of the Lake Township in its infancy in 1865 and was annexed to the city with it in 1889. The community received its name by its location just west of the railroad town of Elsdon at 51st Street and Kedzie Avenue, now Gage Park.

WEST ENGLEWOOD (67) West Englewood about eight miles southwest of the Loop was included in the Town of Lake in 1865. Early development of the area surrounded a nearby subdivision and the present intersection of 63rd Street and Ashland Avenue. After Junction Grove to the east officially became Englewood in 1868, this partially elevated area was known as Englewood-On-The-Hill. The west central parcel of the community today had been owned by the Drexel family of Philadelphia and called the Drexel Estate or Drexel Park. The South Lynn development was platted in 1870 and absorbed Drexel Park. West Englewood was annexed to Chicago as part of Lake Township in 1889.

WEST GARFIELD PARK (26) West Garfield Park was still outside the city limits when the Pennsylvania Avenue Road, now Lake Street, was planked in the 1840s. Still unpopulated until after the Civil War, territory east of Pulaski Road was annexed to the city in 1869, and the new West Side Park Board made public the creation of Central Park to the east. After the assassination of President Garfield in 1885, the name Central Park gave way to Garfield Park and the community was annexed to Chicago in 1889.

WEST LAWN (65) West Lawn lies between Chicago Lawn and Clearing and is historically interwoven with both of them. In 1876 a subdivision was platted by John Eberhart and James Webb called Chicago Lawn and later West Lawn. It was annexed to Chicago as part of Lake Township in 1889.

WEST PULLMAN (53) From 115th Street on the north to the southernmost city limits along the Little Calumet River, West Pullman was originally named for its famous northern neighbor. Early communities in the present area included Kensington and later Gano and West Pullman. Bit by bit, today's West Pullman was annexed to Chicago between 1889 and 1928.

WEST RIDGE (2) Also referred to as North Town or West Rogers Park, the West Ridge area was settled in the 1830s by Phillip Rogers south of what is now Rogers Avenue. Within a decade Luxembourg farmers had started a community, later called Ridgeville, atop the local ridge where Devon today intersects it. West Ridge was incorporated as a village in 1890 and annexed to Chicago three years later.

WEST ROGERS PARK—West Ridge

WEST TOWN (24) The eastern portion of West Town was part of Chicago when it was incorporated in 1837. The main thorofares of West Town were built over old Indian trails. Today's Grand and Elston avenues are two of these, and the old planked road route completed in 1849 now follows Ogden and Milwaukee avenues. The Galena and Chicago Union Railroad had built tracks and run the first train through the area by 1851 when the city limits were extended to Western and North avenues. Activity in the area brought growth, but much of this rapidly deteriorated and became slums. The city limits were extended to include Bloomingdale and Western avenues in 1863 and again to Kedzie Avenue in 1869.

WICKER PARK—West Town

WILDWOOD—Forest Glen

WINNEMAC—Lincoln Square

WOLF POINT—Near North Side

WOODLAWN (42) Just south of the University of Chicago, Woodlawn is about eight miles south of the Loop with Jackson Park on its eastern border. Although the opening of the first Woodlawn train stop at 63rd Street was accomplished in 1862 by the Illinois Central Railway, it was annexed to Chicago in 1889. The Columbian Exposition in 1893 brought unprecedented growth to the area.

WRIGHTWOOD NEIGHBORS—Lincoln Park

BIBLIOGRAPHY

Andreas, A.T. *History of Chicago*. 3 vols. Chicago: A.T. Andreas, 1884-86.

_____. *History of Cook County, Illinois*. Chicago: Andreas, 1884. The most often cited of the histories of Chicago and Cook County with excerpts from primary sources.

Bach, Ira J. *Chicago on Foot*. Chicago: Rand McNally, 1977.

The Chicago Fact Book Consortium. *Local Community Fact Book, Chicago Metropolitan Area*. Chicago: the Univeristy of Illinois at Chicago, 1984. Probably the most important work focusing on Chicago area communities, this volume provides a detailed history of each neighborhood, maps, and statistical tables. The *Fact Book* was designed to fulfill the need for a convenient compilation of a variety of information on local communities within the metropolitan area.

City of Chicago, Department of Development and Planning. *Historic City: The Settlement of Chicago*. Chicago: 1976. This publication describes the pattern of settlement of ethnic groups as Chicago grew, from 1830-1900. Six color coded foldout maps for each chapter show the distribution of nationalities at various periods of Chicago History.

Duis, Perry. *Chicago: Creating New Traditions*. Chicago: Chicago Historical Society, 1976.

_____. *The Saloon: Public Drinking in Chicago and Boston, 1880-1920*. Urbana: University of Illinois Press, 1983.

Greeley, Andrew M. *Neighborhood*. New York: The Seabury Press, 1977.

Grossman, Ron. *Guide to Chicago Neighborhoods*. Piscataway, N.J.: New Century Publishers, Inc., 1981.

Holli, Melvin G. and Jones, Peter d'A. eds. *Ethnic Chicago*. Grand Rapids: William Eerdmans, 1984. This volume provides a close look at the neighborhoods through the eyes of nine authors who are most knowledgeable of ethnic groups represented in the text. The extensive "Notes" serve as research tools in themselves.

Holt, Glen E. and Pacyga, Dominic A. *Chicago: A Historical Guide to the Neighborhoods, The Loop and South Side*. Chicago: Chicago Historical Society, 1979. An interesting look at Chicago's downtown and South Side in pictures and words.

Hunter, Albert. *Symbolic Communities: The Persistence and Change of Chicago's Local Communities*. Chicago: 1974.

Jewell, Frank. *Annotated Bibliography of Chicago History*. Chicago: the Chicago Historical Society, 1979. An excellent bibliographic source with entries grouped under the appropriate community or neighborhood name.

Lane, George A. *Chicago Churches and Synagogues: An Architectural Pilgrimage*. Chicago: Loyola Press, 1981.

Mayer, Harold M., and Wade, Richard C. *Chicago: Growth of a Metropolis*. Chicago: University of Chicago Press, 1969. Considered one of the most important books on Chicago, the volume describes the city's growth to 1969. This book was one of the first books to use photographs and other images to document the history. Almost 1,000 photographs and fifty maps are used to enhance the presentation.

Pacyga, Dominic A. and Skerett, Ellen. *Chicago: City of Neighborhoods*. Chicago: Loyola University Press, 1986. More than a fascinating photograph album and tour guide, this recent publication is a serious study of the neighborhoods. Without overlooking the city's problems, the authors have presented the history and current status of each area. An excellent bibliography of neighborhood sources makes this work especially useful. In words and pictures, it is a lively portrait of Chicago from its past to its present.

CHAPTER 8

Church and Religious Records

C hurch records are acceptable supplements to civil vital records and are considered primary sources in their own right. These sources fill gaps where official records are missing or were never kept, and they often include important facts not recorded in any other source.

Finding the records of the religious congregation to which an ancestor belonged in the Chicago metropolitan area is especially difficult because of the great number of churches and synagogues supported by the enormous population for over 150 years. Chicago, like the rest of America, has been a mixture of national and ethnic groups since the beginning.

Population, geography, and ethnicity are confusing enough; but to complicate matters further, different denominations kept different types of records. For example, presbyteries transferred membership records with the departure of the member. Immigrants commonly chose to worship in their own native language and often would travel to a church where it was spoken. Churches as well as people responded to the dynamics of the city, some closing, consolidating, or moving as neighborhoods changed, while others shifted from their ethnic orientation to accomodate new circumstances. Thus, any researcher having difficulty tracing the church or synagogue of an ancestor might save time by backtracking to study the history of that particular religion in the locale of interest. Though finding religious records may be difficult, it usually repays the time and effort spent. Church records generally predate civil records and often supply valuable information such as birthdates, names of parents, names of sponsors, and sometimes even the town of origin from which individuals emigrated.

An invaluable guide for research in this area is the Historical Records Survey of the Works Progress Administration (WPA). WPA workers inventoried church and public records extant in the 1930s. Their lists for urban churches are especially valuable. For the Chicago area, consult: *Guide to Church Vital Statistics Records in Illinois,* prepared by the Historical Records Survey (Chicago, Illinois, 1942). It is available at the Newberry Library (Call # D2896.41). Although dated, this source still serves to identify churches and records that survived the Chicago Fire of 1871 and outlines existing collections. A typical entry for church vital records would contain the name and address of the institution at the time of the publication, ethnic orientation, and comprehensive dates for each type of vital record. If the organization housed documents from other congregations, the survey noted this and gave a range of dates. A summary of baptisms, marriages, and death records follows for each. In most cases founding dates are listed.

In cases where a church affiliation is not known, other records may serve to locate them. A marriage license from Cook County, for example, will note the name and sometimes the address of the person officiating at the marriage. By consulting a Chicago directory for the same year, the residence of the clergyman may be established, thereby connecting him to a particular congregation. Likewise, religious affiliation can often be determined by death information. If an individual is buried in a cemetery of a particular denomination it is probable that he or she was a member of that denomination. Often that information can be taken a step further when cemetery or obituary information reveals the name of a clergyman, thereby linking the deceased to a church.

Even probate records have been known to provide clues to church affiliation. It is not unusual for people to leave property to their favorite charitable institutions, and mention of this is often included in a will. Accountings of funeral expenditures are frequently included in a probate file, and may also provide invaluable clues which lead to church records. Funeral directors' bills, for example, are often quite detailed and frequently note that carriages were hired for a named minister for a graveside ritual or that carriages were hired for the trip from a particular church to the cemetery. The clues mentioned are not consistently found in these unlikely sources, but an awareness that the possibility of determining religious affiliation by use of these other records makes them worthy of mention.

There are an increasing number of indexes being created to church records. Area genealogical societies are continually working to preserve and make available church records by means of their indexing projects. These indexes and other printed sources relating to religious communities, such as histories published to commemorate the anniversary of a congregation, will also be a means of identifying the place of worship and respective record collections.

Early county histories, ethnic histories, and biographical sketches also provide other background on religious institutions in the local area. Through these descriptions one may trace the church, its development, and ethnic makeup. Modern studies also are a tremendous help, and their bibliographies enhance their utility. George Lane and Algimantes Kezys, *Chicago Churches and Synagogues* (Chicago: Loyola University Press, 1981) single out 125 houses of worship with architectural, historical, or social significance. Further, they provide a detailed description and history of each building and its congregation, ethnic classification, architectural attributes, locality by exact address, and area of city. The acknowledgments and notes give the researcher numerous sources for locating denominational repositiories.

Even though there is no comprehensive guide to American church records, one should mention two major works: August B. Suelflow's, *A Preliminary Guide to Church Records and Repositories*, a standard reference of denominational archives; and, for those with a Roman Catholic interest, the *Official Catholic Directory*, published annually since 1886 by P.J. Kenedy and Sons, which lists American dioceses, parishes, and institutions with their respective addresses. In some instances, successor repositories for closed churches are given. Major libraries and Catholic churches are likely to maintain copies of these volumes. For churches which have changed names and denominated affiliation, consult Julia Pettee's, *List of Churches: Official Forms of the Names for Denominated Bodies with Brief Description and Historical Notes* (Chicago: American Library Association, 1948).

Some church records are available in book or microfilm. The Newberry Library in Chicago has a large collection of sources from the eastern United States as well as from local institutions. Area genealogical society publications, which often include church information and indexes, are usually placed at the Newberry as soon as they become available. The Genealogical Society of Utah has filmed church registers from numerous localities including the Cook County area, and its branch library system allows access in every state to these records.

The Newberry Library has been designated as a repository for microfilms of church registers which are being made available as a result of a program sponsored by the Genealogical Society of Utah and the Council of Northeastern Illinois Genealogical Societies. A program which is in progress will eventually place microfilm copies of the registers of the Catholic parishes of the Archdiocese of Chicago, as well as other large denominational collections, at the Newberry. Also available at LDS branch libraries and the Newberry is the International Genealogical Index (IGI), rich in church registers.

Used in combination with other sources, church vital records may help illuminate even the most perplexing problems. For example, Karl Johnson was known to have lived at a certain address in Chicago for several years near the beginning of the twentieth century, but his death date was unknown. The Works Progress Administration Index to

Chicago Deaths indicated that he died at that address in 1911. This death year led to a certificate which in turn pointed to the cemetery records. The cemetery gave the officiating minister's name, and a directory search identified him as belonging to the Swedish Covenant Church. It had since moved, but inquiries at another congregation of the same denomination pinpointed the new location of the records. Not only did the church have many records on the family, it had a jubilee book with biographical sketches which included Karl Johnson as a founding member. The biography gave his exact birthplace, his date of arrival in this country, and his residence before settling in Chicago in 1884.

A SELECTED BIBLIOGRAPHY ON CHURCH SOURCES

Andreas, Alfred Theodore. *History of Cook County, Illinois.* Chicago: 1884.
Crandall, Dr. Ralph. *Shaking Your Family Tree.* Dublin, N.H.: Yankee Publishing Inc., 1986.
Eakle, Arlene and Cerny, Johni. *The Source: A Guidebook of American Genealogy.* Salt Lake City, Ut.: Ancestry Publishing Company, 1984.
Greenwood, Val D. *The Researcher's Guide to American Genealogy.* Baltimore: Genealogical Publishing Co., 1975.
Otto, Ronald. "Early South Suburban Area Churches," *Source Book.* South Holland, Ill.: South Suburban Genealogical and Historical Society, 1982.
Phillips, George S. *Chicago and Her Churches.* Chicago: 1868.
White, Elizabeth P., C.G. "Report on the Illinois Church Records Card File Project." *Chicago Genealogist* 7, No. 4, (Summer 1975).
Wright, Norman Edgar. *Preserving Your American Heritage.* Provo, Ut.: Brigham Young University Press, 1981.

The census of religious bodies taken in 1916, after the influx of immigrants to America, revealed the following membership statistics for Chicago:

720,000 -Roman Catholic
60,000 -Lutheran
30,000 -Methodist Episcopal
30,000 -Jewish
30,000 -Presbyterian
30,000 -Baptists

Although some useful addresses for other denominations will be provided in this section, the focus of attention will be directed to the dominant religions which are listed above.

ROMAN CATHOLIC RECORDS

The laws of the Catholic Church, the Code of Canon Law, requires that each parish maintain a parochial archive in which the parish sacramental registers are preserved. The III Plenary Council of Baltimore required that this archive be an iron safe. Today this may be a separate room or a fireproof vault. There is no central file for all parish records in the Archdiocese of Chicago, which has jurisdiction over Cook and Lake Counties. All records are obtained from the parish in which a sacramental event took place. The first step then in obtaining a record is to locate the correct parish. If the name of the family parish is not immediately known, there are several useful means for locating the needed registers.

The *Official Catholic Directory, 1886*

Previous directories under various titles and publishers are found in 1833 and forward. This directory is the single most important source for identifying parishes in the United States. Parishes having a resident pastor, including the 444 parishes of the Archdiocese of Chicago, are listed by diocese. Diocesan hierarchy and appropriate offices are shown with addresses and telephone numbers for each. American missionary activities and religious orders of men and women are listed with their addresses. Parish entries include the address, telephone number, name of resident pastors and information regarding any parochial school, student enrollment numbers, and the responsible teaching order. Catholic high schools, colleges, and hospitals, as well as residences for the aged, child caring institutions, residences for the blind, and other special service institutions are also listed under each diocese. In some cases where a parish or other Catholic institution has been closed, the year of closing and the address of the parish or archives holding records are provided.

Addresses for the chancery offices of all of the archdioceses and dioceses are included, so when special problems in locating a parish are encountered an inquiry directed to the chancery may provide additional help. Chancery (Archdiocesan office) personnel do not make searches of individual parish registers, but may be able to answer questions of a general nature. The back of the *Official Catholic Directory* contains an alphabetical list of the cardinals, archbishops, bishops, abbots, regular and secular priests and their residences. A necrology of the religious who have died during the past year is also included. Copies of the *Official Catholic Directory* are available at almost every Catholic parish and institution, as well as major libraries, and the Newberry Library which has copies dating back to about 1880.

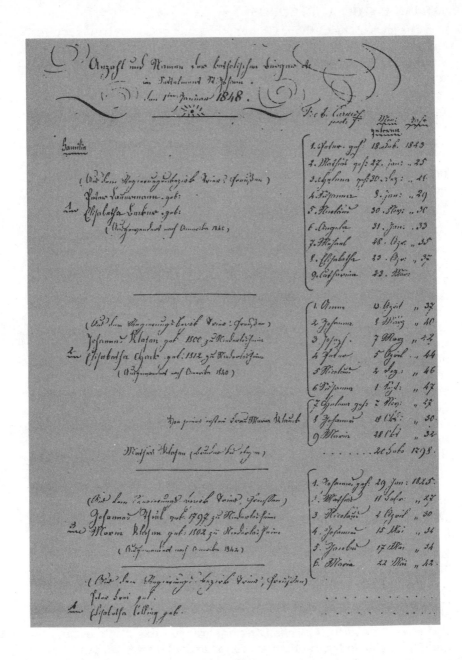

Figure 6. *Catholic Church record, German script—1848*

Selected Bibliography

Archdiocese of Chicago. *Official Directory of the Archdiocese of Chicago.* Chicago: Archdiocesan Pastoral Center. A yearly publication similar to the larger Catholic Directory but which focuses and elaborates on the Archdiocese of Chicago, its parishes and institutions. One of the most important features is a listing of the location of records of closed parishes. It is available for reference at most parishes.

Burgler, J. C. *Geschichte der Kathol. Kirche Chicago's mit Besonderer Berucksichtigung des Katholischen Deutschtums.* Chicago: 1889.

Cleary, Thomas F. "The History of the Catholic Church in Illinois from 1763-1844." Ph.D. Diss., University of Illinois, 1932.

Doretheus Ryan, Sister Mary, O.P. *Development of Catholicity in the Town of Lake.* Chicago: 1942.

Garraghan, Gilbert J. *The Catholic Church in Chicago, 1673-1871.* Chicago: 1921.

Hayes, Francis R.O. "Searching Catholic Records," *Illinois State Genealogical Society Quarterly* VI, No. 2, 1974.

Koenig, Harry C. *A History of the Parishes of the Archdiocese of Chicago.* Chicago: Catholic Bishop of Chicago, 1980. Published on the occasion of the 100th anniversary of the Archdiocese, this two-volume set begins with a description of the establishment of the diocese on 22 May 1843 and the events which led to the creation of the Archdiocese of Chicago on 21 September 1880. The history of what is the the largest Catholic Archdiocese in the United States is followed by a chronology of the founding of the parishes. An individual history of each of the 444 parishes in the Archdiocese is arranged in alphabetical order by name of parish in Chicago, followed by suburban churches in order of town name. The volumes are enhanced with photographs of most of the churches and the clergy serving each parish at the time of the publication.

_____. *Caritas Christi Urget Nos: A History of the Offices, Agencies & Institutions of the Archdiocese of Chicago.* Chicago: Catholic Bishop of Chicago, 1981.

Epstein, Francis J. *A Necrology of Diocesan Priests of the Chicago Archdiocese 1837-1959.* Chicago: Catholic Bishop of Chicago, (ca.1906). An updated, though still undated version by Rt. Rev. Msgr. Malachy P. Foley, P.A., is also extant.

Parot, Joseph John. *Polish Catholics in Chicago, 1850-1920: A Religious History.* Dekalb, Ill.: Northern Illinois University Press, 1981.

Sanders, James W. *The Education of an Urban Minority: Catholics in Chicago, 1833-1965.* New York: Oxford University Press, 1977.

Shanabruch, Charles H. "The Catholic Church's Role in the Americanization of Chicago's Immigrants, 1833-1928." 2 vol. Ph.D Diss., University of Chicago, 1975.

South Suburban Genealogical and Historical Society. *Index to Where the Trails Cross.* South Holland, Ill.: The Society, 1984.

Thomas, Sister Evangeline, ed. *Women Religious History Sources: A Guide to Repositories in the U.S.* New York: Bowker, 1983.

Thornton, Nancy C. "St. James Church and Cemetery," *Historic Illinois* (June 1985).

Old St. Mary's Church was the first Catholic Church in Chicago. The first volumes (1833-1843) of the parish registers were published in the *Illinois Catholic Historical Review* Vol.III, (April 1921): 146-48, 230-33, 404-36: Vol. IV (1921-22): 381-96; Vol.V (July 1922):41, 47-50. A computerized index to the names in the ICHR publication has been compiled by Gail Santroch for the Chicago Genealogical Society and will be published within the year. For general information, contact:

CATHOLIC INFORMATION SERVICE
ARCHDIOCESE OF CHICAGO
155 East Superior
Chicago, IL 60611
(312-751-8204)

CHICAGO CATHOLIC PARISHES TO 1875

Holy Name Cathedral (1845)
730 North Wabash, 60611

St. Adalbert (Polish) (1873)
1650 West 17th Street, 60608

All Saints (1875)
All Saints, St. Anthony of Padua
518 West 28th Place, 60616

St. Anthony of Padua (German)
(1873) (see above)

St. Anne (1865)
153 West Garfield, 60621
(records at St. Charles Lwanga)

Annunciation (1866)
1650 North Paulina, 60622

St. Bridget (1850)
2928 South Archer, 60608

St. Boniface (German) (1864)
921 North Noble, 60622

St. Columbkille (1859)
1648 West Grand, 60622
(closed—records at Holy
Innocents, 743 North Armour)

St. Francis Assissi (1853)
813 West Roosevelt, 60608

Holy Family (1857)
1019· South May, 60607

St. Henry (1851)
6335 North Hoyne, 60645

Holy Trinity (Polish) (1873)
1118 North Noble, 60622

Immaculate Conception (1859)
1415 North North Park, 60610

St. Jarlath (1864)
(records at St. Patricks [Adams])

St. James (1855)
2942 South Wabash, 60616

St. John (1857)
(records at St. James)

St. John Nepomucene (1870)
2953 South Lowe, 60616

St. Josesph (German) (1846)
1107 North Orleans, 60610

St. Margaret of Scotland (1874)
9837 South Throop, 60643

St. Mary (1883)
Old St. Mary's Chapel
21 East Van Buren, 60605

St. Michael (German) (1852)
1633 North Cleveland, 60614

Nativity of Our Lord (1868)
653 West 37th Street, 60609

Notre Dame (French) (1864)
1335 West Harrison, 60607

Our Lady of Sorrows (1874)
3121 West Jackson Boulevard, 60612

St. Patrick (1846)
718 West Adams, 60606

St. Patrick (1857)
9525 South Commercial, 60617

St. Peter (German) (1846)
110 West Madison, 60602

St. Pius V (1873)
1909 South Ashland, 60608

Sacred Heart (1865)
717 West 18th, 60616
(records at Providence of God)

St. Stephen (1869)
825 North Carpenter, 60622
(records at St. John Cantius)

St. Stanislaus Kostka (1867)
1351 West Evergreen, 60622

St. Thomas the Apostle (1865)
5472 South Kimbark, 60615

St. Wenceslaus (1863)
1224 West Lexington
(records at Our Lady of Pompeii)

Note: Nationality listed in parenthesis indicates the ethnic group served by the parish at the time of its founding, but may not be true today. The Diocese of Chicago at this time included the northern half of Illinois. Parishes listed above are only those within the city of Chicago.

NEIGHBORHOOD PARISHES

ANDERSONVILLE—St. Gregory, St. Ita

ALTGELD GARDENS—Our Lady of the Gardens

AUSTIN—St. Lucy (records at St. Catherine of Sienna)

AVONDALE—St. Wenceslaus, St. Hyacinth

BEVERLY—St. Therese, Christ the King, St. Margaret of Scotland, St. Barnabas

BRIDGEPORT—St. George, St. Mary of Perpetual Help, Immaculate Conception B.V.M. (Aberdeen), St. Barbara, St. Bridget, Nativity of our Lord (37th St.), St. David, St. John Nepomucene, All Saints, St. Anthony of Padua

BRIGHTON PARK—St. Agnes, Immaculate Conception (44th), St. Joseph and St. Anne, St. Pancratius, Five Holy Martyrs

CHICAGO LAWN—St. Rita, St. Adrian, Nativity B.V.M., St. Nicholas of Tolentine

EDGEBROOK—Queen of All Saints, St. Mary of the Woods

GAGE PARK—St. Simon, St. Clare de Monte Falco, St. Gall

HEGEWISCH—Anunciata, St. Florian, St. Columba

HUMBOLT PARK—St. Fidelis, St. Mark

HYDE PARK—St. Thomas the Apostle, St. Ambrose

JACKSON PARK—St. Clara, St. Cyril, St. Lawrence

LAKEVIEW—Our Lady of Mt. Carmel, St. Sebastian, St. Ephrem

MCKINLEY PARK—Our Lady of Good Counsel, SS. Peter and Paul (Paulina), St. Maurice MERRIONETTE PARK—St. Christina

N. GREEKTOWN—Queen of Angels, St. Matthias, Transfiguration (Lincoln Square/Ravenswood)

NEWTOWN—St. Vincent de Paul

OLDTOWN—St. Michael, Immaculate Conception (North Park)

PULLMAN—Holy Rosary, St. Anthony, St. Salomea, St. Louis, St. Willibrod

RIVERVIEW—St. Francis Xavier, St. Veronica

ROGERS PARK—St. Margaret Mary, St. Jerome

ROSELAND—All Saints, St. Nicholas, Holy Rosary, St. Louis, Catherine of Genoa

S. GREEKTOWN—St. Patrick (Adams)

SUMMERDALE—St. Eugene

RECORD LOCATIONS FOR CLOSED CHICAGO (IRISH) PARISHES

All Saints
25th Place and Wallace
(Records at All Saints-
St. Anthony
518 West 28th Place, 60616)

St. Anne
55th and Wentworth
(Records at St. Charles Lwanga
153 West Garfield, 60621)

Annunciation
Wabansia Ave. and Paulina
(Records at St. Mary of the Angels
1825 North Wood, 60622)

St. Cecilia
45th and Wells
(Records at St. Charles Lwanga
153 West Garfield, 60621)

St. Charles Borromeo
Roosevelt Road and Hoyne Ave.
(Records at Holy Trinity
916 Wolcott Ave., 60612)

St. Columbkille
Grand Ave. and Paulina Street
(Records at Holy Innocents
743 North Armour Street, 60622)

St. Cyril
64th and Dante
(Records at St. Clara, St. Cyril
6415 South Woodlawn, 60637)

St. Finbarr
14th and Harding Street
(Records at Our Lady of Lourdes
1444 South Keeler Ave., 60623)

St. Jarilath
Jackson Boulevard and
    Hermitage Ave.
(Records at St. Patricks
718 West Adams Street, 60606)

Old St. John
18th and Clark Street
(Records at St. James
2942 South Wabash, 60616)

St. Louis
Polk and Sherman
(Records include many Irish
    names and are at St. Marys
21 West Van Buren Street, 60605)

St. Lucy
Lake Street and Mayfield Ave.
(Records at St. Catherine of
    Siena, St. Lucy
38 North Austin Boulevard
Oak Park, IL 60302)

St. Matthew
Walnut Street and Albany
(Records at Our Lady of the
    Angels
3808 Iowa Street, 60651)

St. Paul
Lexington and Clinton Street
(Records perished in the Chicago
    Fire)

Sacred Heart
19th and Peoria Street
(Records at Providence of God
717 West 18th Street, 60616)

Old St. Stephen
Ohio and Sangamon Street
(Records St. John Cantius
825 North Carpenter Street,
    60622)

St. Theodore
62nd and Paulina Street
(Records at St. Brendan
6714 South Racine, 60636)

NATIONAL (ETHNIC) PARISHES IN CHICAGO
BELGIAN
St. John Berchmans (1903)
2517 West Logan Boulevard, 60647

BOHEMIAN
Blessed Agnes (1904)
(Moravian Czech)
2651 South Central Park, 60623

Our Lady of Good Counsel (1889)
916 North Western, 60622

St. Cyril and Methodius (1891)
5009 South Hermitage, 60609

St. John Nepomucene (1870)
2953 South Lowe, 60609

St. Ludmilla (1891)
2408 South Albany, 60623

St. Procopius (1876)
1641 South Allport, 60623

St. Wenceslaus (1863)
(records at Our Lady of Pompeii)
1224 West Lexington, 60607

St. Vitus (1888)
1818 South Paulina, 60608

Our Lady of Lourdes (1892)
1444 South Keeler, 60623

CROATIAN

Assumption (1901)
(Records microfilmed by GSU)
6005 Marshfield, 60636

Holy Trinity (1914)
(Records microfilmed by GSU)
1850 South Throop, 60608

St. Jerome (1912)
(Records microfilmed by GSU)
2823 South Princeton, 60616

Sacred Heart (1913)
(Records microfilmed by GSU)
2864 East 96th, 60617

St. George (1903)
(Croatians attended St. George until
Sacred Heart was founded, 1913)

DUTCH

St. Willibrod (1900)
11406 South Edbrooke, 60628

FRENCH

St. Louis (1850)

Sherman & Polk Sts.
(Records at Old St. Mary's
21 East Van Buren Street, 60605)

Notre Dame (1864)
1335 West Harrison, 60607

St. John the Baptist (1882)
33rd & Paulina
(Records now at St. Joseph and
St. Anne
2751 West 38th 60632)

St. Louis (1886)
117th Street
(Records at All Saints
10809 South State, 60628)

St. Joseph and St. Anne (1889)
2751 West 38th, 60632

St. John the Baptist (1892)
911 West 50th Place, 60609

Sacred Heart (1911)
11652 South Church
(Records at Holy Name of Mary
11159 South Loomis, 60643)

GERMAN

St. Peter (1846)
110 West Madison Street, 60602

St. Joseph Church (1846)
1107 North Orleans, 60610

St. Henry (1851)
6335 North Hoyne, 60659

St. Michael (Redemptorist)
(1852)
1633 North Cleveland, 60614

St. Francis Assisi (1853)
813 West Roosevelt, 60608

St. Boniface (1864)
921 North Noble, 60622

St. Anthony of Padua (1873)
All Saints, St. Anthony of Padua
518 West 28th Place, 60616

St. Paul (1876)
2127 West 22nd, 60608

St. Augustine (1879)
5045 South Laflin, 60609

St. Alphonsus (1882)
1429 West Wellington, 60657

Immaculate Conception (1883)
3111 South Aberdeen, 60621

St. Aloysious (1884)
2300 West LeMoyne, 60622

St. George (1884)
Wentworth Ave.
(Records at St. Charles Lwanga
153 Garfield Boulevard 60621)

Holy Trinity (1885)
916 South Wolcott, 60612

St. Martin (1886)
5842 South Princeton, 60621

St. Matthias (1887)
2310 West Ainslie, 60625

St. Philomena (1888)
1921 North Kedvale, 60639

St. Francis Xavier (1888)
2840 West Nelson, 60618

St. Teresa (1889)
1037 West Armitage, 60614

St. Maurice (1890)
3615 South Hoyne, 60609

St. Nicholas (1890)
(Records at All Saints
10809 South State, 60628)

Sacred Heart (1894)
7020 South Aberdeen, 60621

St. Clara (1894)
(Records at St. Clara, St. Cyril
6415 South Woodlawn, 60637)

Holy Ghost (1896)
St. Mel, Holy Ghost
22 North Kildare, 60624

Our Lady of Perpetual Help
(1898)
1300 South St. Louis
(closed, records at St. Agatha
3147 West Douglas, 60623)

St. Benedict (1901)
2215 West Irving Park, 60618

St. Raphael (1901)
6012 South Laflin, 60636

St. William (1916)
2600 North Sayre, 60635

HUNGARIAN

Our Lady of Hungary (1904)
9237 South Avalon, 60619

St. Stephen, King of Hungary
(1934)
2015 West August Boulevard,
60622

ITALIAN

Assumption B.V.M. (1881)
323 West Illinois, 60610

St. Mary of Mt. Carmel (1892)
6722 South Hermitage, 60636
(closed, records at
St. Justin Martyr Church
1818 West 71st Street, 60636)

Santa Maria Incornata (1899)

Santa Lucia
3022 South Wells, 60616

Holy Guardian Angel (1899)
(Records at Our Lady of
Pompeii)

Santa Maria Addolorata (1903)
528 North Ada, 60622

Santa Michael the Archangel
(1903)
2325 West 24th Place, 60608

St. Philip Benizi (1904)
357 West Locust, 60610
(Records at St. Dominic)

Holy Rosary (1904)
612 North Western, 60612

St. Anthony (1904)
11533 South Prairie, 60628

Our Lady of Pompeii (1910)
1224 West Lexington, 60604

St. Francis de Paula (1911)
7822 South Dobson, 60619

St. Callistus (1919)
2167 West Bowler, 60612

St. Frances Cabrini
(mission of St. Callistus,
also known as Mother Cabrini,
1936-40;
parish established 1940)
743 South Sacramento Street, 60612

LATVIAN

Our Lady of Algona
2543 West Wabansia, 60647

LITHUANIAN

St. George (1886)
3230 South Lithuanica, 60608

St. Bartholomew (1893)
730 South Lincoln, Waukegan,
60085

Providence of God (1900)
717 West 18th Street, 60616

Holy Cross (1904)
4557 South Wood, 60609

St. Michael (1904)
1644 West Wabansia
(records at Annunciation
1650 North Paulina, 60622)

Our Lady Of Vilna (1904)
2327 West 23rd Place, 60608

St. Joseph (1905)
8801 South Saginaw, 60617

All Saints (1907)
10809 South State, 60628

St. Casimir (1910)
283 East 14th Chicago Heights,
60411

St. Anthony (1911)
1515 South 50th, 60650 (Cicero)

Immaculate Conception (1914)
2745 West 44th Street, 60632

SS. Peter and Paul (1914)
12433 South Halsted, 60628

Nativity, B.V.M. (1927)
6812 South Washtenaw, 60629

POLISH

St. Wenceslaus (1863)
formerly at Halsted and
DeKoven (records at Our Lady of
Pompeii
1224 West Lexington, 60607)

St. Stanislaus Kostka (1867)
1351 West Evergreen, 60622

St. Stephen (1869)
(Records at St. John Cantius
825 North Carpenter, 60622)

Holy Trinity (1873)
1118 North Noble, 60622

St. Adalbert (1873)
1650 West 17th, 60608

St. Mary of Perpetual Help
(1882)
1039 West 32nd, 60608

Immaculate Conception (1883)
2944 East 88th, 60617

St. Josaphat (1884)
2311 North Southport, 60614

St. Joseph (1887)
4821 South Hermitage, 60609

St. Hedwig (1888)
2226 North Hoyne, 60647

St. Casimir (1890)
2226 South Whipple, 60623

St. Michael (1892)
8237 South Shore, 60617

St. John Cantius (1893)
825 North Carpenter, 60622

St. Stanislaus B and M (1893)
5352 West Belden, 60639

St. Hyacinth (1894)
3636 West Wolfram, 60618

SS. Peter and Paul (1895)
3745 South Paulina, 60609

St. Salomea (1897)
11824 South Indiana, 60628

St. Ann (1902)
1814 South Leavitt, 60608

Assumption B.V.M. (1903)
544 West 123rd, 60628

St. Florian (1905)
13145 South Houston, 60633

Holy Innocents (1905)
743 North Armour, 60622

St. John of God (1906)
1234 West 52nd, 60609

Good Shepherd (1907)
2719 South Kolin, 60623

St. Francis Assissi (1909)
932 North Kostner, 60651

St. Barbara (1910)
2859 South Throop, 60608

Sacred Heart (1910)
4600 South Honore, 60609

St. Mary Magdalene (1910)
8424 South Marguette, 60617

Transfiguration (1911)
2609 West Carmen, 60625

St. Wenceslaus (1912)
3400 North Monticello, 60618

Immaculate Heart of Mary (1912)
3824 North Spaulding, 60618

St. Helen (1913)
2315 West Augusta Boulevard,
60622

St. James (1914)
5730 West Fullerton, 60639

St. Ladislaus
5346 West Roscoe, 60641

St. Constance (1916)
5843 West Strong, 60630

St. Bronislava (1928)
8708 South Colfax, 60617

SLOVAK

Assumption B.V.M. (1903)
2434 South California, 60608

St. Joseph Church
720 West 17th Place
(Records at Providence of God
Church
717 West 18th Street, 60616)

St. Michael the Archangel (1898)
4821 South Damen, 60609

Holy Rosary (1907)
100 West 108th Place
(records at All Saints Church
10809 South State, 60628)

St. Cyril and Methodius (1914)
4244 West Walton, 60651

St. John the Baptist (1909)
9129 South Burley, 60617

Sacred Heart (1914)
721 North Oakley, 60612

SLOVENIAN

St. George (1903)
9546 South Ewing, 60617

St. Stephen (1898)
1852 West 22nd Place, 60608

EASTERN RITE CHURCHES

St. Basil Mission (1943) (A Byzantine Rite church serving mainly Ukrainians, attended by St. Michael) 740 East 91st Street 60619

St. Mary (1905)(A Byzantine church of the Ruthenian Rite serving Hungarians and Czechs; Liturgy in Old Slavonic) 4949 South Seeley 60609

St. Michael (1917) (A Byzantine church serving mainly Ukrainians) 12205 South Parnell 60628

Nativity of the Blessed Virgin Mary (1911) (A Byzantine church serving mainly Ukrainians) 4952 South Paulina 60609

St. Nicholas (1906) (A Byzantine church serving mainly Ukrainians) 2238 West Rice 60622

SS. Peter & Paul (1905) (A Byzantine church of the Ruthenian Rite serving mainly Croatians) 3048 South Central Park 60623

St. Joseph (1956) (A Byzantine church serving mainly Ukrainians) 5016 North Cumberland 60656

St. John the Baptist (1910) (A Byzantine church of Melkite Rite, formerly at 1249 South Washtenaw), 200 East North Ave., Northlake, IL 60164

Our Lady of Lebanon (1959) (An Antiochian church of the Maronite Rite serving mainly Lebanese and Syrians) 425 North Hillside, Hillside, IL 60162

SS Volodymyr and Olha (A Byzantine church serving mainly Ukrainians) 739 North Oakley, Boulevard (office: 2247 West Chicago, 60622

Christ the Redeemer (A Byzantine church serving Byelorussians) 3107 West Fullerton, 60647

St. Ephrem (1911) (A Chaldean Rite church serving Syrians and others from the Middle East) 2537 West Bryn Mawr 60659

LUTHERAN CHURCH RECORDS
by Ronald Otto

Lutheranism came to Chicago area communities as it came to other American communities: via the German-speaking immigrants who longed for the comfort of their church in their language. Lutheran churches did exist earlier in the eastern portions of the United States, but as this "Lutheran" church moved westward, it did so with English-speaking congregations. For additional information about the predecesors to this "Lutheran Church in America" organization in Illinois, see "The American Roots of German Lutheranism in Illinois" by E. Duane Elbert in *Illinois Historical Journal* (Summer 1985.) Each of the churches listed at the end of this article began as a German speaking congregation.

According to Robert Wiederaenders in "A History of Lutheranism in Chicago" in Volume II of the *Chicago Lutheran Planning Study* (Chicago: National Lutheran Council, 1965), the first German Protestant minister in this area was the Reverend Jacob Boas (at the time in charge of the Miami, Ohio, Circuit of the Evangelical Association). In August 1837, he preached the first German sermon in Chicago, but no congregation was organized and he returned to Ohio. In 1838, a Prussian, Ludwig Cachend-Ervenberg, became pastor of a German congregation at Dunklee's Grove (today, Addison Township, DuPage) with missions at Long Grove, Arlington Heights, and Bensenville. This last-named place emerged as the home of this known Zion Lutheran, Bensenville. The earliest registers maintained by the Reverend Cachend-Evernberg have been translated by Doctor David Koss (Illinois College, Jacksonville, Illinois) and published in Volume XVII:1 of the *Illinois State Genealogical Society Quarterly*.

Factionalism among German Protestants in Germany carried over in America. Today, one will find in Illinois "Lutheran" Churches belonging to the Missouri Synod, the Wisconsin Synod, the American Lutheran Church and the Lutheran Church in America. In addition to the early Lutheran Churches now organized under the above umbrella organizations, one should also look for Illinois German Protestant Churches which were members of the German United Evangelical Synod of North America. Why so much factionalism? For starters, during the mid-nineteenth century, the early Lutherans (eighteenth century immigrants) were established in the east in English-speaking churches, and more recent immigrants were not comfortable in this "foreign" atmosphere. Simplistically, factionalism here was an extension of factionalism in Germany compounded by the fact that each church here was financially supported by the individual parishioners and not by the state. It was quickly learned that he who pays the fiddler selects the music.

On 27 September 1817, King Friedrich Wilhelm III of Prussia promulgated by court proclamation the "Union" of the Lutheran and Reformed Churches there. Thus the Evangelical Church, the Church of the Prussia Union, came into existence. Vigorous opposition immediately emanated from many sources, such as Klaus Harms, the vehement pastor in Kiel. Opposition to this Union Church continued for decades and resulted in certain migrations by "Old Lutherans" (and others) to the United States and Australia for religious freedom. For more information about the "Old Lutherans" consult: *Nineteenth Century Emigration of "Old Lutherans" from Eastern German (Mainly Pomerania and Lower Silesia) to Australia, Canada and the United States* by Clifford Neal Smith (McNeal, Ariz.: Westland Publications, 1980). While the "Old Lutherans" settled mainly in southeastern Wisconsin, another group, the Saxon Lutherans formed the nucleus of the Wisconsin Synod. For a thorough discussion of the political ramifications of the "Union" Church within Prussia, consider: Bigler, Robert M., *The Politics of German Protestantism: the Rise of the Protestant Church Elite in Prussia, 1815-1848* (Berkley, Calif.: University of California Press, 1972).

The above mentioned German United Evangelical Synod of North America was formed in 1872 by the merger of three factions: Evangelical Synod of the West, Evangelical United Synod of the East, United Evangelical Synod of the Northwest.

The last named was the synod for most of the Evangelical "Union" churches in the Chicago area and its repository to this day is found at Elmhurst College in Elmhurst, Illinois. In 1934, the German United Evangelical had become the United Evangelical Synod and by its merger with the Reformed Church became known as the Evangelical and Reformed Church (E & R). Published sources about the Evangelical United Synod include: *A History of the Evangelical and Reformed Church* by David Dunn et. al. (Philadelphia: The Christian Education Press, 1961); *The German Church on the American Frontier* by Carl Edward Schneider (St. Louis: Eden Publishing House, 1939). "The Origin of the German Evangelical Synod of North America" by Carl Edward Schneider, *Church History* IV:4 (December 1935).

In 1957 another merger took place, this time between the Evangelical and Reformed Church and the Christian Congregational Church, and thus there was formed the United Church of Christ (UCC). To learn the existing churches whose heritage goes back to the "Union" church, consult a current *United Church of Christ Yearbook* available at the nearest UCC Church and at many regional repositories.

Addresses for the repositories of the Evangelical and Reformed Church (today the United Church of Christ) are:

Edens Archives, 475 E. Lockwood Ave., Webster Groves, MO 63119 (the E & R Archives)

Illinois Conference U.C.C., 302 S. Grant, Hinsdale, IL 60521 (for information on area UCC Churches)

Philip Schaff Memorial Library, Lancaster Theological Seminary, Lancaster, PA 17603

Addresses for Lutheran repositories include:

Archives of the American Lutheran Church, Wartburg Theological Seminary, 333 Wartburg Place, Dubuque, IA 52001 (Synods now merged with ALC include: Iowa, Ohio, Hauge, Norwegian, United Norwegian, and Danish (Blair).

Archives of the Lutheran Church in America, Lutheran School of Theology, 1100 E. 55th Street, Chicago, IL 60615 (Synod now merged with LCA: include: Wartburg, Augustana, Chicago, Northern Illinois, and Danish Evangelical).

Concordia Historical Institute, 801 DeMun, St. Louis, MO 63105 (This is the general archives of the Missouri Synod; however, there is also an archives for the Northern District located at 2301 Wolf Road, Hillside, IL).

Wisconsin Lutheran Seminary, 11831 N. Seminary Drive, 65, Mequon, WI 53092 (Archives of the Wisconsin Synod).

For the names of merged synods, the compiler is indebted to Robert Wiederaenders, archivist for the ALC. For additional information about the Missouri Synod Churches listed hereafter (and for information about other northern Illinois Churches of this Synod consult: *The Lutheran Trail* by the Reverend Louis J. Schwartzkopf (St. Louis: Concordia Press, Inc., 1950). For information on Chicago churches as of 1893, consult the listing in Volume XIV:3 of the *Chicago Genealogist*.

The following is a list of existing (and defunct) Chicago area German "Lutheran" churches with founding dates:

1838 Dunklee's Grove (Addison) Zion Lutheran, Bensenville (MS)
1840 Schaumburg–St. Peter's Lutheran
1843 Chicago–St. Paul UCC, Fullerton Pky & Orchard (UCC)
1845 Northbrook–St. Peter UCC, 2700 Willow Road (UCC)
1846 Long Grove–Long Grove UCC, 138 Long Grove Road (UCC)
1846 Chicago–First St. Paul Lutheran (MS)
1846 Palatine–St. John (UCC)
1847 Glencoe–Trinity Lutheran (MS)
1848 Elk Grove–St. John's (MS)
1849 Bensenville–St. John UCC (UCC)
1849 Addison–St. Paul Lutheran (MS)
1849 Coopers Grove–St.John's, 4231 W. 183, Country Club Hills (MS)
1849 Creek–Trinity Lutheran (MS)
1850 Mokena–Immanuel Lutheran (MS)
1851 Roselle–St.John Lutheran (MS)
1852 Richton Park–Immanuel Lutheran, Cicero & Sauk Trail (MS)
1852 Streamwood–Immanuel (UCC)
1854 Chicago–First Immanuel Lutheran, Roosevelt & Ashland (MS)
1854 Eagle Lake–St. John's, Washington Twp, Wisconsin (MS)
1857 Naperville–St. John (UCC)
1857 Joliet–St. Peter's Lutheran (MS)
1858 Monee–St. Paul UCC, 207 Margaret Street (UCC)
1858 Hillside–Immanuel Lutheran (MS)
1858 Dolton–St. Paul Lutheran (MS)

1859 Tinley Park—Trinity Lutheran, 159th & Oak Pk (MS)
1859 Thornton—St. Peter Lutheran (MS)
1859 Niles—St. John's Lutheran (MS)
1860 Arlington Park—St. Peter's Lutheran (MS)
1861 Chicago—Salem UCC, 9717 Kostner, Oak Lawn (UCC)
1862 Burr Ridge—Trinity Ev. Lutheran, German Church Rd (MS)
1862 Seiden Prairie—St. Paul Lutheran, Vollmer Rd, Matteson
1862 Mokena—St. John UCC, 11100 Second St. (UCC)
1862 Blue Island—First Ev. Lutheran, Ann & Grove Sts.
1862 Green Garden Twp.—St. Peter's Ev. now merged with St. Paul
         UCC, Suak Trail, Frankfort (UCC)
1864 Chicago—St. Peter UCC, 5450 W. Diversey (UCC) 1864 Lansing—
         Trinity (MS)
1865 Harlem—St. John Lutheran—today, Forest Park (MS)
1865 Chicago—First Trinity Lutheran (MS)
1865 Beecher—St. Paul's Lutheran (MS)

Note: Kimball Avenue United Evangelical Church of Chicago (1900-1958) has been microfilmed by the Genealogical Society of Utah. The filming is of the original records at the United Congregational Church, Valencia, Pennsylvania.

The following list of Lutheran churches was submitted to the *Chicago Genealogical Society Newsletter* (September 1983) by Ronald Otto. Information appears in the following order: name of church, date of origin, location as of 1900, and current location.

St. Paul (1848)
Superior and North Franklin
(now at: 1301 North LaSalle, 60610)

First Immanuel (1854)
Ashland Boulevard and West 12th
(now at: 1124 South Ashland, 60607)

First Trinity (1865)
South Canal and 25th
(now at: 643 West 31st Street, 60616)

First St. John (1867)
West Superior and Bickerdike, Closed

First Zion (1868)
West 19th and Johnson

St. James (1869)
Fremont and Garfield
(now at: 2048 North Fremont, 60614)

Zion (1870)
Washington Heights
(now at: 9901 South Winston, 60643)

First Bethlehem (1871)
North Paulina and McReynolds
(now at: 1645 West LeMoyne, 60622)

St. Peter (1871)
Dearborn South of 39th
(now at: 7400 South Michigan, 60619)

St. Matthew (1871)
South Hoyne between West 20
and 21st
(now at: 2108 West 21st Street,
60608)

Immanuel (1872)
Colehour (South Chicago)
(now at: 9031 South Houston,
60617)

Bethlehem (1874)
103rd near Ave. G
(now at: 10261 South Ave. H,
60617)

St. John (1875)
1704 West Montrose
4939 West Montrose, 60641

Zion's (1882)
113th and Edbrooke
10858 South King Drive, 60628

St. Luke (1884)
Belmont and Perry
(now at: 1500 West Belmont,
60657)

St. Martini (1884)
West 51st, and South Marshfield
1624 West 51st, 60629

Christ (1885)
North Humbolt and McLean
(now at: 2018 North Richmond,
60651)

St. Paul's (1886)
846 North Menard
(now at: 846 Menard, 60651)

Holy Cross (1886)
South Centre and 31st
(now at: 3116 South Racine,
60608)

Trinity (1887)
Hegewisch
(now at: 13200 Burley, 60653)

St. Mark's (1887)
1114 South California

Emmaus (1888)
North California and Walnut
(now at: 5440 West Gladys,
60644)

St. Andrew (1888)
3650 Honore
(now at: 3650 South Honore,
60609)

St. Stephens (1889)
Englewood and Union
(now at: 910 West 65th, 60621)

Gethsemane (1889)
49th and Dearborn
(now at: 2735 West 79th,
60652)

Bethany (1891)
Humbolt Park Boulevard, and
Rockwell
(now at: 1701 North Narragansett, 60639)

Concordia (1891)
West Belmont and North
Washtenaw
(now at: 2645 West Belmont,
60618)

St. Philip (1893)
Lawrence and North Hoyne
(now at: 2500 Bryn Mawr,
60625)

Bethel (1894)
1076 Hirsch
Hirsch and Springfield

SWEDISH LUTHERAN

The Emigrant Institute of Vaxjo, Sweden began microfilming
Swedish-American church records in the United States in 1968. By 1978,

1,500 congregations had been completed. They filmed records of dissolved and active congregations belonging to the Evangelical Covenant Church of America, the Baptist Conference, and the Luthern Church in America. The films are in the American Lutheran School of Theology, Chicago.

ST. JAMES EVANGELICAL LUTHERAN CHURCH RECORDS, CHICAGO, IL

The Newberry Library has two reels of microfilm records for St. James Evangelical Church. Reel 1 lists confirmations from 1871-95, baptisms from 1870-1931, marriages from 1870-1923, and burials from 1870-80. Reel 2 is a record of burials from 1881-1951.

METHODIST

The archives of the United Methodist Church, including its predecessor denominations is now located at Madison, New Jersey. The archives for a fee accepts genealaogical requests pertaining to clergy, but does not have any local church records, such as membership or baptismal lists. For further information write:

General Secretary
General Commission on Archives and History
United Methodist Church
P.O. Box 127
Madison, NJ 07940

Garrett-Evangelical Theological Seminary Library
2121 Sheridan Rd.
Evanston, IL 60201

For records of the United Methodist Church and its predecessors, Methodist Episcopal, Methodist Protestant, and Evangelical United Brethren, there is a joint library with Seabury-Western Theological Seminary (Episcopal).

CHICAGO METHODIST CHURCHES, 1871 (AND PASTORS)

FIRST
Clark and Washington, W. H. Daniels
Wabash Avenue and Harrison, R. M. Hatfield

TRINITY
Indiana Avenue at 24th, J. H. Bayliss
Indiana Avenue, between 31st and 32nd, Robert D. Sheppard
St. Johns' Oakland, Chas. D. Mandeville

GRACE
N. LaSalle and Chicago Avenue, N. M. Parkhurst

CENTENARY
Monroe west of Morgan, C. H. Fowler
Ada Street, between Lake and Fulton, Thos. R. Stobridge
Park Avenue and Robey, H. W. Thomas

ST. PAUL'S
Maxwell and Newberry, Wm. H. Burns
Halsted Street, near Canalport Avenue,
A. Youker (preaching in both English and German)
Simpson Chapel, Bonfield near C. & L. R. R. crossing,
Homer H. Scoville.
Kickson Street, North Avenue, T. Marsh.

AFRICAN METHODIST EPISCOPAL
Bethel African Methodist Episcopal, 3rd Avenue,
Rev. Henry Brown
Quin's African Methodist Episcopal Church, Jackson and 4th,
W. S. Lankford.

SELECTED BIBLIOGRAPHY

First Methodist Church. Centennial Program. First Methodist Episcopal Church of Chicago. *Commemorating One Hundred Years of Methodist History in Chicago, 1831-1931.* Chicago: 1931.

Lundberg, Gertrude W. "Ministerial Deaths, United Methodist Church, Northern Illinois 1845-1885." *The Chicago Genealogist* 5, No. 3. p. 133.

Norwood, Frederick A. *The Story of American Methodism: A History of The United Methodists and Their Relations.* Nashville: Abington Press, 1974.

Melton, J. Gordon. *Log Cabins to Steeples—The United Methodist Way in Illinois 1824-1974.* Nashville: Parthenon Press, 1974. Details not only the German Conferences, but also the Swedish and Norwegian-Danish. At one time there were four established German Conferences, two of which covered Illinois.

Pennewell, Almer M. *The Methodist Movement in Northern Illinois.* Sycamore, Ill.: 1942.

Schwartz, Elsie, ed. "Records of the Ravenswood United Methodist Church 1872-1972." (Indexed typescript)

Thompson, John. *The Soul of Chicago.* Chicago: 1920.

JEWISH

The Jewish Genealogical Society of Illinois
P.O. Box 481022
Niles, IL 60648
(312-564-1025)

Illiana Jewish Genealogical Society
Attn: Ellen Kahn
3416 Ithaca
Olympia Fields, IL 60461

Chicago Jewish Historical Society
1640 East 50th Street
Chicago, IL 60615
(312-493-7938)

The Jewish Theological College
7135 Carpenter Road
Skokie, IL 60076
(312-674-7750)

Houses the Saul Silber Memorial Library, sources for Rabbinic genealogy, books of Chicago Jewry, Holocaust materials, and Yizkor books.

Spertus College of Judaica
618 South Michigan Avenue
Chicago, IL 60605
(312-922-9012)

Houses the Norman and Helen Asher Library. The collection includes Rabbinic genealogical sources; Yizkor books; sources on Chicago Jewish history; Chicago Jewish periodicals; and microfilm of early twentieth century Yiddish newspapers. Also included in the library are the Chicago Jewish Archives, which contains a large unindexed collections manuscripts, papers from Chicago Jewish organizations, and other material about Jewish life in and around Chicago. Viewing of materials in these archives is only by appointment.

American Jewish Congress
22 West Monroe Street Suite 2102
Chicago, IL 60603
(312-332-7355)
Publishes a Guide to Jewish Chicago

American Jewish Historical Society
2 Thornton Road
Waltham, MA 02154

Hebrew Immigrant Aid Society
200 Park Avenue South
New York, NY 10003
Network of international offices. New York office has microfilm records of every immigrant met by HIAS workers since 1911.

CHICAGO AREA JEWISH CEMETERY GUIDE

Copies of *A Cemetery Guide to Jewish Cemeteries and Non-sectarian Cemeteries with Jewish Sections in the Chicago Area Including a Map of Jewish Waldheim* (1966 edition) published by Piser Menorah Chapels is available for use at Jewish Genealogical Society of Illinois.

SELECTED BIBLIOGRAPHY

American Jewish Congress. *A Guide to Jewish Chicago.* Chicago: 1974.

Associated Jewish Press Bureau. Jewish Directory of Chicago: Containing a Full and Complete List of Congregations, Their Ministers and Members, Also a Complete Manual of the Various Jewish Lodges in the City. Chicago: 1884.

Berkow, Ira. *Maxwell Street: Survival in a Bazaar.* Garden City, N.J.: 1977.

Bernheimer, Charles, ed. The Russian Jew in the United States. Philadelphia: 1905. Deals with Russian-Jewish life in Chicago, Philadelphia, and New York.

Bregstone, Philip P. *Chicago and Its Jews: A Cultural History.* Chicago: 1933.

Chicago Jewish Community Blue Book. Chicago: The Sentinel Publishing Co., ca 1918.

Cutler, Irving. "The Jews of Chicago: From Shetetl to Suburb." *Ethnic Chicago.* ed. Jones, Peter d'A. and Holli, Melvin G. Grand Rapids, Mich.: William B. Eerdmans Publishing Company, 1981.

Eakle, Arlene and Cerny, Johni. *The Source: A Guidebook of American Genealogy.* Salt Lake City, Ut.: Ancestry Incorporated, 1984. Jewish-American Genealogy, pages 602-649

Gutstein, Morris Aaron. *A Priceless Heritage: The Epic Growth of Nineteenth Century Chicago Jewry.* Chicago: 1953.

Heimonvics, Rachel Baron. *The Chicago Jewish Source Book.* Chicago: Follett Publishing Co., 1981.

Korey, Harold. "The History of Jewish Education in Chicago." M.A. thesis, University of Chicago, 1942. A long narrative useful for its WPA newspaper clippings.

Kranzler, David. *My Jewish Roots: A Practical Guide to Tracing Your Genealogy and Family History.* New York: Sepher-Hermon Press, 1979.

Krug, Mark M. "History of the Yiddish Schools in Chicago (1912-53)." *Jewish Education* XXV (Fall 1956): 67-73.

Kurzweil, Arthur. *From Generation to Generation: How to Trace Your Jewish Genealogy and Personal History.* New York: William Morrow and Co., 1980.

Meites, Hyman, ed. *History of the Jews of Chicago.* Chicago: 1924.

Rawidowicz, Simon, ed. *The Chicago Pinkas*. Chicago: 1952.

Rosenthal, Erich. "Acculturation without Assimilation? The Jewish Community of Chicago, Illinois." *American Journal of Sociology* LXVI (Nov. 1960): 275-88.

Rottenberg, Dan. *Finding Our Fathers: A Guidebook to Jewish Genealogy*. New York: Random House, 1986. This pioneer manual is very complete on sources. The bulk of the text lists Jewish surnames found in a variety of sources, indicating countries and related families.

Stern, Malcolm H. *Americans of Jewish Descent: Sources of Information for Tracing Their Genealogy*. Special Publications 20. Washington, DC: National Genealogical Society, 1958. Historic and bibliographic background.

_____. *Jewish Genealogy: An Annotated Bibliography* AASLH Technical Leaflet 138. Nashville: American Association for State and Local History, 1981.

_____. *Tracing Your Jewish Roots*. Cincinnati: American Jewish Archives, 1977. A short manual for beginners.

_____. *First American Jewish Families: 600 Genealogies, 1654-1977*. Cincinnati, Ohio: American Jewish Archives and Waltham, Mass: American Jewish Historical Society, 1978.

PRESBYTERIAN

McCormick Theological Seminary Library
McGaw Library (University of Chicago)
800 West Belden Avenue
Chicago, IL 60614

Holdings include account books, letters, sermons, and other papers pertaining to the Presbyterian Church in the midwestern states.

Presbyterian Historical Society
United Presbyterian Church in the U.S.A.
425 Lombard Street
Philadelphia, PA 19147

Holdings include the Presbyterian Biographical Index, a card index to periodicals, newspapers, and books for both clergy and laymen.

Princeton Theological Seminary
Speer Library
Mercer Street and Library Place
Princeton, NJ 08540

Marjorie Smith compiled an index to the Membership List of the Second Presbyterian Church of Chicago 1842-92 which appeared in the *Chicago Genealogist* III, Nos. 1-4; and Vol. IV, Nos. 1 and 2 (1970-71).

FOURTH UNITED PRESBYTERIAN CHURCH, CHICAGO

The Genealogical Society of Utah has microfilmed records of the Fourth Presbyterian Church, 1892-1900. The microfilm includes session minutes, list of members, and baptisms. (Film #914,074).

SELECTED BIBLIOGRAPHY

Miller, William B. "Church Records of the United States: Presbyterian," a paper delivered at the World Conference on Records and Genealogical Seminar, 5-8 August 1969. Salt Lake City, sponsored by the Church of Jesus Christ of Latter-day Saints.

Stevenson, Andrew. *Chicago: Pre-Eminently a Presbyterian City.* Chicago: 1907.

Union Catalog of Presbyterian Manuscripts Presbyterian Library Association, 1964. Lists Presbyterian and Reformed records.

Writer's Program. Illinois. *A History of the First Presbyterian Church of Chicago, 1833-1941.*

CHICAGO PRESBYTERIAN CHURCHES, 1871

Calvary Presbyterian Church
Indiana Avenue, N.W. and 22nd

First Hyde Park Church
Hyde Park

First Presbyterian
Wabash Avenue between Congress and Van Buren

Eighth Presbyterian Church
Robey, N.W. and Washington

Ninth Presbyterian Church
Ellis

Olivet Church
Wabash Avenue and 14th

Second Presbyterian Church
Wabash Avenue, N.W. and Washington

Seventh Presbyterian Church
Halsted and Harrison

Third Presbyterian Church
W. Washington and Carpenter

Thirty-first Street
Presbyterian Church
Wabash Avenue South of 31st

Reunion Presbyterian
Church
535 Mitchell

Welsh Presbyterian Church
Monore and Sangamon

Fullerton Avenue Church
Fullerton Avenue near Clark

Jefferson Park Church
Adams and Throop

Fourth Presbyterian
Church
Cass Indiana

| Orchard Street Church | Highland Presbyterian Church |
| 194 Orchard | Noble and Erie |

BAPTIST

There is no religious hierarchy in the Baptist Church. Each congregation is autonomous, creating and keeping possession of whatever records it needs. To locate Baptist records, it is sometimes useful to contact churches in the area which are found in the *Yellow Pages,* of a contemporary telephone directory. This approach will not always be productive in city situations where the ethnic makeup of neighborhoods has changed over the years, but it still provides a point to begin research. For additional information contact:

Northern Baptist Theological Seminary Library
100 West Butterfield Road
Oak Brook, IL 60521
Next door to Bethany Theological Seminary—joint library

University of Chicago Divinity School
Swift Hall, 58th Street
Chicago, IL 60614
(312-962-8200)
Originally Baptist, ecumenical

Chicago Metropolitan Baptist Association
Southern Baptist Convention
329 Madison
Oak Park, IL
(312-848-9120)

SELECTED BIBLIOGRAPHY

Bousman, Gary A. "Inclusive Membership in the Churches of the Chicago Baptist Association." M.A. thesis, University of Chicago, 1937.

Dillow, Myron D." A History of Baptists in Illinois, 1786-1845." Ph.D. diss., Southwestern Baptist Theological Seminary, 1965.

Ericson, C. Oscar George. *Harvest on the Prairies: Centennial History of the Baptist Conference of Illinois 1856-1956.* Chicago: 1956.

Hine, Leland D. "Aspects of Change in the Churches of the Chicago Baptist Association, 1931-1935." Ph.D. diss., University of Pennsylvania, 1958.

Stackhouse, Perry J. *Chicago and the Baptists.* Chicago: 1933.

FIRST BAPTIST CHURCH, EVANSTON

The Genealogical Society of Utah has microfilmed records of deaths of the First Baptist Church of Evanston for the years 1865-1960. (Film #907,987)

BRETHREN

HISTORICAL LIBRARY AND ARCHIVES
1451 Dundee Avenue
Elgin, IL 60120

Brethren Historical Library and Archives (BHLA) is the official repository for records created by the Church of the Brethren General Board, Pension Board, and Annual Conference. In addition, it is a research center which makes available books, manuscript collections, and audiovisual items documenting the cultural, socio-economic, theological, genealogical and institutional history of the Brethren. In addition to card catalogs, preliminary inventories for archival records and manuscript collections are maintained. Also available are files on districts and congregations of the Church of the Brethren, a biographical file, and an obituary index (ca. 1851-79). A complete description of the library and archives history, collection, and policies appeared in *Illinois Libraries* 63, No.4 (April 1981).

EPISCOPAL

Individual churches keep their own records. Closed church records are at the church archives:

Diocese of Chicago Episcopal
Archives and Historical Collections
St. James Cathedral
65 East Huron
Chicago, IL 60611
(312-787-6410)

SELECTED BIBLIOGRAPHY

Hall, Francis J. *A History of the Diocese of Chicago, Including a History of the Undivided Diocese of Illinois from Its Origination in A.D. 1835.* Dixon, Ill., n.d.

Hopkins, John Henry. *The Great Forty Years in the Diocese of Chicago, A.D. 1893-1934.* Chicago: 1936.

Schultz, Rima. *The Church and the City: A Social History of 150 Years at St. James, Chicago.* Chicago: R. R. Donnelly, 1986.

EVANGELICAL COVENANT CHURCH OF AMERICA
Archives and Historical Library
5125 North Spaulding Avenue
Chicago, IL 60625
Swedish Covenant

Moody Institute
1609 North LaSalle Street
Chicago, IL 60610

Congregational, United Church of Christ
Chicago Theological Seminary
Hammond Library

5757 South University Avenue
Chicago, IL 60637

Gethsemane United Church of Christ (3617 W. Belle Plaine, Chicago) was founded in 1906 and has been located for most of its life at the corner of Monticello and Belle Plaine. Gethsemane Baptisms have been extracted from the church registers by The Rev. and Mrs. Ray K. Kistler and are being published in the *Chicago Genealogist*. The first segment of the listing (surnames beginning with the letter A) appeared in Vol. XVIII, No. 1 (Fall 1985).

Advent Christian and Millerities
Aurora College Library
Aurora, IL 60507

Orthodox Church in America
Diocese of the Midwest
8200 South County Line Road
Hinsdale, IL 60521
(312-325-6608)

Greek Orthodox Diocese of Chicago
40 East Burton Place
Chicago, IL 60610
(312-337-4130)

Reformed Church of America
(Dutch Reformed Church)
Archives-Commission on History
21 Seminary Place
New Brunswick, NJ 08901

CHAPTER 9

Court Records and Research

T he Circuit Court of Cook County is the largest trial court in the world. At any given time there are up to 300 courtrooms in operation and thousands of people are in contact with the court daily. The volume of paper work created by the metropolitan population is mind-boggling. Court files kept over the years since 1871 when the Chicago Fire nearly swept the old court's file system clean, now number over 75 million and are expanding at a rate of over 5 million a year. Court documents are stored in nine storage locations.

One of the first public buildings in Chicago was the courthouse. The first was built in 1834 and stood until a more suitable replacement could be constructed. The second courthouse, an ornately constructed building, rose on the site of what is now the City Hall-County Building complex at LaSalle and Randolph. That edifice disappeared into ashes in the Chicago Fire along with most of the court's records. Courts carried on business as usual within hours of the holocaust. A third ediface rose quickly as a symbol of the re-birth of the city. The government center still occupied by city and county governments was built 1909-11 and served a dual function as a courthouse until 1965, when the Chicago Civic Center was opened. It occupies a full square block just to the east of the government center. In 1977, it was renamed the Richard J. Daley Center in honor of the late Chicago mayor.

The new thirty story civic center has a half-block square plaza that has become a Loop focal point.and the site of a fivestory-high sculpture by Pablo Picasso. It is also the home of the city's Eternal Flame, dedicated to the memory of Chicagoans who gave their lives in war.

Until 1964, courts were distributed throughout the state on an irregular basis with everything from county-wide courts to justices of the peace. There were over 200 separate courts in Cook County alone. There was a court for Chicago, and others in each of several of the larger suburbs. County-wide courts were responsible for divorces, adoptions, juveniles, criminal hearings, and major law suits. In the suburbs there were police magistrates in local villages and justices of the peace in unincorporated areas. Every single court was an independent entity with separate record-keeping systems. In 1962, voters approved the Judicial Amendment to the Illinois Constitution which created a state-wide court system, effective 1 January 1964, composed of twenty-one judicial circuits. One of these circuits is the Cook County Circuit Court through which every court case must be filed which is brought by or against residents or businesses in the county. Everything from parking tickets to murder trials are heard by this consolidated circuit court. All Cook County trial courts were placed under the supervision of a single chief judge and a single, elected clerk of the court.

The circuit court has two major departments: a county department which hears major cases, and a municipal department which hears less serious matters. Seven divisions comprise the county department: law (major personal injury suits), chancery (injunctions), county (adoptions, elections), probate (wills, estates, guardianships) divorce, juvenile, and criminal. The municipal department is divided into six geographical districts, one for the city of Chicago and five for the suburbs. These courts hear ordinance hearings on felony charges and felony informations.

Recordkeeper for the courts is the clerk of the circuit court, whose office is the largest of its kind in the country. He supplies personnel for all the courtrooms, keeps track of all the paperwork, collects all the court's revenue and is responsible for many of the court's support services such as data processing and microfilming. It takes over 1,750 people to run the circuit court. Prosecutions are handled by the state's attorney. The sheriff is responsible for the serving of legal papers and for maintaining order in the courts.

The administration of justice is a complex matter since there are more than 300 sitting judges and over 6,000,000 cases a year heard in Cook County.

From the first time a lawsuit or criminal charge reaches a filing counter to the day it is finally recorded in a docket book or on a computer file, it is in the hands of the clerk. The process of a case begins when it is logged in, always with a court clerk. It is prepared for its eventual appearance in court and supplementary actions are recorded.

Present records retention regulations allow destruction of some types of records after they reach a certain age (ranging from two and a half years for a traffic case to sixty years for a felony trial record). Disposal schedules were established for millions of obsolete files. All probate, divorce, adoption, and all other records involving the ownership of property are retained forever.

The Cook County Court files are like a mirror of history. Buried away in these archives are the dreams and frustrations of millions of Chicagoans. Buried away also are records of major historical significance such as the original court papers in connection with the commitment of Mary Todd Lincoln, the widow of President Abraham Lincoln. All documents having to do with that case are filed in a special safe in the clerk's office while photostats are kept in the public file. In the same manner, the original will of Francis Mother Cabrini, America's first Roman Catholic saint, was filed with an earlier court.

These files are the foundation of the city's written history. Although the office has authority to burn most of them, it was felt that the records should be preserved. In an effort to identify other important records, Circuit Court Clerk Morgan M. Finley created a Historical Archives Committee composed of thirty-two of the leading urban historians, archivists, and genealogists in the state. This group provided Finley with a sampling technique to preserve enough records to provide a historical profile of the period. It also has recommended destruction of several million files.

When the committee was created, its members included a representative of the Genealogical Society of Utah, a Mormon organization headquartered in Salt Lake City. As a result of meetings with representatives of the society, the clerk engaged in a cooperative venture that eventually will make available microfilm copies of the court's old records. The program which is now several years in progress is saving the public hundreds of thousands of dollars in microfilm costs.

CIRCUIT COURT OF COOK COUNTY

Daley Center, Chicago, IL 60602 (312-443-5500)
Chief Judge, Room 2600
Clerk of Court, Executive Offices, Room 1001

COUNTY DEPARTMENT
LAW DIVISION

Chief Deputy Clerk, Room 801 (312-443-5401)
Information (312-443-5412)
Law Division, Clerk, Room 1201 (312-443-7935)

Files (1981 thru present), Room 801
Files (1977-80), Room 1201
Files (Personal Property Tax), Room 801
All other files, Warehouse
Dockets and Registers (Years 1978 thru present), Room 801
Dockets and Registers Prior to 1978, Room 1201
Index Law (Years 1971 to present), Room 801
Index Law (Years 1964 thru 1970), Room 1201

Index of former Circuit Court Law, Chancery and Divorce prior to 1964, Room 1201

Note: Search the Plaintiff and Defendant Indexes in the Law Division for cases involving law suits, divorces, foreclosures, real estate property controversies, name changes, naturalizations, and the Burnt Record Series. For unexplained reasons, some entries have not been made alphabetically by surname in the indexes, but rather are entered under the letter I—called the INRE file—an abbreviated form of cases filed "In Regard to", or "In the Matter of". Several hundred cases have been filed in this fashion.

Cases older than ten years must be ordered from the warehouse and it usually takes about three working days for files to be brought to the court. Warehouse files are ordered in Room 1201.

The Genealogical Society of Utah has microfilmed the following records which are under the jurisdiction of the Law Division:

Circuit Court Naturalizations (Petition Records), 1906-29 (331 microfilm reels)
Circuit Court Naturalization Records 1871-1925 and Naturalization Indexes 1871-1912 (66 microfilm reels)
Circuit Court Naturalizations (Declarations of Intention) 1874-1929, Indexes 1871-1929 (155 microfilm reels)
Circuit Court Soldier Naturalization Petitions, 1914-1920 (1 microfilm reel)
Circuit Court Burnt Record Series 1871-1932 (3 microfilm reels and more in process of being filmed).

For more information on naturalizations and the Burnt Record Series, see Naturalization Records and Land and Property chapters, respectively.

CHANCERY DIVISION

Presiding Judge, Room 2403
Chief Deputy, Room 802
Deputy Clerk, Room 802
Information (312-443-6284-5)

Files—Chancery (years 1976 to present) Room 802
"Live" Chancery Files (years 1964 to 1975) Room 802
Files—Domestic Relations (years 1976 to present) Room 802
Domestic Relations Files (years 1975 and prior years) in Warehouse
Files of Former Superior Court 1963 and prior years in Warehouse
    Order Warehouse files in Room 802
Dockets and Registers—Chancery and Domestic Relations 1964 to present, Room 802

Former Superior Court Law, Chancery, and Divorce Dockets and Registers 1963 and prior years in warehouse.

Index—Chancery and Domestic Relations (years 1964 to 1983 inclusive), Room 802

Index—Former Superior Court (1871 to 1963 inclusive), Room 802.

Note: Divorce' file numbers are most often found in indexes in Room 802, but may also be found in the Law Division in Room 1201. *Name Changes* are likewise found in the indexes of both divisions.

The Genealogical Society of Utah has microfilmed the following records which were a part of the old Superior Court:

Superior Court Naturalization (Declarations of Intention) 1871-1906 (7 microfilm reels)

Superior Court Naturalizations (Petitions and Records of Military Personnel) 1904-06 (1 microfilm)

Superior Court Naturalizations (Petition Records) 1923-24 (2 microfilm reels)

Superior Court Naturalizations (Petitions and Records) 1906-29 (294 microfilm reels)

Superior Court Naturalizations (Declarations of Intention) 1906-29 (162 microfilm reels)

Superior Court Naturalizations (Indexes) 1871-1906 (2 microfilm reels)

Superior Court Naturalizations (Petitions by aliens under 18) 1904-08 (2 microfilm reels)

Cook County Court Naturalizations (Declarations of Intention) 1874-1906 (25 reels)

Cook County Court Naturalizations (Indexes) 1874-1906 (15 microfilm reels)

COUNTY DIVISION

Presiding Judge, Room 1703
Chief Deputy Clerk, Room 801
Information (312-443-5515)
Clerk's Office, Room 801

Files (years 1980 thru present), Room 801
Files (year 1979 and prior years), Room 1201
Dockets (1933 to present), Room 801
Mental Health Docket and Index (years 1883 to present), Room 801
Index and Dockets—Adoptions (all), Room 801
Index—Tax Deed Petitions (years 1969 to present), 801
Index—Inheritance Tax Returns (years 1969 to present), 801
All other files, dockets and indexes, Room 1201

PROBATE DIVISION

Presiding Judge, Room 1803
Chief Deputy Clerk, Room 1202
Chief Clerk, Room 1202
Information (312-443-6476)
Probate Desk, Room 1202 (312-443-5025)

Files (years 1976 to present), Room 1202
Wills (years 1964 to present), Room 1202

Indexes, Deceased, Incompetent, and Minors Estates, Room 1202

Records which relate to the disposition of an estate after its owners death are called probate records. They will vary in content and value, but these records comprise one of the most consistently helpful research tools when they do exist. All the separate indexes in Room 1202 should be consulted if there is any question as to the existence of probate proceedings.

A person who dies leaving a will is said to be testate and one who dies without a will is intestate. Probate records in Illinois include a document called Proof of Heirship which enumerates applicable heirs — spouses, parents, siblings, children, cousins, or next eligible relatives. The purpose of this testimony is to establish relationships. Notices must be served on persons who have an interest in the estate and their addresses are included. Until recent years, probate files contained an estate inventory which can provide important insights. Index ledgers are bound by year (or other specified time slot) and arranged alphabetically therein. Early indexes are handwritten and are not in strict alphabetical order, but rather in register order by first letters of surnames. More recent indexes are typed and arranged in complete alphabetical order. Files since 1974 are computerized. Files for the last nine years are on hand in Room 1202, but previously filed cases must be ordered from the warehouse and usually take about three or four days to be brought into the Daley Center.

When more than one entry for a particular name is found in a given index with only a number to identify the needed file, it is advisable to take down the docket number and refer to the corresponding docket book. Docket books 1871 to 1892 are available behind the counter in Room 1202, and dockets after that date may be searched in Room 1806. An express elevator to the eighteenth floor near the docket room is located in the Judge's Corridor on the twelfth floor. Each of the separately indexed docket books are numbered and arranged chronologically. These volumes provide case numbers and give a summary of each case; including name of deceased, date of death, executor or administrator of estate, heirs, and other pertinent notes relevant to the

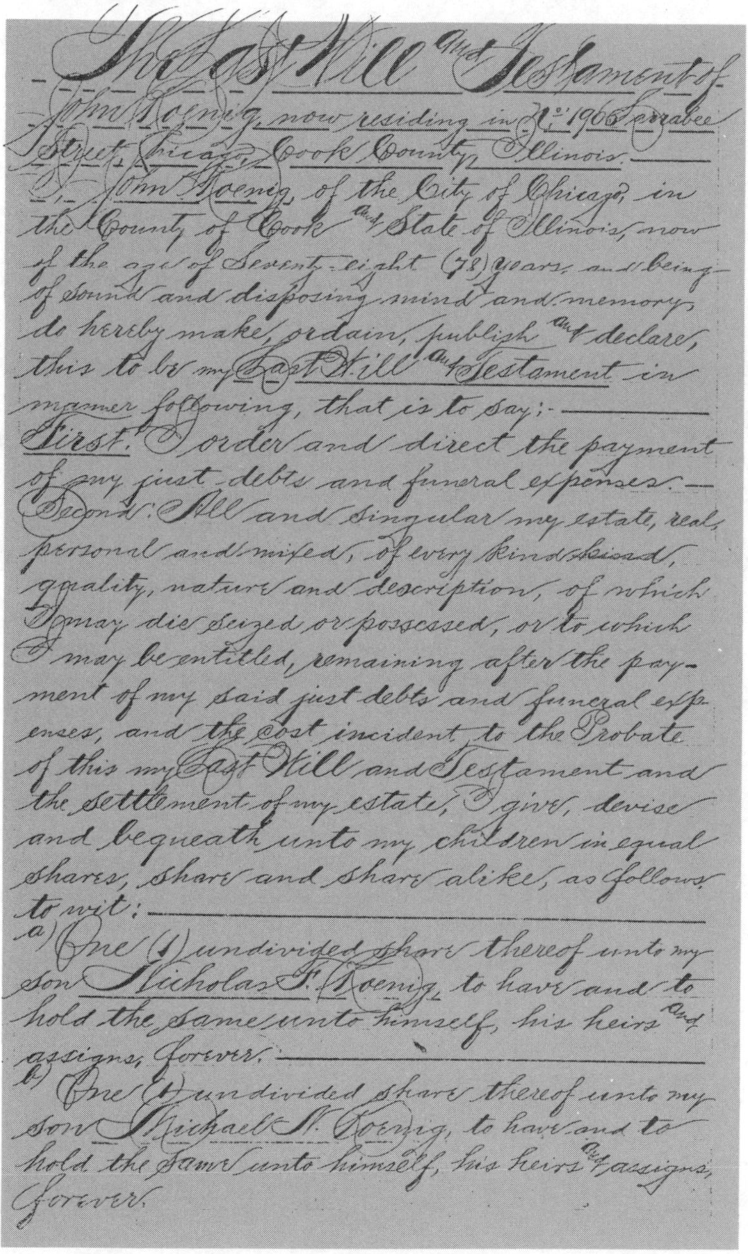

The Last Will and Testament of John Koenig, now residing in No. 1965 Crabee Street, Chicago, Cook County, Illinois.

I, John Koenig, of the City of Chicago, in the County of Cook and State of Illinois, now of the age of Seventy-eight (78) years, and being of sound and disposing mind and memory, do hereby make, ordain, publish and declare, this to be my Last Will and Testament in manner following, that is to say:—

First. I order and direct the payment of my just debts and funeral expenses.—

Second. All and singular my estate, real, personal and mixed, of every kind and, quality, nature and description, of which I may die seized or possessed, or to which I may be entitled, remaining after the payment of my said just debts and funeral expenses, and the cost incident to the Probate of this my Last Will and Testament and the settlement of my estate, I give, devise and bequeath unto my children in equal shares, share and share alike, as follows, to wit:—

a) One (1) undivided share thereof unto my son Nicholas F. Koenig, to have and to hold the same unto himself, his heirs and assigns, forever.—

b) One (1) undivided share thereof unto my son Michael N. Koenig, to have and to hold the same unto himself, his heirs and assigns, forever.

Figure 7. *A 1915 Will from Probate Division, Cook County Circuit Court*

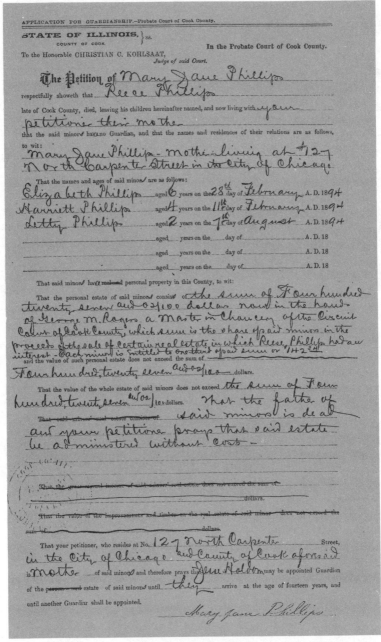

Figure 8. *Guardianship Application, Cook County Probate Court*

case. Docket information will serve to identify correct files which may then be ordered from the clerk back in Room 1202. If names are not found within the Deceased, Minor, or Incompetent Indexes, a search of the Will Books is in order. Will Books are at the far left end of Room 1202 in a free standing book case. Wills filed in Cook County between 1850 and 1915 were indexed by June B. Barekman and published in several issues of the *Chicago Genealogist*, beginning in the fall of 1972 (Vol.5, No. 1). Files listed in that index which pre-date the Chicago Fire of 1871 have not been found, so it is assumed that only the Will Book for 1850-1915 survived.

Files may be photocopied for nominal fees but are not usually ready until the following day. The clerks do provide mail service for an extra charge.

There is an index of approximately 700 entries from Docket Book A, 1871-72 in the probate division. Many of the entries include death dates for individuals who died in years previous to the Chicago Fire of 1871, but whose estates were not probated until after that date, making this an especially valuable source.

The Genealogical Society of Utah has microfilmed the following records from the probate division:

Probate Records 1877-86 (12 microfilm reels)
Probate Records 1877-1923 (283 microfilm reels)
Bonds and Letters of Administration with Wills Annexed 1877-1924 (7 microfilm reels)
Record of Wills 1879-1928 (81 microfilm reels)
Proof of Wills 1882 (1 microfilm reel)
Miscellaneous Probate Records 1913-26 (4 microfilm reels)
Administrator's Bonds and Letters 1877-1931 (66 microfilm reels)
Records of Foreign Wills 1904-22 (9 microfilm reels)
Grants of Guardianship 1877-1923 (17 microfilm reels)
Documentary Records of Guardianships 1877-1923 (73 microfilm reels)
Record of Guardianship Bonds and Letters 1877-1923 (38 microfilm reels)
Miscellaneous Documentary Records 1871-1923 (27 microfilm reels)
Documentary Records-Guardian's Inventories 1880-1923 (29 microfilm reels)

JUVENILE DIVISION
1100 South Hamilton Ave, Chicago, IL 60612
General Information – (312-738-8200)

CRIMINAL DIVISION
2600 South California, Chicago, IL 60608
General Information – (312-890-7100)

UNITED STATES CIRCUIT AND DISTRICT COURT RECORDS

Somewhat less well known than probate or other local court records, are federal court files. The federal courts have traditionally heard cases involving interstate disputes and often served as a court of appeal for litigation which originated at the local level. In addition, the federal courts were usually indexed by plaintiff and/or defendant, making the search a time-consuming project.

The material in a file varies with the significance of the case and the state that it reached during the trial process. But, depositions describing the acquisition and retention of property were not unusual in land disputes, which often appeared as equity suits. These were accompanied many times by maps of the place in question or copies of deeds submitted as exhibits. Such cases can produce literally thousands of pages of testimony and may detail facts about the family and its environment which are unattainable elsewhere. One extraordinary example recorded specifics about the Hyde Park area of Chicago during its settlement years, which had survived in no other form.

Bankruptcy filings included schedules of assets and liabilities, outlining the business and financial dealings of the bankruptcy claimant. Small partnerships and proprietorships, along with personal bankruptcies, comprised the preponderance of cases heard in bankruptcy court. When federal bankruptcy laws were not in effect, "involuntary" bankruptcies were entered as equity proceedings. Federal criminal prosecutions were a minor portion of the case load until the 1920s when prohibition violations swelled the numbers. Other types of federal cases of genealogical interest might include confiscation cases from the Civil War, when the Union government seized the available property of Confederate sympathizers, and personal injury suits against interstate carriers (usually railroads).

The National Archives—Chicago Branch holds the judicial records for the U.S. District Court, Illinois, Northern District, Chicago. Important documentation on such famous trials as that of Al Capone and other less-known cases which were filed between 1871 and 1961 are available at the Chicago branch. If any possibility exists that a person of interest may have been involved in federal litigation, these records can be rich in information and certainly make for fascinating reading. There is no single or general index to the collection and so it is helpful to know the court of origin and the type of case. Most docket books are self-indexed, and so it is sometimes possible—though time-consuming to locate files by searching the dated volumes one-by-one.

RECORDS OF THE SUPREME COURT OF THE UNITED STATES ON MICROFILM

The National Archives—Chicago Branch also has on microfilm (Record Group 267), Dockets and Appellate Files and Indexes of the United States Supreme Court as follows:

Dockets of the Supreme Court of the United States, 1791-1950 (M216; 27 rolls of microfilm). Included are the engrossed dockets of the Supreme Court, 1791-1905, and the single series of dockets that contain entries for original jurisdiction cases, 1829-1905. The dockets after 31 May 1905 record all cases that have come before the court in both original and appellate jurisdictions.

Index to Appellate Case Files of the Supreme Court of the United States, 1792-1909. (M408; 20 rolls).

Each index card gives the names of the parties in each case, the file number, the title of the case, the date the case was docketed, and the date a decision was rendered.

BIBLIOGRAPHY

Eakle, Arlene and Cerny, Johni. *The Source: A Guidebook of American Genealogy.* Salt Lake City: Ancestry Publishing Company, 1984.

Greenwood, Val D. *The Researchers Guide to American Genealogy.* Baltimore: Genealogical Publishing Co., Inc. 1975.

Kirby, Walter W. *Illinois Probate Guide.* Chicago: The author, 1983.

Law Bulletin Publishing Company. *Lawyer's Handbook of Federal, State, and Cook County Courts Surrounding Judicial Circuits and Selected Departments of City of Chicago, County of Cook, State of Illinois, Federal Government.* Twenty-Sixth Edition. Chicago: Law Bulletin Publishing Company, 1983.

McClure, Diane Kotil and Szucs, Loretto Dennis. *Probate Court Records: Cook County, Illinois -Docket Book A, 1871-72.* Chicago: Image Arts, Inc., 1986.

CHAPTER 10

Directories

CHICAGO CITY DIRECTORIES

A lthough Chicago's large population is often an obstacle to researchers, there is one advantage: city directories. The primary value of the directory lies in its usefulness for identifying people in a time and place. The alphabetically arranged publications list adult residents by name, occupation, and address and provide a means of tracing an individual's movements from year to year. A careful study of these yearly editions can reveal an accurate picture of an ancestor's economic and social position as well as giving clues for further research.

The appearance of an individual at the same address for a number of years may indicate home ownership and warrant a search of property records. On the other hand, city people were usually more transient than their rural cousins and frequent moves suggest that they were renters. The appearance and disappearance of a name from city directories from year to year serves to establish a probable time period when the person moved into the area, charts any subsequent moves, and can even pinpoint a death date or departure from the city. If a directory lists James Miller at a particular address in one year and Emma Miller, widow at the same address in the next edition, it would seem fairly obvious that searching for James's death records is in order. The listing of all adult workers in a household is often an important means of identifying other family members. Chicago directories take on extra importance when an address is needed to locate families or individuals in census schedules.

The institution of the city directory is almost as old as the city of Chicago. The first one dates back to 1839 when the city council had the newly-founded city's ordinances printed.
Chicago's first directory was filled with the names of businessmen who had bought subscriptions and was far from complete.

According to the introduction in James W. Norris's *General Directory and Business Advertiser of the City of Chicago for the Year 1844*, it presented "the names of all persons and all firms in the city." Publishers of the 1849-50 directories stated that "there is not a house in the city, that we have not entered or endeavored to", but comparing city directory entries to the Federal Population Census schedules suggests that directory canvassers were not always successful, and part of the mobile population was missed.

In the Foreword to the 1845-46 *General Directory*, J.W. Norris conceded that, "it would be surprising indeed, if, with a population so changeable as ours, with removals and additions almost daily, no names should be found omitted and no residences incorrectly described." Immigrants and boarding house roomers were the most likely to be missed and the most complete information was available for advertisers and established citizens. Canvassing the city for directory information was generally conducted in the last months of the year preceding the publication year, so the collected data was sometimes outdated by the time the volume was printed. In spite of the inaccuracies, city directories remain one of the researcher's most important sources.

Cities often had several directory publishers—Chicago had three in 1871—and all three should be consulted since each may contain unique details. Edward's *Chicago Census Directory* (Chicago: Richard Edwards, 1871) lists not only the name, occupation, and address of the individual, but also provides the ward number, the number of males, females, and total in residence as well as the birthplace of the head of the household. Gager's *1857 Chicago Directory* (Chicago: John Gager and Co.) adds the birthplace and years of residency in Chicago to the usual information. By limiting a search to one directory, you may miss precious clues.

City directories attempted to list every individual and every business in Chicago from 1839 to 1917. The city directories ceased consecutive publication after 1917, though directories did appear in 1923 and 1928-29.

WHERE TO FIND CHICAGO DIRECTORIES

The Chicago Historical Society has the most complete run of Chicago directories in book form. Since many of the original book copies are crumbling due to time, paper content, and heavy usage, they are being replaced with microfilm versions. Photocopies can not be taken of the books.

The Newberry Library has a complete series of Chicago city directories on microfilm, as does the Municipal Reference Library.

The National Archives—Chicago Branch has Chicago city directories for the years 1880, 1890, 1900, 1910, and 1917 on microfilm.

129

Figure 9. *Chicago City Directory*

The South Suburban Genealogical and Historical Society has book copies of Chicago city directories for the years 1877-78, 1892, 1899, 1901-06, 1911, 1913-15, and 1917. Due to their fragile condition, photocopying is not allowed.

Some large university and society libraries have city directories for scattered years. Northwestern University has one of the larger collections.

Microfilm copies of Chicago directories may be purchased from the Photoduplication Department, Joseph Regenstein Library, University of Chicago, 1100 East 57th Street, Chicago, IL 60637.

Dr. George K. Schweitzer, 407 Regent Court, Knoxville, TN 37923 will search Chicago city directories for a fee. Send a stamped, self-addressed envelope for a detailed description of that service.

CROSS REFERENCE DIRECTORIES

Reverse, "criss-cross," or cross reference directories for Chicago are available for the years 1928, 1950, 1952, and 1978 at the Chicago Historical Society. The Chicago Public Library (Social Science and History Division) has cross reference directories for 1955 and the current year. These directories list Chicago streets alphabetically, then numerically, and then by occupant's names. They are useful for determining names of other residents in a household or building of interest.

SUBURBAN AND COMMUNITY DIRECTORIES

Residents outside the Chicago city limits were not included in Chicago directories. It is worth remembering that some present-day Chicago townships and communities were not annexed to the city until as late as the 1880s and the 1890s. The towns of Lake and Bridgeport for example, were not annexed until 1889, and other communities like parts of Cicero were later still in coming within city limits. Some communities published their own directories in scattered years. One such directory is the *Directory of Austin, Illinois* (1897) which was reprinted by the Chicago Genealogical Society. Local community libraries and historical societies are the first places to look for old directories and the Library of Congress has some which are not available anywhere else. Other unique types of directories were published in a rather uneven fashion. An interesting example is the *Southern Cook County, Illinois Farmers Directory—1918*. The alphabetically arranged volume lists heads of households; wife's maiden name; names of children; town and township of residence; geographical description of the farm; and the date (year) that residency was established. The *Southern Cook County Farmers Directory* is available at the South Suburban Genealogical and Historical Society Library.

TELEPHONE DIRECTORIES

Chicago telephone directories are available on microfilm from 1878-1971 at the Chicago Public Library. The 1878 publication for Chicago listed mostly businesses and a handful of individuals who were privileged to own the recently invented luxuries. Most of the population was not represented in telephone books even in later years. As late as 1900, only seventeen people per 1,000 had a telephone, and by 1920 that number had risen to only twenty-three per 1,000. Having a telephone then, as now, did not guarantee inclusion in a telephone book as many elected not to be listed.

MISCELLANEOUS DIRECTORIES

by Diane Schweitzer

American Medical Association. *American Medical Directory*. Chicago: American Medical Association, 1909-Present.

_____. *Chicago Medical Blue Book*. 1937, Chicago: American Medical Association, 1937, 1938, 1952, 1953.

_____. *Polk's Medical Register*, 1890-1917. Chicago: American Medical Association.

Architects and Engineers—Brick Manufacturers and Dealers and Mason Contractors, Carpenters and Builders, Dealers in Stone, Sand, Fireproofing, Plastering, Cement, Asphalt, Lime and Kindred Materials. *Industrial Chicago* 1 (1891): 593-802.

Bench and Bar of Illinois. Chicago: Chicago Bench and Bar Publishing Company, Chicago, 1920.

Banks and Bankers, Prominent Board of Trade Men. Prominent Wholesale Merchants, Other Distinguished Business Men, Distinguished Railroad Men, Sketches of Citizens. *Industrial Chicago* 1894.

Barnum, Gertrude. "The Chicago Woman and Her Clubs." *The Graphic* (May 1893): 343-44.

Barnett, Fremont O. *Politics and Politicians of Chicago, Cook County and Illinois*. Memorial Volume 1787-1887. Chicago: Blakely Printing Company, 1886.

Biographies of Lumbermen. *Industrial Chicago* 3 (1894): 196-580.

Caton, John Dean. *Early Bench and Bar of Illinios*. Chicago: Legal News Company, 1922.

Chicago Medical Society. *History of Medicine and Surgery and Physicians and Surgeons of Chicago*. Chicago: Chicago Medical Society, 1922.

Chicago Social and Club Register. Chicago: Crest Publishers, 1921. Biographical sketches of prominent Chicago women, list of women's clubs, and list of private schools.

Chicago Tribune. *Women of the World's Greatest Newspaper*. Chicago, 1927.

Cook, F. F. *A Retrospect: A Roll Call of Old Settlers, First Group; Men of the Thirties; Men of the Forties; Arrivals About 1850; Names Familiar Today.* N.p., n.d.

Crossley, Frederic B. *Courts and Lawyers of Illinois.* Chicago: the American Historical Society, 1916.

Ffrench, Charles. *Biographical History of the American Irish in Chicago.* Chicago: American Biographical Publishing Company, 1897.

Gale, William H. *List of Chicago Residents Since 1840.* Chicago: n.d.

German Press Club of Chicago. *Prominent Citizens and Industries of Chicago.* Chicago: 1901.

Gilbert, Frank. *Centennial History of the City of Chicago: Its Men and Institutions.* Biographical Sketches of Leading Citizens. Chicago: 1905.

Gilbert, Paul Thomas, and Charles Lee Bryson. *Chicago and Its Makers: A Narrative of Events From The Day of the First White Man to the Inception of the Second World's Fair, With a Chapter on Chicago Hotels and Restaurants* Chicago: F. Mendelsohn, 1929.

Gordon, Charles Ulysses. *Chicago Postmasters, 1831-1897.* Chicago: 1899.

Gosnell, Harold Foote. *Negro Politicians: The Rise of Negro Politics in Chicago.* Chicago: University of Chicago Press, Chicago, 1935.

Hamilton Club, Chicago. *Biographies of All Nominees For Office.* Chicago: The Hamilton Club of Chicago, 1914.

Hill, Josephine D. *A Souvenir of World's Fair Women and Wives of Prominent Officials Connected With the World's Columbian Exposition.* Chicago: The Blocher Company, 1892.

Herringshaw, Clark J. *Herringshaw's City Blue Book of Biography; Chicagoans of 1916, Ten Thousand Biographies.* Chicago: 1916.

Knights of Columbus, Chicago Council No. 182. *Obituary Sketches.* Chicago: 1921.

Linder, Usher F. *Reminiscences of the Early Bench and Bar of Illinois.* Chicago: Chicago Legal News Company, 1879.

Maxwell, Will J. *Fraternity Men of Chicago.* Chicago: Umbdenstock Publishing Company, 1898.

Melville, George W. *Chicago's Semi-Centennial Memorial With Engraved Portraits of the 24 Mayors of Chicago.* Chicago: 1887.

Manufacturers of Sewerage Builders Iron and Lumber Materials, Decorators, Painters and Paint Dealers, Plumbers, Heaters and Ventilators, Roofers, Galvanized Iron Workers, Brass and Iron Furnishers, Glass Dealers, etc. Officials, Building Promoters, Electricians, House Movers and Elevator Dealers. *Industrial Chicago* 2: 642-817.

Mosher, Charles D. *Centennial Historical Album, 1876, Containing Photographs, Autographs and Biographies.*

Old Tippecanoe Club of Chicago. *Chicago: Press of the Peerless Printing Company, 1889.*

Palmer, John McAuley. *The Bench and Bar of Illinois.* Chicago: Lewis Publishing Company, 1899.
Press Club of Chicago. *Official Reference Book.* Chicago: Chicago Press Club, 1922.
Rex, Frederick. "List of mayors, city clerks, attorneys, treasurers, aldermen from 1837-1937". Chicago Municipal Reference Library, 1937.
Rothermel, Charles T. *Portraits and Biographies of the Fire Underwriters of the City of Chicago.* Chicago: Monarch Printing and Binding Company, 1895.
Sketches of Manufacturers, Memoirs of Business Men. *Industrial Chicago* (1894): 3, 723-821.
University of Illinois Medical School. "Student Records From Medical School, M.S. and Ph.D. Thesis Reports, 1905-1975."
Who's Who In Chicago and Illinois. 1905, 1911, 1917, 1926, 1931, 1936, 1941, 1945. Chicago: A.N. Marquis Company.
Wilke, Franc Bangs. *The Chicago Bar.* Chicago: 1872.
Winchell, Samuel Robertson. *Chicago Past and Present, A Manual For The Citizen, the Teacher and the Student; History,*
Government Officials, Their Duties and Salaries. Chicago: A. Flanagan Company, 1906.

BIBLIOGRAPHY OF CHICAGO DIRECTORIES

Associated Jewish Press Bureau. *Jewish Directory of Chicago Containing A Full and Complete List of Congregations, Their Ministers and Members, Also a Complete Manual of the Various Jewish Lodges in the City.* Chicago: 1884.
Barrett, E.G. *H.C. Chandler and Co.'s Railroad Business Directory of Chicago, Milwaukee, Green Bay, St. Paul and Intermediate Points.* Indianapolis: 1867.
Baldwin's Chicago Guide and Business Directory. Chicago: G.S. Baldwin & Co., 1867 [also 1869].
Black's Blue Book; Names, Adresses and Phone Numbers of Colored Homes, Also A Classified List of Colored Businesses and Professional People. Chicago: n.d.
Bohemian-American Hospital Association. *Directory and Almanac of the Bohemian Population of Chicago.* Chicago: 1915.
Board of Education, City of Chicago. *Chicago School Directory, 1895-96.* Chicago: John F. Higgins, 1895. Lists Board of Education members, administrators, salaries names of schools in city, addresses, enrollment, directions from public transportation, directory of teachers, where they taught, home addresses. Directories also available for 1900-01, 1901-02, 1902-03, 1908-09, 1928-29.

The Bon-Ton Directory Giving the Names in Alphabetical Order, Addresses and Hours of Reception of the Most Prominent and Fashionable Ladies Residing in Chicago and Its Suburbs. Chicago: Blakely, Brown & Marsh, 1879-80.

Brayton, J. H. *Directory of Englewood, Illinois, Comprised Within the Limits of Indiana Avenue and Halsted Street, 55th and 71st Streets.* Englewood, Ill.: Tousley, Denison & Tousley Steam Printers, 1882.

Brown, C. *Brown's Gazeteer of the Chicago and Northwestern Railway, and Branches, and of the Union Pacific Railroad. A Guide and Business Directory.* Chicago: Bassett Brothers Steam Printing House, 1869.

Business Directory of Burned District. Chicago: O. W. Richardson, Chicago: 1871.

Chicago Business Directory and Commercial Advertiser, 1859. Edited by Smith and DuMoulin. S.C. Griggs & Co., Chicago, Illinois, 1871. Business directories are also available for 1839, 1844, 1853-57, 1859-1917, 1923, 1928-29.

Chicago Association of Commerce. *Official Directory and Market Guide, Containing Alphabetical Classified and Trade Lists, Complete Membership of the Chicago Association of Commerce. Chicago.* N.p., n.d.

Chicago Bicycle Directory: A Reference Book of the Trade, 1898: Containing an Alphabetical List of Manufacturers, Jobbers, Dealers, Repairers, Maker of Parts. . .And All Local Cycling Clubs. Chicago: Carr & Mensch, 1898.

Chicago Church Federation. *Year Book and Directory of the Chicago Church Federation.* Chicago: 1925.

Chicago City Directory Company. *Chicago Blue Book of Selected Names of Chicago and Suburban Towns. . .For the Year Ending 1890.* Chicago: 1882.

Chicago Directory of Lodges and Benevolent Societies for 1883. Containing the name and the time and place of meeting of every lodge in the city of Chicago and the name and address of individual members of the same. Chicago: C.F. Lichtner & Bro., 1882.

The Chicago Manufacturers, Importers and Wholesalers Directory for 1889. Chicago: R. R. Donnelley & Sons, 1889.

The Chicago Society Directory and Ladies Visiting and Shopping Guide, Containing the Names and Addresses of Ladies Residing in Chicago and Vicinity. Chicago: Ensign, McClure & Co., 1876.

The Churches of Chicago. A Complete Directory of the Churches of Chicago, Their Location, Name and Residence of Clergy, Hours of Service, Etc. Chicago: Lakeside Press, 1878.

Danenhower's Chicago City Directory for 1851. Chicago: W. W. Danenhower, 1851. Contains an alphabetical list of the mechanics and businessmen with their several places of residence, also brief notices of the religious, literary, and benevolent associations of the city, military, fire department, etc.

Directory of Directors in the City of Chicago, 1900-01. Chicago: Audit Company of New York, 1900.

Directory of Licensed Real Estate Dealers of Chicago, 1890-91. Chicago: 1891.

Edward's Chicago Business Directory: Embracing a Classified List of All Trades, Professions and Pursuits in the City of Chicago For the Year 1868-69. Chicago: 1868.

Edwards, Richard. *Chicago Census Report And Statistical Review, Embracing a Complete Directory of the City, Showing the Number of Persons in Each Family, Male and Female, Birthplace and Ward Now Residing In, With a Vast Amount of Valuable Statistical, Historical and Commercial Information.* Chicago: R. Edwards, 1871.

The Elite Directory and Club List of Chicago, 1884-1885. Chicago: The Elite Directory Co., 1884.

Elite of Chicago; Reversed Directory. Chicago: The Elite Directory Co., 1881.

Fleischman Floral Company. *Chicago Automobile Directory.* Chicago: 1906.

Full Account of the Great Fire and New Business Directory of Leading Houses. Chicago: Northwestern Publishing Co., 1872.

The Guests' Business Reference Book, A Directory of the First Wholesale and Retail Stores and Leading Places of Business in Chicago, 1870-71, Chicago: P.L. Hanscom & Co., 1870.

Harris, Isaac Counselor. *The Colored Men's Professional and Business Directory of Chicago and Valuable Information of the Race in General.* Chicago: I.C. Harris, 1885.

Jefferson's Chicago Business Directory for 1868-69. Chicago: H.A. Newcombe & Co., 1885.

Kopfman, Harold R. *The Masonic Directory of Illinois, 1970. Ladies Exclusive Directory and Calling List,* Chicago: Swalm, Powers & Co., 1895.

Lampkins, Mrs. M. *Mrs. M.G. Lampkins Lawyers Directory of Chicago.* Chicago: 1875. Also available 1877-78, 1880-81.

The Merchants of Chicago. List of First Class Houses, Jobbers and Manufacturers. Chicago: 1865.

Manahan, C. F. & Co. *Classified Directory of the Chicago Furniture Trade and Kindred Lines. A Complete List of Firms Manufacturing Each Line of Goods, 1895.* Chicago: Bureau of Furniture Statistics, 1895.

Polk's Chicago Directory. . .A Buyers Guide and A Complete Classified Business Directory. Chicago: 1923.

Polk's Chicago Numerical Street and Avenue Directory, Including Names of Householders, Occupants of Office Buildings and Places of Business, Also a Complete Street and Avenue Guide. Chicago: R. L. Polk & Co., 1929.

Printing Trades Blue Book. . .A Business Directory for Busy People. Chicago: A. F. lewis & Co., 1910.

Rhea's New Citizens Directory of Chicago, Illinois and Suburban Towns, Also other Towns and Cities. Chicago: W. S. McCleland, 1908.

Richardson and Connorton's Commercial Pocket Directory of Chicago. Business Directory of Burned District. Chicago, 1872.

Rock Products Company. *Chicago Builders Guide; Directory of Chicago Architects, Contractors, and Building Material Dealers.* Chicago, 1912.

Schoff, S. *The Glory of Chicago—Her Manufactories.* Chicago: Knight & Leonard, 1873. A list of factories, locations and number of employees.

Selected Directory of the Italians in Chicago, Market Guide and Yearly Information Bulletin, Listing 4,500 Firms, Stores and Professional Men. Chicago, 1929-1933.

Simm's Blue Book and National Negro Business and Professional Directory. Chicago: James N. Simms, 1923.

Spencer, W. S. *W. S. Spencer's Chicago Business Directory for 1864-65* Chicago: J. N. Dean's, 1864. Also a reprint of the business directory for 1843.

Swalm, Powers & Co., *Ladies Exclusive Directory and Calling List.* Chicago: 1895.

Udall & Hopkins Chicago City Directory for 1852 & 1853, Comprising an Alphabetical Directory. . .A List of City, State and U.S. Officers, Notices of the Various Societies, Associations and Institutions; Military and Fire Departments, etc. Chicago: Udall & Hopkins, 1852.

Walton's Legal Directory for Chicago and Cook County. Chicago: Gunthorp-Warren Printing Co., 1907.

Washington, Lucious William. *The Chicago Negro Business Men and Women and Where They Are Located,* Chicago: Flanders Printing Company, 1912.

Western News Company. *The Great Conflagration, A Complete Account of the Burning of Chicago. Containing Descriptions of the Scenes, Incidents and Accidents of the Fire* [With a Business Directory and List of the Principal Business Houses in their Present Locations]. Chicago: The Western New Co., 1871.

West Side Elite Directory and Calling List. Chicago: Thomas Cushing & Co., 1884.

West Side Society Directory. Chicago, 1890.

The Woman's Blue Book, Representing a List of Societies, Clubs and Socially Inclined Women of Chicago and the Suburbs. Chicago: Woman's Blue Book Company, 1913.

CHAPTER 11

Ethnic Sources

From the date of the city's founding, the foreign-born element has played an essential part in the life of Chicago and Cook County. In its formative years, approximately one-half of the population of the city was made up of persons born in the old world. Ethnic groups have had an integral part in the development of the metropolitan area, and they have made an indelible mark on its character. Evidence of the ethnic presence can be found in the following sources:

GENERAL MULTI-ETHNIC COLLECTIONS

Chicago Historical Society
Clark Street and North Avenue
Chicago, IL 60614
(312-642-4600)

Books, manuscripts, maps, newspaper clipping file, photograph collection concerning the various population groups. See Appendix for Chicago Historical Societies.

Chicago Municipal Reference Library
City Hall, Room 1004
121 North LaSalle Street
Chicago, IL 60602
(312-744-4492)

Newspaper clipping file beginning in 1956 includes ethnic groups.

Chicago Public Library
425 North Michigan Avenue
Chicago, IL 60611
(312-269-2900)

Important collection of printed information on the various ethnic groups. See Appendix for Chicago Public Library.

The Chicago Public Library
Newspapers and Periodicals Center
425 North Michigan Avenue, 60611
(312-269-2913)
Has available a list of all current foreign and ethnic newspapers as well as some ethnic newspapers which are now defunct.

The Newberry Library
60 West Walton
Chicago, IL 60610
(312-943-9090
See Appendix for The Newberry Library.

University of Illinois at Chicago Library
801 South Morgan Street
Chicago, IL 60680
(312-996-2716)

Large collection of multi-ethnic materials pertaining especially to the Chicago area.

AFRO-AMERICAN SOURCES

The Afro-American Genealogical and Historical Society of Chicago
Post Office Box #A3027
Chicago, IL 60690

The DuSable Museum of Afro-American History
740 East 56th Place
Chicago, IL 60637
(312-947-0600)

Johnson Publishing Company Library
820 South Michigan Avenue
Chicago, IL 60605

Over 8,000 volume library of books by and about black Americans, microfilmed black newspapers dating back to 1863, clipping file on black experience in America dating back thirty years and selected from over 200 newspapers and journals.

Carter G. Woodson Regional Library
Vivian G. Harsh Collection
9525 South Halsted Street
Chicago, IL 60628
(312-881-6910)

Over 30,000 books and bound periodicals, 7,867 titles on microfilm, pamphlet and clipping collections, Chicago Afro-American Union Analytic Catalog, manuscript, tape, graphics, and newspaper collection.

Most of the Chicago area college and university libraries have special Black Studies collections.

SELECTED BIBLIOGRAPHY

Aschenbrenner, Joyce. *Lifelines: Black Families in Chicago.* Prospect Heights, Ill.: Waveland Press, 1975.

Berlin, Ira. *Slaves Without Masters.* New York: Pantheon Books, 1974.

Black Studies: Select Catalog of National Archives and Records Service Microfilm Publications. Washington, D.C.: General Services Administration, 1983.

Black's Blue Book: Names, Addresses and Phone Numbers of Colored Homes, Also a Classified List of Colored Businesses and Professional People. Chicago. n.d.

Blockson, Charles L. and Fry, Ron. *Black Genealogy.* Englewood Cliffs, N.J.: Prentice-Hall, 1977.

Chicago Public Library. Special Collections Divison. "The Black Soldier in the Civil War." A checklist and bibliography of sources.

Eakle, Arlene and Cerny, Johni. "Black Ancestral Research," *The Source: A Guidebook of American Genealogy.* Salt Lake City, Ut.: Ancestry Publishing Company, 1984.

Drake, St. Clair. "Churches and Voluntary Associations in the Chicago Negro Community." Mimeograph. Chicago: 1940.

Drake, St. Clair and Cayton, Horace. *Black Metropolis: A Study of Negro Life in a Northern City.* New York: 1945.

Frazier, Edward Franklin. *The Negro Family in Chicago.* Chicago: 1932.

Gossnell, Harold Foote. *Negro Politicians: The Rise of Negro Politics in Chicago.* Chicago: University of Chicago Press, 1935.

Harris, Isaac Counselor. *The Colored Men's Professional and Business Directory of Chicago and Valuable Information of the Race in General.* Chicago: I.C. Harris, 1885.

Rose, James, and Alice Eichholz. *Black Genesis.* Detroit: Gale Research, 1978.

Simm's Blue Book and National Negro Business and Professional Directory. Chicago: James N. Simms, 1923.

Spear, Allan H. *Black Chicago.* Chicago: The University of Chicago Press, 1967.

Washington, Lucious William. *The Chicago Negro Business Men and Women and Where They are Located.* Chicago: L.W. Flanders Printing Company, 1912.

AMERICAN INDIAN SOURCES

The Newberry Library
   Edward E. Ayer Collection of Americana and American Indians and Center for the History of the American Indian

60 West Walton
Chicago, IL 60610
(312-943-9090)

The National Archives—Chicago Branch
7358 Pulaski Road
Chicago, IL 60629
(312-581-7816)

SELECTED BIBLIOGRAPHY

American Indians: A Select Catalog of National Archives Microfilm Publications. National Archives Trust Fund Board. U.S. General Services Administration, 1984.

Eakle, Arlene and Cerny, Johni. *The Source: A Guidebook of American Genealogy.* Salt Lake City, Ut.: Ancestry Publishing Company, 1984. "Records Relating to Native American Research" by George J. Nixon.

Hill, Edward E. *Guide to Records in the National Archives Relating to American Indians.* Washington, D.C.: National Archives & Records Service, 1981.

Strong, William Duncan. *The Indian Tribes of the Chicago Region.* Chicago: The Field Museum of Natural History, 1926.

BOHEMIAN SOURCES

Bohemian-American Hospital Association. *Directory and Almanac of the Bohemian Population of Chicago.* Chicago: 1915.

Goldsborough, Robert. "The Bohemians." *Chicago* VI,1 (Spring 1969): 46-52.

McCarthy, Eugene Ray. "The Bohemians in Chicago and Their Benevolent Societies, 1875-1946." M.A. thesis, University of Chicago, 1950.

CANADIAN SOURCES

DuPage County (IL) Genealogical Society. *Genealogy and Canadian Sources.* The Society, 1984. One of the best compilations of Canadian materials available.

Kennedy, Patricia and Roy, Janine. *Tracing Your Ancestors in Canada.* Public Archives of Canada. Revised in 1984.

Lost in Canada?
Mrs. Joy Reisinger C.G.R.S.
1020 Central Avenue
Sparta, WI 54656

This Canadian-American query exchange is designed to help American researchers, working on Canadian immigrant lines, get in touch with others working on their lines, and also help Canadians searching in America. A quarterly publication.

CHINESE SOURCES

Chicago Public Library
Chinatown Branch
2314 South Wentworth
Chicago, IL 60616
(312-326-4255)

Ling Long Museum
2238 South Wentworth
Chicago, IL 60616
(312-225-6181)

SELECTED BIBLIOGRAPHY

Fan, Ting C. *Chinese Residents in Chicago*. San Francisco: R & E Research Associates, 1974.

Fang, John T. C. *Chinatown: Handy Guide: Chicago*. Chicago: The Chinese Publishing House, 1959.

Li, Peter S. *Occupational Mobility and Kinship Assistance: A Study of Chinese Immigrants in Chicago*. San Francisco: R & E. Research, 1977.

Liang, Yuan. "The Chinese Family in Chicago." M.A. thesis, University of Chicago, 1951.

Wilson, Margaret Gibbons. "Concentration and Dispersal of Chinese Poplulation of Chicago, 1870 to the Present." Ph.D. diss., University of Chicago, 1969.

CZECHOSLOVAKIAN SOURCES

Chicago Public Library
Toman Branch
4005 West 27th Street
Chicago, IL 60623

Special collection with focus on Czech community.

Czechoslovak Society of America
2701 South Harlem Avenue
Berwyn, IL 60402

Museum and library, folk costumes, handicrafts, arts, Czech language newspapers and periodicals published in Chicago.

Illinois Benedictine College
Theodore Lownik Library
5700 College Road
Lisle, IL 60532   (312-968-7270)

Fourteen thousand books, manuscripts, and periodicals on Slavic studies, Czech literature, Czech Bibles, and Bohemian materials.

SELECTED BIBLIOGRAPHY

Bicha, Karel D. "The Survival of the Village in Urban America: A Note on Czech Immigrants in Chicago to 1914." *International Migration Review* V, 1 (Spring 1971): 72-74.

Droba, Daniel. *Czech and Slovak Leaders in Metropolitan Chicago.* Chicago: 1974. Subtitled "A Biographical Study of 300 Prominent Men and Women of Czech and Slovak Descent." Arranged by occupations.

Hletka, Peter. "The Slovaks of Chicago." *Slovakia* XIX, 42 (Oct. 1969): 32-63. Lists Slovak institutions and leaders with a list of Slovaks known to have been Chicago residents 1890-1900.

Horak, Jakub. "Assimilation of Czechs in Chicago." Ph.D. Diss., University of Chicago, 1920.

International Exposition Chicago, 1933 Incorporated. *World's Fair Memorial of the Czechoslovak Group.* Chicago: 1933. History of the Czech community and biographical sketches of leaders, with photographs. Available at the Chicago Public Library.

Palickar, Stephen J. "The Slovaks of Chicago." *Illinois Catholic Historical Review* IV, 2 (Oct. 1921): 180-96.

Reichman, John J. ed. *Czechoslovaks of Chicago.* Chicago: 1937.

Schlyter, Daniel M. *A Handbook of Czechoslovak Genealogical Research.* Provo, Ut.: Press America, 1985.

Vraz, Vlasta, ed. *Panorama: A Historical Review of Czechs and Slovaks in the United States of America.* Cicero, Ill.: Czechoslovak National Council of America, 1970.

DUTCH

The South Suburban Genealogical and Historical Society Library
P.O. Box 96
South Holland, IL 60473
(333-9474)

Has a considerable amount of material for the area of Dutch settlement in Chicago.

The Chicago Public Library, Cultural Center and Special Collections has material on predominently Dutch neighborhoods and settlements such as Roseland.

SELECTED BIBLIOGRAPHY

DeJong, Gerald F. *The Dutch in America, 1609-1974.* The Immigrant Heritage of America Series. Boston: Twayne Publishers, 1975.

Ettema, Ross. *The Dutch in South Cook County Since 1947*. South Holland, Ill.: Park Press, 1984.

Nijhoff, Martinus. *The Hollanders in America*. San Francisco: R & E Research Associates, 1972.

Vanderbosch, Amry. *The Dutch Communities of Chicago*. Chicago: 1927.

ENGLISH

The Newberry Library
60 West Walton
Chicago, IL 60610

Has a particularly strong collection of British material, guides, maps, and transcriptions.

The Chicago Genealogical Society and the DuPage Genealogical Societies have British special interest groups.

SELECTED BIBLIOGRAPHY

Filby, P. William. *American & British Genealogy & Heraldry* 3rd ed.; Boston: New England Historic Genealogical Society, 1983.

Pelling, George. *Beginning Your Family History*. 3rd edition Devon, England: 1982. Available from the Federation of Genealogical Societies, P.O. Box 220. Davenport, IA 52805.

FINNS

Arra, Esa. *The Finns in Illinois*. Translated by A. I. Brask. Mills, Minn.: 1971.

GERMAN SOURCES

Palatines to America—Illinois Chapter
P.O. Box 3884
Quincy, IL 62305

SELECTED BIBLIOGRAPHY

Bullard, Thomas. "Distribution of Chicago's Germans 1850-1914." M.A. thesis, University of Chicago, 1969.

Chicago und sein Deutschthum. Cleveland, 1901-1902. German Press Club of Chicago. *Year Book of Chicago*, Published to commemorate the twentieth anniversary of its organization. Chicago: 1933.

Gross, Jacob. " A German Family in Chicago: 1856." *Chicago History* 4, No. 10 (Winter 1956-57).

Hofmeister, Rudolph A. *The Germans of Chicago*. Champaign: 1976.

Jentz, John B. "Bread and Labor: Chicago's German Bakers Organize." *Chicago History* XII, No. 2 (Summer 1983): 24ff.

Keil, Hartmut, and Jentz, John B. *German Workers in Industrial Chicago, 1850-1910: A Comparative Perspective.* DeKalb, Ill.: Northern Illinois University Press, 1983.
Townsend, Andrew Jacke. *The Germans of Chicago.* Chicago: 1932.
Wellauer, Maralyn A. *German Immigration to America in the Nineteenth Century: A Genealogist's Guide.* Milwaukee, Wis.: Roots International, 1985.

GERMAN RESEARCH
by Ronald L. Otto

To research a German-born ancestor in Cook County, one must utilize all aspects of this publication. For, with the major exception of church records and the possible exception of fraternal organization records, separate Cook County records for the German-born were not maintained. Thus, one would begin research as any other genealogical endeavor—with family records—and then proceed to vital statistics, court records and on to federal census records. Many Cook County vital and probate records are on microfilm available at LDS (Mormon) Branch Libraries. If the ancestor was here in 1900, I would start the search with a review of the 1900 Illinois Soundex to find the specific entry for the ancestor, and then extract all others of the same surname in Cook County or elsewhere in Illinois. Sooner or later you will use this surname information. If the surname has too many listings, select the other entries of the same generation as the ancestor that of the parents. The 1900 Soundex (and the full census data) will provide a specific location, names and approximate ages of wife and children, and the approximate year of immigration. This will be useful for future research.

German-American church records in Cook County are probably the most valuable records for researching the German-born ancestor. Fortunately, most German-American religious organizations carried over the European tradition of detailed church records. And, particularly as to congregational records prior to 1880, German villages were often included in various entries; 1880 is merely a rule of thumb. Consult the individual church records. By the 1870s, German born and educated ministers were being replaced by German-American-educated ministers, and less emphasis was placed on the origins of the parishioners.

The church records most used by genealogists are baptismal, marriage, and burial. These, of course, are useful if the family you seek is detailed therein. Again, include everyone of the same surname in your extracts. Sooner or later, you will use this information. *Extract, don't abstract.* All detail will prove useful. When you later return to complete abstracts, the records may no longer be available to you. Be sure to include sponsors at baptisms and witnesses at marriages. Although half were neighbors, the other half were relatives. Which were which? Surnames do not always answer the question.

Do not forget confirmation records. One experienced researcher noted that, in his research, the baptism of a certain ancestor was not in the church records. From a burial record he knew the year of birth. By checking the confirmation records thirteen years after the birth year, he found his ancestor and the names of that ancestor's parents. Yes, some of these early Chicago area church records are in German (or Latin in Catholic Churches). However, if the information therein is important to you, you will learn to read these records. For help, consult: *How To Read German Church Records Without Knowing Much German*, by Arta F. Johnson, and *If I Can You Can Decipher Germanic Records*, by Edna M. Bentz. Both are available at most genealogical book vendors.

It is most important, if at all possible, to do the searching yourself. No one else has your interest in your family nor your knowledge of the family names.

If you are not local to Cook County, most churches will respond to written inquiries; but all churches have staff limitations and cannot or will not provide extensive research. Always include a modest contribution with each request. Remember, negative research takes as much time as positive, and neither party is satisfied if the desired information is not found. If you can not research yourself, it is better to hire a professional researcher from the area to do the search where you seek more than a few events. Whoever does the search must deal with the temperment of the one who controls the records. Tact and diplomacy are essential not only for your effort, but also for those who follow.

Most early church records for Cook County are located at the church itself or at a nearby successor to a defunct church. A few of the records have been microfilmed and some are found at the archives. For example, the Archives of the Missouri Synod; Concordia Historical Institute, 801 DeMun Avenue, St. Louis, MO 63105, holds microfilmed copies of the registers of the earliest Lutheran Chicago Churches in Chicago, First Saint Paul and First Immanuel. The institute also offers useful pamphlets on German research and on the use of their archives. Two other Lutheran Archives for Cook County church records are: Archives of the American Lutheran Church, Wartburg Theological Seminary, 333 Wartburg Place, Dubuque, IA 52001 and Archives of the Lutheran Church in America, 1100 East 55th Street, Chicago, IL 60615.

A local repository for the Northern Illinois District of the Missouri Synod holds the records of the now defunct First St. John's Lutheran Church and is located at 2301 Wolf Road, Hillside, IL 60162. The registers of St John's Lutheran (Cooper's Grove) in today's South Cook County community of Country Club Hills have been microfilmed and are found at the Grande Prairie Library in Hazel Crest, IL. Microfilmed records for St. James Evangelical Lutheran Church, which was organized in 1869 and then located at Fremont and Garfield in Chicago, are found at the Newberry Library.

The best method to locate the Cook County church which holds the records you seek is to review a denominational directory of current churches and addresses and then compare such addresses to a current map of Chicago or your Cook County area of interest. The best map for this purpose is *Geographia's Complete Street Atlas of Chicago and Vicinity*, available at most Chicago rare book stores. Because street names changed you will occassionally need to refer to a nineteenth century map. Usually a denominational directory will provide one with the date of commencement of each church. However, the commencement date is not always the date the extant records begin. If you are not local to Cook County, visit a nearby church of the denomination you seek to look at the current directory. Remember the modest contribution.

A current telephone book is a second choice for locating the church you seek. For Cook County, several telephone directories must be considered. Another method is to review publications of Cook County genealogical societies. For example, the *Chicago Genealogist* XIV 3 (1982) has a listing of Chicago churches of all denominations as of the year 1892. It is a reprint of the list in Martin's *World's Fair Album-Atlas*. For South Cook County, the South Suburban Genealogical and Historical Society has a separate publication listing churches, township by township. The list was compiled by this author.

Information about Chicago churches will be found in the nineteenth century (and early twentieth) Chicago directories. Usually the name of the church pastor is given. This is useful information to locate the specific church you seek when you hold a baptismal certificate or a marriage license with the name of the pastor. The Chicago Public Library and the Chicago Historical Society Library each hold Chicago city directory collections.

To gain a broad perspective of the location of the early Cook County churches of various denominations, all published Cook County histories will provide some information. These histories and genealogical publications are listed elsewhere in this book. Good sources to consult are: Schwab and Thoren, *History of the Illinois Conference of the Evangelical Church 1937* (Harrisburg, Pa.: Evangelical Press, 1937) these Evangelical Churches; became E.U.B. and today are United Methodist; Schwartzkopf, Louis J., *The Lutheran Trail* (St. Louis: Concordia Press, 1950) covers only Missouri Synod churches; Mielton, J. Gordon, *Log Cabins to Steeples—The United Methodist Way in Illinois 1824-1974* (Nashville, Tenn.: Parthanon Press, 1974); and Elbert E. Duane, "The American Roots of German Lutheranism in Illinois," *Illinois Historical Journal* 97 (Summer 1985).

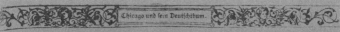

Chicago und sein Deutschthum.

Nach seiner Rückkehr im Mai 1868 betrieb Herr
[G]ottfried einen Handel mit Fahrbauten und im August 1870 brachte er die Saladin'sche Brauerei an der
[Eck]e der Archer und Stewart Avenue käuflich an sich.
Die ungeheuren Schwierigkeiten, welche sich ihm an-
[fäng]lich entgegenstellten, überwand er mit Fleiß und
[sel]tener Energie und seine Kundschaft vergrößerte sich
[so] derartig, daß er zwei große Eishäuser bauen
[muß]te. Im Frühjahr 1884 errichtete er westlich von
[der] bisherigen Brauerei ein großes fünfstöckiges Ge-
[bäu]de, welches mit allen modernen Verbesserungen,
[be]sondere mit seinen eigenen werthvollen Erfin-
[dun]gen, ausgestattet wurde. Einen schweren Kampf
[hatt]e Herr Gottfried mit fast allen Brauereien des
[Land]es zu bestehen, welche sein Patent auf eine Pich-
[mas]chine ausnützten, ohne ihm eine Entschädigung
[dafü]r zu bezahlen. Er gewann in allen Instanzen
[und] es wurde ihm eine bedeutende Entschädigungs-
[sum]me zugesprochen. Im Juni 1881 wurde die Fir-
[ma] unter dem Namen „Gottfried Brewing Company"
[inco]rporirt.
[H]err Gottfried war nicht nur ein tüchtiger und
[erfol]greicher Geschäftsmann, sondern spielt auch im
[öffen]tlichen Leben eine hervorragende Rolle. Er ist
[Mit]glied der Lessing Loge der Freimaurer, der Hoff-
[nun]gs Loge J. O. O. F., der Knight Templars, Vo-
[na]Ritter, des Germania Männerchors, des Chi-
[cago] Schützenvereins und Mitglied und Gründer des
[Turn]vereins „Vorwärts. Seine bedeutenden Erfolge
[hat] Herr Gottfried nicht nur seinen geschäftlichen
[Fähig]keiten und seinem ehrenwerthen Charakter,
[sond]ern auch seinem liebenswürdigen Wesen, seiner
[Gefä]lligkeit und seiner offenen Hand für wohlthätige
[Zwe]cke und gemeinnützige Bestrebungen zu danken.
[Sei]ne Gattin, welche ihm acht Kinder schenkte, war
[ihm] stets eine treue und intelligente Gehülfin.
[A]dolph und Ferdinand, der Erste der älteste, der
[zwe]ite der jüngste Sohn, starben jung; Karl, der
[jetz]t älteste Sohn, jetzt Secretär der Gottfried Brew-
[ing] Company, verheirathete sich vor fünf Jahren mit
[He]dwig Brand, einer Tochter des Herrn Ru-
[dol]ph Brand. Febronia, die älteste Tochter, ist die
[Gatt]in des Herrn Karl Meißschneider, welcher in Au-
[rora] wohnt; Ida, die zweite, ist die Wittwe des vor
[einig]en Jahren verstorbenen Herrn Karl Ortmeyer;
[Mar]garete, die dritte Tochter, ist die Gattin des
[Herr]n John H. Weiß, Präsidenten der Gottfried
[Brew]ing Company; Mathilde, die vierte Tochter, ist
[mit] Herrn A. G. Glock, von der Firma Hansell-El-
[kin] Foundry Company verheirathet, und Maud, die
[jüng]ste, heirathete kürzlich Herrn Philipp Brand, ei-
[nen] Sohn des Herrn Rudolph Brand.

Fridolin Madlener.

Als Fridolin Madlener am 27. Januar 1897 seine Augen für immer schloß, verlor das Deutschthum
Chicago's einen Vertreter, der in geschäftlichen und

Fridolin Madlener.

geselligen Kreisen sich eines ebenso allgemeinen als
wohlverdienten Ansehens erfreute und dessen zu früh-
es Hinscheiden nicht nur ein herber Schlag für seine
Familie war, sondern auch in der ganzen Stadt auf-
richtiges Bedauern erregte. Seines gütigen Herzens,
seiner stets offenen Hand wegen war er bei Reichen
und Armen gleich beliebt und sein sonniges, stets hei-
teres Temperament erwarb ihm sowohl im Geschäfts-
leben, als auch im geselligen Verkehr zahlreiche
Freunde.

Fridolin Madlener wurde am 3. Mai 1836 in
Ueberlingen, am Bodensee, Baden, geboren. Hier
lebten und starben seine Eltern Michael und Marga-
retha Madlener. Die Familie war eine angesehene
und alte, und der Vater, welcher das Geschäft eines
Müllers betrieb, bestimmte seinen Sohn Fridolin für
die kaufmännische Laufbahn. Im Jahre 1856 kam
der junge Madlener nach Chicago und verlegte sich
vor allen Dingen auf die Erlernung der englischen
Sprache und da er sich auch zugleich mit den hiesigen
Geschäftsmethoden bekannt machen wollte, besuchte er
das Dyrenfurth'sche Business College, das erste derar-
tige Institut in Chicago. Er erlangte eine An-

Figure 10. *Chicago und Sein Deutschthum—1902 (courtesy The Newberry Library)*

As mentioned before, all Cook County histories should be considered; however, for German research, two are particularly useful: Hofmeister, Rudolf A.; *The Germans in Chicago* (Champaign, Ill.: Stipes Publishing Co., 1976); and *Chicago und Sein Deutschum* (Cleveland: German American Press, 1902). The sole limitations of the latter is that it is written in German. The former has an extensive bibliography. For south Cook County ancestry (German or other), consider the manuscript "Southern Cook County and History of Blue Island Before the Civil War" by Ferdinand Schapper. This manuscript is several hundred pages long and includes personal data (unavailable elsewhere) on hundreds of south Cook County families. It is available at the Chicago Historical Society Library.

One Lutheran denomination can cause some confusion for researchers. In Chicago, Cook County, and northeast Illinois during the nineteenth century, a number of German Protestant congregations associated with the United Evangelical Synod of the Northwest. Its archives were located at its seminary at Elmhurst College, Elmhurst (DuPage), Illinois. In 1872, this synod merged with others to form the German Evangelical Synod of North America. In 1934 a merger of this synod with the Reformed Church resulted in the Evangelical and Reformed Church and the designation of "E and R" for its individual congregations. In 1957 the E and R Church merged with the Christian Congregational to form the United Church of Christ. Today most of these former Evangelical, then E and R Churches are now designated "U.C.C." . Consult a *United Church of Christ Yearbook* for dates of commencement of area "E and R" churches. A useful history of the Evangelical (Union) Church is: Schneider, Carl Edward; *The German Church on the American Frontier*. (St. Louis: Eden Publishing House, 1939).

The archives of this Evangelical E & R Church are: Eden Archives, 475 E. Lockwood Avenue, Webster Groves, MO 63119. Some local information is also found at the Elmhurst College Library, but no defunct church registers are there (apparently). Remember to distinguish the Evangelical (Union) churches, later E and R, and Evangelical Association (today United Methodists) Churches.

On its way to becoming United Methodist, the Evangelical Association merged with the United Brethren Church to form the E.U.B Church. Some Cook County family information can be found in: *Index to the Subjects of Obituaries abstracted from "Der Christliche Botsshafter" of the Evangelical Church 1836-1866*, by Mrs. E. R. Seder of Naperville, Illinois. A copy of this book can be found at the Newberry Library.

German Catholic churches have extensive records of baptisms, confirmations, marriages, and burials. One must, however, remember that where no "German" congregation existed, these events will be found in a nearby Catholic church whether Irish or whatever. Useful information will be found in *Finding Your Chicago Ancestor* by Margaret O'Hara (1982) and in *A History of the Parishes of the Archdioceses of Chicago* (1980). Additional Catholic records information will be found elsewhere in this book.

For three years, I have been compiling for the newsletter of the Chicago Genealogical Society (P.O. Box 1160, Chicago, IL 60690) the column, German Interest Group News, and occasionally I will receive correspondence from someone just beginning their research. For the beginner, a useful introduction to Germanic research will be found in Konrad, J., *German Family Research Made Simple* (Summit Publications, P.O. Box 222, Monroe Falls, OH 44282). It has an excellent section for locating the village of origin. To assist in locating this elusive village, consider also my "Locating the Village of Origin for an Immigrant Ancestor" in *Chicago Genealogist* XIV, 1 (Fall 1981). The two-volume set by Larry Jensen, *Genealogical Handbook of German Research* provides an introduction to many aspects of German research and is keyed to the microfilm collection of the Genealogical Society of Utah (LDS). This set is available from most genealogical book vendors and from the author (P.O. Box 441, Pleasant Grove, UT 84062).

The beginner (and the advanced researcher) can be helped by the series of taped programs from various conferences. There are several on the subject of German research. To obtain a catalog, write (enclose a self-addressed, stamped envelope) to TRIAD, 700 S. 5th, Pekin, IL 61554. A society without geographic boundaries that can assist is the German Research Association, P.O. Box 11293, San Diego, CA 92111. They publish *The German Connection* three times yearly. Another national society with both a quarterly and a newsletter is, Palatines to America, Capital University Box 106, Columbus, OH 43209. A separate newsletter (six times a year) is published by the Illinois Chapter of Palatines to America, P.O. Box 3884, Quincy, IL 62305. Do not be misled by the name Palatines; it is generic and includes all German-speaking people regardless of period of immigration. To gain an overview of German-American research in the United States, I highly recommend: *Bibliography & Source Materials for German-American Research* (1982) by Dr. Arta F. Johnson, 153 Aldrich Road, Columbus, OH 43214. Available from the author and most genealogical book vendors.

Local society publications are helpful to both the beginner and the experienced German researcher. Cumulative subject indexes for the *Chicago Genealogist* and for *Where The Trails Cross* have recently been published. Write to the Chicago Genealogical Society and the South Suburban Genealogical and Historical Society. The quarterly of the Illinois State Genealogical Society publishes articles about Cook County and German research. In volumes XVII, no. 1 (Spring 1985), they published the earliest "Lutheran" Church registers for the Cook County area. The registers were those kept in 1838/39 by the Rev. Cachend Ervenberg. A fifteen-year subject index for the ISGS quarterly will be found in Volume XV, no. 3 (Fall 1983).

Both the beginning and the advanced researcher of German genealogy must develop an ability to use gazetteers. They are essential to furthering your research. Let's say that you now know the name of your ancestor's village of origin. You have looked at the Mormon (LDS) geographic indexes, but they hold no records for your village of interest. Ah, but if you had consulted a gazetteer you would have learned that the Evangeliches (or Katholiches) Kirche for your ancestors was not in "your village" but in the adjoining village of"_____" and a search of those same Mormon geographical indexes (there are more than one) will inform you that the records of this church are available on microfilm. Or, perhaps, wills are available once you know the "R.B." Maybe you will find civil records in still another community. To assist your use of gazetteers, consult the pamphlet of the Genealogical Society of Utah: "Gazetteers – The German Empire (1871-1918)." It is available at most LDS branch libraries. Each branch also has at least one gazetteer on permanent loan. The film numbers for *Meyers Orts-und-Verkeras-Lexicon* are: 0496640 (localities A-K) 0496641 (localities L-Z).

At the Newberry Library, *Meyers* is found on the open shelves and *Ritter's Geogrpahisch-Statistiches Lexicon* is under call number fg 005.741. Should you have the need to convert the German name of a village east of the Oder/Niese River to the current Polish name, the mechanics of how to use the LDS branch library collection to so convert are found under *Poland-Prussia: How to Locate Vital Records of Former Prussian Areas of Poland in the Mormon Genealogical Library* by Daniel M. Schlyter. This seven-page booklet is available from Genealogy Unlimited, Inc. 789 S. Buffalo Grove Rd., Buffalo Grove, IL 60089. One of the tools suggested by Schlyter is Mueller's *Directory of Localities Across the Oder-Niese Under Foreign Administration*. This 1958 publication is found as LDS microfilm #1,045,448. While utilizing the collection of an LDS branch library, remember to check the International Genealogical Index (IGI).

As with other genealogical research, German research information will be found in the major Chicago area libraries. Little fraternal organization information seems to be available. Consult the Chicago Historical Society Library and the Newberry Library. To flesh out the genealogical skeleton of a German workingman in Cook County, consider *German Workers in Industrial Chicago, 1850-1910: A Comparative Perspective*, Hartmut Keil and John B. Jentz, Editors (DeKalb, Ill.: Northern Illinois University Press, 1983). It is a book that describes the everyday life of the ancestors of most of us – the German workingman and woman – doing their best to raise a family and to enjoy life.

GREEKS

Abbott, Grace. " A Study of the Greeks in Chicago." *The American Journal of Sociology* (November 1909): 379-93.

Burgess, Thomas. *Greeks in America*. An Account of Their Coming, Progress, Customs, Living, and Aspirations. American Immigration Collection, Series #2. New York: Arno Press, 1970.

Chicago Board of Education. "Greek American." Ethnic Studies Process. Chicago: 1972.

Diacou, Stacy, ed. *Hellenism in Chicago*. Chicago: The United Hellenic American Congress, 1982.

Kopan, Andrew T. "The Greeks of Chicago and the Great Fire." Chicago: 1971. (mimeographed)

_____. "Education and Greek Immigrants in Chicago, 1892-1973: A Study in Ethnic Survival." M.A. thesis, University of Chicago, 1974.

Kourvetaris, George A. *First and Second Generation Greeks in Chicago*. Athens: 1971.

Mistaras, Evangeline. "A Study of First and Second Generation Greek Out-Marriage in Chicago." M.A. thesis, University of, Chicago, 1950.

Petrakis, Harry Mark. "Chicago's Greeks, the Warmth of Halsted Street." *Chicago Tribune Magazine*, 4 August 1974.

Saloutos, Theodore. *The Greeks in the United States*. Cambridge: 1964. Mostly Chicago.

Yeracaris, Constantine A. "A Study of the Voluntary Associations of the Greek Immigrants of Chicago from 1890 to 1948 with Special Emphasis on World War II and the Post War Period." M.A. thesis, University of Chicago, 1950.

IRISH SOURCES

Irish American Heritage Center
4626 North Knox Avenue
Chicago, IL 60630
(312-282-7035)

Chicago Irish Ancestry (CIA)
c/o The Newberry Library
60 West Walton
Chicago, IL 60610

Irish Interest Group
c/o The Chicago Genealogical
   Society
P.O. Box 1160
Chicago, IL 60690

The Irish American News
   (newspaper-monthly)
P.O. Box A66218
Chicago, IL 60666 (312-359-5302)

IRISH PERSONAL NAME INDEX

Biographies and obituaries of Chicago Irish are the sources of an extensive index compiled by John Corrigan. Information has been extracted principally from *The Chicago Inter Ocean, The Chicago Citizen, The South Side Sun, Lake Vindicator, The Sun,* and the *New World* (Chicago Archdiocese) newspapers. Additional data has been extracted from published Chicago sources and personal research. Send a self-addressed, stamped envelope for more information and fee schedules to: John Corrigan, 1669 West 104th Street, Chicago, IL 60643.

DePaul University
Lincoln Park Campus Library
2323 North Seminary
Chicago, IL 60614

Irish studies collection includes educational materials pertaining to the history, literature, and culture of Ireland.

SELECTED BIBLIOGRAPHY

Cross, Robert. "Chicago's Irish: Swimming in the Mainstream." *Chicago Tribune Magazine* (17 September 1978): 38ff.
Duff, John B. *The Irish in the United States. Minorities in American Life Series.* Belmont, Calif.: Wadsworth Publishing Company, Inc., 1971.
Falley, Margaret Dickson. *Irish and Scotch-Irish Ancestral Research.* Evanston, Ill.: The Author, 1962.
Fallows, Marjorie R. *Irish Americans: Identity and Assimilation.* Ethnic Groups in America Series. Englewood Cliffs, N.J.: Prentice Hall, Inc., 1979.
Ffrench, Charles, ed. *Biographical History of the American Irish in Chicago.* Chicago: 1897.
Funchion, Michael F. *Chicago's Irish Nationalists, 1881-1890.* New York: 1976.
Griffin, William D. *A Portrait of the Irish in America.* New York: Charles Scribner's Sons, 1981.
Heraldic Artists, Ltd. *Handbook on Irish Genealogy.* Dublin: Heraldic Artists, Ltd., 1978.
Maguire, John F. *Irish in America.* American Immigration Collection, Series #1. New York: Arno Press, 1971.
Meachen, Edward. "Irish Historical Sources at the Newberry." *Origins* I, No. 2 (December 1984).
O'Day, Edward J. "Tracking Irish Immigrant Ancestors." *Illinois State Genealogical Society Quarterly* XVI, No. 4 (Winter 1984): 192ff.
O'Grady, Jospeh P. *How The Irish Became Americans. The Immigrant Heritage of America Series.* Boston: Twayne Publishers, (n.d.).

Piper, Ruth M. "The Irish in Chicago 1848 to 1871." M.A. thesis, University of Chicago, 1936.

Wittke, Carl. *The Irish in America.* Localized History Series. New York: Teachers College Press, 1968.

ITALIAN SOURCES

Italian Cultural Center
1621 39th Avenue
Stone Park, IL 60165
(312-345-3842)

Publishes American Italian Historical Association Newsletter.

Italians in Chicago Project
Department of History
University of Illinois at Chicago
Box 4348, Chicago, IL 60680
(312-996-3144)

The Project Traveling Exhibit was created from 5,000 items from 300 donors. The material suggests the variety and texture of Italian-American culture, creating a feeling of nostalgia for the warm family lives of the hard-working immigrants, their children, and the Chicago experience. Copies of all collected materials and the oral history tapes and transcriptions are on file at the Manuscripts Department of the Library at the University of Illinois at Chicago. A permanent version of the exhibit is at the Italian Cultural Center.

SELECTED BIBLIOGRAPHY

Chicago Board of Education. "Italian Americans." In *Ethnic Studies Process.* Chicago: 1972.

Candeloro, Dominic. "Chicago's Italians: A Survey of the Ethnic Factor 1850-1985," unpublished paper, 1985.

_____. "Suburban Italians: Chicago Heights, 1890-1975." In *Ethnic Chicago.* ed. Jones, Peter d'A. and Holli, Melvin G. Grand Rapids, Mich.: William B. Eerdman's Publishing Company, 1981.

_____. "Villa Scalabrini: Citadel of Italian American Ethnicity." unpublished paper, 1984.

Graham, Jory. "The Italians." *Chicago* VI, 4 (Winter 1969): 72ff.

Lopreato, Joseph. *Italians Americans: Ethnic Groups in Comparative Perspective.* New York: Random House, 1970.

Nelli, Humbert S. *Italians in Chicago, 1880-1930.* New York: 1970.

Lord, Eliot. *The Italians in America.* San Francisco: R & E Research Associates, 1970.

Quaintance, Ester Crockett. "Rents and Housing Conditions in the Italian District of the Lower North Side of Chicago, 1924." M.A. thesis, University of Chicago, 1925.

Reed, Robert D. *How and Where to Research Your Ethnic-American Heritage: Italian Americans*. The Author, 1979.

Sager, Gertrude E. "Immigration: Based Upon a Study of the Italian Women and Girls of Chicago." M.A. thesis, University of Chicago, 1914.

Schiavo, Giovanni E. *The Italians in Chicago: A Study in Americanization.* Chicago: 1928.

Vecoli, Rufolph John. "Chicago's Italians Prior to World War I: A Study of Their Social and Economic Adjustment." Ph.D. Diss., University of Wisconsin, 1962.

Wright, Caroll D. *The Italians in Chicago*. N.Y.: Arno Press, 1970.

Zaloha, Anna. " A Study of the Persistence of Italian Customs among 143 Families of Italian Descent, Members of Social Clubs at Chicago Commons." M.A. thesis, Northwestern University, 1937.

JAPANESE

Nagata, Kiyoshi. "A Statistical Approach to the Study of Acculturation of an Ethnic Group Based on Communication Oriented Variables: The Case of Japanese-Americans in Chicago." Ph.D. Diss., University of Illinois Urban, 1969.

Nakane, Kenji. *History of the Japanese in Chicago*. Chicago: 1968. (In Japanese).

Nishi, Setsuko Matsunaga. "Japanese American Achievement in Chicago: A Cultural Response to Degradation." M.A. thesis, University of Chicago, 1947.

Osako, Masako M. "Japanese-Americans: Melting into the All-American Pot?," in *Ethnic Chicago*. Jones, Peter d'A and Holli, Melvin G. eds. Grand Rapids, Mich.: William B. Eerdman's Publishing Company, 1981.

Uyeki, Eugene Shigemi. "Process and Patterns of Nisei Adjustment in Chicago." Ph.D. Diss., University of Chicago, 1953.

JEWISH SOURCES

(See Church and Religious Records Chapter)

LITHUANIAN SOURCES

Balzekas Museum of Lithuanian Culture
6500 South Pulaski
Chicago, IL 60629
(312-582-6500)

Museum and library, folk arts, handicrafts, memorabilia, weapons, costumes, ten thousand volumes on Lithuanian history and humanities, genealogical society information.

SELECTED BIBLIOGRAPHY

Consulate General of Lithuania. *Lithuanians in Chicago*. Chicago, n.d.
Fainhauz, David. *Lithuanians in Multi-Ethnic Chicago, Until World War II*. Chicago: Lithuanian Library Press, Inc., 1977.
Kezys, Algimantas. *A Lithuanian Cemetery*. Chicago: Loyola University Press, 1976.
Krisciumas, Joseph. "Lithuanians in Chicago." M.A. thesis, DePaul University, 1935.
Raece, Helen. "A Dream of Freedom." *Chicago Tribune Magazine* (30 April 1978): 23-30.

MEXICAN SOURCES

De Curutchet, Marta Isabel Kollman. "Localization of the Mexican and Cuban Population of Chicago." Ph.D. Diss., University of Chicago, 1967.
Jordan, Lois B. *Mexican Americans*. Littleton, Colo.: Libraries Unlimited, Inc., 1973.
Pacyga, Dominic A. and Skerrett. *Chicago City of Neighborhoods: Histories and Tours*. Chicago: Loyola University Press, 1986.
Ropka, Gerald W. " The Evolving Residential Pattern of the Mexican, Puerto Rican and Cuban Population in the City of Chicago." Ph.D. Diss., Michigan State University, 1973.
Sussman, Sue. "The Mexicans." *Chicago* 6, No. 3 (Fall 1969).

NORWEGIAN SOURCES

Andersen, A. W. *The Norwegian-Americans. The Immigrant Heritage of America Series*. Boston: Twayne Publishers, 1975.
Blegen, T. C. *Norwegian Migration to America: The American Transition*. Northfield, Minn., 1940.
Qualey, Carlton C. *Norwegian Settlement in the United States*. American Immigration Collection, Series #2. New York: Arno Press, 1970.
Strand, Algot E., comp. *A History of the Norwegians of Illinois*. Much information about Chicago and its Norwegian community.
Wellauer, Maralyn A. *Tracing Your Norwegian Roots*. Milwaukee, Wis.: The Author, 1979.

POLISH SOURCES

Polish Museum of America
984 North Milwaukee Avenue
Chicago, IL 60622
(312-384-3352)

Hours: Monday thru Saturday 1:00 to 4:00 p.m.
        Sunday from 12 noon to 5:00 p.m.
        Closed Good Friday and Christmas Day

Library open: 10:00 a.m. to 4:00 p.m. week days only. Researchers should call the library in advance to specify their requirements. (Polish art, costumes, religious artifacts, memorabilia of Polish leaders.) The library houses fifteen thousand volumes on Poland and Poles of Chicago. Geographical dictionaries of Poland, histories of churches and villages, Polish heraldry, Polish biographical dictionaries, Polish Army Daily Order Books, and anniversary books of Chicago parishes are some of the subjects included in the collection.

> Polish Genealogical Society
> 984 North Milwaukee Avenue
> Chicago, IL 60622

The Polish Genealogical Society was organized in 1978 to promote interest in Polish genealogy, and to provide an exchange of information among researchers. The Society publishes a semiannual *Polish Genealogical Society Newsletter* and a *Polish Genealogical Society Bulletin*. It holds quarterly meetings and workshop sessions. Members and nonmembers are invited to submit Ancestor Index Cards to be included in a master index of Polish ancestors.

> Polish National Alliance Library—Archives
> 1520 West Division Street
> Chicago, IL 60622
> (312-276-0700)

Circulating library of eighteen thousand books in English and Polish; archival materials; rare books from Poland and information on Poles of Chicago.

SELECTED BIBLIOGRAPHY

Ames, Mary Boczon, *How to Research Your Personal Polish Family History*. New Carrollton, Md.: The Author, 1976.

Andrea, M. "The Societies of St. Stanislaw Kosta Parish, Chicago." *Polish American Studies* IX 1/2 (Jan.-June 1952): 27ff.

Emmons, Charles Frank. "Economic and Political Leadership in Chicago's Polonia: Some Sources of Ethnic Persistence and Mobility." Ph.D. Diss., University of Illinois at Chicago, 1971.

Fox, Paul. *Poles in America: American Immigration Collection*, Series #2. New York: Arno Press, 1970

Frazin, Judith R. *A Translation Guide to 19th Century Polish Language Civil Registration Documents (Birth, Marriage and Death Records)*. Niles, Ill.: The Jewish Genealogical Society, 1985.

157

Gnacinski, Jan and Len. *Polish and Proud: Tracing Your Polish Ancestry.* West Allis, Wis.: Janlen Enterprises, 1979.

Golembiewski, Thomas E. *Index to Polish American Family Biographies Found in Jubilee Books of St. Stanislaus Kostka Parish, and Holy Trinity Parish.* Chicago: The Polish Genealogical Society, 1982.

_____. *The Study of Obituaries as a Source for Polish Genealogical Research.* Chicago: The Polish Genealogical Society, 1984.

Hollowak, Thomas L. and Hoffman, William F. *Index to the Obituaries and Death Notices Appearing in the* Dziennik Chicagoski 1890-1899. Chicago: The Polish Genealogical Society. 1984.

Hollowak, Thomas L., ed. *Polish Directory for the City of Chicago 1903.* Chicago: The Polish Genealogical Society, 1981.

Inviolata Ficht, Sister M. "Noble Street in Chicago: Socio-Cultural Study of Polish Residents within Ten Blocks." M.A. thesis, DePaul University, 1952.

Kantowicz, Edward R. *Polish-American Politics in Chicago 1888-1940.* Chicago: University of Chicago Press, 1975.

Konrad, J. *Polish Family Research.* Munroe Falls, Oh.: Summit Publications, 1982.

Kowallis, Otto K. *A Genealogical Guide and Atlas of Silesia.* Logan, Ut.: Everton Publishers, Inc., 1976.

Lagodzinska, Adela. *The Polish Heritage and the Future of Chicago.* Chicago: Polish Women's Alliance of America, 1953.

Lewanski, Richard C. *Guide to Polish Libraries and Archives.* Irvington, N.Y.: Columbia University Press, 1974.

Lopata, Helena Znaniecki. *Polish Americans: Status Competition in an Ethnic Community. Ethnic Groups in American Life Series.* Chicago: Claretian Publications, 1972.

_____. "The Function of Voluntary Associations in an Ethnic Community: 'Polonia'." In *Contributions to Urban Sociology.* edited by Ernest W. Burgess and Donald J. Bogue. Chicago: 1964.

Magierski, Louis. "Polish American Activities in Chicago 1919-1939." M.A. thesis, University of Illinois Urbana, 1940.

Michalski, Diane Marie. "The Family in a Polish-American Community in Chicago." M.A. thesis, University of Chicago, 1942.

Nowosielski, Janina Eugenia. "The Changes in the Residential Pattern of the Polish Population in Chicago, Illinois as a Measure of Acculturation." M.A. thesis, Northeastern Illinois State College, 1971.

Obal, Thaddeus J. *A Bibliography for Genealogical Research Involving Polish Ancestry.* Hillsdale, N.J.: the Author, 1978.

Ortell, Gerald A. *Polish Parish Records of The Roman Catholic Church.* Astoria, N.Y.: The Author, 1979.

Ozog, Julius John. "A Study of Polish Home Ownership in Chicago." M.A. thesis, University of Chicago, 1942.

Parot, Joseph John. *Polish Catholics in Chicago, 1850-1920: A Religious History.* DeKalb, Ill.: Northern Illinois University Press, 1981.

Pawlowski, Eugene Joseph. "The Polish American Element in the Politics of Chicago." M.A. thesis, Northwestern University, 1970.

Peckwas, Edward A. *Collection of Articles on Polish Heraldry.* Chicago: The Author, 1978.

Poles of Chicago, 1837-1937: A History of One Century of Polish Contribution to the City of Chicago, Illinois. Chicago: Polish Pageant, 1937.

Slowiak, Walter J. "A Comparative Study of the Social Organization of the Family in Poland and the Polish Immigrant Family in Chicago." M.A. thesis, Loyola University, 1950.

Tobiasiewicz, Maryellen. Poles in Chicago. *Chicago Genealogist* XV, Nos. 2-4 (Winter 1983, Spring and Summer 1984).

Wellauer, Maralyn A. *Tracing Your Polish Roots.* Milwaukee, Wis.: The Author, 1979.

RUSSIAN SOURCES

Hall, Thomas Randolph. "The Russian Community of Chicago." *Papers in Illinois History* XLIV, (1937).

_____. "Russians in Chicago." Unpublished manuscript, Pierce Papers, Regenstein Library, University of Chicago.

Mehr, Kahlile B. and Schlyter, Daniel M. *Sources for Genealogical Research in the Soviet Union.* Buffalo Grove, Ill.: Genun Publishers, 1983.

SCOTTISH SOURCES

MacMillan, Thomas C. "The Scots and Their Descendants in Illinois." *Illinois State Historical Society Quarterly* XXVI (1919): 31-85.

McLeod, Dean L. "Success In Tracing Your Scottish Ancestors." *The Genealogical Helper* (January-February 1980).

Northwest Orient. *Tracing Your Scottish Ancestry.* Northwest Orient Airlines, 1983.

Stuart, Margaret. *Scottish Family History: A Guide to Works of Reference on the History and Genealogy of Scottish Families.* Genealogy Unlimited, Inc. 789 Buffalo Grove, IL 60089 (312-541-3175). Lists several titles and maps for Scottish research.

SWEDISH SOURCES

Swedish–American Historical Society
5125 North Spaulding Avenue
Chicago, IL 60625
(312-583-5722)

The purpose of the society is to stimulate and promote interest in Swedish–American contributions to the history and growth of the United States, collect and preserve documents and other valuable material, encourage historical research, and sponsor publications that will keep this heritage alive and strong.

The society published a quarterly known as the *Swedish Pioneer Historical Quarterly*, a respected, frequently quoted journal available in university and other libraries throughout the United States and abroad.

The archives is a research center, established in 1968, which contains a rich documentary record of the Swedish-American experience. Emphasis is given to records of the Swedish American experience in Chicago, once "the world's second largest Swedish city." These holdings have provided a resource for scholars, students, genealogists, and American and Swedish journalists, among others. Materials include letters, diaries, family histories, organization records, newspapers, periodicals, pamphlets, music, photographs, books, oral histories, and reference files. The archives is open to the general public daily, and research is encouraged.

The Office and Archives of the Swedish-American Historical Society are open Monday—Friday and are located at, though independent of, North Park College. For additional information write or phone the above address.

SELECTED BIBLIOGRAPHY

Beijbom, Ulf. *Swedes in Chicago: A Demographic and Social Study of the 1846-1880 Immigration.* Stockholm: 1971.

_____. "Chicago's Swede Town -Gone But Not Forgotten." *The Swedish Pioneer Historical Quarterly* (October 1964): 144-58.

_____. "Scandanavians in Chicago 1850-1860." *The Swedish Pioneer Historical Quarterly* (January 1963): 163-74.

Hemdahl, Reuel G. "The Swedes in Illinois Politics: An Immigrant Group in an American Political Setting." Ph.D. Diss., Northwestern University, 1940.

Johansson, Carl-Erik. *Cradled in Sweden: A Practical Help for Genealogical Research in Swedish Records.* Rev. ed. Logan, Ut.: Everton Publishers, 1977.

Nelson, Helge. *The Swedes and the Swedish Settlements in North America.* Lund: 1943.

Olson, Ernst W. *The Swedish Element in Illinois. Survey of the Past Seven Decades.* Chicago: Swedish American Biographical Publishers, 1917.

Olsson, Nils William. "Tracing Your Swedish Ancestry," *Swedish Pioneer Historical Quarterly* 13 (1962). Reprint ed. Stockholm: Royal Swedish Ministry of Foreign Affairs, 1965.

_____. "First Swedes in Chicago (1838-50)." *American Swedish Monthly* XLII, 6 (June 1948): 81-82.

Scott, Eleanor Torell. "The Influence of Swedish Settlers on a Community in Greater Chicago." *The Swedish Pioneer Historical Quarterly* (January 1954): 13-19.
Stephenson, George M. "The Stormy Years of the Swedish Colony in Chicago Before the Great Fire." *Illinois State Historical Society Quarterly* XXXVI (1929): 166-84.

UKRAINIAN

Ukrainian National Museum
2453 West Chicago Avenue
Chicago, IL 60622
(312-276-6565)
Hours: Sunday noon–3 p.m. (4:30 p.m. when culture bus is in service)

SELECTED BIBLIOGRAPHY

Kochman, Thomas, and Semchyshyn, Miroslav. *Ukrainians in Illinois.* Chicago: Ukrainian Bicentennial Committee, 1976.
Pleshkewych, Dan. "Ukrainians in Chicago: Immigration and Assimilation." Northeastern Illinois University unpublished paper, 1975.

BIBLIOGRAPHY

Allswang, John Myers. *The Political Behavior of Chicago's Ethnic Groups 1918-1932.* New York: Arno Press, 1980.
Baxter, Angus. *In Search of Your European Roots.* Baltimore: Genealogical Publishing Co., Inc., 1985.
Chicago Public Library. "Omnibus Project." Work Progress Administration. *The Chicago Foreign Language Press Survey: General Description of Its Contents.* Chicago: 1942.
City of Chicago. Department of Development & Planning. *Historic City, The Settlement of Chicago.* Chicago: Department of Development & Planning, 1976. Describes pattern of settlement of various ethnic groups as Chicago grew from 1830 to 1900. Excellent color-coded maps showing distribution of groups and cultural population at various times.
_____. *The People of Chicago, Who We Are and Who We Have Been.* Chicago: Department of Development & Planning, 1976. Contains census information on foreign born in Chicago 1837-1970.
Cressey, Paul Frederick. "The Succession of Cultural Groups in the City of Chicago." Ph.D. Diss., University of Chicago, 1930.
Eakle, Arlene, and Cerny, Johni. *The Source: A Guidebook of American Genealogy.* "Tracking Immigrant Origins," Salt Lake City: Ancestry Publishing Company, 1984.

Galford, Justin B. "The Foreign Born and Urban Growth in the Great Lakes, 1850-1950: A Study of Chicago, Cleveland, Detroit, and Milwaukee," Ph.D. Diss., York University 1957.

Greeley, Andrew M. "The Unwanted Who Proved Indispensable." *Chicago Tribune Magazine* (23 May 1976): 26ff.

_____. *Ethnicity in the United States.* New York: John Wiley and Sons, 1974.

Holli, Melvin G. and Jones, Peter d' A. *The Ethnic Frontier: Essays in the History of Group Survival in Chicago and the Midwest.* Grand Rapids, Mich.: William B. Eerdmans Publishing Company, 1977.

Hull House Maps and Papers: By Residents of Hull-House. New York, 1970. Maps included show the ethnic composition and income level of families in the area. Also included are essays by residents which treat sweat shops, child labor, Bohemians, Italians, etc.

Jones, Peter d' A. and Holli, Melvin G. *Ethnic Chicago.* Grand Rapids, Mich.: William B. Eerdman's Publishing Company, 1981. The editors have arranged the essays into two sections: "cultural pluralism" and "the melting pot." Contents include: "Irish Chicago: Church, Homeland, Politics, and Class-The Shaping of an Ethnic Group, 1870-1900." by Michael Funchion; "The Jews of Chicago: From Shtetl to Suburb" by Irving Cutler; "Greek Survival in Chicago: The Role of Ethnic Education, 1890-1980" by Andrew T. Kopan; "Ukrainian Chicago: The Making of a Nationality Group in America" by Myron Bohdon Kuropas; "Suburban Italians: Chicago Heights, 1890-1975" by Dominic Candeloro; "Irish Chicago: The Multiethnic Road to Machine Success" by Paul Michael Green; "The Great War Sinks Chicago's German Kultur" by Melvin G. Holli; and "Japanese-Americans: Melting into the All-American Pot?" by Masako M. Osako.

Kiang, Ying-Cheng. "Distribution of the Ethnic Groups in Chicago." *American Journal of Sociology* LXIV, 34 (Nov.1968): 292-96.

National Archives Trust Fund Board. *Immigrant and Passenger Arrivals: A Select Catalog of National Archives Microfilm Publications.* Washington, D.C.: National Archives Trust Fund Board, 1983.

Pacyga, Dominic A. and Skerrett, Ellen. *Chicago: City of Neighborhoods.* Chicago: Loyola University Press, 1986.

Roberts, Robert E. T. *Chicago's Ethnic Groups.* Chicago: 1965.

Smith, Jessie Carney, ed. *Ethnic Genealogy.* Westport, Conn.: Greenwood Press, 1983.

Wasserman, Paul, editor. *Ethnic Information Sources of the United States.* Detroit: Gale Research, 1976. One volume work combining different types of information about ethnic groups and peoples. Categories for groups include: foreign government organizations in the United States; research centers; museums and special libraries; ethnic festivals; and bibliographies.

Wynar, Lubomyr R. *Encyclopedic Directory of Ethnic Organizations in the United States.* Littleton, Colo.: Libraries Unlimited, 1976.

For Additional Information on Particular Groups, See Churches and Religious Records Chapter.

CHAPTER 12

State of Illinois Sources for Cook County

by Sandra Hargreaves Luebking

T wo repositories and two societies offer holdings and publications which are of interest to Cook County researchers. The repositories are the Illinois State Archives and the Illinois State Historical Library, both located in Springfield, the state capital. Societies of importance are the Illinois State Genealogical Society and the Illinois State Historical Society. Both will be found to have helpful publications with news and articles about Chicago.

ILLINOIS STATE ARCHIVES

Several record groups created, administered, or simply deposited at the state level have specific application to research activity in Cook County. The records discussed in this section are held by the Illinois State Archives, Springfield IL 62756.

This category would include the name index to early records; records resulting from the sale of public domain lands; war indexes and veteran's burial lists; Civil War Military Enrollments; muster rolls; World War I Draft Registration and State Council of Defense Records; Supreme Court case files and criminal records; and the Illinois Historical Records Survey of the Work Projects Administration.

A publication essential to understanding both the characteristics and arrangements of Illinois archival material is *Descriptive Inventory of the Archives of the State of Illinois,* by Victoria Irons and Patricia C. Brennan (Springfield: Illinois State Archives, 1978). This may be purchased from the Archives for $20. Checks should be made payable to the Secretary of State. A pamphlet titled "Genealogical Records and Mail Research Policy of the Illinois State Archives" is available without charge upon request.

Mail inquiries or search requests should be limited to only one or two specific items at a time. Designate the specific record to be searched and provide the complete name(s) of the person(s) sought. Submit no more than two names per request and do not send a second request until you have received an answer to the first.

Personal visits are encouraged. The Illinois State Archives building is located south of the capitol, west of the Centennial Building, and north of the Illinois State Museum in Springfield. The Archives is open from 8:00 to 4:30 Monday through Friday and most Saturdays 8:00 to 3:30.

In the descriptions which follow, numbers preceded by "RG" and shown in parenthesis are record group number assignments which will aid in accessing the particular set of holdings described.

NAME INDEX TO EARLY ILLINOIS RECORDS

This is a cumulative card file, by individual name, of all extant Illinois state and federal census records from 1810 through 1855. Also included are names from early house and senate journals, the governor's executive records, election returns, and other state documents. The file contains well over 1.5 million index cards.

NORTHEASTERN LAND DISTRICT OFFICE

The Northeastern Land District Office was created at Chicago by an Act of Congress of 26 June 1834 and operated through 31 July 1855. The area had formerly been contained in the Danville district and was comprised of part of those lands lying north of the line separating townships thirty and thirty-one north of the baseline for the second and third principal meridians.

The Illinois State Archives holds receipt entries, correspondence, and account books for the receiver of the general land office as well as original tract books and abstracts of the surveyor's field notes.

A search of the remarkable Archives Public Domain Computer Conversion Project microfiche (see following) will provide the researcher with details on the first purchase of land from the federal government. However, some individuals were prevented from original purchases and their names will not appear in this source. Therefore, a search of the ledgers concerning preemption claims (RG 952.326; RG 952.327; RG 952.328 and RG 952.329) might reveal evidence of disputes involving another individual's right to own or purchase a specific tract of land.

The preemption claims ledgers are not indexed and are best searched in person. The collection consists of less than three volumes and 2 1/2 cubic feet of declaration statements. (The latter being RG 952.327).

PUBLIC DOMAIN COMPUTER CONVERSION PROJECT

First purchases of land in Illinois from the federal government are now indexed alphabetically by the purchaser's name in this statewide finding aid. In addition to federal sales, school lands sold by the state government and some county swamp lands are included. Also available in the archives reference room are two other arrangements: an alphabetical list of Cook County purchasers and a list by legal description giving section, township, and range numbers within Cook County.

WAR INDEXES AND VETERAN'S BURIAL LISTS

There are separate indexes for the Indian, Black Hawk, Mexican, Civil, and Spanish-American wars.

The Honor Roll of Veteran's Buried in Illinois lists veterans of all wars buried in Illinois. Although the file is incomplete and contains errors, it is the single most comprehensive source to burials. The 1956 edition contains three volumes for Cook County which the archives will examine upon request.

A recent publication, *Index to Roll of Honor, Cook County, Illinois* provides the names and death dates of soldiers, sailors, and marines buried in Cook County from the Revolutionary War through World War I. (Markham Publications, P.O. Box 521018, Salt Lake City, UT, 84152-1018.) This indexes a 1929 edition of the *Honor Roll of Veterans Buried in Illinois*.

CIVIL WAR MILITARY ENROLLMENTS

On 3 May 1861 the state legislature approved an act requiring county assessors to list all able-bodied male citizens between the ages of eighteen and forty-five who were subject to militia duty. The information within these enrollment registers is limited to names and classification of volunteer or reserve.

The following year, in August 1862, General Order No. 99 issued by the U.S. War Department required state governors to prepare lists of able-bodied male citizens between eighteen and forty-five. Although Illinois was already preparing similar lists, the federal decree added requirements for listing age and occupation, as well as a remarks section pertaining to possible exemption from duty.

None of these lists are indexed. Most Cook County entries will be found on rolls #30-287 where they are listed by town. Additional Cook County names will be found randomly mixed with entries for adjacent DuPage and Will Counties on roll #1012407.

When requesting a search of these enrollments, you must indicate a specific township location.

MILITARY MUSTER ROLLS

The Indian wars muster rolls for Illinois units contain only the names of men who served. The Black Hawk (RG 301.7) and Mexican wars (RG 301.8) include names, county of residences, and sometimes remarks. Civil War and Spanish-American War rosters will provide a physical description, residence, nativity, and service dates; for Spanish-American War, (Muster-Out Rolls are in RG 301.89), the name of next-of-kin is also shown.

WORLD WAR I DRAFT REGISTRATION

World War I draft registration was required of all able-bodied males by the Federal Selective Service Act of 18 May 1917. The archives has these records on microfilm. These lists include name, address, date and place of birth, occupation, citizenship status, name and address of nearest relative, and a brief physical description. Cook County names are not indexed, but arranged alphabetically under draft board number. Lists are extant for ninety-five Cook County draft boards. Provide the archives with the full name, 1917 address, and city ward number.

STATE COUNCIL OF DEFENSE RECORDS

On 2 May 1917 the State Council of Defense was created to assist and cooperate with the Council of National Defense. Of the many files, clippings, and lists which resulted from their work, at least four pertain directly to Cook County. Each covers only the latter half of 1917 and continues through 1918 (except Military Affairs Committee Administrative which go through 1919). Each measures one cubic foot or less in size. None are indexed.

Military Affairs Committee Administrative Files go through 1919 and include correspondence between committee officials and Illinois Volunteer Training Corps (IVTC) officers. Among other topics are the development of Polish and Bohemian corps units and a list of IVTC units in Cook County and their officers, and a list of all IVTC commissioned officers. (RG 517.13)

The *Cook County Members' Register* is a one-volume alphabetical register of members of several Committees of the State Council of Defense which shows each member's name, address occupation, and committee affiliation. (RG 517.21)

The Cook County Neighborhood Committee and Volunteers Files lists the names, addresses, and some telephone numbers of committee chairman, vice chairman, secretary, treasurer, and volunteers. (RG 517.39)

The Cook County Neighborhood Committee Entertainers Files lists names, addresses, and telephone numbers of musicians, singers, and music teachers. Their instrument or the specialty of each is also shown. (RG 517.41)

SUPREME COURT OF ILLINOIS

Record Group 901 consists of case files for every case heard before the Supreme Court of Illinois between 1820 and 1936. These cases are primarily appeals. However, original jurisdiction is assigned to this court in cases relating to revenue, cases of mandamus, and in impeachment cases required to be tried before it (original jurisdiction for impeachment was withdrawn in 1870). (RG 901.1)

Cases are indexed by appellant or petitioner and will occasionally provide information of a genealogical nature. Abstracts of cases appear in issues of the *Illinois State Genealogical Society Quarterly*. The years 1819-31 appeared in *ISGSQ* 6 (Spring and Summer 1974); 1832-34 in *ISGSQ* 17 (Winter 1985); and 1835-36 in *ISGSQ* 2 (Summer 1986).

CRIMINAL RECORDS

A comprehensive listing of registers, petitions, and other records maintained by the department of corrections appears in the Spring 1986 issue of *Illinois State Genealogical Society Quarterly* XVIII, No. 1, "Criminal Records of Illinois in the Illinois State Archives" by Robert S. Johnston. In addition to providing titles and record group numbers, Johnston lists "Convicts in the Illinois State Prison Who Have Been Pardoned, Died or Escaped 1 January 1855 to 31 December 1856." It is worth noting that forty-seven percent of these convicts were from Cook County. Similar lists will be found in subsequent quarterlies.

Access to some of these records is restricted by the Freedom of Information Act (Public Act 83-1013) and the Unified Code of Corrections (Revised Statutes of the State of Illinois, chapter 38).

ILLINOIS HISTORICAL RECORDS SURVEY OF THE WORKS PROJECT ADMINISTRATION

Record Group 954 contains data and inventory work sheets from unpublished inventories compiled by fieldworkers as part of the Illinois Historical Records Survey. This survey sought to locate and describe federal, state, county, municipal, and church archives in Illinois. The inventories for Cook County have not been published but are available in manuscript form at the archives. While there is no information of a genealogical nature in these inventories, they do serve to establish the presence and location of a particular record at the time of inventory.

The Cook County Archives were inventoried by record title, dates, quantity, arrangement, type of indexing, contents, and location by fieldworkers between 1936 and 1942. (RG 954.7) In addition, research material and preliminary essays include drafts of historical sketches of Cook County and Chicago and legal essay material on county officials and county courts. (RG 954.9)

A list of Cook County municipal archives inventoried includes: Bellwood, Berwyn, Blue Island, Brookfield, Chicago, Cicero, Crestwood, Des Plaines, Dixmoor, Evanston, Forest Park, Franklin Park,

La Grange, Lyons Township, Maywood, Melrose Park, Oak Park, Park Ridge, River Forest, Riverside, Summit, Tinley Park, Westchester, and Westmont. The information provided on each form included title and creation or inclusive dates of items inventoried, description and form of recording, size and condition, and location at the time of inventory.

ILLINOIS STATE HISTORICAL LIBRARY

An estimated four million manuscript items, consisting of 200 large collections and over 2,000 smaller ones, are housed in the library rooms in the lower level of the old state capitol at Springfield. Most items date from 1818, the year of Illinois statehood, and relate to all phases of Illinois history. The library is known particularly for its fine holdings relating to Abraham Lincoln; papers of political leaders and other state officials; and military collections from the Black Hawk War and the Civil War.

Of particular interest to Chicago area researchers is the library's fine collection of Cook County newspapers on microfilm. More than 300 titles are available for the city of Chicago alone, ranging from the 26 November 1833 *Democrat* through current times. Holdings include scattered issues for more than three dozen Chicago ethnic newspapers. An excellent finding aid can be found in the March 1985 issue of *Illinois Libraries*, available from the Illinois State Library, Springfield 62756.

The library is open to the public from 8:30 to 5:00, Monday through Friday.

ILLINOIS STATE GENEALOGICAL SOCIETY

More than 2,500 persons comprise the membership of the Illinois State Genealogical Society which was organized in 1968. The society publishes ten newsletter issues and four issues of their quarterly each year. The annual index to the quarterly aids in finding surname and Chicago or Cook County references. Membership information is available from the Society, P.O. Box 157, Lincoln, IL 62656.

ILLINOIS STATE HISTORICAL SOCIETY

The Illinois State Historical Society is a private nonprofit corporation organized in 1899 to collect, preserve, and disseminate information concerning the history of Illinois. Members receive a discount on publications sold by the society, the quarterly *Illinois Historical Journal* and the bimonthly newsletter, the *Dispatch*. The quarterly often contains book reviews and articles of historical interest concerning Chicago. For information contact the society, Old State Capitol, Springfield IL 62701.

BIBLIOGRAPHY

Irons, Victoria, and Patricia C. Brennan. *Descriptive Inventory of the Archives of the State of Illinois*, Springfield: Illinois State Archives, 1978.

Stark, Sandra M. "Newspapers in the Illinois State Historical Library," *Illinois Libraries* 67, no. 3 (March 1985).

Volkel, Lowell M., "Genealogical Sources in the Illinois State Archives," *Illinois Libraries* 68, no. 4 (Spring 1986).

CHAPTER 13

Land and Property Records

L and records meet the needs of researchers in different ways and contain a variety of genealogical and historical data. They are a major source of information for many family history studies and provide primary source material for local history as well. They are closely related to probate and other official court records and should be investigated in connection with them. Land and property are leading issues in settlement of estates and the majority of civil cases in the courts deal with real and personal property. Although land records will rarely yield vital statistics, they will in many instances provide the only proof of family relationships. Often they will include the names of heirs of an estate (including daughters' married names, and a widow's subsequent married name) as well as referring to related probates and other court cases by number and court name. Additionally, in Cook County where other sources are information are sometimes scarce, the land records take on extra importance. Occasionally these documents will disclose former residences and more often will provide the new addresses of the grantors or heirs at the time of the sale of the property.

Deeds and other instruments affecting property are deposited in the office of the county recorder where they are filed as public record. Through these records a researcher may trace the ownership of land. As with other official records for Cook County, property records were destroyed in the Chicago Fire of 1871, and therefore no records are available from the county recorder previous to that year.

Recorder of Deeds, Cook County
County Building
118 North Clark Street—Room 120
Chicago, IL 60602
(312-443-5050)

Hours: Monday—Friday 9:00 a.m. to 5:00 p.m. closed weekends and holidays.

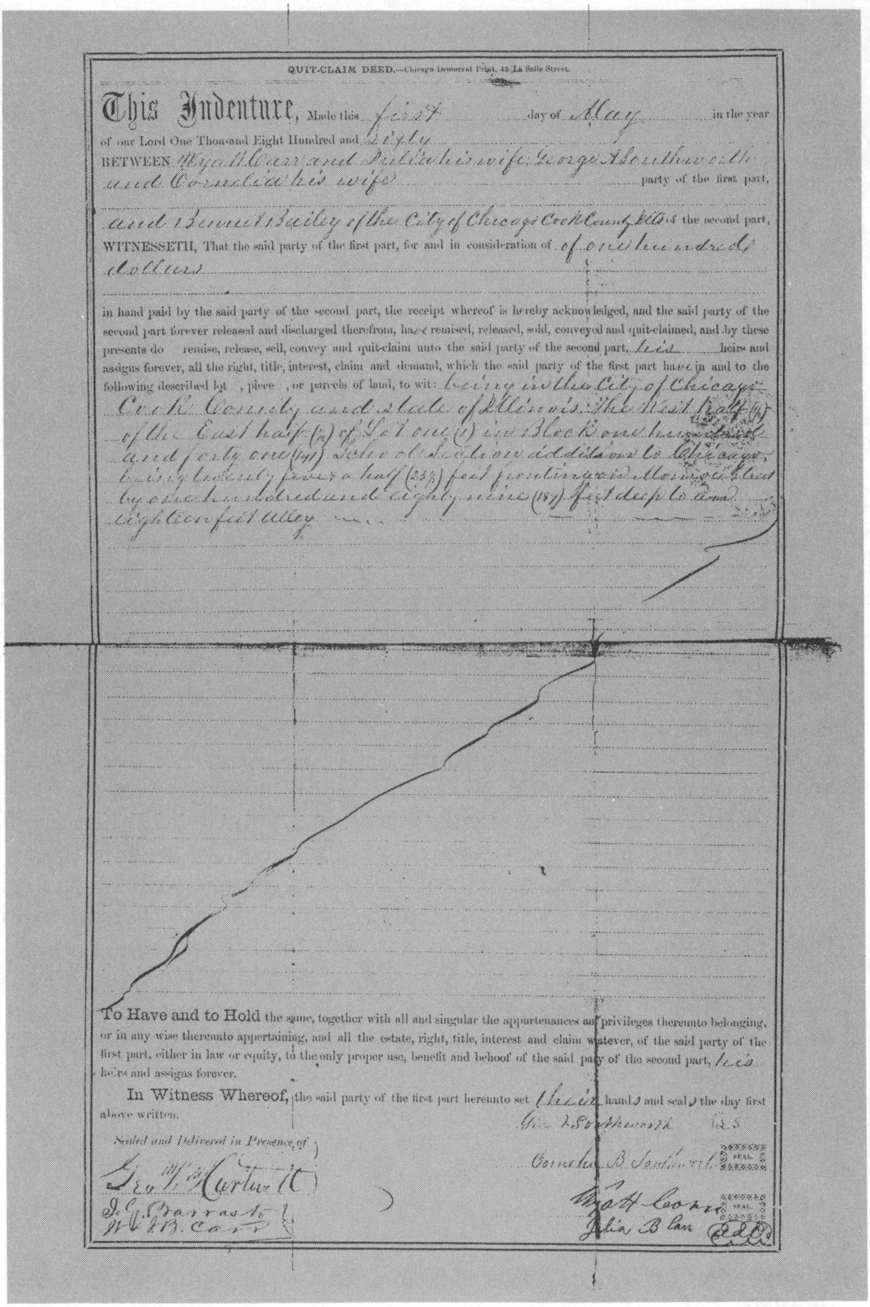

QUIT-CLAIM DEED.—Chicago Democrat Print, 45 La Salle Street.

This Indenture, Made this first day of May in the year of our Lord One Thousand Eight Hundred and Sixty

BETWEEN Wyatt Carr and Julia his wife, George A Southworth and Cornelia his wife party of the first part,

and Bennet Bailey of the City of Chicago Cook County Ills of the second part,

WITNESSETH, That the said party of the first part, for and in consideration of of one hundred dollars

in hand paid by the said party of the second part, the receipt whereof is hereby acknowledged, and the said party of the second part forever released and discharged therefrom, have remised, released, sold, conveyed and quit-claimed, and by these presents do remise, release, sell, convey and quit-claim unto the said party of the second part, his heirs and assigns forever, all the right, title, interest, claim and demand, which the said party of the first part have in and to the following described lot , piece , or parcels of land, to wit: being in the City of Chicago Cook County and state of Illinois. The West half (½) of the East half (½) of Lot one (1) in Block one hundred and forty one (141) School Section addition to Chicago, being twenty five & half (25½) feet fronting on Monroe Street by one hundred and eighty nine (189) feet deep to an eighteen feet alley

To Have and to Hold the same, together with all and singular the appurtenances and privileges thereunto belonging, or in any wise thereunto appertaining, and all the estate, right, title, interest and claim whatever, of the said party of the first part, either in law or equity, to the only proper use, benefit and behoof of the said party of the second part, his heirs and assigns forever.

In Witness Whereof, the said party of the first part hereunto set their hands and seals the day first above written.

Sealed and Delivered in Presence of

Geo. W. Cartwright
J. G. Barrasto
W. B. Carr

Geo. A Southworth [SEAL.]
Cornelia B Southworth [SEAL.]
Wyatt Carr [SEAL.]
Julia B Carr [SEAL.]

Figure 11. *Ante-Fire Chicago Deed (personal papers)*

Because of the tremendous population of the metropolitan Chicago area, locating property by grantee and grantor index is impractical. To obtain land records in Cook County, a legal description of the property is necessary. Although street addresses are important, they are not sufficient to locate property since records are indexed geographically by township. Addresses may be obtained from directories, from probate and other court cases, as well as from personal documents.

A full legal description of the property can be obtained in one of three places: (1) County Treasurer's Office, Room 112, County Building, (2) County Clerk's Office, Room 434, County Building, or (3) City of Chicago Bureau of Maps and Plats, City Hall, Room 803, 121 North LaSalle. (Located in the other side of the City/County Building). There is a minimal charge for the address/legal description conversion.

The following is a recommended procedure to find recorded documents:

1. Present a legal description of the property to the Recorder's Tract Department which is located in the basement of the south concourse. Use the stairs in Room 120. The elderly or handicapped may use the elevator which is located in the center aisle of Room 120.

2. If no legal description is available, go to the treasurer's office, room 112. By giving the person at the counter the address or permanent tax index number, you will obtain the legal description.

3. Present the legal description to the Tract Department. A clerk at the desk just inside the door will translate the legal description and provide the number of the ledger to be consulted in the tract department. Transactions are filed chronologically so that by scanning several pages of a tract book, the history of ownership of the property can be traced. When the correct tract book is located, look under the section and block number. For each document, the following information is posted: document number, grantor, grantee, type of instrument, date of instrument, date of filing and description.

4. Taking the document number from the tract book, proceed to the microfilm library in the south concourse of the basement. Paging books are used to locate the microfiche of the original document. The first digit or digits of the document number refer to the book number, the middle numbers to the page, and the last numbers to the line. The numbers found recorded in the paging books refer then to still another book and page. These last numbers must be recorded on a slip of paper and ordered from the clerk. A clerk will bring you the microfiche which you can search on one of several microfiche readers in that same room.

5. Once a document is identified on the microfiche, copies may be ordered. Since these documents are usually copied for legal purposes they are certified, which makes it expensive if many pages are requested. Most deeds are two to four pages in length. With proper authorization, copies can be made without the extra expense of certification.

6. Copies are priced at the microfilm room. A statement from a clerk in that department must then be taken to the first floor, room 120, to the cashier's cage. Take a paid receipt to counter six where you will receive a copy of the order receipt. Additional charges are added if documents are to be mailed. Documents ordered can be picked up forty-eight hours after the order is placed at counter six.

Property records can be tricky and the above steps need careful attention. One number copied incorrectly can throw off the entire process.

ABBREVIATIONS USED IN DESCRIBING THE INSTRUMENTS POSTED IN THE COOK COUNTY RECORDER'S TRACT INDICES

Accpt—As Trustee
Aff'd—Affidavit
Agmt—Contract for Deed or other purposes
App'mt—Appointment as Trustee
Assm't—Assignment
Bill—Suit filed in Circuit or Superior Court
Ch'cy—Suit filed in Circuit or Superior Court
C.M.—Chattel Mortgage
C of I—Certificate of Incorporation
C of R—Certificate of Redemption
Consent—(Generally by Trustee)
D—Deed
Dec'd—Deceased (Probate Court Case # in document column)
Ded—Dedication of alley
D in T—Deed in Trust
Div—Divorce Proceedings
D of T—Deed of Trust (Trust Deed)
Extn—Extension of Mortgage
Invty—Inventory of Estate
Judgmt—Judgement
LR—Land Registration under Torrens System
Grant—Form U.S. Government
MD or Mast.D.—Master in Chancery Deed
MS or Mast S—Master in Chancery Sale
Mtg.—Mortgage

Petn—Petition (by County Clerk or Treasurer to collect back taxes or
   Declaration of Bankruptcy)
QC—Quit Claim
R or Rel—Release Deed
Resgn—Resignation (As Trustee, Receiver, etc.)
Satis—Satisfaction of Lien or Judgement
Schedule—An instrument in Bankruptcy
Sub or Subdvn—Plat of Subdivision
SWD—Special Warranty Deed
TD—Trust Deed (Mortgage)
Tx D—Tax Deed
Tx S—Tax Sale
TR D—Trustees Deed
WD—Warranty Deed

THE CHICAGO FIRE AND PROPERTY RECORDS

At the time of the Chicago Fire of 1871, the Cook County Courthouse
was on the same site as the present combination county courthouse
(often called County Building) and City Hall. It has been suggested that
the records of the recorder's office were not removed from the courthouse at the time of the fire because of their tremendous weight and
there was not sufficient time for their removal after it became apparent that the "fireproof" courthouse was doomed to destruction.

Shortly after the fire, the county recorder secured the new set of
maps and tract books and was ready to start anew the recording of
deeds and other instruments. But because so many of the property
owners had no deeds to record, their documents having been destroyed
by the fire, the recorder was comparatively helpless.

Emergency legislation was needed. Accordingly, on 9 April 1872,
the state legislature enacted a law known as the "Burnt Record Act"
which provided methods for the reestablishment of property records.
The act stipulated, among other things, that the owner of a property
whose deed had not been destroyed could rerecord the document, that
copies of court orders of transfer could be accepted by the recorder as
valid, and that the county board might purchase from abstract companies any existing maps, tract books, or other official entries, and have
them recorded in behalf of the property owner.

The most important provision, however, was the one stipulating
that in cases of destroyed records, the claimant of a property could go
into any court in the county having chancery (court of record) jurisdiction, present whatever evidence he could muster to support his claim,

STATE OF ILLINOIS   )
) SS:
COUNTY OF COOK   )

IN THE CIRCUIT COURT OF COOK COUNTY.

TO THE r MARCH TERM A.D. 1915.

TO THE HONORABLE
    THE JUDGES OF SAID CIRCUIT COURT OF COOK COUNTY
                IN CHANCERY SITTING:

Your petitioner, ELSA MADLENER, of the City of Chicago,
in the County of Cook and State of Illinois, respectfully represents unto Your Honors that she is the owner, in fee simple, of
the following described real estate situated in the City of
Chicago, in the County of Cook and State of Illinois, to-wit:

          Lot Forty-two (42) in E. K. Rogers'
    Subdivision of Lots One (1) and Two (2) in Block
    Five (5) in Duncan's Addition to Chicago, together
    with Block One (1) in the Canal Trustees' Subdivi-
    sion of the West half (W½) and the West half (W½)
    of the Northeast quarter (NE¼) of Section Seventeen
    (17), Township Thirty-nine (39) North, Range Fourteen
    (14) East of the Third Principal Meridian.

Your petitioner further represents that she acquired her
title to the said premises in the manner following:

That said premises, together with other lands, were selected by the commissioner of the general land office, under the
direction of the President of the United States, as a portion of
those lands intended to be granted by the United States to the
State of Illinois by act of the Congress of the United States,
approved March 2, 1827 entitled: "An Act to grant a quantity of
land to the State of Illinois for the purpose of aiding in opening a canal to connect the waters of the Illinois River with those of

Figure 12. *Burnt Record Series, Cook County Circuit Court*

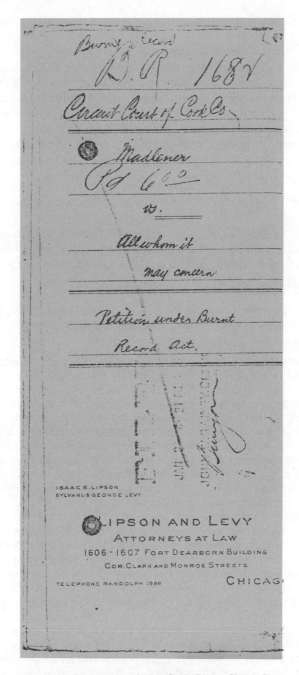

Figure 13. *Burnt Record Series, Cook County Circuit Court*

and, if the judge was satisfied, the judge was to issue whatever order necessary proclaiming ownership. The court order then could be recorded with the county recorder.

The best evidence of this nature proved to be the records kept by private abstract and title guarantee companies, of which there were three in operation in Chicago. These records, mostly of tract book nature, had been compiled throughout the years as properties changed hands and new deeds were recorded. A sworn statement by the abstractor, certifying that a person was shown by the abstractor's books to be the owner of a certain parcel of property, would satisfy the court.

THE BURNT RECORD SERIES

The Genealogical Society of Utah has microfilmed the Burnt Record book series 1871-1932 (which are the result of the Burnt Records Act previously described) with indexes on forty-nine microfilm reels. The original records which are available through the Law Division of the Circuit Court (Room 1201) must be ordered from the warehouse.

ANTE-FIRE RECORDS FOR COOK COUNTY

Everett Chamberlin in his book, *Chicago and Its Suburbs*, (Chicago: T.A. Hungerford & Co., 1874), described the preservation of some of the records by the abstract companies:

> Chase Brothers. At the time of the fire this was still the leading abstract firm in town, employing a force of 25 men, and having accumulated a collection of 300 volumes of indexes, 230,000 pages of letterpress copies of abstracts in all, some three tons of manuscripts. The fire came, and destroyed a portion of these books, but fortunately the most valuable parts saved from the flames by other conveyances mentioned below.
>
> Shortall & Hurd. Mr. Shortall arrived at the place where his precious books were stored at midnight. . . .Observation already told him that the safeguards which had been thrown around his property were not, as had been supposed, sufficient. The only safety lay in removing the books beyond the district likely to be burned over.
>
> What to do for a means of conveyance? For Shortall, tho versed in all manner of legal conveyances, was not equal to this emergency without help from a conveyancer of a more literal or physical type. But the carters were the greatest men in town that night, and in the vicinity of Larmon block none could be got, for love or money, to move those books. The only other resort was in the rear pocket of Shortall's trowsers. He drew it forth—a revolver! and requested the nearest carter to come alongside and anchor while his craft could be filled with books from upstairs.
>
> By keeping this instrument carefully trained upon the commander of the unknown craft, Shortall was able to hold him there while the boys of the office brought down most of the books, and while the flames roared and the walls toppled around them. A friend came to the rescue after a

while, with a wagon more commodious and a driver more trustworthy than the one whom Shortall had impressed into his service. The latter was, therefore, honourably discharged and reasonably paid. The friend's wagon was driven off in the direction of safety, and the books were saved. A great many loose crannies in our land titles were thereby made snug and tight, and Shortall's fortune was made. The exertions by which the other sets of abstract books were saved were scarcely less brave and praiseworthy.

Jones & Sellers. The books of Messrs. Jones & Sellers which were also contributed to the joint library of archives from which the most of our land titles are now verified, were started at a later period than either of the two sets referred to above. . . .These books, like those of the other firms named, were rescued by dint of great exertion from the consuming element, hardly any portion being lost in any case except those least valuable, viz., copies of abstracts.

ALLIANCE FORMED

The fire over, and every scrap of the public records gone up in the fiery whirlwind, the abstract men were not long in perceiving that they held the key to the land title situation. It was found that by combining their books a record could be made up which would afford not only a complete chain of title of every tract in Cook county, but would also furnish very full evidence relative to the effect of all judgments—in fact a thoro inquest could be made by means of these books into all the strong and weak points of possession, claim, or conveyance. The three firms therefore lost no time in forming an alliance, and in making themselves ready to serve the public.

The combined books of the three firms were leased on 1 December 1872 to Messrs. Handy, Simmons and Company. In 1879, this firm became Handy and Company, and in 1887 was succeeded by Title Guarantee and Trust Company. This latter company became the owner of all the ante-fire records of Cook County and in 1901, through further consolidations, the records became the property of Chicago Title and Trust Company (now Chicago Title Insurance Company).

CHICAGO TITLE INSURANCE COMPANY RECORDS
111 West Washington Street, 3rd Floor
Chicago, IL 60602
(312-630-2283)

The Chicago Title Insurance Company is one of the largest title insurers in the country. The downtown Chicago office holds records for some 1,600,000 parcels of land in Cook County, including the only surviving sets of Ante-Fire Tract and Copy books. The company's collection of copy books contains information abstracted from the original documents filed in the Cook County Recorder's Office. Copy books

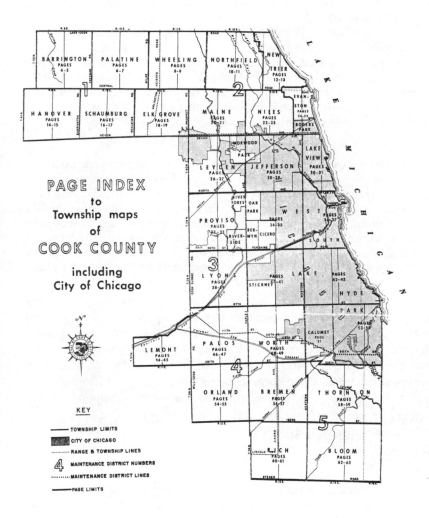

Figure 14.

summarize the original instruments listing grantor, grantee, description of the conveyances and the encumbrances, and, at times, sketches of the recorded plats.

Tract Books (geographic indexes) are used since the population of Cook County makes the use of grantor/grantee indices impractical. The Ante-Fire Tract Books contain recorded data starting with the issuance of the original government patent to 8 October 1871, the date of the Great Chicago Fire. Post-fire tract books contain recorded data from 9 October 1871 through 30 August 1974. Commencing 1 September 1974, the data from recorded instruments has been posted into the Chicago Title Insurance Company's computerized record keeping system. This data is posted against the permanent index number assigned to real estate by the Cook County Clerk.

All recorded data may be obtained from the records of the Chicago Title Insurance by utilizing the various searches sold by the company. In addition, the company's tract books are available for use by researchers who are well versed in using land records. Such use of these documents is by appointment only.

PUBLIC DOMAIN RECORDS

The staff of the Illinois State Archives has completed the Public Domain Computer Conversion Project which includes information from over 550,000 original sales of public lands in Illinois. Access to the records by surname of purchasers is available by mail from the state archives. The Chicago Public Library and the South Suburban Genealogical Society have copies of the index for Cook County. It should be noted that these records cover only the original purchases from the federal government.

The original sales records had been written in over 100 large bound volumes that were accessioned by the Archives in the 1950s from the Auditor of Public Accounts. The auditor had held them since the 1870s when the federal government gave the records to the state.

Information entered for each sale includes name of purchaser and identification number, type of sale, description of land purchased, number of acres, price per acre, total price, male or female purchaser, date of purchase, county or state of residence of purchaser, and volume and page of original land record.

Once the name has been located, land purchases can be located on a map of Illinois. Illinois State Archives staff can provide photocopies of printout listings to a patron along with a map on which to locate the purchase for a small photocopy fee. (Persons requesting land purchase information should address inquiries to: Information Service/Reference, Illinois State Archives, Archives Building, Springfield, IL 62756).

NATIONAL ARCHIVES–CHICAGO BRANCH LAND RECORDS

The National Archives–Chicago Branch has some records of land purchases which cover only the initial transfer from the Federal Government. The land records include those for Illinois, Indiana, Ohio, and Wisconsin and are in the form of cash receipts, certificates, and credit applications. Then name of the land office and certificate of purchase number is needed to access these records which are entered in the volumes by date.

BIBLIOGRAPHY

Eakle, Arlene, and Johni Cerny. *The Source: A Guidebook of American Genealogy*. Salt Lake City: Ancestry, Inc., 1984.

Greenwood, Val D. *The Researchers Guide to American Genealogy*. Baltimore: Genealogical Publishing Co., 1975.

Hammersmith, Mary P. "Those Menacing Metes and Bounds Surveys." *Genealogy* (October 1978). Indianapolis: Indiana Historical Society, Genealogy Section.

Oran, Daniel. *Law Dictionary for Non-Lawyers*. St. Paul, Minn.: West Publishing Co., 1975.

Smith, Clifford Neal. "Reconstructing Chicago's Early Land Records." *Illinois State Genealogical Society Quarterly* 5, No. 4 (Winter 1973): 217-21.

White, Elizabeth P. "Early Land-Entry Records." *Illinois State Genealogical Society Quarterly* 8, No. 1 (March 1976): 19-22.

White, Elizabeth P., and Henry G. R. White, "Land Records Revisited." *Illinois State Genealogical Society Quarterly* 10, No. 4 (Winter 1978): 181-93.

CHAPTER 14

Maps and Geographical Finding Aids

A solid knowledge of the geography of the locality is essential to the success of any genealogical or historical research project. Contemporary maps are usually good for starting out, but they will not resolve the problems encountered in locating Cook County and Chicago towns, communities, neighborhoods, and street names that have changed since the nineteenth century. Street numbering and ward boundaries have also changed, and villages were incorporated at different times, adding to the confusion.

A critical factor in Chicago research is the street numbering change which took place in 1909. Ignorance of that change can completely alter the results of research. A complete explanation of the numbering change is given later.

CURRENT MAPS

Chicago and suburban telephone directories have detailed sectional maps.

Cook County Clerk—Maps and Tax Redemption Department
County Building
118 North Clark Street
Chicago, IL 60602
(312-443-5640)

The county clerk's office has the most complete set of Cook County maps.

City of Chicago
Department of Public Works—Bureau of Maps and Plats
121 North LaSalle Street—Room 803
Chicago, IL 60602
(312-744-4996)

Besides all of the city maps, the Bureau of Maps and Plats has a street name change file and a cross-reference index to old and new house numbers.

City of Chicago—Municipal Reference Library
City Hall—Room 1004
121 North LaSalle Street
Chicago, IL 60602
(312-744-4992)

Chicago Convention and Tourism Bureau, Inc.
McCormick Place-on-the-Lake
Chicago, IL 60616
(312-225-5000)

Rand McNally Map Store
23 East Madison Street
Chicago, IL 60602-4497
(312-267-6868)

The store has a number of Cook County and Chicago maps and detailed atlases. Call or visit for map descriptions.

OLD MAPS AND GEOGRAPHICAL FINDING AIDS

Chicago Historical Society
Clark at North Avenue
Chicago, IL 60614
(312-642-4600)

The society has the most extensive collection of old Chicago and Cook County maps. A map notebook entitled "A Listing of Maps of the City of Chicago" is on the open-shelf in the society library. Maps in the notebook are arranged by the following subject order:

Date: 139 entries for the years 1812-1975
Prehistory and geology: 53 entries
Fire of 1871: 3 entries
World's Columbian Exposition: 34 entries
Annexation and accretion: 11 entries
Cemeteries: 8 entries
Fort Dearborn: 27 entries
General (political, postal, real estate, etc.): 45 entries
Communities (alphabetically by name, from Albany Park to Wood-
    lawn): 163 entries
Ward maps (1851-1975): 23 entries
Historical and pictorial maps: 47 entries
Industries: 46 entries

Maps of Individual Wards (showing election precincts): 12 pages
of entries (about 60 entries per page)
Institutions (schools, churches, hospitals, etc.)
Other subject headings include Parks, population and sociology,
portage, transportation, waterworks and sanitation.

Not included in the notebook, but of considerable importance, are
the Fire Insurance Maps for Chicago which are at the Chicago Historical Society. The Sanborn Map Company produced some 700,000 sheets
of detailed maps for 12,000 cities and towns in North America from 1867
to the present. These maps were used by insurance agents to determine hazards and risk in underwriting specific buildings. Each map is
produced on a large oversized sheet in pastel colors: olive drab for
adobe, pink for stone, blue for brick, yellow for wood, gray for iron.
Size, shape, and construction of homes, businesses, and farm buildings; locations of windows, doors, firewalls, roof types; widths and
names of streets; property boundaries; ditches, water mains, and sprin-
kling systems; and other details are clearly indicated. Individual residents do not appear on the maps by name, although specific addresses
are shown. Businesses appear by name. Once you find your ancestor
or subject of interest in the census or city directory, you can determine
precisely what house or business the family lived or worked in. The
Library of Congress also has a large collection of fire insurance maps.

CITY OF CHICAGO—OLD AND NEW NUMBERS

The new numbering plan passed by the City Council, 22 June 1908
to be in force and effect 1 September 1900, makes Madison Street from
Lake Michigan to the city limits on the west the base line for numbering all north and south streets and streets running in a northerly or
southerly direction. For east and west streets, the base line is State
Street from the southern city boundary to North Avenue, thence
extended by an imaginary line through Lincoln Park and Lake
Michigan.

Eight-hundred (800) numbers are assigned to each mile or 100 numbers to each one eighth mile, commencing with No. 1 at the north line
of Madison, etc. In like manner, the numbers on east and west streets
commence with No. 1 at the east line of State and run east to the lake,
and west to the city limits.

Previous to the 1909 numbering change, Chicago streets were
divided in a more confusing manner which used physical boundaries
such as the branches of the Chicago River to determine the numbering system. Moran's *Dictionary of Chicago* (1892), which is available at
the Chicago Municipal Library, provides a detailed explanation of the
old numbering. The Chicago Historical Society, the Chicago Municipal

Library, and the Chicago Public Library have guides which convert old and new street numbers.

STREET NAME CHANGES

Many Chicago streets and portions of streets have undergone name changes. Other streets have completely disappeared when expressways were built over them.

The Chicago Municipal Library has a street name file which gives the origins of Chicago street names, street name changes, and dates when street name changes took effect. Similarly, the Chicago Historical Society has a file and notebook with several thousand street name changes listed.

MAPS FOR CENSUS SEARCHING

The Newberry Library, the Chicago Public Library, and the National Archives—Chicago Branch all have some maps to aid in locating addresses in census years. Of these, the Newberry Library map collection is the most complete. (See chapter on Census Records.)

BIBLIOGRAPHY

Cummings, Kathleen Roy. *Architectural Records in Chicago*. Chicago: The Art Institute of Chicago, 1981.

Kirkham, E. Kay. *A Handy Guide to Record Searching in the Larger Cities of the United States*. Logan, Ut.: Everton Publishers, 1974. Includes an 1850-55 and an 1878 map and street guide for Chicago.

Sherwood, Arlyn. "Cartographic Materials for Genealogical Research: An Overview of Resources at the Illinois State Library." *Illinois Libraries* 68, No 4, (April 1986): 267-72.

CHAPTER 15

Military Records

I n July 1803, a detachment of United States infantry soldiers under the command of Capt. John Whistler and Lt. James Swearingen established Fort Dearborn at the mouth of the Chicago River. Thus began Chicago's recorded military history. Many of Cook County's earliest settlers were Revolutionary War veterans who had been anxious to own land and brought their families from the eastern states to settle here. From their very inception, Chicago and Cook County have contributed great numbers of men and women to serve in the armed forces, and this involvement has generated many useful records. Military personnel records often supply the most genealogically valuable information, and as with other federally created records, these records are generally more reliable than most other sources.

The term "military records" refers to any and all records of all branches of armed services including Army, Navy, Coast Guard, Air Force, and Marine Corps. These records fall into two general catagories: military service records and veteran's benefits. As with other groups of American records, there is little uniformity in military records. Though some indexes do exist, identifying persons who served from this heavily populated metropolitan area is more complicated. Most pre-World War I military service and related records are kept at the National Archives in Washington, D.C., and those from World War I and after are at the National Personnel Records Center in St. Louis, Missouri. Although these two facilities hold the bulk of military records, there are many microfilm and book publications available locally which can provide the necessary foundation to begin research for an individual's military history.

For detailed descriptions of military records, their content and use, the following general guides are suggested:

Eakle, Arlene and Cerny, Johni. *The Source: A Guidebook of American Genealogy.* Salt Lake City, Ut.: Ancestry Publishing Company, 1984.

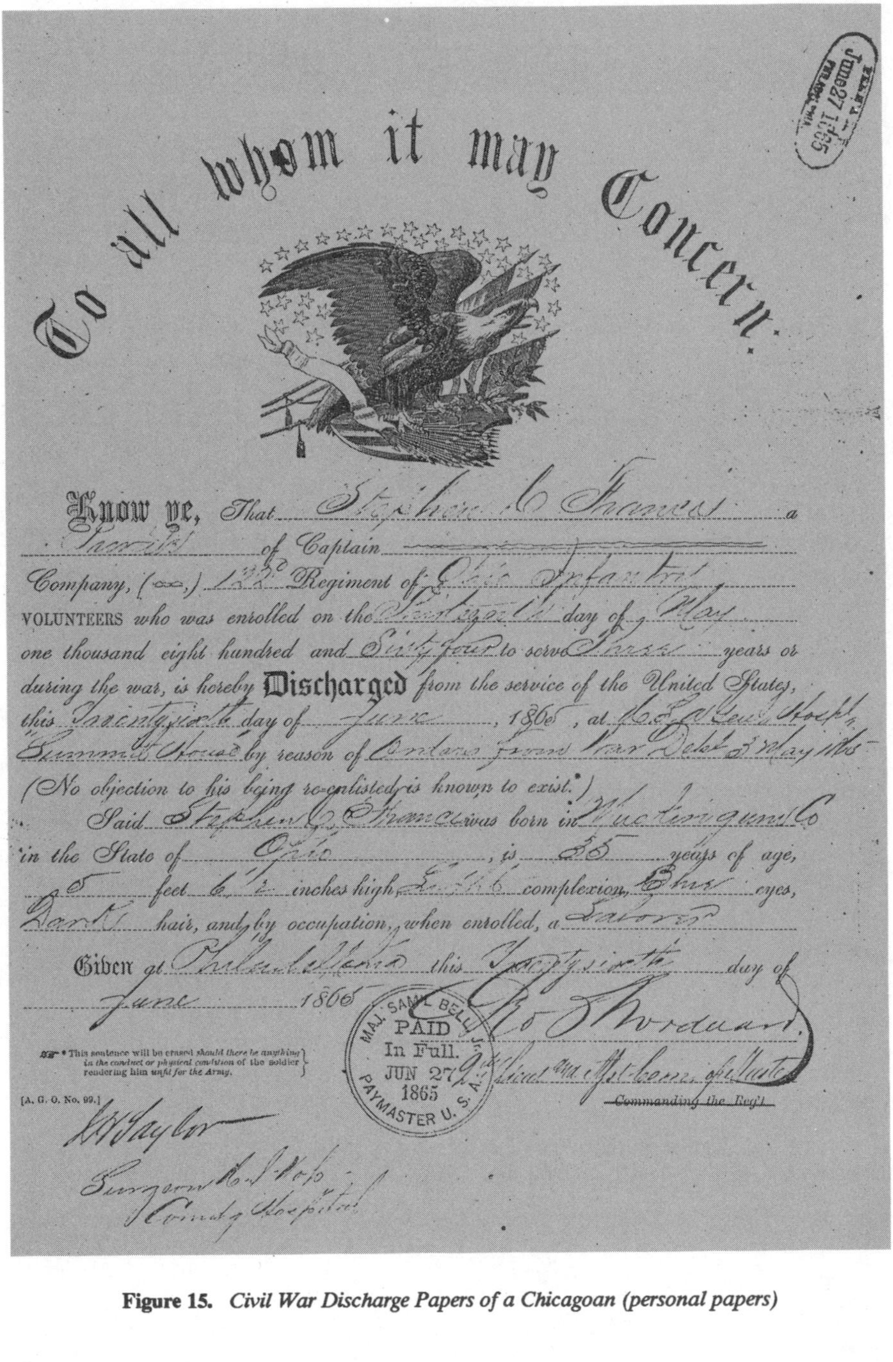

Figure 15. *Civil War Discharge Papers of a Chicagoan (personal papers)*

Greenwood, Val D. *The Researcher's Guide to American Genealogy.* Baltimore: Genealogical Publishing Co., Inc., 1975.

National Archives and Records Service. *Guide to Genealogical Research in the National Archives.* Washington, D.C.: National Archives Trust Fund Board, 1982.

National Archives and Records Administration. *Military Service Records: A Select Catalog of National Archives Microfilm Publications.* Washington, D.C.: National Archives Trust Fund Board, 1986.

MILITARY SERVICE AND PENSION RECORDS

Effective 1 April 1984, all requests for copies of military service records held by the National Archives, Washington, DC must be submitted on NATF Form 80. NARA will research the request, prepare copies of any records located, and hold the copies for three weeks or until payment is received, whichever is sooner. As soon as records are located and copied, the researcher will receive a bill and instructions for making a remittance. Researchers should also submit a separate NATF Form 80 for each pension, bounty-land, or compiled military service record desired. Copies of NATF Form 80 may be obtained by writing to Reference Services Branch (N–R), National Archives and Records Administration, Washington, DC 20408.

GENERAL MILITARY INFORMATION SOURCES FOR CHICAGO AND COOK COUNTY

Andreas, Alfred T. *History of Chicago.* 3 vols. Chicago: A.T. Andreas, 1884-86. Provides a good general history of Chicago military, especially for regiments that served during the Civil War.

_____. *History of Cook County, Illinois.* Chicago: A.T. Andreas, 1884. Good general history of military, but this volume encompasses all of Cook County.

REVOLUTIONARY WAR SOURCES

Revolutionary War pension and bounty-land-warrant application files, and compiled service records of soldiers who served in the American Army During the Revolutionary War, are available on microfilm at the National Archives–Chicago Branch.

DAR Directory–Illinois. Information is compiled by member's name. This source includes a veteran's index, but is difficult to use unless the submitting member's name is known. It is available at the Newberry Library and other area libraries.

DAR Patriot Index. 2 vols. (Washington, D.C.: by the Society, vol. 1, 1966; vol. 2, 1979). These volumes include name of the patriot, with available dates of birth, death, marriage (and to whom), residence, and type of service rendered. The set is available at the Newberry Library.

DAR Index of the Rolls of Honor. 4 vols., 1916-40 (Washington D.C.: by the Society, 4 in 2). These are also available at the Newberry Library.

Meyer, Virginia M. *Roster of Revolutionary War Soldiers and Widows Who Lived in Illinois Counties.* Chicago: the Author, 1962.

Neagles, James C. *Summer Soldiers: A Survey & Index of Revolutionary War Courts-Martial.* Salt Lake City: Ancestry, Inc., 1986.

Schweitzer, George K. *Revolutionary War Genealogy.* Knoxville, Tenn.: George K. Schweitzer, 1982.

WAR OF 1812

The index to compiled service records of volunteer soldiers who served during the War of 1812 is available at the National Archives, Chicago Branch, as is the set of War of 1812 Military Bounty Land Warrants, 1815-58.

Illinois Adjutant General. *Record of Services of Illinois Soldiers in the Black Hawk War, 1831-32, and in the Mexican War, 1846-48.* [With an appendix of the Illinois Militia, Rangers, and Riflemen in Protecting the Frontier from the Ravages of the Indians from 1810-13]. By Isaac H. Elliott, Adjutant General, Springfield, 1882.

"Illinois Index, Soldiers of 1812, Illinois." Compiled by Willard R. Matheny. (Springfield, 1947). Typescript in Newberry Library.

U.S. General Land Office. "Lands in Illinois to Soldiers of the Late War. (War of 1812)." 26th Cong., 1st sess., 1840. House Doc. 262.

Schweitzer, George K. *War of 1812 Genealogy.* Knoxville, Tenn.: George K. Schweitzer, 1982.

Walker, Homer A. *Illinois Pensioners List of the Revolution, 1812, and Indian Wars.* Washington, D.C.: (1955?) Contents include names of soldiers, widows, and heirs.

MEXICAN WAR

The index to compiled service records of volunteer soldiers who served during the Mexican War is available on microfilm at the National Archives-Chicago Branch.

CIVIL WAR

Index to compiled service records of volunteer Union soldiers who served in organizations from the State of Illinois is available on microfilm at the National Archives—Chicago Branch. The index gives soldier's name, rank, and unit in which he served. With this

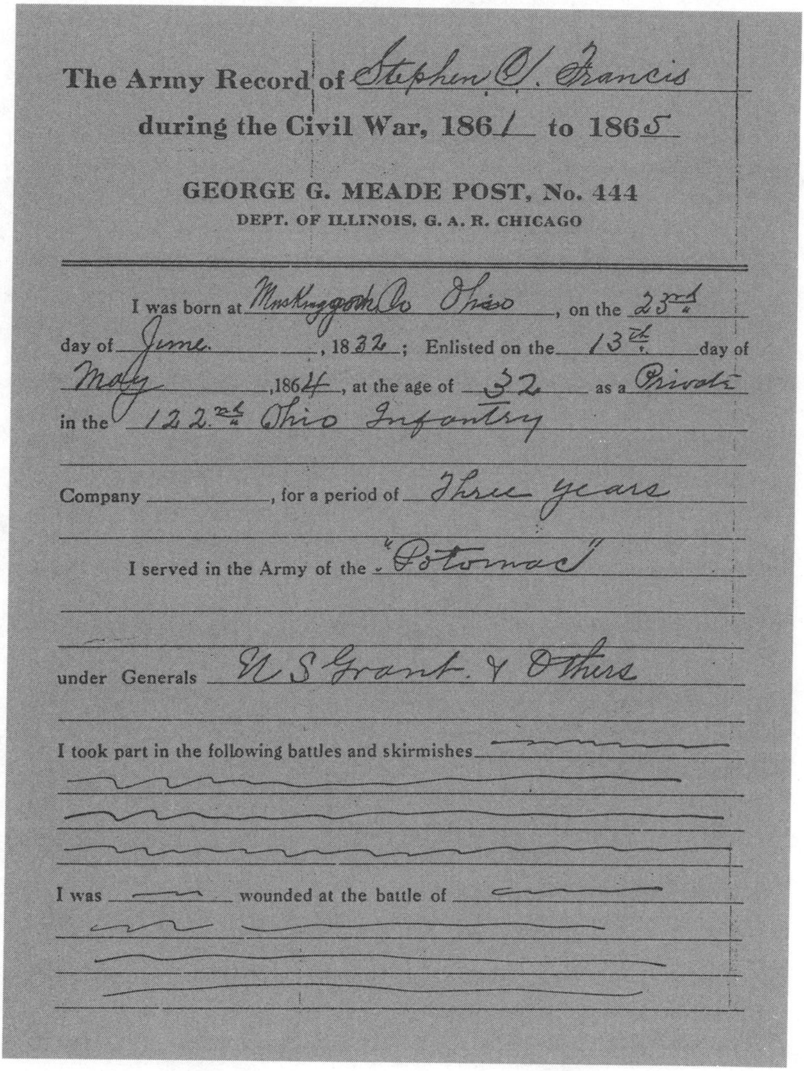

The Army Record of *Stephen C. Francis*

during the Civil War, 186*1* to 186*5*

GEORGE G. MEADE POST, No. 444
DEPT. OF ILLINOIS, G. A. R. CHICAGO

I was born at *Muskingum Co Ohio*, on the *23rd*
day of *June*, 18*32*; Enlisted on the *13th* day of
May, 186*4*, at the age of *32* as a *Private*
in the *122nd Ohio Infantry*

Company _____, for a period of *Three years*

I served in the Army of the *"Potomac"*

under Generals *U S Grant & Others*

I took part in the following battles and skirmishes _____

I was _____ wounded at the battle of _____

Figure 16. *Chicago G.A.R. Post Application (personal papers)*

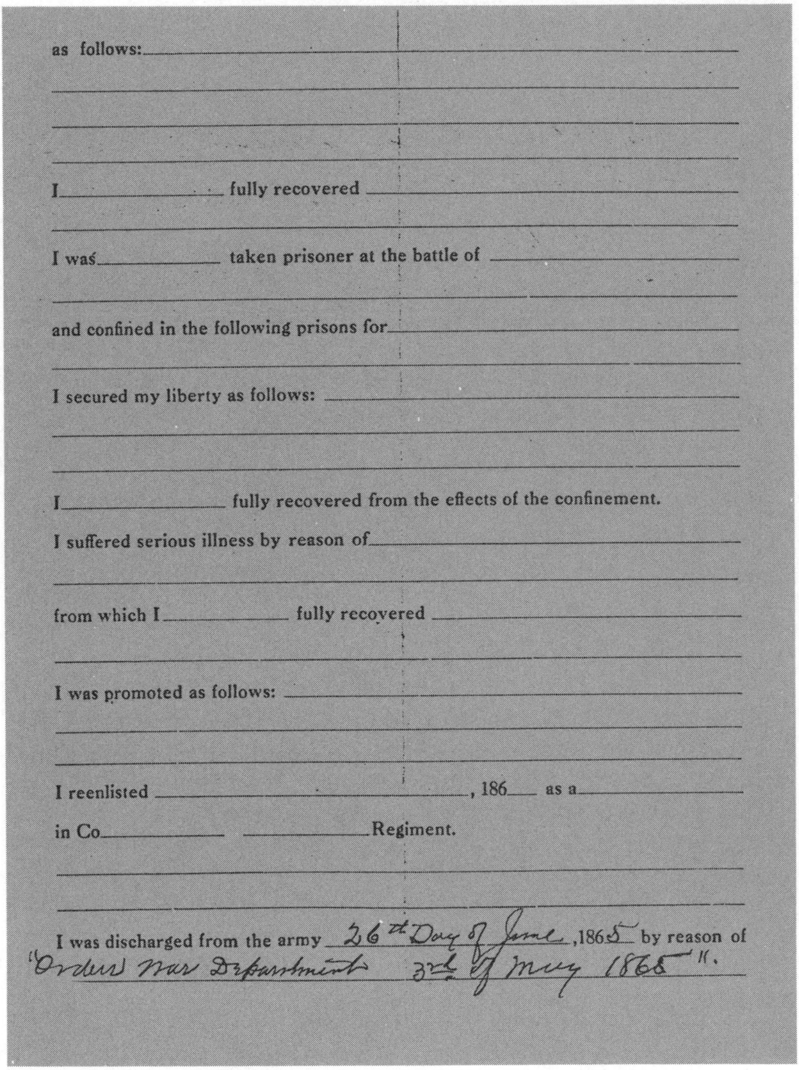

as follows:_____

_____

_____

I_____ fully recovered _____

I was_____ taken prisoner at the battle of _____

and confined in the following prisons for_____

I secured my liberty as follows: _____

_____

I_____ fully recovered from the effects of the confinement.

I suffered serious illness by reason of_____

from which I_____ fully recovered _____

I was promoted as follows: _____

_____

I reenlisted _____, 186___ as a_____

in Co_____ _____Regiment.

_____

I was discharged from the army *26ᵗʰ Day of June*,186*5* by reason of
Orders War Department   3ʳᵈ of May 1865 ".

Figure 17. *Chicago G.A.R. Post Application (personal papers)*

State any incidents or circumstances connected with your army life which might be of interest:

I was, detailed during most of my Service to Hospital duty at Camp. Distribution near Alexandria Va. where I nursed and cared for the sick wounded and suffering

Figure 18. *Chicago G.A.R. Post Application (personal papers)*

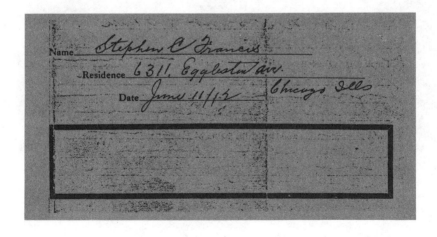

Figure 19. *Chicago G.A.R. Post Application (personal papers)*

information, additional military records may be obtained by writing to the National Archives in Washington.

Common names are frequently a special problem, especially when a state-wide index is being used. To narrow a search and identify individuals who served from Cook County, the following list may be useful:

Cook County Regiments—Infantry

12th Regiment-Companies A,D,I,K
19th Regiment-Companies A,D,E,G,I,K
23rd Regiment-Companies B,C,F,G,H,I,K
24th Regiment-Companies A,C,D,E,F,G,H
37th Regiment-Companies D,G,I
39th Regiment-Companies F,G
42nd Regiment-Companies B,C,E,F,G,H,I,K
43rd Regiment-Company D
44th Regiment-Companies E,K
51st Regiment-Companies A,K
55th Regiment-Company B
57th Regiment-Companies C,E,G
58th Regiment-Companies A,B,D,E,F,H
59th Regiment-Company K
65th Regiment-Companies D,H,K
67th Regiment-Companies B,D,E,G,I
69th Regiment-Companies C,E
72nd Regiment-Companies A,B,C,D,E,F,H,K
82nd Regiment-Companies A,B,C,D,E,G,H,I
88th Regiment-Companies A,B,C,D,E,F,G,H,I,K
89th Regiment-Companies C,K
90th Regiment-Companies C,E,F,G,H,I
113th Regiment-Companies A,C,E,G
127th Regiment-Companies B,G,H
132nd Regiment-Companies B,G,H,I,K
134th Regiment-Companies A,C,D,E,F,G,I,K
142nd Regiment-Company A
147th Regiment-Companies D,H
153rd Regiment-Companies F,G,I
156th Regiment-Companies A,C,E,I,K
Sturgis Rifles

Cook County Cavalry Units

4th Regiment-Companies A,B
9th Regiment-Companies D,F,L
10th Regiment-Company D

12th Regiment-Companies A,D,H,I
13th Regiment-Companies A,B,C,D,E
Thielman's Cavalry-Companies A,B
29th Regiment U.S. Colored-Companies B,C,D

Cook County Artillery

1st Regiment-Batteries A,B,E,H,L,M
2nd Regiment-Batteries L,M
Chicago Board of Trade Battery
Chicago Mercantile Battery

SELECTED BIBLIOGRAPHY

The Chicago Public Library. *One Hundred Important Additions to the Civil War and American History Research Collection.* Chicago: The Chicago Public Library, 1978. See Appendix C on Chicago Public Library — Cultural Center.

Chicago Public Library, Special Collections Division. *The Black Soldier in the Civil War.* Chicago: Chicago Public Library, 1986. Three page checklist and bibliography which is available from the Chicago Public Library.

Civil War Centennial Commission of Illinois. *Illinois Units in the Civil War.* Springfield, Ill.: State of Illinois, 1962.

Schweitzer, George K. *Civil War Genealogy.* Knoxville, Tenn.: George K. Schweitzer, 1982.

Szucs, Loretto D., Bobko, Kathryn, Stoddard, John, and Murdoch, Sharon, compilers. *List of Pensioners—Chicago & Cook County, Illinois—January 1, 1883.* Chicago: Chicago Genealogical Society, 1985. Most of the pensions are for Civil War service. The name of each pensioner is given, together with the cause for pension, the post office address, the rate of pension per month, and the date of the original allowance. The publication is available from the Chicago Genealogical Society.

CIVIL WAR DRAFT RECORDS

In 1863, the federal draft system was created. Men between the ages of twenty-five and forty, both citizens and aliens who had declared their intent to naturalize, were eligible for the Civil War draft. Males who were twenty to thirty-five and unmarried were required to serve unless physically disabled. Males who were seventeen to twenty could serve with the permission of a parent or guardian. The draft applied to men residing in the United States under Union control. The lists which were created are arranged by state, then by county. To obtain records, it is necessary to provide the name of the individual, the state from which he served, the county and the congressional district for the county in which a man lived, the city (including the ward number which can sometimes be found by using the 1860 census) or the town name if it is outside of Chicago. Requests must be submitted to: Navy and Old Army Branch, National Archives and Records Administration, Washington, DC 20408. The Congressional district number can be obtained by consulting the *Congressional Directory for the Second Session of the 38th Congress of the U.S.* (Washington, D.C.: for the Joint Houses of Congress, 1865).

THE CIVIL WAR AND AMERICAN HISTORY RESEARCH COLLECTION

Special Collections Division
The Chicago Public Library
78 East Washington Street
Chicago, IL 60602
(312-269-2926)

The Civil War and American History Research Collection is a major resource of the special collections division. The collection was formally established in 1975 with the assistance of the Chicago Civil War Round Table. The Grand Army of the Republic research material was the basis of the collection and included a rich variety of exhibit and research materials: manuscripts, documents, broadsides, photographs, sheet music, published reminiscences, official records, and other contemporary and retrospective accounts of the Civil War. The Grand Army of the Republic collections also included: firearms, swords, military accessories, military uniforms, medical and musical instruments. This collection presents a very personal look at the Civil War: letters from young recruits to their families, diaries and personal narratives. Portions of the Civil War and American History Research Collection are on display twice a year in a rotating permanent exhibition entitled "A Nation Divided: The War Between the States, 1861-1865."

WORLD WAR I SELECTIVE SERVICE RECORDS

When the United States became involved in World War I in 1917, all males between the ages of eighteen and forty-five were required to register for the draft. More than 24 million of these selective service records are on file at the National Archives—Atlanta Branch. They are filed by state and then by draft board. To obtain a copy of the selective service records, you must supply the full name of the individual and the city or county in which they were living at the time of registration. Street addresses (available from the 1917 Chicago Directory) must also be supplied for those who were resident of the city. Requests may be made to National Archives—Atlanta Branch, 1557 St. Joseph Avenue, East Point , GA 30344. A check for $5.00 made out to the National

Archives Trust Fund must accompany each request. The Illinois State Archives also has a set of these Draft registrations.

ILLINOIS SOLDIERS AND SAILORS HOME

The home at Quincy was established in 1885 by an act of the general assembly to provide subsistence and a home for honorably discharged and disabled veterans of the Mexican and Civil Wars. In later years, Illinois veterans of all wars became eligible for admission, and beginning in 1903 wives of veterans could also be admitted. These records have been indexed and are available in book form as well as at the Illinois State Archives. The book gives the individual's name, registry number, rank, company regiment, length of service, amount of pension, age, disability, county admitted from, birthplace, occupation, marital status, literacy, date of admission, and status in some cases. Also included is information on getting copies of the soldier's complete file.

Volkel, Lowell M. *Illinois Soldiers and Sailors Home at Quincy 1887-1898.* Indianapolis: by the author, 1980.

_____. *Illinois Soldiers and Sailors Home at Quincy, 1898-1908.* Utica, Ky.: McDowell Pulications, 1985.

_____. "Illinois Soldiers and Sailors Home at Quincy, 1908-1910." *Illinois State Genealogical Society Quarterly* (Summer and Fall 1985).

AMERICAN BATTLE MONUMENTS COMMISSION

Upon request, the American Battle Monuments Commission, Washington, DC 20314 will research its files, those of the Department of the Army, the Veteran's Administration, and the Department of the Interior for the place of permanent interment of World War I and World War II dead. It will also provide information concerning the place of commemoration of the missing in action and the lost or buried at sea of World War I, World War II, Korea, or Vietnam. Additionally, the commission provides relatives upon request with a photograph of the gravesite in the commission cemetery, or the section of the Tablets of the Missing where an individual is commemorated by name mounted on a color lithograph of the cemetery or memorial concerned. A booklet describing the cemetery or memorial in detail accompanies the lithograph.

ILLINOIS SELECTIVE SERVICE 1940-47

Kleber, Victor. *Selective Service in Illinois 1940-1947.* Springfield: State of Illinois, (1949?).

A complete history of the operation of the Selective Service System in Illinois from its inception on 16 September 1940 to its termination 31 March 1947. The volume includes a list of individuals serving on each of the local boards in Illinois with several hundred from Chicago and Cook County. A copy is available at the National Archives – Chicago Branch.

CHAPTER 16

Naturalization Records

Although alien naturalization records are considered a valuable source of information, it should be noted that these records vary greatly in content. Generally speaking, the very early naturalizations contain sparse information that is of genealogical value. In most pre-nineteenth-century documents only the name of the individual, his native country, and the date of the naturalization are given. Rarely will the town of origin be supplied. It was not until 1906, when naturalization laws became uniform, that one can expect to find more personal details in these documents. Those immigrants who could write left their descendants a signature to remember them by, while the illiterate could only leave their mark.

Some early papers, however, can be goldmines of information for the genealogist. During certain early periods and in certain courts, it was required that the applicant give his age, the town of his birth, the date of emigration, the port from which he sailed and where he arrived in this country. In most papers of intent, places of residence, and dates were given that would enable the genealogist to chart the immigrant's progress across this country to the final place of residency and citizenship. Often included with the final oath papers, a Declaration of Intent will be found which shows that the applicant had begun the proceedings in one state and completed the requirements when final residency was established in another state.

Naturalization records can sometimes serve as a key to locating a military service file. Some final papers will contain a description of the veteran, his state, and the regiment in which he served. Although this is what all genealogists would like to find, many records contain far less information. A great number of people applying for citizenship were listed as having arrived from Great Britain and Ireland, and that, in fact, could mean that he emigrated from England, Ireland or any British Colony or that he had merely resided in Canada before entering this country. Prussia is commonly listed as the place of origin in naturalization records. Little help comes from this vague locality identification, and the disappointed researcher is left with the problem of narrowing the search to the ancestor's exact town of origin within what was then Prussia.

The first step in determining whether to search for naturalization records is to be reasonably sure that the individual in question was a naturalized citizen. While the 1870 census may lend a clue to citizenship, the census records for 1900 through 1930 show the year of immigration, and the 1920 schedules include the year of naturalization. The 1900 and 1910 schedules reveal only whether or not individuals were naturalized, but no date is given in these years.

The Declaration of Intention or "first papers" were frequently completed and filed with a court soon after immigration. Logical places to look for many of those documents would be in port cities. After the required length of stay in America (usually five years), the immigrant was required once more to go into a court and file his "final papers." These consisted of a petition for citizenship with the required affidavits. Included was a witnessed statement that he had resided in this country and state for the required period of time. Part of this petition was an oath of allegiance to the Constitution of the United States. The Certificate of Naturalization was then issued after the court had satisfied itself that legal requirements had been met. This certificate then became a court record and may be the only document left to the searcher when other documents may have been lost or destroyed. Some courts did retain a "stub" or receipt of certificate.

Certain groups of people became naturalized without the necessity of filing a declaration of intention. Wives and children of naturalized males generally became citizens automatically until 1906. There were provisions, though, for later naturalization of persons who arrived in this country while still a minor. Those who served in the United States military forces also could become citizens after an honorable discharge without the need to file a declaration of intention in advance. An act of 22 September 1922 removed marriage as a cause for citizenship. A married woman now had to be naturalized on her own.

From the first naturalization in this country in 1673, the process of naturalization is quite cumbersome and records have suffered somewhat because of overlapping jurisdictions.

The records of naturalization in the U.S. District Courts are mostly still in the courts but are, in some cases, in the custody of various federal record centers. The records of naturalizations in the state courts are still in the court's custody almost without exception. County courts, criminal courts and every other existing court may need to be searched for naturalizations, and in some cases these records have been turned over to libraries, historical societies, or warehouses for storage.

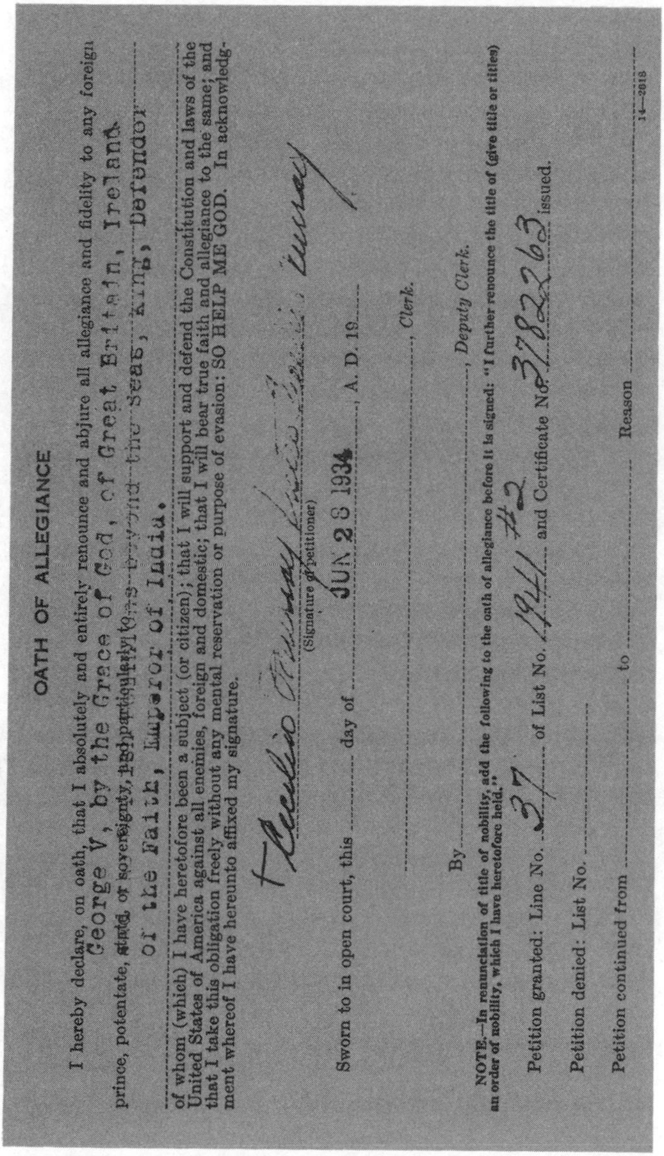

OATH OF ALLEGIANCE

I hereby declare, on oath, that I absolutely and entirely renounce and abjure all allegiance and fidelity to any foreign prince, potentate, state, or sovereignty, and particularly to George V, by the Grace of God, of Great Britain, Ireland and the British Dominions beyond the Seas, King, Defender of the Faith, Emperor of India.

of whom (which) I have heretofore been a subject (or citizen); that I will support and defend the Constitution and laws of the United States of America against all enemies, foreign and domestic; that I will bear true faith and allegiance to the same; and that I take this obligation freely without any mental reservation or purpose of evasion: SO HELP ME GOD. In acknowledgment whereof I have hereunto affixed my signature.

_____
(Signature of petitioner)

Sworn to in open court, this _____ day of _____ JUN 28 1934 _____ A. D. 19____

_____, Clerk.

By _____, Deputy Clerk.

NOTE.—In renunciation of title of nobility, add the following to the oath of allegiance before it is signed: "I further renounce the title of (give title or titles) an order of nobility, which I have heretofore held."

Petition granted: Line No. 37 of List No. 1941 #2 and Certificate No. 3782263 issued.

Petition denied: List No. _____

Petition continued from _____ to _____ Reason _____

14—2818

Figure 20. *Post 1906 Naturalization Oath (courtesy National Archives—Chicago Branch)*

TRIPLICATE   No. 86925

UNITED STATES OF AMERICA

DECLARATION OF INTENTION
(Invalid for all purposes seven years after the date hereof)

UNITED STATES OF AMERICA   In the .... DISTRICT .... Court

NORTHERN DISTRICT OF ILLINOIS } ss: THE UNITED STATES at CHICAGO

I, CECELIA MURRAY - - Sister Cecelia Murray

now residing at ____6337 Harvard Avenue, Chicago, Illinois,____
occupation ____nun____, aged ____51____ years, do declare on oath that my personal description is:
Sex __female__, color __white__, complexion __fair__, color of eyes __grey__
color of hair __brown__, height __5__ feet __1__ inches; weight __130__ pounds; visible distinctive marks
____none.____

race ____Irish____; nationality ____British____
I was born in ____Brewers Mills, Canada,____ on ____May 16, 1880____
I am __not__ married. The name of my wife or husband is _____;
we were married on _____ at _____; she or he was
born at _____ on _____, entered the United States
at _____ on _____, for permanent residence therein, and now
resides at _____. I have _____ children, and the name, date and place of birth,
and place of residence of each of said children are as follows:

_____

I have __not__ heretofore made a declaration of intention: Number _____, on _____
at _____ (Name of court)
my last foreign residence was ____Kingston, Canada,____
I emigrated to the United States of America from ____Kingston, Canada,____
my lawful entry for permanent residence in the United States was at ____Port Huron, Michigan,____
under the name of ____Sister Cecelia Murray____, on ____July 15, 1908____
on the vessel ____G. T. RR____
I will, before being admitted to citizenship, renounce forever all allegiance and
fidelity to any foreign prince, potentate, state, or sovereignty, and particularly,
by name, to the prince, potentate, state, or sovereignty of which I may be at the
time of admission a citizen or subject; I am not an anarchist; I am not a
polygamist nor a believer in the practice of polygamy; and it is my intention in
good faith to become a citizen of the United States of America and to reside
permanently therein; and I certify that the photograph affixed to the duplicate
and triplicate hereof is a likeness of me: So HELP ME GOD.

X Cecelia Murray, Sister Cecelia Murray

Subscribed and sworn to before me in the office of the Clerk of said Court,
at __Chicago, Illinois__ this __26__ day of __Oct.__
anno Domini 19__31__. Certification No. __11 30394__ from the Commissioner of Naturalization showing the lawful entry of the declarant for permanent
residence on the date stated above, has been received by me. The photograph
affixed to the duplicate and triplicate hereof is a likeness of the declarant.

Sister (Miss) Cecelia Murray

[SEAL]

Form 2202-L-A.
U. S. DEPARTMENT OF LABOR
NATURALIZATION SERVICE

Charles M. Bates,
Clerk of the U. S. District Court.
By _____ Deputy Clerk.

Figure 21. *Post 1906 Declaration of Intention (courtesy National Archives—Chicago Branch)*

In a case where the citizen who had been naturalized, or the alien who was seeking naturalization, filed a homestead claim or applied for a passport, these applications are normally in the U.S. National Archives. These records will provide the name of the court in which the naturalization took place.

Between 1777 and 1790, each state handled its own naturalization laws. The United States established its first law in the matter in 1790. Through the years and in different jurisdictions the laws changed back and forth. Political issues and vote fraud forced a stricter law in 1906. After this time valuable genealogical information can be found in applications.

As with other Cook County records, early naturalizations were destroyed in the Chicago Fire of 1871. The existing records begin shortly after this and have been continuously maintained from November 1871 until December 1929 when the local courts lost jurisdiction. Naturalization, and a great number of naturalization records after this date to the present are kept by the National Archives—Chicago Branch, 7358 South Pulaski Road, Chicago, IL 60629, (312-581-7816).

The Chicago Branch also has the Soundex Index for naturalizations for this area. The index covers the time period from 1871 to 1950, and although the vast majority of the records are for Cook County, some are for other states. Originally, this area which was known as Immigration and Naturalization Services District #9, served parts of Illinois, Indiana, Iowa, and Wisconsin as well as Cook County. The Genealogical Society of Utah completed the microfilming of the Naturalization Soundex Index in May 1986.

Other Chicago branch acquisitions are the county, superior, circuit, and criminal court naturalizations from Cook County. These are dexagraph (negative photostat) copies of the original records from 1871 to 1906. A distinct advantage of the branch is that records may be photocopied.

Some late naturalizations for Cook County are still in the possession of the circuit court. For a search of those records, contact:

Mr. Robert A. Williams, Supervisor
Law Division, Circuit Court of Cook County Room 1201,
Richard J. Daley Center
50 West Washington
Chicago, IL 60602
(312-443-7935)

The Genealogical Society of Utah has microfilmed naturalizations which are still under the jurisdiction of the Cook County Courts. See Court Records and Research chapter for a more detailed listing of the naturalizations which have been microfilmed.

The Chicago Branch also has some naturalizations for the northern, eastern, and southern districts of Indiana; the eastern and western districts of Michigan; the northern and southern districts of Ohio; and the western district of Wisconsin (although most of this collection was recalled to Wisconsin).

The circuit and district courts for the eastern district of Michigan (Detroit) have been indexed for the years 1837-1903, and these original indexes as well as the documents are at the Chicago branch.

UNITED STATES DISTRICT COURT–CHICAGO
Naturalizations
Room 2062
219 South Dearborn
Chicago, IL 60604
(312-435-5697)

The U.S. District Court–Chicago maintains an index to all naturalizations which took place in the court from 1871 to the present. Additionally, access to any naturalization which took place after 1959 in the U.S. District Court must be obtained from this address.

CALUMET CITY COURT NATURALIZATION INDEX

Nine volumes of Calumet City naturalizations which were temporarily stored in a local library basement were recently donated to the South Suburban Genealogical Society in South Holland. The records, which date from about 1906-52, were indexed by Joan Alguire. Although the great majority of the immigrants represented in this file are of Italian and Polish origin, many other nationalities are included.

It is interesting to note that most of the Declarations of Intention of the individuals included in the collection were taken out in other states and cities (presumably where the immigrants first settled) and the final papers were completed in the Calumet City Court.

Index cards which were compiled from the original documents include: name of the immigrant, exact date, and place of birth, occupation, port of departure, vessel name, last foreign residence, port of entry in the U.S., date of entry in the U.S., marital status, and names of spouse and children.

The alphabetically arranged card index and the original papers are available for use at the South Suburban Genealogical and Historical Society library:

South Suburban Genealogical and Historical Society
P.O. Box 96
Roosevelt Community Center
161st Place and Louis Avenue
South Holland, IL 60473
(312-333-9474)

CHICAGO HEIGHTS NATURALIZATIONS

Original naturalization records for nearly four thousand individuals who completed citizenship requirements in Chicago Heights are presently held by the Chicago Heights Public Library. The Declaration of Intention and Petition books which cover the time period between 1907 and 1954 have been indexed by the South Suburban Genealogical Society. The "Index to the Declarations of Intention" has been published in the society's quarterly publication *Where the Trails Cross*. The Index to Declarations for individuals whose names begin with letters A-O appear in Vol. 10:2 (Winter 1980): 66-93. Letters O-Z appear in Vol. 10:3 and 4 (Spring/Summer 1980): 168-83. The Index to Chicago Heights Naturalization Petitions appears in *Where the Trails Cross*, Letters A-MAL in Vol. 11:1 (Fall 1980). Letters MAL-Z in Vol. 11:2 (Winter 1980).

The Chicago Heights Public Library
15th Street and Chicago Road
Chicago Heights, IL 60411
(312-754-0323)

Hours: Monday-Friday 9:00 a.m.—9:00 p.m.
Saturday 9:00 a.m.—5:00 p.m.
Sunday (Sept.—May) 1:00 p.m.—5:00 p.m.

Photocopies of naturalization records may be made for a very nominal fee. The library will provide copies by mail for a fee of $2.00 per name searched, and a large, stamped, self-addressed envelope. Make checks payable to Chicago Heights Public Library.

BIBLIOGRAPHY

Eakle, Arlene and Cerny, Johni. *The Source: A Guidebook of American Genealogy*. Salt Lake City: Ancestry Publishing Company, 1984.

Neagles, James C., and Lila Lee. *Locating Your Immigrant Ancestor*. Logan, Ut.: Evertons, 1975.

Newman, John J. *American Naturalization Processes and Procedures 1790-1985*. Indianapolis, Ind.: Family History Section—The Indiana Historical Society, 1985.

Szucs, Loretto Dennis. "Naturalization Records of the Circuit Court of Eastern Michigan 1824-1906," *Detroit Society for Genealogical Research Magazine* 49 No. 1 (Fall 1985); Vol. 49, No. 2 (Winter 1985); and Vol. 49 No. 3 (Spring 1986).

_____. "Naturalization Records of the District Court of Eastern Michigan, Detroit," *Detroit Society for Genealogical Research Magazine* 46, No. 1 (Fall 1982); and Vol. 46, No. 2 (Winter 1982).

CHAPTER 17

Newspapers

The researcher who ignores newspapers misses a great mass of valuable material. They are an excellent source for family and local history, giving accounts of events from a contemporary point of view. The newspaper takes on added importance when official public records have been destroyed as they were in the Great Chicago Fire of 1871. They became essential in reconstructing the history of Chicago. A great number of newspapers have come and gone, and some collections are missing or not accessible. However, many now-defunct papers as well as contemporary publications have been microfilmed and are available as an important resource. The following list includes the most important collections for the Cook County area, but it is sometimes necessary to seek out the needed issues in specialized libraries, museums, or at the original publishing company.

All of the libraries included in this listing have additional newspaper holdings which extend to other interests and geographical areas. The Chicago Public Library Newspapers and General Periodicals Center, for example, has a wide selection of contemporary American, ethnic, and foreign newspapers. Only the major indexes and newspaper collections considered relevant to research in the Cook County area are mentioned here.

NEWSPAPERS AT THE CHICAGO HISTORICAL SOCIETY

Aftonbladet Skandia 9/17/1890−6/1/1891
(Chicago) *American* 7/17/1840−10/19/1842
Arlington Heights Herald 9/21/1961−10/12/1961
Broad Ax 8/31/1895−9/10/1927
Centennial of the North-Western Territory 11/1793−6/1796
Citizen 1/14/1882−5/16/1914
Clipper 4/9/1870−3/24/1877; 12/31/1881−1/6/1883; 4/1884-10/1884;
    4/1892−3/9/1893
Conservator 1882-83; 1886
Defender 1909 to the present

(Weekly Chicago) *Democrat* 11/26/1833–12/14/1842; 1/25/1843–
    12/30/1845; 1/5/1847–11/2/1847; 1/4/1848–7/27/1861
(Chicago Daily) *Democrat* 2/27/1840–1/18/1842; 6/30/1847–12/25/1852;
    loose issues 1853-55; 2/26/1856–12/27/1856; 3/11/1857–7/24/1861
Egyptian Republican 1/1939–12/1948
(Chicago) *Express* 8/2/1881–11/29/1881; 12/13/1881–12/27/1881;
    1882-1886 (lacking 9/5, 9/12,and 9/19/1885); 12/13/1890–12/20/1890;
    1891; 1/2/1892–1/30/1892
Faderneslandet 1/4/1879–1/31/1880
Fiaccola La 9/5/1912–2/10/1921
Fosterlandet 11/4/1891–9/25/1907
Framat 1/8/1890–10/28/1891
Gem of the Prairies 5/29/1844–1852
Genius of Universal Emancipation 2/26/1839–9/13/1839
Hemfrid 11/21/1889–12/29/1892
Chicago Herald 3/1/1859–10/21/1859; 5/10/1881–12/31/1889;
    5/1/1893–2/28/1901; 4/1901–12/1932
Hyde Park Herald 4/29/1882–8/7/1886; 1/5/1884–6/28/1884;
    8/14/1886–3/29/1889; 9/6/1918–12/28/1934; 4/16/1936–12/27/1940;
    2/2/1941–4/15/1953
Illinois Gazette 9/25/1819–1830 (incomplete)
Illinois State Journal 1/2/1856–6/30/1860
Illinois Swede & Nya Verlden 4/24/1869–1/5/1874
Inter-Ocean 3/27/1872–5/7/1914
L' Italia 4/28/1886–5/27/1889; 1/1/1901–12/25/1909; 1/1/1910–12/29/1918
(Chicago Daily and Chicago Evening) *Journal* 8/31/1844- -4/21/1845;
    9/30/1845–12/31/1845; 6-9 and 11-12/1847; 1/1848–12/1849;
    1/3/1853–6/27/1854; 10/2/1854–3/31/1855; 1/3/1856–3/31/1856;
    10/1/1856–6/30/1857; 1/2/1858–9/1867; 7/1/1868–12/31/1897;
    7/1/1898–12/30/1916; 6/1/1921–8/21/1929
Labor Enquirer 2/23/1887–8/18/1888
(Chicago) *Labor News* 5/1919–3/2/1923
Liberator 9/3/1905–4/15/1906
Little Fort Porcupine and Lake County Visitor 3/4/1845–10/2/1847
Chicago Evening Mail 7/1/1885–12/1895
Messaggiere Italiano Dell 'Ouest 10/1/1869–2/10/1869
Mormon newspapers (Illinois)–No dates given
(Chicago Daily) *News* 12/1/1875–3/4/1978
North Shore News 9/20/1902–7/7/1911
(Chicago Evening) *Post* 4/29/1890–10/29/1932
Il Proletario 1905–8/1921
Republican 1/1/1916–10/21/1922
Rights of Labor 1886-93
Sentinel 11/15/1883–12/6/1883; 12/20/1883–12/27/1883; 1/84–10/1884

Skandia 6/11/1890—6/24/1891
(Chicago) *Socialist* 3/11/1899—4/6/1907
Sporting and Theatrical Journal 3/1/1884—9/20/1884; 6/20/1885
Steel Labor 1936-41
(Chicago) *Sun* 5/2/1884—3/21/1909; 12/4/1941—1/31/1948
(Chicago) *Sun Times* 2/1/1948 to present
Svenska Arbetaren 12/30/1882—11/1/1884
Svenska Nyheter 10/1/1901—6/26/1906
Svenska Tribunen 9/20/1877—12/26/1889
Svenska Varlden 3/11/1904—2/28/1908
(Weekly Chicago and Daily Chicago) *Times* 1/16/1855—7/20/1859;
    8/20/1857—6/30/1858; 10/1/1858—12/1858; 4/1/1859—3/31/1860;
    3/9/1861—12/31/1861; 1/1/1871—12/1894
(Chicago) *Tribune* 4/23/1849—7/13/1853; 9/1/1853—9/30/1854;
    1/11/1855—9/20/1856; 1/7/1857 to the present
Watchman of the Prairies 8/10/1847—2/22/1853
Western Citizen 7/26/1842—7/19/1855
Western Herald 4/1/1846—8/1/1849
Western Pioneer and Baptist Standard Bearer 7/1835—12/13/1838
(Chicago) *Whip* 6/24/1919—12/30/1922
Woodlawn Booster 7/13/1932—12/30/1959
Worker's Digest 9/27/1935—9/25/1936
(Chicago Evening) *World* 1906—10/25/1907; 1908-12

NEWSPAPERS AT THE CHICAGO PUBLIC LIBRARY

Chicago American, 1950-69
Chicago Daily American 4/1839; 1/1840—4/1840; 1841-42
Chicago Daily News 1876-1978
Chicago Daily Times 1929-48
Chicago Defender (Daily edition) 1956—
Chicago Defender (Weekly edition) 1909—
Chicago Democrat 1833-39
Chicago Democratic Press 1852-58
Chicago Evening Post 1890-1932
Chicago Express 10/1842—9/1843
Chicago Foreign Language Press Survey (approx.) 1861-1938
Chicago Herald 1914-18; 5/1893—3/1895
Chicago Herald-American 1939-69
Chicago Herald and Examiner 1919-38
Chicago Inter-Ocean 1872-1914
Chicago Journal 1846-1929
Chicago Mail 1885-95
Chicago Maroon 7/1970—6/1971
Chicago Reader October 1971—

Chicago Record 1881-1901
Chicago Record-Herald 1901-14
Chicago Sun 12/1941–1/1948
Chicago Sun Times 1855-94
Chicago Times Herald 1895-1901
Chicago Today 4/1969–10/1974
Chicago Tribune 1849–

NEWSPAPER INDEXES AND NEWSPAPER-RELATED SOURCES AT THE CHICAGO PUBLIC LIBRARY

CURRENT NEWSPAPER DIRECTORIES

Ayer Directory of Publications. Philadelphia: Ayer Press. (Annual)
National Directory of Weekly Newspapers. New York: American Newspaper Representatives, Inc. (Annual)

UNION LISTS OF NEWSPAPERS

Newspapers in Microform 1948-1972. 2 vols. Washington: Library of Congress, 1973.
Gregory, Winifred, ed. *American Newspapers 1821-1936.* New York: Reprint Corp., 1967.
Brigham. Clarence S. *History and Bibliography of American Newspapers 1690-1820.* Westport, Conn.: Greenwood Press, 1976.

NEWSPAPER INDEXES, 1972–

Newspaper Index. Wooster, Oh.: Bell & Howell.

Includes indexing for the *Chicago Tribune, The Los Angeles Times, The Times-Picayune* (New Orleans), and *The Washington Post.*

Bell & Howell's Newspaper Index to the Chicago Sun-Times. 1979–. Wooster, Oh.: Bell & Howell.

NEWSPAPER INDEXES, PRE-1972

Index. Chicago Democratic Press, 1855
Index. Chicago Record-Herald, 1904-12
Index. New York Times, New York: New York Times Co., 1851
Palmer's Index to The Times Newspaper. (London): 1790-1905. Vadus Kraus Reprint Ltd.
Official Index to The Times (London). 1906–; London: The Times Publishing Co.

MISCELLANEOUS NEWSPAPER INDEXING

Obituaries Index New York Times, 1858-1968. New York: New York Times Co. 1970.
Personal Name Index to the New York Times Index 1851-1974. Succasunna, N.J.: Roxbury Data Interface.

CHICAGO MUNICIPAL LIBRARY

The Library has copies of the *Chicago Tribune* only from 1972, at which time the index for that newspaper began.

NEWSPAPERS AT THE NEWBERRY LIBRARY

Advance 1876-89
Chicago Arbeiter Zeitung 5/1879–12/1889
Chicago Daily Democratic Press 1855 Index
Chicago Daily News 1/1879–12/1935
Chicago Daily News (Morning Edition) 3/21/1881–3/1901 *Chicago Evening Post* 6/15/1894
Chicago Evening Post (Friday Literature Review) 3/1909– 2/28/1913
Chicago Journal (also titled *Chicago Evening Journal*) 1854-1859 (Film available at Chicago Historical Society; bound volumes in Special Collections)
Chicago Overseas Tribune 1943-46
The Chicago Record (title varies) 3/21/1881–3/27/1901
Chicago Republican 6/30/1865–3/23/1872
Chicago Sun Book Week 11/1942–9/1947
Chicago Times (also titled *Chicago Daily Times*) 1857-84 Film available at Chicago Historical Society; bound volumes in Special Collections
Chicago Tribune 1876-84; 2-3/1914; 1928-39.
Chicago Tribune 1940-64
Chicago Tribune Book World 9/1967–12/1970, Indexes
Chicago Weekly Journal 1878-94
Chicagoer Arbeiter Zeitung 5/1879–12/1889
Die Freie Presse 1872-98
Illustrated Graphic News 1885-87
Illinois Staats-Zeitung 1861-1901
Inter-Ocean 1/1880–5/7/1914 (ended)
Ipavia Independent 1896-98 (missing 11/4/1896; 11/11/1896; 11/18/1896; 2/10/1897–2/17/1897; 3/3/1897– 3/3/1897; and 8/25/1897)
Lockport Telegraph 5/6–11/6/1850
Der Volksfreund 6/19–9/8/1878; 8/14–8/28/1879.
Weekly Chicago Times 1/16/1855–7/20/1859

COLLEGE AND UNIVERSITY NEWSPAPER COLLECTIONS

All of the area colleges and universities have some kind of newspaper collection and most have microfilm copies of the *Chicago Tribune* and the *New York Times*. In addition to the major dailies, institutional libraries generally have special collections which often include smaller local newspapers serving the community in which the school is located. The following list is offered as an example.

GOVERNORS STATE UNIVERSITY NEWSPAPER HOLDINGS
Governors State University
Park Forest South, IL 60466
(312-534-5000)

Billboard 1894-1940
Chicago Daily News 1971-73
Chicago Defender (City Edition) 1909-67
Chicago Defender 1921-67
Chicago Sun Times 1971 –
Chicago Today 1971-74
Chicago Tribune 1849 –
Christian Science Monitor 1908 –
The Era 1/1851 – 9/1939
Illinois State Journal 1971-73
London Times 1900-74
London Times Educational Supplement 1960-76
New York Times 1851 –
Park Forest Star 1961 –
Variety 1940-72
Wall Street Journal 1958 –

Governors State University Library also has the *Chicago Tribune Index, The New York Times Index* and the *New York.*

NEWSPAPERS IN THE ILLINOIS STATE HISTORICAL LIBRARY
Since 1959 the Illinois State Historical Library has acquired over 60,000 reels of newspaper microfilm. Back files of newspapers are acquired from various sources, microfilmed, and added to the library's collection. Current newspapers are received on subscription, either in original form or on microfilm. *Illinois Libraries* 67, No. 3 (March 1985) lists all of these newspaper acquisitions held by the historical library. There 297 newspaper titles for Chicago alone and the rest of Cook County is also well represented. Some of the included newspapers such as *Happy Hours* (10/11/1871) are but a single issue, some exist for a few years, and others like the *Chicago Tribune* are almost complete runs. *Illinois Staats-Zeitung* for the German readership, the *Citizen* which catered to the Irish, and several other ethnic titles are represented in the listing for Chicago. Neighborhood papers such as the *Beverly Review* and the *Logan Square Herald* also appear in limited numbers. Argo-Summit, Barrington, Blue Island, Lemont, Melrose Park, Midlothian, Niles, Oak Lawn, Western Springs, and Wilmette are among other Cook County towns included in newspaper listings.

OBITUARY SOURCES

The following libraries and historical societies have indexed obituaries. These are unpublished sources and therefore do not appear in major obituary reference sources. Some libraries maintain separate obituary files such as that of the South Suburban Genealogical Society, and some are intermixed with the general card catalog such as that of the Chicago Historical Society. See Historical Societies and Libraries appendixes for addresses.

> Arlington Heights Public Library
> Balzekas Museum of Lithuanian Culture
> Chicago Historical Society
> Chicago Municipal Reference Library (clipping file)
> Evanston Historical Society
> Evanston Public Library
> Illinois State Historical Society
> Oak Park Public Library
> South Suburban Genealogical and Historical Society
> Winnetka Public Library

IRISH OBITUARIES

Biographies and obituaries of Chicago Irish are the source of an extensive index compiled by John Corrigan. Information has been extracted principally from the *Chicago Inter-Ocean, The Chicago Citizen,* the *South Side Sun, Lake Vindicator,* the *Sun* and the *New World* (Catholic Archdiocesan newspaper). Additional data has been extracted from published Chicago sources and personal research. Send a self-addressed, stamped envelope for more information and a fee schedule to: John Corrigan, 1669 West 104th Street, Chicago, IL 60643.

PUBLISHED COOK COUNTY OBITUARIES

Carlock, Mabe. "Obituaries: Attorneys and Physicians, Cook County, Illinois, January-September 1952," (Copied from *Chicago Tribune.*) Oak Park, Ill.: 1952.

Chicago Genealogical Society. Newspaper Research Committee. *Vital Records from Chicago Newspapers, 1833-1839.* Chicago: Chicago Genealogical Society, 1971.

_____. Newspaper Research Committee. *Vital Records from Chicago Newspapers, 1840-1842.* Chicago: Chicago Genealogical Society, 1972.

_____. Newspaper Research Committee. *Vital Records from Chicago Newspapers,1843-1844.* Chicago: Chicago Genealogical Society, 1974

_____. Newspaper Research Committee. *Vital Records from Chicago Newspapers, 1845.* Chicago: Chicago Genealogical Society, 1975.

_____. Newspaper Research Committee. *Vital Records from Chicago Newspapers, 1846.* Chicago: Chicago Genealogical Society, 1976.

Chicago Sun Times. Newspaper Index. Wooster, Ohio: Bell and Howell Company, 1979—(monthly).

Chicago Tribune. Newspaper Index. Wooster, Ohio: Bell and Howell Company, 1972—(monthly).

Daily Democratic Press. *The Chicago Daily Democratic Press Index for the Year 1855.* Chicago: Works Project Administration, 1940.

Daughters of the American Revolution. *Cook County Genealogical Records.* 4 vols. Chicago: Daughters of the American Revolution, 1972. 1 contains Obituaries from *Oak Leaves* (Oak Park, Illinois) July-November 1943. Vol. 4 contains Obituaries from the *Evanston Index* (Evanston, Illinois) 1873-75, 1880-87.

Epstein, Francis James. *Decet Meminisse Fratrum: A Necrology of the Diocessan Priests of the Chicago Archdiocese, 1844-1936.* Chicago, Ill.: J.F. Higgins Printing Co., 1937.

Fergus, Robert. "Obituary Compiled by Robert Fergus Before 1900: Names, Places, Dates and Ages at Death of Some of Chicago's Old Settlers Prior to 1843, and Other Well-Known Citizens. Who Arrived After 1843, Together With Others Prominently Connected With Illinois History." *Chicago Genealogist* VII, No. 3 (Spring 1975): 96-101.

Grimes, Marilla R. "Items from Oneida County, New York Newspapers Having an Illinois Reference (1860)." *Illinois State Genealogical Society Quarterly* VII, No. 2 (1976).

Hollowak, Thomas L., and Hoffman, William F. *Index to the Obituaries and Death Notices Appearing in the* Dziennik Chicagoski *1890-1899.* Chicago: The Polish Genealogical Society, 1984.

Knights of Columbus, Chicago Council No. 182. *Obituary Sketches.* Chicago: 1921.

Koss, David. "Chicago Obituaries in *Der Christliche Botschafter,* 1844-1971." *Chicago Genealogist* (Summer 1979).

Newbill, Leona Hopper. *Early Settlers of LaGrange, Illinois and Vicinity.* 2 vols. LaGrange, Ill.: 1941.

BIBLIOGRAPHY

Ayer Directory of Publications. (Published annually, without interruption since 1869.)

Chicago. Center for Research Libraries. *Catalogue: Newspapers.* Chicago: The Center, 1978.

Illinois. "Newspapers in the Illinois State Historical Library," *Illinois Libraries* 67, No. 3 (March 1985).

Szucs, Loretto Dennis. "Newspapers" in *The Source: A Guidebook of American Genealogy.* Salt Lake City: Ancestry Publishing Company, 1984. 406-26.

_____. "Newspapers," in *Source Book.* South Holland, Ill.: The South Suburban Genealogical and Historical Society, 1983.

University of Chicago Library. "Newspapers in Libraries of Chicago, a Joint Checklist." Chicago: University of Chicago Document Section, 1936

CHAPTER 18

Occupational and Business Resources

T The following examples represent some of the more commonly requested and most available occupational and business resources for the Cook County area. Original records, archives, and published sources exist for others, but space does not permit the inclusion of all. The Chicago Historical Society offers the best starting place for the investigation of professional records. Subject headings (by business or occupational name) in the card catalog include a great number of entries listing publications and manuscripts to further research.

PHYSICIANS

American Medical Association
535 North Dearborn Street
Chicago, IL 60610

The American Medical Association which is headquartered in Chicago has a card file of over 1 million entries concerning American physicians. Membership in the A.M.A. was not a prerequisite to inclusion in the index. Biographical information on the cards often includes obituary notices, a history of the individual's medical education, evidence of residences where medicine was practiced, and birth and death dates. The library/archives will research the files for a nominal fee (per half hour). The fee includes copies of biographical information (if applicable) and addresses of other organizations to pursue the research.

The *American Medical Directory*, published by the American Medical Association, has existed since 1906. It was not published annually, but is most useful for the years it was published.

SELECTED BIBLIOGRAPHY

Chicago Medical Society. *History of Medicine and Surgery and Physicians and Surgeons of Chicago 1803-1922*. Chicago: Biographical Publishers Corp., 1922.

Sperry, I. M. *Distinguished Physicians & Surgeons of Chicago.* A Collection of Biographical Sketches of Many of the Eminent Representatives Past & Present of the Medical Profession of Chicago. Chicago: Beers Publishers, 1904.

University of Illinois Medical School. *Student Records from Medical School, M.S. and Ph. D. Thesis Reports, 1905-1975.* Chicago: 1976.

DENTISTS

American Dental Association
Bureau of Library Services
211 East Chicago Avenue
Chicago, IL 60611
(312-440-2642)

FIREMEN

The Retirement Board of the
Firemen's Annuity and Benefit Fund of Chicago
180 North LaSalle Street, Suite 701
Chicago, IL 60601
(312-726-5823)

SELECTED BIBLIOGRAPHY

Bushnell, George D. "Chicago's Rowdy Firefighters." *Chicago History* II, 4 (Fall/Winter 1973): 232-41.

Little, Kenneth. *Chicago Fire Department Engines: Sixty Years of Motorized Pumpers, 1912-1972.* Chicago: 1972

McQuade, James S. *A Synoptical History of the Chicago Fire Department.* Chicago: 1908.

LAW

Chicago Bar Association
29 South LaSalle Street
Chicago, IL 60603
(312-782-7348)

SELECTED BIBLIOGRAPHY

Caton, John Dean. *Early Bench and Bar of Illinois.* Chicago: Legal News Company, 1922.

Crossley, Frederic B. *Courts and Lawyers of Illinois.* Chicago: The American Historical Society, 1916.   •

Linder, Usher F. *Reminiscences of the Early Bench and Bar of Illinois.*
Chicago: Chicago Legal News Company, 1879.
Wilke, Franc Bangs. *The Chicago Bar.* Chicago: 1872.

POLICE

The Secretary
The Police Pension Fund
221 North LaSalle Street, Room 1626
Chicago, IL 60601
(312-744-4149)

SELECTED BIBLIOGRAPHY

Flinn, John Joseph. *History of the Chicago Police.* New York, 1973.
Biographical sketches included.

PULLMAN RECORDS

Over one million documents for Pullman Standard workers are at the
South Suburban Genealogical and Historical Society. The records date
from the late 1800s to the mid-1950s and cover the shops located on
111th Street, and Cottage Grove in Chicago, two shops in Hammond,
Indiana, and those of the Michigan City, Indiana, shop. The personnel
records vary somewhat in content but most have considerable information that is of genealogical and historical value. Some files list only
birth dates, while others give physical descriptions, family relationships, educational background, previous employment, and even
include birth certificates or other proofs of age. Immigrants' files
frequently include the date of arrival in the U.S., ship name, and
naturalization information and documents. Historically, the collection
reflects the nationality, race, sex, and working conditions of a labor
force before government regulation and scrutiny. The collection is not
open to the public or organized for research purposes, but the society
is involved in alphabetizing the files and a microfilming project is
underway. The Newberry Library has yet another group of Pullman
records. The organization of the Newberry collection also makes
retrieval of information for individuals difficult.

RAILROAD RETIREMENT BOARD

Railroad Retirement Board
844 Rush Street
Chicago, IL 60611

CALDWELL & BRANNOCK. Americans certainly hold the power in the business circles of New York, and it has been ascertained that this same rule applies with force in Chicago, where two natives of this city, the above named, are found engaged as dealers in fine wines, spirits and cigars, at 156 Wells Street and 118 and 120 E. Kinzie Street, the former place having been established June 5, 1888, and the latter in July, 1889. Eight capable and polite bar men are employed in these two places, and both sample rooms are finely fitted. The Wells Street room is 40x60 feet, with attractive stained glass front and cherry furniture, while the Kinzie Street house is 40x80 feet in space and is attractively arranged. Both of the partners are Foresters and formerly conducted a cafe in this city. A good business is done at the Wells Street place, and a still more extensive trade is transacted at the Kinzie Street sample room, and every facility is afforded patrons

J. Caldwell.   J. Brannock.

to seek enjoyment, the spirits, wines and cigars being of the highest grade, while a palatable luncheon awaits all comers. They have built up a good trade, and are certainly among the popular men in their line. The Kinzie Street establishment is known as the American Hotel, and has excellent accommodations for 150 persons. It is a popular place for captains, mates and engineers of lake boats and sailing vessels to winter at, when the lakes are frozen and unnavigable. Railroad men, conductors, etc., make it their headquarters and find every accommodation here for their comfort and ease. The American House contains fifty neatly furnished rooms, and guests are treated with every consideration. Mr. Caldwell is a gentleman now enjoying the prime of an active and successful business career, and he is regarded as a man of sound business judgment. His genial manners and obliging disposition have made him a wide circle of patrons and friends, who are wont to daily visit his Kinzie Street place, which is located nearly opposite the Chicago & North-Western railroad depot.

E. J. AND JOHN P. GRACE, two young gentlemen, conduct the fine sample room at 727 W. North Avenue, the former brother having been born in Chicago and the latter in Ireland. Their sample room was established in 1889 by a Mr. Harsken, who was succeeded by Addison & Douglass. On March 1, 1891, Peterson & Grace came in, and on June 17, 1891, the Brothers Grace took possession. Prior to entering upon their present arduous duties these gentlemen were engaged in the capacity of salesmen for the wholesale clothing house of Cohn, Wampold & Co. Their place is 25x70 feet in space and finely arranged, well kept, orderly, patronized by a most desirable class of people, and their wines, spirits and cigars are the choicest to be had in the market. They were raised in this ward, where their father is a well-known politician, and both of the brothers are very popular and active young politicians, John P. Grace being the captain of the Fourteenth Ward Democratic Club and a warm friend and supporter of Alderman Jackson. The sample room is the trysting place for the leading Democrats of this vicinity. The Messrs. Grace are successful because they deserve it, and it is only a matter of time before they will both be nominated and elected to political offices.

Figure 22.

The Retirement Board did not begin operations until the mid-1930s, therefore records are limited to individuals who were either associated with the rail industry at or since that time, or who were receiving a private rail pension which was assumed by the Board in 1937. The retirement board's records are arranged by the railroad employee's social security number, and are extremely difficult to locate by name only. For further information see "Genealogical Research and the U.S. Railroad Retirement Board" by Bill Poulos in *Ancestry Newsletter* III, No. 5 (September-October 1985).

There are several railroad archives in the Chicago area; however, most of these manuscript collections are not organized for retrieval of information regarding individuals at the present time.

BIBLIOGRAPHY

Album of Genealogy and Biography, Cook County, Illinois. Chicago: Calumet Book & Engraving Co., 1897.

Appleton, John B. *The Iron and Steel Industry of the Calumet District.* Urbana, Ill.: 1927.

Barnett, Fremont O. *Politics and Politicians of Chicago, Cook County, Illinois. Memorial Volume 1787-1887.* Chicago: Blakely Printing Company, 1886.

Bate, Phyllis A. "The Development of the Iron and Steel Industry of the Chicago Area, 1900-1920." Ph.D. Diss.,University of Chicago, 1948.

Biographical Sketches of the Leading Men of Chicago. Chicago: Wilson & St. Clair, 1868.

Biographical Sketches of the Leading Men of Chicago. Chicago: Wilson, Pierce & Co., 1876.

Chicago Historical Society. *Chicago Photographers 1847-1900 as Listed in Chicago City Directories.* Chicago: Chicago Historical Society, 1958.

Currey, Josiah Seymour. *Manufacturing and Wholesale Industries in Chicago.* Chicago: Thomas B. Poole Co., 1918.

Darling, Sharon. *Chicago Metalsmiths.* Chicago: Chicago Historical Society, 1978.

_____. *Chicago Furniture: Art, Craft & Industry 1833-1983.* Chicago: Chicago Historical Society in association with W. W. Norton & Company, 1984.

Eakle, Arlene and Cerny, Johni. *The Source: A Guidebook of American Genealogy.* Salt Lake City: Ancestry Publishing Co., 1984. ("Business and Employment Records" by Kory L. Meyerink and "How to Find Business and Employment Records" by Arlene H. Eakle. Both chapters offer lists of places to write for employment records, some background on record keeping practices, suggestions on how to get desired information, and what to expect from these collections.

Frueh, Erne Rene. "Retail Merchandising in Chicago, 1833-1848." *Journal of the Illinois State Historical Society* 2 (June 1939): 149-72.

Fleming, I. A. *Chicago Stock Exchange: An Historical Sketch with Biographies of Its Leading Members.* Chicago: 1894.

Flinn, John J. *Handbook of Chicago Biography.* Chicago: 1893.

German Press Club of Chicago. *Prominent Citizens and Industries of Chicago.* Chicago: German Press Club of Chicago, 1901.

Gilbert, Frank. *Centennial History of the City of Chicago: Its Men and Institutions.* Chicago: Inter-Ocean Publishing Co., 1905.

Gilbert, Paul Thomas, and Bryson, Charles Lee. *Chicago and Its Makers.* Chicago: F. Mendelsohn, 1929.

Heckler, Edwin L. *The Meat Packing Industry.* Boston: 1944.

History of Chicago, and Souvenir of the Liquor Interest: The Nation's Choice for the Great Columbian Exposition, 1893. Chicago: Belgravia Publishing Co, 1891.

Jackson, Elisabeth Coleman, and Curtis, Carolyn. *Guide to the Burlington Archives in the Newberry Library, 1851-1901.* Chicago: The Newberry Library, 1949.

James, Frank Cyril. *The Growth of Chicago Banks.* 2 vols. New York: 1938.

Jewell, Frank. *Annotated Bibliography of Chicago History.* Chicago: Chicago Historical Society, 1979.

Mohr, Carolyn Curtis. *Guide to the Illinois Central Archives in The Newberry Library, 1851-1906.* Chicago: The Newberry Library, 1951.

Monchow, Helen C. *Seventy Years of Real Estate Subdividing in the Region of Chicago.* Chicago: 1939.

Mosher, Charles D. *Centennial Historical Album, 1876.*

Nash, Jay Robert. *People to See: An Anecdotal History of Chicago's Makers and Breakers.* Piscataway, N.J.: New Century Publishers,Inc., 1981.

O'Grady, R. P. *Chicago and Cook County Official Republican Directory and Sketch Book, 1900.* Chicago: R. P. O'Grady, 1900.

Parkhurst, M. S. *History of the Yards, 1865-1953.* Chicago: 1953.

Rex, Frederick. Chicago Municipal Reference Library. *Chicago, 1937.* List of mayors, city clerks, attorneys, treasurers, and aldermen for 1837-1937.

Rice, Wallace. *The Chicago Exchange: A History.* Chicago: 1923.

Rothermel, Charles T. and Co. *Portraits and Biographies of Fire Underwriters of the City of Chicago.* Chicago: Monarch Printing and Binding Company, 1895.

Schoff, S. *The Glory of Chicago—Her Manufactories.* Chicago: Knight and Leonard, 1873.

Schroder, H.L., and Forbrick, C. W. *Men Who Have Made the Fifth Ward.* Chicago: 1895.

Sketches of Manufacturers, Memoirs of Business Men. *Industrial Chicago.* Chicago (1894).

Taylor, Charles Henry. *History of the Board of Trade of the City of Chicago.* Chicago: Robert O. Law Co., 1917.

Who's Who in Chicago and Illinois. 1905, 1911, 1917, 1926, 1931, 1936, 1941, 1945. Chicago: A. N. Marquis Company.

Wood, David Ward. *Chicago and Its Distinguished Citizens.* Chicago: 1881.

World's Columbian Exposition Souvenir. Chicago: North American Engraving and Publishing Co., 1895.

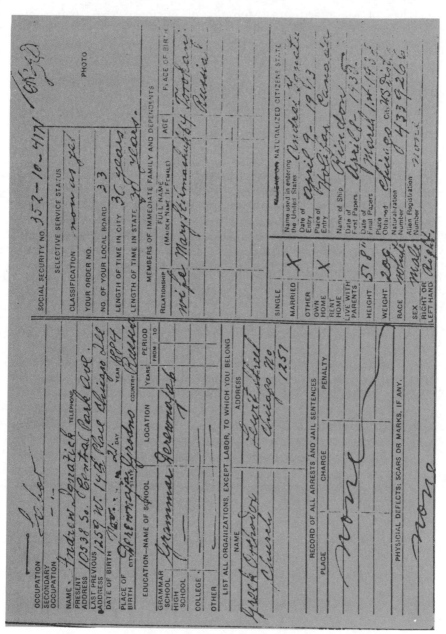

Figure 23. *Employment record (courtesy South Suburban Genealogical & Historical Society)*

CHAPTER 19

Societies: Fraternal, Social and Patriotic

by *Linda Stone Lamberty*

A s a source, organization and society records can be a complicated and time-consuming avenue to pursue. However, once the more conventional sources have been exhausted—which can often happen in Cook County when one's subject predates the 1871 Chicago Fire—patience and perserverance with this "last resort" can unearth enough information to keep you going.

There are many types of organizations, formed for as many reasons. Some are job-oriented; many are ethnic. Some are social groups, perhaps with philanthropic aspects, and vice versa; while others formed for some mutual benefit, such as insurance, but also may have social functions; and so on. The information recorded by each varies as well. Basically, unless historical or genealogical in origin, they have one thing in common: data was not recorded for the benefit of outsiders doing personal research, and whoever maintains that information has other duties to perform than answering phone calls and letters. Whatever information can be gleaned from those kind souls who do make the effort to help should be received graciously. (It should be noted that Masonic Grand Secretaries are among those who generously respond to numerous inquiries.)

First of all, it is necessary to determine whether an individual being researched was associated with any organized groups. If family members cannot be of help, clues can be found within the context of a death notice, obituary, biographical note in a printed source, a probate record, headstone, or amongst personal possessions. Especially in early years when a death notice might provide scant information, reference to a deceased "brother" (which would give the name of the lodge, etc.) can often be found under "Fraternal Notices" in the classified section of the newspaper. Papers or jewelry may bear crestlike insignias containing initials or words.

Under close examination, old photographs, previously unnoticed rings, medallions, watch-fobs, etc., can become significant. Sometimes painstaking research is necessary to identify the social organizations represented. Bear in mind that it is possible for someone to belong to more than one of a similar type of organization, and that within one group there can even be different bodies holding separate records. Before requesting information from an organization it is important that it be fully researched if the most is to be made of it as a record source.

In local libraries such as the Newberry and the Chicago Historical Society under the headings, "Associations," "Clubs," "Fraternities," "Lodges," "Organizations," "Societies," etc., a variety of printed sources can be found. Some are specifically devoted to particular clubs, lodges, etc. Check most sources, including printed histories and directories of the time, under the same headings. A. T. Andreas' *History of Chicago* gives detailed histories of organizations in the city, and his *History of Cook County, Illinois* describes many of the same existing in the suburbs, up to about 1885. Use of encyclopedias can be most helpful if your field of interest includes established national or international groups such as the Masons or Oddfellows. An understanding of the development and mechanisms of such complex organizations can sometimes lead to additional records otherwise ignored. Present-day directories of associations providing at least current addresses are also available; and today's *Yellow Pages* include many, though possibly under a similar, but different, name.

If the group you seek no longer exists, it is necessary to determine where their records may have been deposited. Fraternal lodges will often consolidate with another lodge, which should then retain any records of the first lodge. Records of other groups may have come to rest in a local library or historical society, or perhaps even in some loyal individual's basement or attic. Many records were not kept at all, and fires and floods have destroyed many of the records that were intended for posterity. Should your sleuthing lead you to one of these bleak conclusions, all hope is still not gone. If significant dates can be determined in the history of a club, research of local newspapers, especially nostalgia columns, might provide further data. Clubs may have published newsletters, magazines, or histories of their own, copies of which may yet be retained by other institutions. This can be a good source for obituaries or biographical notes on milestone birthdays or anniversaries of individual members.

It would be impractical to attempt to detail all sources pertinent to the many social groups in Chicago and Cook County over the years. However, a few suggestions and examples follow in the hope that concepts set forth in this chapter will help to form a reusable pattern for further research.

ANCIENT FREE AND ACCEPTED MASONS

Freemasonry originated centuries ago as a stonecraft. With craftsmen travelling about the country to work it was necessary to develop some secret means (word or handshake) to differentiate apprentices and fellows of the craft from cowans (workmen who had not been apprenticed or had been poorly taught). The lodge in their home jurisdiction was a workshop as well as a place to relax and speak freely, thus necessitating a bond of secrecy between fellows to protect themselves from employers and nonmasons.

With the decline of cathedral building in the seventeenth century, many of these groups became purely social and admitted men, called Speculative Masons, who had not worked in stonecraft. As nonoperatives gained in numbers, these gentlemen Masons became known as Accepted Masons. Between 1737 and 1907 about sixteen English princes of royal blood had joined the brotherhood, and over the years many of the world's elite in government and society have been acknowledged among the Masonic fraternity.

Rites and ceremonies are based upon the building craft and personal development of high morals and benevolence. Belief in one God is a requirement of membership, as is adherance to the laws of the land. Freemasonry is not permitted in communist and certain other countries. Some Protestant bodies have declared Freemasonry incompatible with Christianity, while the Catholic Church has even threatened its members with excommunication for joining.

The organizational structure of Freemasonry in the United States is unique. Though Masonic lodges existed here during the colonial years, they were governed by provincial Grand Lodges whose grand masters were under the Masonic authority in Great Britain. After the Revolutionary War, the provincial grand bodies declared themselves independant, each confining itself within state boundaries and there remaining supreme in Masonic matters. Thus, in each state is a Grand Lodge governing the Blue Lodges (so called because of their official color, and comprised of Masons having achieved the first three degrees) with no nationwide or world-wide authority above it.

In 1805, the first Masonic Blue Lodge established in what is now Illinois was at Kaskaskia, and in December of 1822 at Vandalia, a Grand Lodge was instituted. This was discontinued in about 1828 after such a storm of controversy over the order had swept the country that the Masonic society more or less dispersed. (Out of this situation was born the Anti-Masonic party which helped to form the Whig party in 1834.) However, it was not until 1846 that an Anti-Masonic Society was organized in Illinois. Politically driven, this group chose to warn voters by publishing names of known Masons. Remaining Masonic factions survived "underground" until about 1835 when they began to regroup. In April of 1840, an Illinois Masonic Grand Lodge was again established by 127 members of six lodges about the state. There were certainly Masons living in Chicago before the creation of lodges in the city, and while degrees could still be conferred by a required number of Masons of required degree and standing, without lodges there would have been no record here of their actions as Masons.

Of the first Chicago Blue Lodges chartered in the early 1840s, two (LaFayette #18 and Oriental #33) remained by 1850. By 1875 there were thirty-four Blue Lodges in the city and ten in surrounding Cook County. (The number following the name of a lodge pertains to the sequence in which charters were granted by the state Grand Lodge.) Thus, even if the name of a particular lodge was changed it should still bear the same number, unless it surrendered its charter or consolidated with another lodge. Note: A member who is listed as *dimitted* in lodge (or chapter, etc.) records (a date is usually given) has requested that his name be removed often, so that he may move on to another lodge. A member who is listed as *suspended* has been removed from the roster, perhaps for not paying his dues.

Illinois Grand Secretary
Grand Lodge A.F. & A.M.
P.O. Box 4147
Springfield, IL 62708

This office has records for every Mason in Illinois since 1840. When a Blue Lodge stops working, its records are usually taken over by the office of the Grand Secretary. However, fires in 1850 and 1870 left only the (annual) Grand Lodge proceedings for research. In records after 1871, some dates and places of birth and death are available. The individual records system did not originate until about 1930.

Upon receipt of the Third Degree (Master Mason), a Blue Lodge Mason has the option to improve himself by earning additional degrees in the York Rite or Scottish Rite (not mutually exclusive). With each degree, principles of morality and craft are further developed, and the Mason is eligible for membership in other (appendant) Masonic societies. It is, however, to the Blue Lodge records of the State Grand Secretaries that most researchers apply for information. This is still the best initial source to try. Beyond that, research is confined to individual lodge records and proceedings (many of which have suffered fires and floods even recently) which usually give little information that does not relate to Masonic activities. But, if you are desperate for clues, this may still be worthy of pursuit.

The York Rite is a name (not an organization) describing the Capitular, Cryptic (optional), and Templar Rites. Each is comprised of named and numbered degrees culminating in the Thirty-third Degree, or Knight Templar. (The Templar Rite is exclusively Christian). The Capitular chapters, Cryptic councils, and Templar commanderies each come under the authority of a state Grand Body, which in turn answers to a nation-wide general Grand Body; though these grand bodies do not retain records on individual members of the subordinate groups.

In the Scottish Rite the lodges, councils, chapters, and consistories progressively confer the fourth through the thirty-second degrees. These bodies are governed by a Supreme Council. The Thirty-third Degree (honorary, in recognition of outstanding services) in the Scottish Rite is conferred upon individuals by the governing Supreme Council and may not be requested.

The first Surpreme Council of the Scottish Rite was established at Charleston, South Carolina, in 1801. Though Scottish Rite degrees existed earlier, before this time there was no governing body organized around them.

Though a parent body, a Supreme Council is composed of active Thirty-third Degree Masons and elects its own members. While each member of the council is the highest officer in his own state, this body is self-perpetuating and not represented by its subordinates.

The United States was entitled to only one supreme council, but due to difficulties of travel in colonial times, a second was established by the first. The northern jurisdiction now governs all states (termed "orients") north of the Ohio and east of the Mississippi, while Charleston governs the southern jurisdiction of all remaining states and territories. For information pertaining only to Thirty-third Degree Masons of the Scottish Rite in the Northern Jurisdiction:

Supreme Council of the Scottish Rite
P.O. Box 519
Lexington, MA 02173

APPENDANT ORDERS

The preceding described Masonic organizations represent the fundamental Masonic society. Beyond the Blue Lodge and the York and Scottish Rites are over one hundred independant organizations (especially prevalent in the United States) for men, women, and children whose membership depends in some way (familial) upon a good standing in one of the three primary Masonic organizations. A few among the most notable are the Order of the Eastern Star (includes women), Imperial Council of the Ancient Arabic Order of Nobles of the Mystic Shrine—otherwise known as "Shriners" (thirty-second degree Masons or Knights Templar), the Order of DeMolay (boys) and the Order of Job's Daughters (girls). The National League of Masonic Clubs has also chartered many of the hundreds of such local organizations. English Masons are forbidden to affiliate with these extra-curricular appendant societies.

The majority of the fraternal organizations existing in the country at the time were represented in Chicago by 1883, when at least 570 various lodges were listed in the city directory. A general descriptive history of many of these groups can be found in the *Fraternal Directory* (San Francisco: The Bancroft Co., Publishers, 1889). In the *Chicago Directory of Lodges for the Year 1883* (Chicago: C. F. Lichtner & Bro.) can be found a list of the lodges in Chicago that year, including memberships of many.

THE CALUMET CLUB

The history of the Calumet Club and accounts of its receptions, wrought with splendor, should make interesting research and reading, even for those whose ancestors were not among the hosted and toasted of the city.

Chartered by the state of Illinois in 1878, the Calumet Club was organized on the near South Side of Chicago as a gentlemen's social club and was open to early and distinguished settlers of the city.

As early as the 1850s, and again in 1871, an attempt was made to organize an old settlers' society, but it was not until May of 1879 that the Calumet Club was able to achieve some success in a similar endeavor. An invitation to a reception was extended to settlers who had come to Chicago as adults before 1840. This reception became an annual event under the direct supervision of qualifying old settlers who were members of the Calumet Club. In May 1885, the invitations to this event numbered almost 450, and the collection of relics and records of pioneers had grown to notable proportions. It is unfortunate that so much was destroyed by a fire in 1893 (after which an even more impressive structure was erected).

Another established event at the Calumet Club was the annual art reception, where, in December 1885, ninety-five paintings were displayed.

Although membership in 1885 numbered 581 regular and twenty-eight nonresidents, and had eventually risen as high as 800, this number was reduced by the year 1917 to about 100. In November of that year the Calumet Club closed its doors as a social institution forever. (An indexed account of the first reception in 1879, including a list of those invited, with addresses, and a list of those who attended can be found in *Reception to the Settlers of Chicago Prior to 1840 by the Calumet Club of Chicago*. The list of those who attended includes date of arrival, birthplace and present age and address. See Andreas' *History of Chicago* for 1885 lists of old settlers and additional information. Of these three, the first list consists of males and their addresses. Over and above wives of these old settlers, the second lists single ladies and ladies with names of their deceased husbands, as some had remarried by this time, and their addresses. The last, being chronological, cites deaths of pioneers between May 1879 and November 1885. At least the first two include out-of-towners.

PATRIOTIC SOCIETIES

SONS OF THE AMERICAN REVOLUTION (S.A.R.)

National Society, S.A.R.
1000 South Fourth Street
Louisville, KY 40203

As a result of the centennial celebrations to occur in 1876, a state society, Sons of the American Revolution was proposed in San Francisco, California, in 1875. Organized there on 4 July 1876, it was the first of many subsequently formed in other states. The national society was not formed until 1889, at which time efforts were made to begin a state society in Illinois. In January 1890, through receptions at the Iroquois and Union League Clubs in Chicago, the formation of the Illinois Society, Sons of the American Revolution was finally accomplished.

Objectives being purely patriotic and social, applicants were required to be male, twenty-one years of age, a citizen of good repute and lineally descended from an active and recognized soldier or patriot of the American Revolution.

DAUGHTERS OF THE AMERICAN REVOLUTION (D.A.R.)

National Society, D.A.R.
1776 D Street, N.W.
Washington, DC 20006

With similar eligibility requirements, the National Society, Daughters of the American Revolution (D.A.R.) was organized in 1890 due to a defeat of a motion to admit women into the S.A.R. Within a year, the first chapter in Chicago had been organized. In 1895, the D.A.R. created the Children of the American Revolution (C.A.R.).

In addition to its many charitable, educational, and historically preservational activities, one ongoing project of the D.A.R. is the acquisition of transcripts of old bible records, regardless of whether or not they apply to a patriotic family. These are maintained at the D.A.R. library in Washington. Numbered D.A.R. *Lineage Books* and *Lineage and Revolutionary Record Books* (containing lineages of members), as well as *The Patriot Index* (listing Revolutionary War patriots), bound and indexed periodically, can be found on the open shelves at the Newberry

Library. While the D.A.R. itself no longer accepts all documentation cited in earlier applications, this is still a good source of information. It should be noted that the excellent D.A.R. Library in Washington, D.C. is closed during April to all but members. Staff will not do research, but will send a list of individuals who will do research for a fee. Staff will, however, send photocopies of up to thirty specified pages, per day, for a copy fee per page. Recent catalogs of the contents of the library have been published by the D.A.R. Any eligible woman at least eighteen years of age interested in membership can apply to the address above to contact a chapter in her area. In all cases, a self-addressed stamp envelope (SASE) should be included.

THE ILLINOIS ATHLETIC CLUB (I.A.C.)

Founded and organized by Chicago Mayor William Hale "Big Bill" Thompson and a small group of friends and businessmen desiring a place to exercise, relax, and entertain, the Illinois Athletic Club was chartered by the state of Illinois in 1904. Their only assets being a box of cigars and an architect's plan and sketch (done in good faith), this ingenious group led the press to believe that something big was already in the works. With the ensuing publicity, the needed applicants for membership began showing up. Ground broke in February 1905 and construction was completed in November 1907 on the impressive twelve-story structure still standing at 112 South Michigan Avenue. With facilities to accomodate quite a variety of sports, the club sponsored many accomplished athletes, including some Olympic champions.

After many years of making a name and a place for itself in the history of the city and the nation, in the face of financial difficulties the I.A.C. recently sold out to the Charlie Fitness Club chain. As part of the new owner's efforts to expand and improve the existing facilities, much of the history of the Illinois Athletic Club, in the form of trophies and other memorabilia, has been preserved and emphasized in glass-enclosed cases. Most importantly to researchers, the entire collection of the club magazine (1911 to end) has been retained. If given a specific date, this publication can be searched for birth, marriage and death notices (often lengthy) for the cost of the photocopy. For further details contact:

Charlie Fitness Club & Hotel
112 South Michigan Avenue
Chicago, IL 60603
Attn: Mary Lambertino
(include SASE)

CHAPTER 20

Vital Records

V ital records are documents which verify the significant events in human life: birth, marriage, and death—regardless of where they are found. Vital statistics, as considered here, are the official records created and maintained by government agencies at local, state or national levels. Whether found in the county clerk's office or in a newspaper, vital records are prime sources for documenting the life of an individual.

Compulsory registration of vital statistics did not begin until 1 January 1916 in Illinois; however, a large percentage of births, deaths, and marriages were registered with Cook County in earlier years.

The Chicago Fire of 1871 destroyed the Cook County Court House and the official documents which had been recorded and filed previous to that date. For verification of events which were registered prior to the fire, or for information on events not officially registered, alternative solutions are often available. You may find birth, marriage, or death information in church records, histories, biographies, Bibles, newspapers, employment records, military records, and cemeteries. Approximate birthdates can be obtained from census and school records.

BUREAU OF VITAL STATISTICS

COOK COUNTY
Lower Concourse
118 North Clark Street
Chicago, IL 60602
(312-443-7790)

Hours: Monday—Friday 9:00 a.m.—5:00 p.m.
Saturday, Sunday, and Holidays—Closed

The Cook County Clerk is legally responsible for preserving and making available vital records generated within the county limits. It is the job of the Bureau of Vital Statistics to receive, process, and store these vital records. Because of the huge volume of records created by the metropolitan population—over forty million—searching of the birth, marriage, and death indexes by individuals is impractical. Cook County exercises home rule and cannot allow the free access which is taken for granted in some less-populated Illinois counties. On a typical day, one thousand vital statistics requests are processed by the county clerk's office, giving it the distinction of the world's busiest vital statistics office.

Since 1 December 1984, a fee of $5.00 is required for a three year search of each vital record. (Note that all fees are subject to change.) The current fee includes one certified copy of the record if it is found. Additional copies are $2.00 each. A certified notice that a particular search has been made will be issued in instances when a record cannot be found. Under Illinois State law, search fees are not refundable, even when a vital record is not located.

The increased use of vital records for fraudulent purposes has, in recent years, necessitated more vigilant enforcement of Illinois State Statutes, and these changes are reflected in the forms for requesting vital records in Cook County as of April 1986. Although the newer restrictions may seem inconvenient, they serve to protect us from those who would use our records for false identification. The Cook County Bureau has a policy of cooperation with genealogists. Persons who can present proof of membership in an Illinois genealogical society may obtain records by indicating that a requested document will be used for genealogical purposes only. The more information supplied when requesting a form, the better the chances of positive results. It is generally understood that genealogists do not always have all the information which is requested on the forms issued to secure a certificate, and some exceptions are made in these cases. In early years, a baby yet unnamed at the time of the birth was registered and a record will be entered with "Baby" as a first name. Often, a baby's name was changed after due reflection on the part of the parents, and a name used later in life will not be the name registered with the county. As in any other records, clerical errors and difficult handwriting make searches more difficult, if not impossible.

BIRTH RECORDS

Birth records were destroyed along with other official vital statistics in the Chicago Fire. Further complicating a search is the fact that in early years, fewer births were registered since babies were often born at home with only a midwife in attendance.

A typical Cook County birth certificate in the 1870s provided the child's name; number of children of this mother; race and sex; date and

STANLEY T. KUSPER, JR., County Clerk

Form CB

REQUEST FOR PHOTOSTATIC COPY OF

BIRTH RECORDS

Before Filling Out Application Be Certain BIRTH Occurred in Cook County

Name _____
     First Name   Middle Name   Last Name

Date of Birth _____

Place of Birth _____

Name of Father _____

Maiden Name of Mother _____
     First Name   Middle Name   Last Name

I, the undersigned do hereby certify that as the person whose record is sought, or as the parent, guardian, or legal representative of the person, am legally entitled according to the Illinois State Statute [Chap. 111-1/2, Sec. 73-25(4)(b)] to receive the requested certified copy.

_____
Name of Person Requesting Copy

                                _____
                                  Signature of Person Requesting Copy

_____
Address

_____
City

                                  _____
                                  Relationship of Person Requesting Copy

Please Enclose Self Addressed
Stamped Envelope

Kindly Mail Certificate to:

Name _____

Address _____

City_____ **State** _____ **Zip Code** _____

Statutory Fee for All Searches is $5,.00 for each 3 Year period searched.
If Record is Found a Certified Copy Will Be Mailed Free of Charge.
Additional copies are $2.00 each.

Make Remittance by Money Order or Check, Payable to:

STANLEY T. KUSPER, JR., County Clerk
Bureau of Vital Statistics (Lower Randolph Street Concourse)
118 North Clark Street, Chicago, Illinois 60602

445

Figure 24. *Application for Birth Record (may be photocopied)*

place of birth; nationality; place of birth; age of each parent; full and maiden name of mother and her residence; full name of father and his occupation; name and address of the medical attendant; and the date of the birth registration. Information provided on birth certificates changed little over the years until about 1920. At that time, more questions (mostly of a medical nature) were added to city and county forms.

The Genealogical Society of Utah has microfilmed the following birth records:

Cook County (Illinois). County Clerk. Chicago birth registers, 1871-1922. Microfilm of original records at the Cook County Courthouse, Chicago, Illinois, arranged by certificate number within each year. (906 microfilm reels).

Cook County (Illinois). County Clerk. County birth records, 1878-94. Microfilm of original records at the Cook County Courthouse, Chicago, Illinois.

For indexes to Cook County births on microfiche, check the Genealogical Library Catalog (GLC) Locality fiche or the author-title indexes under Cook County Clerk. Birth record indexes 1871-1916. Arranged by certificate number within each year. (31 microfilm reels).

NORTHWESTERN MEMORIAL HOSPITAL ARCHIVES BIRTH RECORDS

The Genealogical Society of Utah has microfilmed thousands of birth records and case records of the Chicago Maternity Center from 1896-1933. The records include those of the Maxwell Street Dispensary, the Newberry Clinic, Chicago Lying-In Hospital, and the Stockyards Clinic.

The records contain the only copies of birth certificates of a number of persons born in the area, including Jack Ruby, the killer of John F. Kennedy's accused assassin Lee Harvey Oswald. Because Chicago did not require registration of babies born at home prior to 1915, Northwestern Memorial has the only record of thousands of births during the thirty-five year period.

Chicago (Illinois) birth records, 1896-1933. Microfilm of original records in the Northwestern Memorial Hospital, Chicago, Illinois. (14 microfilm reels).

Cook County (Illinois). County Clerk. County birth registers, 1916-22. (34 microfilm reels).

For indexes to Cook County births on microfiche, check the Genealogical Library Catalog (GLC) Locality fiche or author-title indexes under Cook County Clerk, birth record indexes 1871-1916. Cook County (Illinois). County Clerk.

Cook County (Illinois). County Clerk. Chicago delayed birth indexes, 1871-1948. Microfilm of original records at the Cook County Courthouse, Chicago. Not in strict alphabetical order, (7 microfilm reels).
Cook County (Illinois). County Clerk. Birth corrections and indexes, 1871-1915. Microfilm of original records at the Cook County Courthouse, Chicago, Illinois. Not in strict alphabetical order. Includes some actual birth records. (17 microfilm reels).
Cook County (Illinois). County Clerk. Birth corrections and delayed births 1916-18. Microfilm of original records at the Cook County Courthouse, Chicago, Illinois. (21 microfilm reels).

MARRIAGE RECORDS

Marriage records begin in 1871 in Cook County. Upon completion of a request form, a copy of the marriage license (if found) will be furnished. Information provided on marriage licenses has not changed from when records began to the present time. The names of the bride and groom, their respective towns or cities of residence, and their ages are given. Some of the most helpful information often comes from the information provided by the individual who officiated at the marriage. By linking the name of the minister, priest, or rabbi with the congregation to which he belonged, additional religious records may be located which will often lead to other family relationships. The exact address of the person officiating was added in the 1920s. Unfortunately, the specific addresses of brides and grooms were not furnished on the license. Marriages performed by a justice of the peace present a more difficult problem. Records which may have been kept of those marriages performed by a justice of the peace would have remained in his possession and it has not been my experience to locate any of those collections.

Unlike other Illinois counties, the marriage applications in Cook County are not any more complete than the marriage licenses. It was not until the 1920s then the exact birthdates of brides and grooms were added. In 1962, marriage applications changed and specific addresses of brides and grooms were provided. It was not until 2 January 1968 that a Cook County marriage application asked for birthplaces, and the names of the applicant's parents.

Marriages in Cook County were indexed from 1871 to 1878 by males only. This means that unless the groom's name is known, a long and tedious page-by-page search must be made to locate a record. In some cases, the ledgers have faded, to a degree making microfilming impossible.

STANLEY T. KUSPER, JR., County Clerk

Form CM   REQUEST FOR PHOTOSTATIC COPY OF

MARRIAGE RECORDS

Before Filling Out Application Be Certain MARRIAGE Occurred in Cook County

Name of Husband

_____

First Name   Middle Name   Last Name

Wife's Name at Time of Marriage

_____

First Name   Middle Name   Last Name

Date of Marriage _____

Date License Issued _____

Place of Marriage _____
                          City, Town or Village

I, the undersigned do hereby certify that I am a person, or a duly authorized agent of a person, who is legally entitled to the marriage certificate requested above, as specified by State Statute.

_____
Name of Person Requesting Copy

                          _____
                          Signature of Person Requesting Copy

_____
Address

_____   _____
City   Relationship of Person Requesting Copy

                          Please Enclose Self Addressed
Kindly Mail Certificate to: Stamped Envelope

Name _____

Address _____

City _____ **State** _____ **Zip Code** _____

Statutory Fee for All Searches is $5,.00 for each 3 Year period searched.
If Record is Found a Certified Copy Will Be Mailed Free of Charge.
Additional copies are $2.00 each.

Make Remittance by Money Order or Check, Payable to:

STANLEY T. KUSPER, JR., County Clerk

Bureau of Vital Statistics (Lower Randolph Street Concourse)
118 North Clark Street, Chicago, Illinois 60602

445

Figure 25. *Application for Marriage Record (may be photocopied)*

The Genealogical Society of Utah has microfilmed the following marriage records:

Cook County (Illinois). County Clerk. Marriage licenses, 1871-1920; index, 1871-1916. Microfilm of the original records at the Cook County Courthouse, Chicago.

Beginning in 1894, marriage licenses of the city of Chicago are separated from other licenses of Cook County. Within each sequence of 100 numbers, the Cook County licenses come first, followed by licenses from Chicago. Licenses are arranged numerically and chronologically. Some licenses in correct chronological order are misnumbered. Spade marks on licenses indicate numbering problem. Most years have out of order licenses indicated as "misc." Prior to 1894, licenses were held by the Clerk of the County Court. A few licenses are for the time prior to the Chicago Fire. Female indexes did not begin until 1878. (709 microfilm reels)

ALTERNATIVE SOURCES FOR MARRIAGE RECORDS

Alguire, Joan L. *Some Cook County Marriages Prior to the Fire.* South Holland, Ill.: The South Suburban Genealogical and Historical Society, 1981. Abstracts of 423 marriage licenses issued within the year before the 1871 Chicago Fire. Includes index. Microfilmed by the Genealogical Society of Utah (1 microfilm reel).

Newbill, Leona Hopper. "Cook County, Illinois Marriage License Records 1870-1880." Typescript with bride and groom index. Microfilmed by the Genealogical Society of Utah (1 microfilm reel).

MICROFILM OF TRANSCRIPT RECORDS IN THE CUSTODY OF SAM FINK

A microfilm copy of a typescript, "Chicago Marriage and Death Index," compiled by and in the custody of Sam F. Fink, has been microfilmed by the Genealogical Society of Utah and is available at LDS branch libraries and at the Newberry Library. The marriage portion of the index was duplicated and appears twice on the film—just as it does in the original volume. Information for the marriage and death index was compiled from the *Chicago Tribune, Chicago Evening Journal, Chicago Democrat, Chicago Examiner, Chicago Evening Post, Chicago Record Herald, Chicago Daily News, Chicago Examiner,* and the *Inter-Ocean.* The Marriage Index covers the years 1833 to 1871. The Death Index covers the years 1856 to 1889. The film will be found in the LDS Locality Catalog under Illinois, Cook, Vital Records Indexes—Chicago Marriage and Death Indexes in the custody of Sam Fink—#1321939.

CHICAGO MARRIAGES IN CROWN POINT, INDIANA 1915-1940
by Herbert H. Post

An estimated 175,000 marriages, many of them couples from Chicago and environs, took place in Crown Point, Indiana, during the period 1915 to 1940. Four justices of the peace in Crown Point, not far from Chicago, advertised "quick, painless marriages" at minimal costs. They advertised in Chicago and other midwest city newspapers and on the Pathe News Service newsreels (the equivalent of today's television commercial). Elopement and marriage in Crown Point became the "in" thing to do and thousands of Chicagoans were attracted to Crown Point for marriage in what became known as the "Marriage Mills". Rudolph Valentino and the Mills Brothers are among the celebrities who were married at Crown Point in the heyday of the operation.

The years 1937 to 1940 were the busiest. Illinois had passed a tough blood test law in 1937 and, with war clouds gathering in Europe, many Chicago area couples took advantage of the quick marriages available at nearby Crown Point. Crown Point was then accessible by trolley car and the "Marriage Mills" operated twenty-four hours a day.

In 1940, Indiana passed a marriage law requiring blood tests and a three-day waiting period. Thus the "Marriage Mills" ground to a sudden and permanent halt.

Crown Point is the county seat of Lake County, Indiana. The very early years of the "Marriage Mill" records can be readily accessed through the WPA's Index to Marriage Records, Lake County, Indiana, 1805-1920 inclusive, in nine alphabetically arranged volumes. These can be found at the Newberry Library, the Indiana Room at the Lake County Public Library, and at the Allen County Public Library, 900 Webster Street, Fort Wayne, IN 46302.

Records from 1920 to 1940 can be obtained by writing to the Recorder's Office, Marriage Clerk, Lake County Government Center, 2293 North Main Street, Crown Point, IN 46307. Their records are indexed by years and they will make a three-year search of their index. They ask that you submit the name of both the bride and groom and the date of the marriage.

SELECTED BIBLIOGRAPHY
Swisher, Charles W. and Swisher, Mable Wise, ed. *Crown Point, Indiana 1834-1984, The Hub City.* Crown Point: 1984.

_____. *Souvenir of Crown Point's Anniversary, 1834-1959, 125 Years.* Crown Point: 1959.

Works Progress Administration. *Index to Marriage Records, Lake County, Indiana* 1850-1920, 1939. 9 vols.

"The Marrying Squires of Crown Point." *The Lake County Star.* 18 April 1974.

DEATH RECORDS

As with other "official" vital statistics, death records are available in Cook County from 1871. Death records are often the easiest to access since dates of those events were conscientiously recorded and are often to be found by locating the date in indexes. In many ways, death records are some of the most helpful since what is recorded on a death certificate, mortician's record, coroner's record, cemetery record, in a probate, obituary, or a church record will lead to important information about the deceased as well as serving to identify other family members. There is no strict order in which death records should be searched, but it is often a matter of beginning with the known facts and working toward the unknown. If an exact death date is known, a copy of a death certificate is the best starting point as it should provide important data concerning the individual as well as the place of burial.

Cemetery research will often serve to identify other family members who may be buried in the same plot. Probate records provide exact death dates and often the place of burial as well as listing widows, heirs, previous marriages. Additionally, probates have the advantage of being indexed by year in Cook County. Chicago Deaths 1871-1933 is an index which makes it possible to find death dates for a great percentage of Chicagoans who died within that time period (see Genealogical Society of Utah microfilms listed later in this chapter.) Detailed discussion of mortician's records, coroner's records, cemetery records, probates, obituaries, and church records will be found under appropriate headings in this volume.

DEATH CERTIFICATES

A typical death certificate from Chicago or Cook County (both are issued from the Cook County Bureau of Vital Statistics) from the 1870s will provide: the full name, age, sex, marital status, and occupation of the deceased. The date and hour of death as well as the cause and the duration of the disease are listed. The street address and the ward, nationality and place of birth, and length of residence in this state were other questions asked on the standard forms. The place and date of burial and the name and address of the undertaker are other valuable pieces of information sources which were noted on a certificate of death. It was not until 1910 that the names and birthplaces of the deceased's parents were included on death certificates.

The Genealogical Society of Utah has microfilmed the following death records:

Cook County (Illinois). County Clerk. Chicago death certificates, 1878-1915. Microfilm of original records in the Cook County courthouse, Chicago, Illinois. (655 microfilm reels)

STANLEY T. KUSPER, JR., County Clerk

REQUEST FOR PHOTOSTATIC COPY OF

Form CD

DEATH RECORDS

Before Filling Out Application Be Certain DEATH Occurred in Cook County

Name _____

First Name   Middle Name   Last Name

Date of Death _____

Place of Death _____

City, Town or Village

I, the undersigned do hereby certify that I am a person, or a duly authorized agent of a person, who has a personal or property right interest in the death certificate, and am legally entitled to the certificate, as specifed by Illinois State Statute [Chap. 111-1/2, Sec. 73-25(4)(d)].

_____

Name of Person Requesting Copy

_____

Signature of Person Requesting Copy

_____

Address

_____

City

Relationship of Person Requesting Copy

Please Enclose Self Addressed
Stamped Envelope

Kindly Mail Certificate of Death to:

Name _____

Address _____

City _____ **State** _____ **Zip Code** _____

Statutory Fee for All Searches is $5,.00 for each 3 Year period searched.
If Record is Found a Certified Copy Will Be Mailed Free of Charge.
Additional copies are $2.00 each.

Make Remittance by Money Order or Check, Payable to:

STANLEY T. KUSPER, JR., County Clerk

Bureau of Vital Statistics (Lower Randolph Street Concourse)
118 North Clark Street, Chicago, Illinois 60602

 445

Figure 26. *Application for Death Record (may be photocopied)*

Certificates are divided into four-month periods (Jan.-Apr., etc.), and numbering begins over for each period. Earliest years may be divided into two periods of six months each. After obtaining a name and date from the microfiche index, it will be necessary to look in the appropriate sequence of numbers. For example, John Doe died in June 1911, and his certificate number is listed as being 1001. His death certificate would be found in the second numbering sequence for 1911 (May-Aug.). Certificates are arranged numerically. Many certificates are missing or filmed out of sequence. Certificates for some months are arranged alphabetically by first letter of surname. Some county certificates are filed with city certificates.

Cook County (Illinois). County Clerk. Death record indexes, 1871-1916. Microreproduction of original indexes at the Cook County Courthouse, Chicago, Illinois. (70 microfiche)

Cook County (Illinois). County Coroner. Coroner's death records, 1879-1904. Microfilm of original records at the Cook County courthouse, Chicago, Illinois. Records for each month are arranged alphabetically by first letter of surname.

Chicago (Illinois). Board of Health. Chicago Deaths 1871-1933. (13 microfilm reels) Alphabetical listing of Chicago city and county deaths returned to the clerk includes name, address, date of death, and register number. (The register number no longer applies and should not be included when filling out a request form for a death certificate.) (13 microfilm reels). This is, without any question, the quickest means of finding a death date for individuals in Chicago. It is not, however, all inclusive; but it does include some Chicagoans who died out of town, and stillbirths.

The criteria for inclusion of deaths on this list is yet unknown despite an investigation by the author. It would seem that they are burial permits and their respective registration numbers with the Chicago Board of Health. This would explain the fact that the numbers do not agree with death certificate numbers. Additionally, it would provide a reason for the inclusion of out of town deaths as well as the absence of some persons who died in Chicago, but whose names do not appear in the index. Death certificates for persons who appear on the list with an out-of-town address cannot be obtained in the Cook County Bureau of Vital Statistics even though the names appear on the Chicago Death Index, but must be ordered from the city or county listed after the name of the individual. Those included in the list with out-of-town are almost always found to be buried in a Chicago area cemetery.

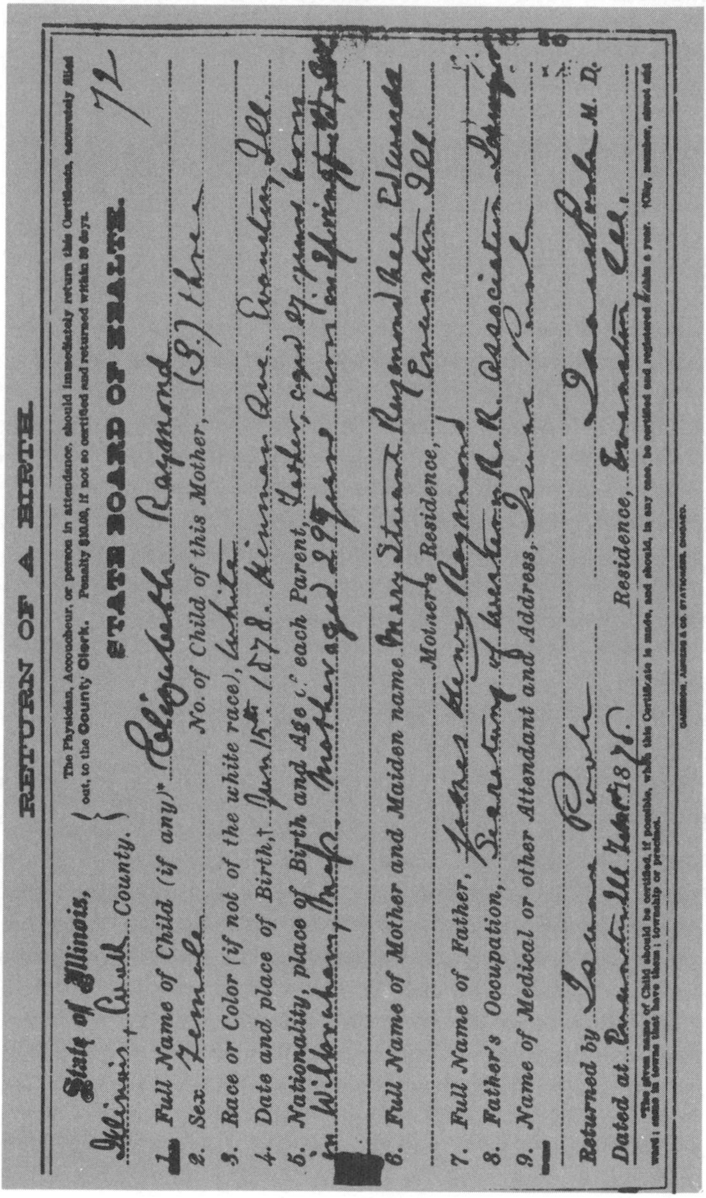

Figure 27. *Cook County Birth Record—1878*

ALTERNATIVE SOURCES OF VITAL RECORDS
CHICAGO BOARD OF HEALTH

The Chicago Board of Health, located in the lower level of the Daley Center, maintains only Chicago vital statistics. Chicago birth records are available in that office from 1955 to the present for a $10 fee. Chicago death records are available from 1961 to the present for the same amount.

Cook County suburban cities and towns (outside of Chicago) also maintain their respective sets of vital statistics; however, they are for relatively recent years. Records filed with the state are at:

STATE OF ILLINOIS
Office of Vital Records
Illinois Department of Public Health
Springfield, IL 62761

The Chicago Genealogical Society has compiled a "Chicago Ancestor File: 1974-84," which contains records of over 10,000 ancestors who were residents of Chicago. Contributed by more than 1,250 of their descendants, it was compiled and indexed by the Chicago Genealogical Society. Each entry shows the name of the ancestor; date and location of birth, death, or marriage; name of spouse; parents' names; dates of residency in Chicago; and the name and address of the person submitting the information. The 381-page volume was published and is available for sale by the Chicago Genealogical Society, P.O. Box 1160, Chicago, IL 60690. Data which has been collected since the publication of the "Chicago Ancestor File 1974-1984" is being printed in the society's quarterly publication, *The Chicago Genealogist*.

VITAL RECORDS FROM CHICAGO NEWSPAPERS

In seven volumes covering the years 1833 to 1848, the Chicago Genealogical Society has published vital statistics which appeared in Chicago newspapers. Data included in each of the separately sold books includes marriage and death information, thereby making it possible to recreate the records destroyed by the 1871 Chicago Fire. All volumes are indexed. Vol. I, 1833-39; Vol. II, 1840-42; Vol. III, 1843-44; Vol. IV, 1845; Vol.V, 1846; Vol.VI, 1847; Vol. VII, 1848.

DEATH NOTICES FROM LITHUANIAN NEWSPAPERS, 1900-1979

The Balzekas Museum of Lithuanian Culture has the original index which was also microfilmed by the Genealogical Society of Utah and found under "newspapers" in the Genealogical Library Catalog (GLC).

INDEX TO IRISH NAMES FROM CHICAGO NEWSPAPERS

An index of Chicago Irish names is being compiled primarily from personal sources, newspapers, and other printed sources by John

Corrigan. The index, which is constantly growing, consists of over 8,000 names and includes hundreds of death notices and obituaries. Many of the names appearing in the index do not appear in other major sources, making this an especially valuable research tool. Newspapers covered in the index include *The Chicago Inter-Ocean, The New World, The Chicago Citizen, The South Side Sun* and the *Lake Vindicator.* For more information send a stamped, self-addressed envelope to: John Corrigan ,1669 104th Street, Chicago, IL 60643.

INDEX TO POLISH OBITUARIES AND DEATH NOTICES

Hollowak, Thomas L., and Hoffman, William F. *Index to the Obituaries and Death Notices Appearing in the* Dziennik Chicagoski 1890-1899. Chicago: Polish Genealogical Society, 1984. An especially valuable tool since many of the names included did not appear in English language newspapers. Available for sale from the Polish Genealogical Society, 984 N. Milwaukee, Chicago, IL, 60622.

INDEX TO THE *CHICAGO RECORD HERALD* DAILY AND SUNDAY (1904-12)

The index is to the date, part, page, and column and is alphabetical by subject. It does not include paid death notices or other vital statistics, but may pinpoint death dates of persons who gained notoriety for any reason such as accident, fire, suicide, and murder victims. Available at the Chicago Historical Society.

DAILY DEMOCRATIC PRESS INDEX—1855

The *Chicago Daily Democratic Press* Index—1855 was prepared by the Omnibus Project, Division of Professional and Service Projects, Works Progress Administration under the sponsorship of The Chicago Public Library. It does not include paid death notices or other vital statistics, but may pinpoint death dates of persons who gained notoriety for any reason, such as accident, fire, suicide, and murder victims. Available at the Chicago Historical Society.

CHURCH VITAL STATISTICS

A *Guide to Church Vital Statistics in Illinois*, prepared by the Illinois Historical Records Survey, Division for Community Service Programs, Works Projects Administration in 1942, lists vital statistics which were found in churches in Illinois. (See Church and Religious Records chapter.)

CORONER'S INQUEST RECORDS
   by Patricia Kathryn Szucs

The Office of the Medical Examiner
County of Cook

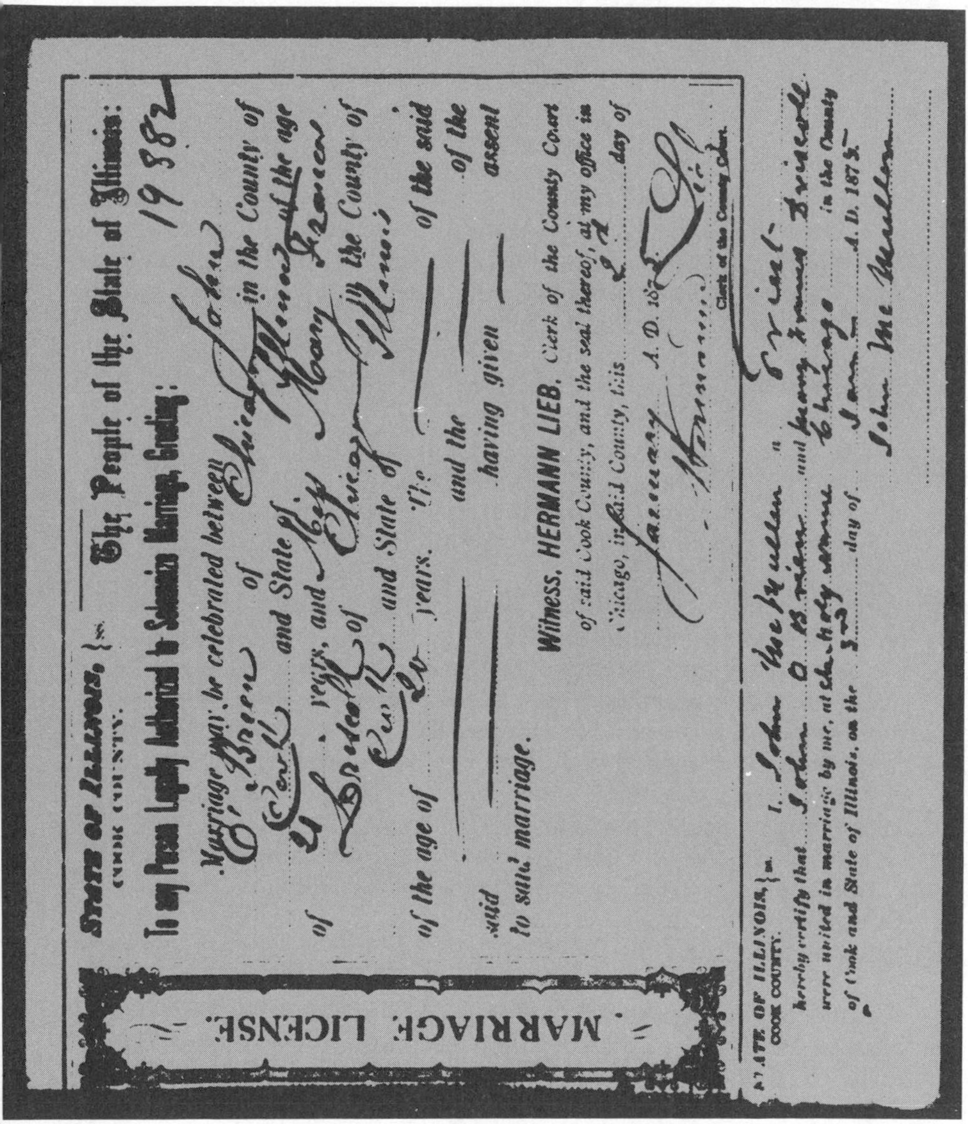

MARRIAGE LICENSE.

STATE OF ILLINOIS, } ss.
COOK COUNTY.

The People of the State of Illinois:

To any Person Legally Authorized to Solemnize Marriage, Greeting:

1988

Marriage may be celebrated between O'Brien John of Chicago in the County of Cook and State of Illinois of the age of 21 years, and Miss Mary Frances Driscoll of Chicago in the County of Cook and State of Illinois of the age of 20 years. The of the said and the of the said having given assent to said marriage.

Witness, HERMANN LIEB, Clerk of the County Court of said Cook County, and the seal thereof, at my office in Chicago, in said County, this 2d day of January A. D. 1875

Hermann Lieb
Clerk of the County Court.

STATE OF ILLINOIS, } ss.
COOK COUNTY.

I, John McMullen a Priest hereby certify that John O'Brien and Mary Frances Driscoll were united in marriage by me, at Chicago in the County of Cook and State of Illinois, on the 3d day of Jan A. D. 1875.

John McMullen

Figure 28. *Cook County Marriage License—1875*

2121 West Harrison
Chicago, IL 60612
(312-666-0500)

Coroner's inquest records are rarely mentioned and seldom used. When researching a violent, unknown, or unnatural death, these records may contain a wealth of information not easily found in other sources.

Inquest records in Cook County are available from 1878 to the present. Until 1910, these records were in bound ledgers. These ledgers are not as extensive as later records, but they do include some personal data. On 6 December 1976, the inquest records came under the jurisdiction of the first Cook County Medical Examiner. When this occurred, there was no longer a determination of guilt included in the record as there often was in the coroner's verdict.

Beginning in 1911, individual inquest files were kept which include many personal details. If they were properly completed, the files include the individual's full name, the date of inquest, and a list of names, addresses, and occupations of witnesses and jurors. A "Statistical History of the Deceased" included: the address of the individual, age, sex, color, marital status, birthplace, how long they were in the city and the U.S., name and birthplace of father, maiden name and birthplace of mother, date of death, date of accident, hour of accident, mental and physical condition, height, weight, extent of education, religion, housing conditions, occupation, employer, past occupation, wages or salary due, amount of life insurance, value of personal and real estate property, military service, number and ages of dependents, cause of death, cause of accident or catastrophe, place of accident and death, name of company or persons involved in death, and more. The doctor's statement, which is attached to the file, may in itself include several pages of physical details.

The testimony of a witness may give a detailed account of the death. A special insight into the character of the individual and his lifestyle may be revealed when the witness happens to be a relative or someone who knew the decedent.

Some of the most notorious murder cases in the country are documented in the coroner's collection. Many times they provide the missing link to an unsolved police case. Among these records was found the long-lost John Dillinger autopsy report, after an absence of decades.

Catastrophe records are grouped together by name of disaster (Our Lady of Angels Fire, railroad accidents, airplane crashes, etc.), and then by individual names involved. Records for early years are contained in single volumes for an entire year, but files for the last two fill great bookcases in a large room. The early ledgers and records have suffered water damage and crumble when they are touched, and there are no other copies. No effort has been proposed to microfilm or otherwise preserve these documents.

When requesting a case file, the date of death or inquest must be known. Cases prior to 1974 are stored in a warehouse and it usually takes a couple of days to have them brought to the medical examiner's office for viewing. Photocopies may be requested for a fee.

CEMETERY RECORDS

Cemetery records are very useful for establishing death dates and for obtaining clues to other vital statistics. See chapter on cemetery records.

FUNERAL DIRECTOR'S RECORDS

Records from 398 funeral homes in Cook County have been surveyed by Kirk Vandenburg of the South Suburban Genealogical and Historical Society. During the process of the survey, every attempt was made to locate records of funeral homes that have changed names or gone out of business. Plans are underway to publish this valuable compilation. For further information, send a stamped, self-addressed envelope to South Suburban Genealogical and Historical Society, P.O. Box 96, South Holland, IL 60473.

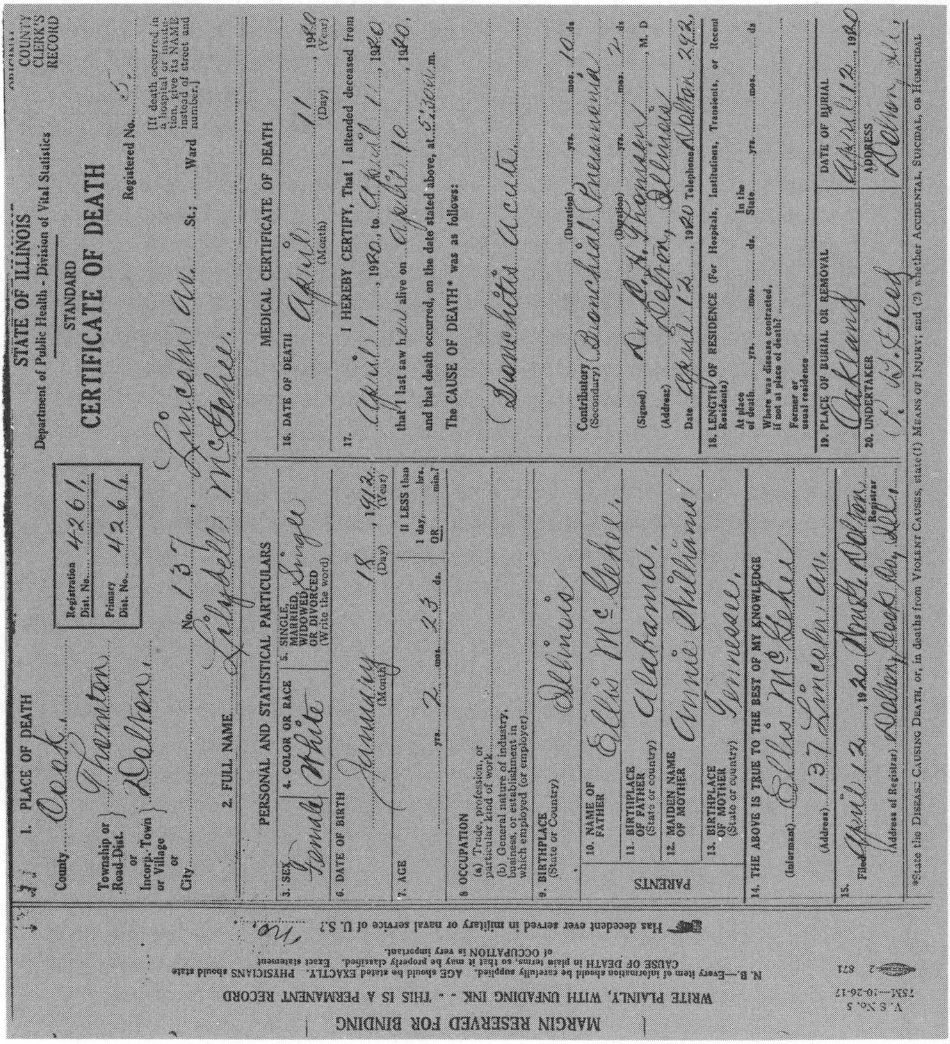

STATE OF ILLINOIS
Department of Public Health - Division of Vital Statistics
STANDARD
CERTIFICATE OF DEATH

Registered No. ...5...

1. PLACE OF DEATH

County ....Cook....

Township or Road-Dist. ....Thornton....

or Incorp.-Town or Village ....Dolton....

City ....

[If death occurred in a hospital or institution, give its NAME instead of street and number.]

2. FULL NAME ....Lizbeth McAhee....

No. ..137.. ..Lincoln Av.. St., ... Ward

PERSONAL AND STATISTICAL PARTICULARS

Registration Dist. No. ..4261..

Primary Dist. No. ..4261..

3. SEX ....Female....

4. COLOR OR RACE ....White....

5. SINGLE, MARRIED, WIDOWED, OR DIVORCED (Write the word) ....Single....

6. DATE OF BIRTH ....January 18, 1918.... (Month) (Day) (Year)

7. AGE ..2.. yrs. ..2.. mos. ..23.. ds. If LESS than 1 day, ...hrs. OR ...min.?

9. OCCUPATION
(a) Trade, profession, or particular kind of work.
(b) General nature of industry, business, or establishment in which employed (or employer)

8. BIRTHPLACE (State or Country) ....Illinois....

PARENTS

10. NAME OF FATHER ....Ellis McAhee....

11. BIRTHPLACE OF FATHER (State or country) ....Alabama....

12. MAIDEN NAME OF MOTHER ....Annie Williams....

13. BIRTHPLACE OF MOTHER (State or country) ....Tennessee....

14. THE ABOVE IS TRUE TO THE BEST OF MY KNOWLEDGE

(Informant) ....Ellis McAhee....

(Address) ....137 Lincoln Av.....

15. Filed ....April 12, 1920.... ....Annal Dolton.... (Address of Registrar) Dolton Cook Co. Ill. ....Registrar

---

MEDICAL CERTIFICATE OF DEATH

16. DATE OF DEATH ....April 11, 1920.... (Month) (Day) (Year)

17. I HEREBY CERTIFY, That I attended deceased from ....April 1, 1920, to April 11, 1920.... that I last saw h... alive on ....April 10, 1920...., and that death occurred, on the date stated above, at ....5 A.M.... m.

The CAUSE OF DEATH* was as follows:
....Bronchitis Acute.... (Duration) ..yrs. ..mos. ..10.. ds.

Contributory (Secondary) ....Bronchial Pneumonia.... (Duration) ..yrs. ..mos. ..2.. ds.

(Signed) ....Dr. A. H. Thomas...., M. D

(Address) ....Dolton, Illinois....

Date ....April 12, 1920.... Telephone ....Dolton 292....

18. LENGTH OF RESIDENCE (For Hospitals, Institutions, Transients, or Recent Residents)

At place of death .....yrs. .....mos. .....ds. In the State .....yrs. .....mos. .....ds.

Where was disease contracted, if not at place of death ....

Former or usual residence ....

19. PLACE OF BURIAL OR REMOVAL ....Oakland.... DATE OF BURIAL ....April 12, 1920....

20. UNDERTAKER ....F. H. Seed.... ADDRESS ....Dolton, Ill.....

---

*State the DISEASE CAUSING DEATH, or, in deaths from VIOLENT CAUSES, state (1) MEANS OF INJURY; and (2) whether ACCIDENTAL, SUICIDAL, OR HOMICIDAL.

Has decedent ever served in military or naval service of U. S.?

N. B.—Every item of information should be carefully supplied. AGE should be stated EXACTLY. PHYSICIANS should state CAUSE OF DEATH in plain terms, so that it may be properly classified. Exact statement of OCCUPATION is very important.

WRITE PLAINLY, WITH UNFADING INK. - - THIS IS A PERMANENT RECORD

MARGIN RESERVED FOR BINDING

V. S No. 5
7SM—10-26-17
2 871

Figure 29. *Cook County Death Record—1920*

CHAPTER 21

Miscellaneous Sources and Addresses

CHICAGO ANCESTOR FILE

R ecords of over 10,000 ancestors who were residents of Chicago were contributed by more than 1,250 of their descendants. *Chicago Ancestor File: 1974-1984* shows dates and locations of births, marriages, and deaths. The names and addresses of submitters in the compilation make it possible to exchange surname information. The 381-page volume is available for purchase from the Chicago Genealogical Society, P.O. Box 1160, Chicago, 60690.

HOSPITAL INFORMATION

The Northwestern Memorial Group Archives
516 West 36th Street
Chicago, IL 60609
(312-908-3090)

The Northwestern Archives has records of some of the older and now defunct hospitals. The Genealogical Society of Utah has microfilmed part of the hospital collection which included birth records. (See chapter on Vital Records). The archives are open Monday through Friday from 8:30 a.m. to 5:00 p.m. Call for further information regarding holdings, finding aids, and access to collections. Photocopy and microform copies are available for materials not restricted. See Rima Schultz "Discoveries in the Stacks" *Origins* I, No.3 (April 1985): 6-7, for a complete description of the holdings.

MARITIME

Chicago Maritime Society
5508 South Lake Park Avenue
Chicago, IL 60637
(312-667-6666)

The Chicago Historical Society
Clark at North Streets
Chicago, IL 60614
(312-642-4600)

The Society has a great number of publications cataloged which provide a sound basis for maritime research.

National Archives-Chicago Branch
7358 Pulaski Road
Chicago, IL 60629
(312-581-7816)

The National Archives-Chicago Branch has Records of the Bureau of Marine Inspection for Illinois, 1865-1952. Certificates of enrollment and licensing of commercial vessels and yachts; oaths taken by owners and masters; records of mortgages and bills of sale of vessels; and correspondence regarding vessel documentation are arranged chronologically.

Feltner, Charles E. and Feltner, Jeri Baron. *Great Lakes Maritime History: Bibliography and Sources of Information.* Dearborn, Mich.: Seajay Publications, 1982.

This bibliography is a valuable source for anyone interested in Great Lakes maritime history. There are over one thousand entries organized in twelve categories which include: reference works; great lakes history; ship history; directories and registers; shipbuilding and ship construction; shipwreck history; U.S. Government organizations; charts, maps and cartography; newspapers and periodicals; photographic collections; special topics; archives, societies and museums.

PASSENGER LISTS OF SHIPS ARRIVING AT AMERICAN PORTS

The National Archives-Chicago Branch has the largest collection of microfilmed passenger lists in the Chicago area. The Port of New York arrivals (1820-1897) form the greatest number of films, but the recently acquired Galveston arrivals (1896-1951) are a formidable addition to the passenger list series. Copies of Lists of Passengers Arriving at Miscellaneous Ports on the Atlantic and Gulf Coasts and at Ports on the Great Lakes (Chicago not included), 1820-1873 is unindexed and constitutes the smallest part of the collection which is arranged by Port. The Archives has most of the major passenger list index series which have recently been published.

PRINTS AND PHOTOGRAPHS

The charm of photographs is that they communicate with us in a universal language. Any family or local history is enhanced by the

255

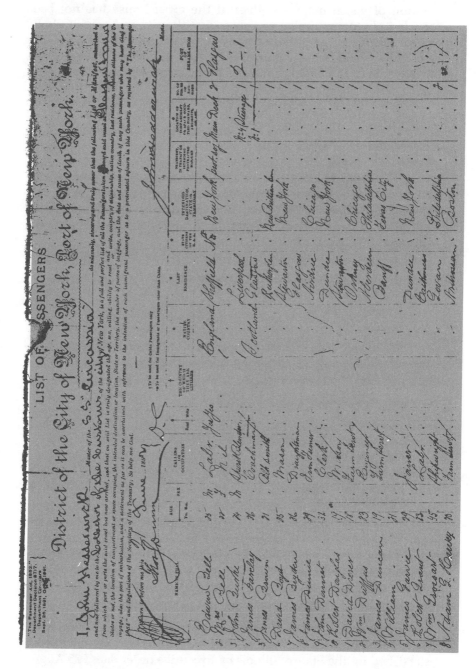

Figure 30. *New York Passenger List—1892 (courtesy National Archives—Chicago Branch)*

addition of visual materials. Even if the exact house has not been recorded photographically, to know what the city and neighborhood looked like in our grandfather's day adds another dimension to our research. Several libraries and commercial enterprises make it possible to obtain copies of old prints and photographs of the Chicago area.

The Chicago Historical Society
Prints & Photographs Collection
Clark at North Avenue
Chicago, IL 60614
(312-642-4600)

In hundreds of file drawers and thousands of carefully labeled folders rest nearly one million photographs, prints, posters, and broadsides of the Chicago Historical Society's Prints and Photographs Collection. Catalogued by geographical areas and by subject, the pictures can be purchased for a nominal cost.

The Chicago Public Library
Cultural Center, Special Collections
78 East Washington Street
Chicago, IL 60602
(312-269-2900)

The Chicago Public Library Special Collections Division has thousands of old Chicago neighborhood photographs to choose from and copies can be purchased very reasonably.

TAX RECORD SOURCES

Real Estate Tax
Cook County Assessor's Office
County Building
118 North Clark Street, Room 301
Chicago, Illinois 60602
(312-443-5306)

The Assessor appraises Cook County property for tax purposes and records dating from 1955 to the present are filed at that office. Unimproved property as well as property with buildings is filed by Permanent Real Estate Number. Older records are housed at the warehouse and are difficult to access.

Internal Revenue Assessment Lists for Illinois, 1862-1866

On sixty-three rolls of this microfilm publication are reproduced bound volumes of tax assessment lists for the thirteen collection districts established for the State of Illinois by Executive order dated 25 August

1862. The lists were created in the offices of assessors of Internal Revenue during the period 1862-66.

The Internal Revenue Act of 1 July 1862 was intended to provide Internal Revenue to support the Government and to pay interest on the public debt. Monthly, specific, and *ad valorem* duties were placed on manufactures, articles, and products ranging from ale to zinc. Monthly taxes were levied on the gross receipts of transportation companies; on interest paid on bonds; on surplus funds accumulated by financial institutions and insurance companies; on gross receipts from auction sales; and on sales of slaughtered cattle, hogs, and sheep. Gross receipts from newspaper advertisements were subject to quarterly tax. Annual licenses were required for all trades and occupations, and annual duties were placed on carriages, yachts, billiard tables, and gold and silver plate. An annual tax was also levied on all income in excess of $600, and legacies and distributive shares of personal property were made taxable. Stamp duties were imposed on legal and business documents and on medical preparations, playing cards, perfumery, and cosmetics.

The act also authorized the establishment of the Office of Commissioner of Internal Revenue in the Treasury Department to superintend the collection of taxes and to prepare regualtions, instructions, and forms used in assessing and collecting taxes.

All persons, partnerships, firms, associations, or corporations submitted to the assistant assessor of their division a list showing the amount of annual income, artilces subject to the special tax or duty, and the quantity of goods made or sold in volume. Lists are not included for every division or every month.

These records are part of Record Group 58, Records of the Internal Revenue Service, in the National Archives and are available at the National Archives-Chicago Branch. Cook County is District One, on microfilm roll numbers 1 and 2.

Internal Revenue Service Records 1905-19

The National Archives-Chicago Branch has Records of the Internal Revenue Service, Illinois, 1905-19. These records are in bound volumes and are arranged by district and thereunder chronologically. They are part of Record Group 58.

VOTER LISTS—VOTER REGISTRATION

Cook County Clerk—Election Department
118 North Clark Street, Room 402
Chicago, IL 60602
(312-263-3163)

A list of Cook County Voters of 7 August 1826 was publishd in the *Chicago Genealogist* II, No. 2 (Dec. 1969), and a list of voters in the first city election in Chicago was published in *Genealogical Sources in Chicago, Illinois 1835-1900* (Chicago: The Chicago Genealogical Society, 1982).

Lurie Index of Chicago Voters, 1937

The Lurie Index was part of a private collection which was microfilmed by the Genealogical Society of Utah, and as far as it can be determined, the LDS film is the only public access to this source. The LDS catalog description follows:

Lurie Index of people in Chicago in 1937 as well as all of the voters-'registration for Chicago. Addresses are included. Tucson, Arizona, 38 reels of microfilm. Nos. 0933501-0933538.

Some Voter Registration Lists for early years survive in Cook County warehouses, but are not accessible. Others are in the custody of private sources. They are difficult to use, even when found as they are arranged by address, ward, and precinct number. A typical example is:

Precinct Register of Voters
October 17, 1940
Ward 42, Precinct 1
West Division Street
708—Modica Sam, 1st r
712—Craven Gar Rev., 1st Fl
712—Evans Ada, 2nd Fl
712—Gordnen Annie M, 2nd Fl
712—Martin Marie, 2nd Fl
712—McCullough Charles r
712—Miller Lee, 2nd Fl
712—Ward Preston r
712—Williams Allen r

COOK COUNTY SCHOOL RECORDS

For Cook County schools outside the city of Chicago, records must be obtained from the local school districts. Addresses of district administrative offices can be obtained from public libraries serving the area of interest.

Chicago and Cook County high schools keep their own records as do all private elementary and high schools.

CHICAGO PUBLIC SCHOOL RECORDS

Chicago Public Schools
Division of Records Services

1819 West Pershing Road 2C(n)
Chicago, IL 60609
(312-890-7722, 8748, or 8444)

Apply in person or write for records. A fee and a stamped, self-addressed envelope must be enclosed with the request form.

Chicago Public Schools
Bureau of Libraries
1819 West Pershing Road 4C(n)
Chicago, IL 60609

The Chicago Public Schools Professional Library provides a collection of professional material related to the field of education. All Chicago Public School employees may use and withdraw materials. The public is invited to use the collection on a noncirculating basis. Of special interest to genealogists and historians is the archival material in the library which includes Proceedings of the Chicago Board of Education from 1867 to 1945 (microfiche and some hard copies). Ruling superintendents were required to submit annual reports which included faculty names and salaries; textbooks used in schools; and statistical charts. Lists of graduating students in the proceedings add value to these records which are often used as the basis for writing school histories. The *Manual of Public Schools* a yearly publication available for scattered years from 1869 to 1941, lists names and often the addresses of all teachers in the system. Employment records are kept by the Teacher Personnel Department at the above address.

Archives and Manuscript Collections

L ibraries, repositories, and information centers included in the following list were chosen because of the nature of the respective collections, access, and usefulness for genealogical or historical research. Though considered an important resource, corporation archives were not included as they are more readily found by consulting current directories. Of equal importance, but also omitted from this listing, are the archives of many religious orders. Further information on their collections will be found in the Church and Religious Records chapter.

Alexian Brothers Hospital Archives
600 Alexian Way
Elk Grove Village, IL 60007
(312-640-7550)

American Medical Association Library and Archives
535 North Dearborn
Chicago, IL 60610
(312-645-4999)

American Police Center and Museum
1130 S. Wabash
Chicago, IL 60605
(312-431-0005)

Archdiocese of Chicago Archives
5150 Northwest Hwy.
Chicago, IL 60630
(312-286-7038 Ex. 210)

Art Institute of Chicago-Ryerson and Burnham Archives
Michigan at Adams Street
Chicago, IL 60603
(312-443-4777

Balzekas Museum of Lithuanian Cultures
6500 South Pulaski Road
Chicago, IL 60629
(582-6500 or 847-2441)

Barrington Area Historical Soc.
218 West Main Street
Barrington, IL 60010
(312-381-1730)

Chicago Architecture Foundation
1800 South Prairie
Chicago, IL 60616
(312-326-1393)

Chicago Board of Education
1819 Pershing Road
Chicago, IL 60609
(312-890-8000)

Chicago Historical Soc. Library and · Manuscripts Collection
Clark Street at North Avenue
Chicago, IL 60614
(312-642-4600, ext. 19)

Chicago Jewish Historical Soc.
1640 East 50th Street
Chicago, IL 60615
(312-493-7938)

Chicago Maritime Soc.
5508 South Lake Park Avenue
Chicago, IL 60637
(312-667-6666)

Chicago and Northwestern Historical
Society and Archives
1812 Hood Avenue
Chicago, IL 60660
(312-743-1159)

Chicago Public School Special Collections
78 East Washington Street
Chicago, IL 60602
(312-269-2906)

Chicago Sun-Times Public Service Bureau
401 North Wabash, Room 110
Chicago, IL 60611
(312-321-2031)

Chicago Tribune Archives
Tribune Tower, Room 1231
435 North Michigan Avenue
Chicago, IL 60611
(312-321-2031)

City of Chicago Commission on Chicago
Historical and Architectural
Landmarks
320 North Clark Street, Room 800
Chicago, IL 60610
(312-744-3200)

City of Chicago Department of Planning
City Hall, Room 1000
121 North LaSalle Street
Chicago, IL 60602
(312-744-4160)

City of Chicago Department of Public
Works Bureau of Engineering
320 North Clark Street, Room 700
Chicago, IL 60610
(312-744-3544)

City of Chicago Municipal Reference
Library
City Hall, Room 1004
121 North LaSalle Street
Chicago, IL 60602
(312-744-4992)

Cook County Hospital Archives Health
Science Library Nurses' Residence
1900 West Polk Street
Chicago, IL 60612
(312-633-7538)

The John Crerar Library
35 West 33rd Street
Chicago, IL 60616
(312-225-2526)

Croatian Ethnic Institute, Inc.
4851 South Drexel Boulevard
Chicago, IL 60615
(312-373-2248)

Czechoslovak Heritage Museum
2701 South Harlem Avenue
Berwyn, IL 60402
(312-562-2595)

DePaul University Archives
2323 North Seminary
Chicago, IL 60614
(312-341-8088)

Des Plaines Historical Society and
Museum
789 Pearson Street
Des Plaines, IL 60016

Du Sable Museum of African and
Museum
740 East 56th Place
Chicago, IL 60637
(312-947-0600)

Elmhurst Historical Museum
120 East Park Avenue
Elmhurst, IL 60126
(312-833-1457)

Episcopal Church Archives
65 East Huron
Chicago, IL 60611
(312-787-6410)

Max Epstein Photography Archive
The Joseph Regenstein Library
Room 420, University of Chicago
1100 East 57th Street
Chicago, IL 60637
(312-753-2887)

Evangelical Covenant Archives and
Historical Library
5125 North Spaulding Avenue
Room 25
Chicago, IL 60637
(312-583-2700, ext. 287)

The Evanston Historical Soc.
225 Greenwood Street
Evanston, IL 60201
(312-475-3410)

Glenview Area Historical Soc.
1121 Waukegon Road
Glenview, IL 60025
(312-724-2235)

Grand Army of the Republic Memorial
Hall
Chicago Public Library
Special Collections
78 East Washington Street
Chicago, IL 60602
(312-269-2926)

Hedrich-Blessing
11 West Illinois Street
Chicago, IL 60610
(312-321-1151)

Historical Pictures Service, Inc.
17 North State Street
Chicago, IL 60602
(312-346-0599)

Historic Pullman Foundation, Inc.
11111 South Forestville Avenue
Chicago, IL 60628
(312-785-8181)

Hyde Park Historical Soc.
5437 South Lake Park Avenue
Chicago, IL
(312-493-1893)

Illinois Institute of Technology Archives
31 Perlstein Hall
10 West 33rd Street
Chicago, IL 60616
(312-567-3039)

Illinois Labor History Soc.
2800 Sheridan Road
Chicago, IL 60657
(312-248-8700)

Illinois State Archives
Archives Building
Springfield, IL 62756
(217-782-3641)

Irish-American Heritage Center
4626 North Knox
Chicago, IL 60630

K. and S. Photo Graphics
180 North Wabash Avenue
Eighth Floor
Chicago, IL 60601

Kenilworth Historical Soc.
415 Kenilworth Avenue
Kenilworth, IL 60043
(312-251-2565)

La Grange Area Historical Soc.
444 South LaGrange Road
P.O. Box 613
La Grange, IL 60525
(312-482-4248)

Loyola University Archives
6525 Sheridan Road
Chicago, IL 60626
(312-508-2661)

Lutheran Church in America Archives
1100 East 55th Street
Chicago, IL 60601
.(312-667-3500)

MAC (Midwest Archives Conference)
Archives
Northwestern University
Library Archives
Evanston, IL 60201
(312-491-3136)

Marquis Who's Who
200 East Ohio Street
Chicago, IL 60611
(312-787-2008 ext. 253)

Matteson Historical Soc.
813 School Avenue
Matteson, IL 60443
(312-791-4476)

Midwest Nursing Library
Research Center
College of Nursing, Room 1042
845 South Damen Avenue
Chicago, IL 60612
(312-996-8005)

Moody Bible Institute Library
820 North LaSalle Street
Chicago, IL 60610
(312-329-4140)

Mundelein College Archives
6363 Sheridan Road
Chicago, IL 60660
(312-262-8100)

National Archives
Washington, DC 20408
(202-523-3218)

National Archives-Chicago Branch
7358 South Pulaski Road
Chicago, IL 60629   .
(312-581-7816)

National Baha'i Archives
Baha'i House of Worship
100 Linden Avenue
Willmette, IL 60091
(312-869-9039)

Newberry Library
Modern Manuscripts
60 West Walton
Chicago, IL 60610
(312-943-9090)

Northeastern Illinois University
Library
5500 North St. Louis
Chicago, IL 60625
(312-583-4050 ext. 479)

Northwestern Memorial Hospital Archives
516 West 36th Street
Chicago, IL 60609
(312-908-3090)

Northwestern University Library
Special Collections, Archives
1935 Sheridan Road
Evanston, IL 60201
(312-492-3635)

Oak Lawn Historical Soc.
9526 South Cook Avenue
Oak Lawn, IL 60453
(312-425-3424)

Oak Park Public Library
834 Lake Street
Oak Park, IL 60301
(312-383-8200)

Palatine Historical Soc.
224 East Palatine Road
Palatine, IL 60067
(312-991-6460)

Polish Museum of America
984 Milwaukee Avenue
Chicago, IL 60622
(312-384-3352)

Printer's Row Printing Museum
715 South Dearborn
Chicago, IL 60605
(312-987-1059)

Ravenswood-Lake View Historical
Association
4544 North Lincoln Avenue
Chicago, IL 60625
(312-728-8652)

Ridge Historical Soc.
10621 South Seeley Avenue
Chicago, IL 60643
(312-881-1675)

Rush Presbyterian-St. Luke Medical
Center
1753 West Congress Parkway
Chicago, IL 60612
(312-942-7214)

Society of American Archivists
600 South Federal
Suite 504
Chicago, IL 60605
(312-922-0140)

South Holland Historical Soc.
16250 Wausau Avenue
South Holland, IL 60423
(312-596-2722)

South Shore Historical Soc.
7566 South Shore Drive
Chicago, IL 60649
(312-375-1699)

South Side Irish Parade and Heritage
Foundation
10926 South Western Avenue
Chicago, IL 60643
(312-238-1969)

South Suburban Genealogical and
Historical Soc.
P.O. Box 96
South Holland, IL 60473
(312-333-9474)

Spertus College of Judaica
618 South Michigan
Chicago, IL 60605
(312-922-9012 ext. 65)

Swedish Pioneer Archives
5125 North Spaulding
Chicago, IL 60625
(312-583-5722)

University of Chicago Library Special
Collections
1100 East 57th Street
Chicago, IL 60637
(312-962-8705)

University of Illinois at Chicago
Library
P.O. Box 8198
801 South Morgan, Room 220
Chicago, IL 60607
(312-996-2756)

University of Illinois
Medical Center Archives
1750 West Polk Street
Chicago, IL 60612
(312-996-8977)

Wilmette Historical Museum
565 Hunter Road
Wilmette, IL 60091
(312-256-5838)

Winnetka Historical Soc.
P.O. Box 142
768 Oak
Winnetka, IL 60093
(312-446-0497)

Historical Societies

THE CHICAGO HISTORICAL SOCIETY

Clark Street at North Avenue
Chicago, IL 60614
Telephone 312-642-4600

HOURS:

Exhibition Galleries	Mon.-Sat.: 9:30 a.m. to 4:30 p.m. Sun: Noon to 5:00 p.m.
Research Collections	Tues.-Sat.: 9:30 a.m. to 4:30 p.m.

A large portion of the materials collected during the early years concerns general American history as well as the history of other localities. Through the years the society has placed increasing emphasis on Chicago as the predominant, though not exclusive, subject for its collections.

The first building of the Chicago Historical Society opened on 19 November 1868 on the northwest corner of Ontario and Dearborn. Three years later, the structure and all of its contents were destroyed in the Great Chicago Fire. Collecting began again, and the Society rebuilt a new and massive Romanesque building on the original site in 1896. In 1920, the society purchased the fabulous collection of Charles H. Gunther, a Chicago candy manufacturer who had bought everything from fifteenth-century books to an entire Civil War prison, including Abraham Lincoln's carriage and Benjamin Franklin's typesetting stick. In 1932, the Chicago Historical Society moved to its present location in Lincoln Park.

THE MUSEUM

From the anchor of the Santa Maria to George Washington's waistcoat to the extensive Civil War and Lincoln collections, American history is represented through a variety of original materials, exhibitions, and publications at the Chicago Historical Society. The oldest Chicago-related item in the manuscript collection is a letter written by Robert Cavalier de La Salle from "Checagou," and dated 1 September 1683.

Other artifacts and writings ranging from the days of Fort Dearborn to the more contemporary collections of the United Steelworkers of America, are also part of the Society's holdings.

RESEARCH RESOURCES

Library holdings include more than 120,000 books and pamphlets, 20,000 volumes of newspapers and periodicals, 10,000 maps and atlases, 50,000 pieces of printed ephemera such as theater and concert programs, 14,000 broadsides and posters, 50,000 prints, 900,000 photographs, 9,900 reels of microfilm, and 10,000,000 manuscripts (correspondence and other records of individuals, institutions, and organizations). The Museum Research Collection includes more than 12,000 costume items, 1,500 paintings and sculptures, and 10,000 artifacts.

The research collections concern all aspects of life in Chicago from the early nineteenth century to the present including business and industry, labor, social welfare, politics, architecture, and music. All types of materials useful for research or exhibit are represented, from Chicago directories and trade catalogs to architectural drawings and TV newsfilm.

THE LIBRARY

While Chicago dominates the library collection, other areas of Cook County and Illinois are well represented. The collection includes the basic sources: general histories of the state, counties, and towns; traveler's journals and descriptions; accounts of important organizations and agencies; and similar materials. The library does acquire, on a selective basis, some materials concerning the Civil War and Abraham Lincoln.

THE LIBRARY REFERENCE COLLECTION

The Library Reference Collection is an extensive group of books and articles assembled to answer basic questions about Chicago history. The collection is located in the society's main reading room for easy access.

The items in the reference collection were chosen because they provide a substantial amount of information on Chicago topics without requiring extensive use of primary sources. The easiest way to identify material on the subject of your research is to consult a copy of the *Annotated Bibliography of Chicago History*. Several copies are available on the tables in the reading room. This bibliography, arranged by subject, lists and describes many of the items in the reference collection. To find your subject look at the table of contents and select the section that relates to your topic. If the society owns an item, the call number for it will be written in the margin. All of the materials marked with call numbers are housed in the reference collection. Obviously, additions have been made to the collection since the publication date, and not all of the entries in the card catalog will be found in the bibliography. The card catalog is still the key finding aid.

The society's library has some unique sources for researchers interested in biographical information. Among these are: membership directories and yearbooks from Chicago clubs and associations, high school yearbooks, Civil War regimental histories for Illinois, newsletters from Chicago companies, and anniversary (centennial, jubilee) publications from churches, banks, etc. All can be located by using the card catalog.

NEWSPAPERS

Files of Chicago newspapers are very extensive, but of course, not complete. The library has Chicago's first newspaper, the *Chicago Democrat*, from the inaugural issue in 1833 until it ceased publication in 1861. Many other extinct newspapers and ethnic and foreign-language newspaper files are there. A list of the library's newspaper holdings in microfilm is available on each table in the reading room. A related collection is the clipping file, consisting of about thirty-seven file drawers of clippings selected from major Chicago newspapers and arranged by subject. Materials in the clipping file date from the 1930s, and clippings are added to the file on a weekly basis. A list of the subject headings used in arranging the file is available on each table in the reading room.

DIRECTORIES

City directories, which attempted to list every individual and every business in Chicago from 1839 to 1917, are kept in the reading room. The city directories ceased consecutive publication after 1917, though directories did appear in 1923 and 1928-29. Since many of the original book copies are crumbling due to time, paper content and heavy use, they are being microfilmed. For directory information after 1917 readers must rely on the telephone directories which are available on microfilm or microfiche. The society holds reverse or "criss-cross" directories arranged by address for the years 1928, 1950, 1952, 1978, and 1984.

Located next to the city directories on the open shelves are the *Who's Who in Chicago* and the *Chicago Blue Book* which provide information on Chicago's most prominent residents. In addition, there are many directories not located in the reading room. These holdings can be identified by looking in the card catalog under the name of a city or county and noting those with the subheading "Directories", i.e., Evanston, Illinois. Directories.

MAPS

The society's map collection includes some 150 Illinois county atlases, 4,000 nineteenth- and twentieth-century maps, of which one half cover Chicago and one half cover Illinois counties. There are special maps for Chicago outline wards, school districts, park district land, and cemeteries. Maps which define ward and boundary changes for the city and surrounding areas were published annually and are listed chronologically. A collection of Chicago area fire insurance atlases is the largest in the area. In addition to Chicago fire insurance atlases, the society also has some for the suburbs and other Illinois towns. The library has a bibliography, *Checklist of Printed Maps of the Middle West to 1900*, Vol. 4, Illinois, which includes its holdings of nineteenth-century published maps. A notebook in the reading room lists the library's nineteenth- and twentieth-century unpublished Chicago maps.

MANUSCRIPTS

Extensive holdings of manuscripts constitute one of most valuable research resources. These collections consist of the correspondence, memoranda, internal reports, and other unpublished files accumulated through the years by Chicago organizations, institutions, firms, and individuals. These manuscript collections provide first-hand accounts in much more detail than most publications.

Treasures in the manuscript collection include: documents dated as early as 1635 concerning French explorations and settlements near the Great Lakes; Indians in the Chicago area; records of the Illinois and Michigan Canal; the early Galena and Chicago Union Railroad; and more recently records of contemporary institutions and organizations. The diversity of the collection is evidenced by such collections as those of Senator Paul H. Douglas; the Illinois Manufacturers Association; the United Charities of Chicago; Welfare Council of Metropolitan Chicago; Jewish Community Centers of Chicago; Afro-American Police League; and the Polish-American Democratic Organization to name a few.

PRINTS AND PHOTOGRAPHS

Another important resource is the Prints and Photographs Collection, which includes over 1 million images. Here are prints engravings, lithographs, broadsides, and motion picture films which relate to Chicago history from the early nineteenth century to the present. The collection is the largest source for pictorial information concerning the history of Chicago and the surrounding area.

SOCIETIES SERVING THE METROPOLITAN AREA

American Police Center and Museum
1130 South Wabash
Chicago, IL 60605

Historical Society and Museum of Arlington Heights
500 North Vail Ave.
Arlington Heights, IL 60004

Balzekas Museum of Lithuanian Culture
6500 Pulaski Road
Chicago, IL

Barrington Historical Society
111 West Station Street
Barrington, IL 60010

Bartlett Historical Society
P.O. Box 257
Bartlett, IL 60103

Blackhawk Chapter
National Railway Historical Society
P.O. Box A-3795
Chicago, IL 60690

Blue Island Historical Society
c/o Blue Island Public Library
2433 York
Blue Island, IL 60406

Bremen Historical Society of Tinley Park
P.O. Box 325
Tinley Park, IL 60477

Broadview Historical Society
2230 South 17th Ave.
Broadview, IL 60153

Brookfield Historical Society
8820 Brookfield Ave.
Brookfield, Il 60513

Buffalo Grove Historical Society
150 Raupp BoulevBuffalo Grove, IL 60090

Calumet Historical Society
11210 South Parnell
Chicago, IL 60628

Center for Photographic Arts Ltd.
364 West Erie
Chicago, IL 60610

Chicago and Northwestern Historical Society
1812 Hood Ave.
Chicago, IL 60660

Chicago Historical Society
Clark Street at North Ave.
Chicago, IL 60614

Chicago Jewish Historical Society
5457 South Hyde Park Boulevard
Chicago, IL 60615

Chicago Lawn Historical Society
3230 West 63rd Place
Chicago, Il 60638

Chicago School of Architecture Foundation
1800 South Prairie Ave.
Chicago, IL 60616

Des Plaines Historical Society
P.O. Box 225
Des Plaines, IL 60016

DuSable Museum of African American
History
740 East 56th Place
Chicago, IL 60637

Elk Grove Historical Society
399 Biesterfield
Elk Grove Village, IL 60007

Elmwood Park Historical Society
c/o Elmwood Park Library
Elmwood Park, IL 60635

Evanston Historical Society
225 Greenwood Street
Evanston, IL 60201

Field Museum of Natural History
East Roosevelt Road and South
Lake Shore Dr.
Chicago, IL 60605

The Historical Society of Forest Park
c/o Dr. Frank Orland, President
519 Jackson Boulevard
Forest Park, IL 60130

Frank Lloyd Wright Home and Studio
Foundation
951 Chicago Ave.
Oak Park, IL 60302

Franklin Park Historical Society
9564 Schiller Boulevard
Franklin Park, IL 60131

Glencoe Historical Society
Glencoe Public Library
320 Park Ave.
Glencoe, IL 60022

Glenview Area Historical Society
1121 Waukegan Road
Glenview, IL 60025

Glessner House
1800 South Prairie Ave.
Chicago, IL 60616

Grand Army of the Republic Museum
78 East Washington Street
Chicago, IL 60602

Greek Heritage Foundation
110 South Dearborn
Chicago, IL 60603

Harvey Area Historical Society
14622 Wallace Street
Harvey, IL 60426

Historic Pullman Foundation, Inc.
11111 South Forrestville Ave.
Chicago, IL 60628

Hyde Park Historical Society
c/o Mrs. John R. Davey
5748 South Harper Ave.
Chicago, IL 60637

Illinois Funeral Service Foundation
Museum
515 North Dearborn
Chicago, IL 60610

Illinois Labor History Society
600 South Michigan Ave.
Chicago, IL 60605

Italian Cultural Center
1621 North 39th Ave.
Stone Park, IL 60165

Jane Addams' Hull-House
750 South Halsted
P.O. Box 4348
Chicago, IL 60680

Kenilworth Historical Society
415 Kenilworth Ave.
Kenilworth, IL 60043

LaGrange Area Historical Society
440 South LaGrange Road
P.O. Box 613
LaGrange, IL 60525

Landmarks Preservation Council
407 South Dearborn Street
Chicago, IL 60605

Lansing Historical Society
P.O. Box 1776
Lansing, IL 60438

Historical Society of
Lawndale-Crawford
c/o Toman Branch Chicago Public
Library
4003 West 27th
Chicago, IL 60623

The Lemont Area Historical Society
306 Lemont Street
P.O. Box 126
Lemont, IL 60439

The Lexington Group in Transporta-
tion History
Graduate School of Management
Northwestern University
Evanston, IL 60201

Ling Long Museum
2238 South Wentworth
Chicago, IL 60616

Lyons Historical Commission
P.O. Box 129
Lyons, IL 60534

Maine West Historical Society
c/o Social Science Department
Maine Township High School West
1755 South Wolf Road
Des Plaines, IL 60018

Matteson Historical Society
813 School Ave.
Matteson, IL 60443

Maurice Spertus Museum of Judaica
618 South Michigan Ave.
Chicago, IL 60605

Maywood Historical Society
202 South 2nd Ave.
Maywood, IL 60153

Melrose Park Historical Society
P.O. Box 1453
Melrose Park, IL 60161

Morton B. Weiss Museum of Judaica
KAM Isaiah Israel Congregation
1100 East Hyde Park
Chicago, IL 60615

Morton Grove Historical Society
P.O. Box 542
Morton Grove, IL 60053

Mount Prospect Historical Society of Elk
  Grove and Wheeling Townships
P.O. Box 81
Mount Prospect, IL 60056

National Trust for Historic Preservation
407 South Dearborn
Chicago, IL 60610

Northbrook Historical Society
1776 Walter's Ave.
Northbrook, IL 60062

Norwood Park Historical Society
Roden Branch Library
6079-83 North Northwest Highway
Norwood Park, IL 60631

Oak Lawn Historical Society
9526 South Cook Ave.
Oak Lawn, IL 60453

The Historical Society of Oak Park and
  River Forest
P.O. Box 771
Oak Park, IL 60303

Oriental Institute
1155 East 58th Street
Chicago, IL 60637

Palatine Historical Society
P.O. Box 315
Palatine, IL 60067

Palos Historical Society
c/o John F. Rodgers
12021 South 93rd Ave.
Palos Park, IL 60464

Park Ridge Historical Society
c/o Paul Carlson
140 Euclid
Park Ridge, IL 60068

Polish Museum of America
984 North Milwaukee Ave.
Chicago, IL 60622

Poplar Creek Historical Society of
  Hoffman Estates
c/o Hoffman Estates Village Hall
1200 North Gannon Drive
Hoffman Estates, IL 60196

Public Works Historical Society
1313 East 60th Street
Chicago, IL 60637

Ravenswood–Lake View Historical
  Society
North Park College
5000 North Spaulding Ave.
Chicago, IL 60625

Ridge Historical Society
c/o R.J. White
10621 South Seely Ave.
Chicago, IL 60643

Riverside Historical Society
107 Bloomingdale Road
Riverside, IL 60546

Skokie Historical Society
8331 Springfield
Skokie, IL 60076

Society of American Archivists
801 South Morgan
Chicago, IL 60680

South Holland Historical Society
P.O. Box 48
South Holland, IL 60473

South Shore Historical Society
7651 South Shore Drive
Chicago, IL 60649

Stone Park Historical Association
Village Hall
1629 North Mannheim Road
Stone Park, IL 60165

Swedish Museum
5248 North Clark
Chicago, IL 60640

Swedish Pioneer Historical Society
5125 North Spaulding Ave.
Chicago, IL 60625

Village of Thorton Historical Society
P.O. Box 34
Thorton, IL 60476

Ukrainian Institute of Modern Art
2247 West Chicago Ave.
Chicago, IL 60622

Western Springs Historical Society
916 Hillgrove Ave.
Western Springs, IL 60558

West Side Historical Society
115 South Pulaski Road
Chicago, IL 60624

Wheeling Historical Society
84 South Milwaukee Ave.
Wheeling, IL 60090

Wilmette Historical Society Museum
825 Green Bay Road
P.O. Box 96
Wilmette, IL 60091

Winnetka Historical Society
P.O. Box 142
Winnetka, IL 60093

Historical Society of Woodlawn
Woodlawn Branch
Chicago Public Library
6247 South Kimbark Ave.
Chicago, IL 60637

Chicago Public Library

425 North Michigan Avenue
Chicago, IL 60611
(312-269-2900)
Hours: Monday-Thursday: 9:00 a.m.-7:00 p.m.
Friday: 9:00 a.m.-6:00 p.m.
Saturday: 9:00 a.m.-5:00 p.m.

THE SOCIAL SCIENCES AND HISTORY DIVISION, 12th Floor

History Section: The History Section includes the broad fields of numismatics, archives, seals, heraldry, travel, genealogy, general biography, and an excellent collection on Native Americans and American history including the Library of American Civilization collection on ultrafiche.

Travel: The travel collection includes a self-help Travel Information and Planning Center which contains copies of current airline, hotel, and travel guides. In addition, there are books describing cities and countries of the world as well as books on ancient civilizations and archeology. Reference atlases and maps are also available.

Chicago History: The Chicago collection consists primarily of noncirculating. Circulating materials are available in the open stack area. A reference clipping file on Chicago and files on local history and streets bring together out-of-the-way information to those interested in Chicagoana. Chicago City Directories for the years 1839, 1843-1917, 1923, 1928/29, and Chicago Telephone Directories for the years 1878-1971 on microfilm (1972 + in hard copy) help those trying to trace ancestors or locate former business establishments. U. S. Census Population Schedules are available for Cook County for the years 1850, 1860, 1870, 1880, 1900 and 1910 in this section. Little known, but very useful for quick reference, is the microfilm collection of 101 Illinois county histories filed in the department. There are county histories for other states in the closed stack area as well as the *Journal of the Illinois State Historical Society;* Wisconsin Historical Collections; *New York Genealogical and Biographical Record;* Massachusetts Historical Society Collection; and the *New England Historical and Genealogical Register* among other important genealogical and historical works.

Genealogy: The Genealogy collection places emphasis on "how to" books. Family histories as such are not collected, except for those of famous American families.

Biography: The Biography collection is strong and contains many collected biographies, biographical dictionaries, and indexes such as the Who's Who series and the *Biography and Genealogy Master Index*. This collection offers a good starting place when the only known information is a person's name. Other subject divisions have biographies of noted persons in their subject fields.

Maps: Approximately 2,000 maps comprise the divisional map collection. Street and road maps of the United States are available together with atlases and gazeteers, for research and reference.

Periodicals: The book collection is augmented and strengthened by a periodical collection of over 1,400 titles.

THE GENERAL INFORMATION SERVICES DIVISION, 12TH FLOOR

The reference services and collections of this division are separated into three major units: the Bibliographic and Interlibrary Loan Center, the Information Center, and the Newspapers and General Periodicals Center.

Bibliographic and Catalog Information (312-269-2807)

To learn if the library owns a particular title, call the Catalog Information Desk. The staff will check up to three titles per call. When the requested book is owned by the library, the staff will provide the call number and location of the branch or division in which the book can be found. If a particular book, article, or needed piece of information is not available at a branch or in a subject division of The Chicago Public Library, it can often be obtained from another library through interlibrary loan.

Information Center (312-269-8200)

The staff of the Information Center provides quick, up-to-date information from reference sources covering all subject areas. Almanacs, dictionaries, business directories, handbooks, and encyclopedias are in the 1,400 volume collection. This book collection is updated and supplemented by clippings from local newspapers. Topics in these clippings files range anywhere from acupuncture to zoos. The Information Center also maintains special files on topics of local interest such as clubs and organizations in the Chicago area, places to pick fresh fruits and vegetables in season, and current information on "things to do" in Chicago. The Information Center typically answers questions such as: the date of Chicago's biggest snowfall; a senator's address; the star of a particular movie; or the distance from Chicago to Miami.

Newspapers and General Periodicals Center

The Newspapers and General Periodicals Center has collections of newspapers, periodicals, indexes, and almanacs covering a broad range of subjects in many different languages. The Newspaper collection includes over 260 current papers from every state and fifty foreign countries. Many U.S. and Chicago ethnic newspapers are received as well as community newspapers from Chicago and the suburbs. Retrospective newspaper holdings include full microfilm runs of the major Chicago newspapers, the *New York Times* and the *Times* (London). Indexes for the *New York Times* from 1851, the *Times* (London) from 1790, and the *Chicago Tribune* from 1972 can also be found in this unit.

The center has complete holdings of many general magazines, including the various weekly news magazines. Some of these holdings date back to the mid-nineteenth century.

Among the special research materials included in this unit are the Foreign Language Press Survey, the Underground Newspaper Microfilm Collection, and the microcard collection of Early American Newspapers, 1704-1820.

Microfilm reader-printers producing copies ranging in size from a full newspaper page to a letter size sheet are available. Prices are nominal.

BUSINESS/SCIENCE/TECHNOLOGY DIVISION

Business/Labor Histories

Listed in the catalog under company name or union are several sources applicable to genealogical or historical research. Of note is a six-volume set entitled *Industrial Chicago* (Goodspeed Publishing Co. 1891-96). Volumes are devoted to building, lumber, manufacturing, judicial, and legal professions. Also useful is the *Certified List of Domestic and Foreign Corporations* (Illinois Secretary of State, 1902—present). Company names are listed alphabetically. Included in the listing is the address of the principal office of the company, the president or manager, the corporate secretary of the company, and each of their addresses.

Computer-Assisted Reference Center (CARC)

CARC has access to more than 200 online databases. Most of these have at most twenty years of records and are automated indexes to secondary or periodical literature. Several are potentially helpful, however. *Biography Master Index* is an index to more than 370 biographical dictionaries and directories. *Dissertation Abstracts Online* includes an author guide to almost every American dissertation accepted at an accredited institution since 1861. *America: History and Life* indexes and summarizes articles from numerous local, state, and special interest historical journals. CARC charges fees for its services and an appointment must be made.

GOVERNMENT PUBLICATIONS

This library is a congressionally designated depository for U.S. Government Documents. The Government Publications Department receives materials from the United States government, State of Illinois, city of Chicago, and Cook County. The Collection totals over 1,000,000 items. Nearly 100 percent of the publications available to libraries through the U.S. Government Printing Office's depository program are currently selected. Arrangement is by the Superintendent of Documents (SUDOC) classification scheme.

The Chicago Public Library became an Illinois depository with the inception of the state depository program in 1968. Prior to the depository act, CPL had built a strong collection which dates from 1826. Arrangement is by an Illinois Documents Classification scheme. In the local collection comprehensive coverage of the city of Chicago and Cook County publications is attempted. Arrangement is by issuing agency and title.

The department has an extensive collection of Congressional reports, documents, hearings, and committee prints dating from the nineteenth century. A complete run of the Congressional Record and its predecessors is available.

Many U.S. agencies have issued statistical publications for many years. Depending on the agency, these are available for various time periods. In addition, all U.S. statistical publications indexed in the *American Statistics Index* (1973-) are available on microfiche. Many Illinois state, Cook County, and Chicago agencies also issue statistical reports.

The department does not have a complete law library. However, law-related titles include: *U.S. Code, Code of Federal Regulations, Federal Register,* administrative decisions of U.S. agencies, *U.S. Reports* (cases adjudged in the Supreme Court), copies of Congressional bills (1981-), *Illinois Revised Statutes, Illinois Register, Illinois Law and Practice,* and the *Chicago Municipal Code.*

Many of the indexes to government publications are available in outline format through the Computer-Assisted Reference Center. Among the indexes available online are American Statistics Index, Congressional Information Service Index, Commerce Business Daily, GPO Monthly Catalog, NTIS and Legi-Slate. The Government Publications Department offers unique access to the Illinois Bill Status System.

Government Publications are for room-use only. Most documents will be loaned to libraries affiliated with The Chicago Public Library/Chicago Library System and member libraries of the Illinois Library and Information Network through special arrangement or through interlibrary loan.

THE CHICAGO PUBLIC LIBRARY CULTURAL CENTER

78 East Washington Street
Chicago, IL 60602
(312-269-2900)

Hours: Monday-Thursday: 9:00 a.m.-7:00 p.m.
Friday: 9:00 a.m.-6:00 p.m.
Saturday: 9:00 a.m.-5:00 p.m.

With a collection of over half a million books, exhibit halls, theater, and Renaissance architecture, The Chicago Public Library Cultural Center is the city's major showcase for the arts. The center offers programs (including frequent presentations on history and genealogy) and exhibits on a wide variety of subjects. The Literature and Language Sections, the Audiovisual Center, the Thomas Hughes Children's Library, the Art and Music Sections and Special Collections are housed at the cultural center.

SPECIAL COLLECTIONS

Reference Hours: 12:00 p.m.-4:00 p.m. Mon.-Fri. Appointments can be made for other times.

The Special Collections Division showcases The Chicago Public Library's rarest and most valuable materials—fine books, manuscripts, historical archives, art works, and museum artifacts. The division's facilities include the Grand Army of the Republic Memorial Hall, a recently renovated reading room, and stack areas equipped with special security and environmental controls necessary to protect its fragile holdings. With the addition of significant private donations and limited purchasing, holdings comprise over 30,000 bound volumes plus 2,000 linear feet of archival and over 1,000 artifactual materials. Special strengths are: the American Civil War; Chicago and the Neighborhoods; over 4,000 photographs (the majority of which are in the Neighborhood Collection);

Book Arts; and Collecting. The library actively purchases books, manuscripts, and artifacts for the Civil War Collection.

Civil War Collections

Civil War holdings include the Grand Army of the Republic Memorial Collection, acquired from Civil War veterans in 1948, and the Civil War and American History Research Collection, founded in 1975 with the assistance of the Chicago Civil War Round Table. This collection has grown rapidly through such significant gifts as the library of Joseph and Jennifer Lutz (over 5,000 volumes) and that of Civil War author Bruce Catton. Highlights of this strong research collection include over 700 histories of individual Civil War regiments (many out-of-print and difficult to locate), antislavery pamphlets, manuscript records of the Army of the Potomac, audio tapes of Civil War Round Table programs, the complete Official Records of the War of the Rebellion, and nearly 7,000 monographs on the military aspects of the war.

The Grand Army of the Republic Memorial Hall is located adjacent to the reading room. Military gear, medical and musical instruments, photographs, graphics, sheet music, manuscripts, maps, printed ephemera, and other items from the Civil War and American History collections are exhibited here. "A Nation Divided: The War Between the States, 1861-1865" is one of the exhibits which is featured at least once every year.

Chicago Collections

The division's Chicago collections makes available to both researchers and casual readers significant materials on the city's literary, social, cultural, economic, and political history (including maps, photographs, trade catalogs, ephemera, newspapers, artifacts, and manuscripts as well as books).

The Chicago Authors and Imprints Collection features early and private press editions of major Chicago authors—Sandburg, Dreiser, Hecht, Farrell, Starrett, and others—together with related manuscripts, advance copies, page proofs, as well as works by lesser known authors. Pre-1900 imprints and private press productions further aid in studying Chicago's literary and publishing history.

The Chicago Theater Arts and History Collection includes the Goodman Theater archives (1925-present), theater scrapbooks, thousands of programs, playbills, and broadsides for the legitimate theater, vaudeville, and other amusements (1847-present).

The World's Columbian Exposition Collection is a significant and heavily used research collection of several hundred pamphlets, photographs, published volumes, and manuscript papers of Fair officials James Ellsworth and George Woodbury. There is also a small collection on the Century of Progress Exposition.

A major archival project funded by the Dr. Scholl Foundation has preserved and reorganized significant neighborhood and local history resources, beginning with Ravenswood-Lake View Historical Collection at Sulzer Regional Library. The "Cities within a City" project has brought all of the neighborhood branch collections to special collections. The West Side Historical Collection is the most recent to be processed.

BIBLIOGRAPHY

Orlando, Thomas A., and Gecik, Marie. *Treasures of The Chicago Public Library.* Chicago: The Chicago Public Library, 1977. Includes an introduction to the Special Collections.

Gazetteer of Cook County

I n 1795 an act of Congress required a survey of the Northwest Territory in preparation for offering public lands for sale. With meridians as reference lines, land was marked off into squares six miles on each side. These congressional, or survey, townships have never been units of government; but their boundaries have been used as the basis for school districts, civil townships, road districts, election districts, and statistical reports. Most civil townships within Cook County are based on these Congressional District lines. Early settlers from the east brought with them the New England concept of the town as the general purpose unit of government. As a result, eighty-five township counties, including Cook County, and seventeen commission counties, were established in Illinois in 1848. Thirty-eight civil townships were established as political divisions of Cook County. The eight Civil Townships within the city of Chicago have become inactive, although the congressional township lines remain.

ALSIP—Worth Township; Zip Code 60658; south of Chicago on the Calumet Sag Channel; incorporated in 1927.

ARLINGTON HEIGHTS—Elk Grove, Palatine, and Wheeling townships; Zip Code 60005; northwest of Chicago; settled in the 1830s and incorporated in 1887.

AUBURN—Town of Lake

AVONDALE—Jefferson Township

BANDOW—Jefferson Township

BARRINGTON—Barrington and Palatine townships, Cook-Lake County line; Zip Code 60010; thirty-two miles northwest of Chicago and founded in 1845. Early pioneers in Barrington included Quakers; some came from Great Barrington, Massachusetts, from which it derives its name. Main Street in Barrington is the dividing line of Cook and Lake counties.

BARRINGTON HILLS—Barrington Township; encompasses thirty square miles of Cook, Lake, McHenry, and Kane counties; Zip Code 60010; incorporated in 1959.

BARRINGTON TOWNSHIP—Presently comprised of Barrington (pt.); Barrington Hills (pt.); Hoffman Estates (pt.); Inverness (pt.); and South Barrington.

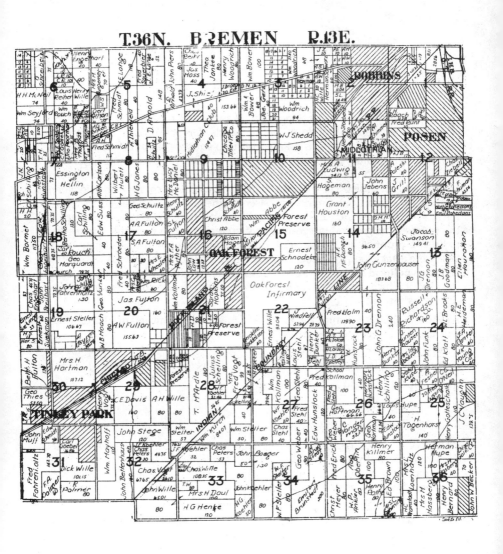

Figure 31. *Bremen Township, Cook County—ca. 1880*

BARTLETT – Hanover Township; Cook-DuPage county lines; Zip Code 60103; thirty-one miles west of the Chicago Loop; founded in 1873 by Luther Bartlett, the first postmaster, who also bought the land in 1844; incorporated in 1891.

BENSENVILLE – Leyden Township; Zip Code 60106.

BEDFORD PARK – Lyons and Stickney townships; Zip Code 60638; west of Chicago; incorporated as a village in 1940.

BELLWOOD – Proviso Township; Zip Code 60104; thirteen miles west of Chicago; the first enterprise in town was a blacksmith shop (1870); incorporated in 1900.

BERKELEY – Proviso Township; Zip Code 60163; west of Chicago; Incorporated in 1924, it was named for Berkeley, California.

BERWYN – Berwyn Township; Zip Code 60402; ten miles west of Chicago; named for a town in Pennsylvania; chartered in 1908.

BERWYN TOWNSHIP – presently comprised of Berwyn City.

BLOOM – See Chicago Heights

BLOOM TOWNSHIP – presently comprised of Chicago Heights; East Chicago Heights; Flossmoor (pt.); Glenwood (pt.); Homewood (pt.); Lansing (pt.); Lynwood; Olympia Fields (pt.); Park Forest (pt.); Sauk Village; South Chicago Heights; and Steger.

BLUE ISLAND – Bremen, Calumet, Thornton, and Worth townships; Zip Code 60406; located on the Calumet Sag Canal; south of Chicago. Blue Island was first settled in 1835 by German and Italian pioneers and was named for the ridge upon which it grew. The ridge is a glacial remnant on the otherwise flat Chicago Lake Plain; At times a blue haze could be seen enveloping the densely wooded ridge which rose like an island from the surrounding marshlands; Blue Island became incorporated in 1872.

BREMEN TOWNSHIP – presently comprised of Blue Island (pt.); Country Club Hills (pt.); Crestwood (pt.); Harvey (pt.); Hazel Crest (pt.); Homewood (pt.); Markham (pt.); Midlothian; Oak Forest; Orland Park (pt.); Posen (pt.); Robbins (pt.); and Tinley Park (pt.).

BRIDGEVIEW – Lyons, Palatine, Stickney and Worth townships; Zip Code 60455; southwest of Chicago; Bridge View was incorporated in 1947.

BRIGHTON PARK – Town of Cicero

BROADVIEW – Proviso Township; Zip Code 60153; west of Chicago; incorporated as a village in 1910.

BROOKFIELD – Lyons, Proviso, and Riverside townships; Zip Code 60513; west of Chicago; founded in 1893 following extensive land purchases by members of the Ogden, Armour, McCormick, and Rockefeller families; then known as Grossdale, but the name was changed to its present form in 1905.

BUFFALO GROVE – Wheeling Township; Zip Code 60090; Lake and Cook county line; fifteen miles northwest of Chicago in an agricultural area noted for feed-grains.

BURBANK – Stickney Township; Zip Code 60459.

BURNHAM–Thornton Township; Zip Code 60633; at the Indiana line just north of Calumet City.

BURR OAK–See Calumet Park

BURR RIDGE–Lyons Township

CALDWELL'S RESERVE–Jefferson Park and Niles Townships

CALUMET CITY–Thornton Township; Zip Code 60409; twenty miles south of Chicago on the Indiana border. Calumet City proper was platted in 1833 but owed much of its growth to the real estate boom of the 1920s. The city developed as part of the residential-industrial complex of Gary-South Chicago-Hammond. It was called West Hammond until 1924 when it gained its present name, which is derived from the French meaning "peace-pipe of the Indians".

CALUMET PARK–Calumet and Thornton townships; Zip Code 60643; south of Chicago. Originally known as Burr Oak, the name was changed to Calumet Park in 1925.

CALUMET TOWNSHIP–Until 5 March 1867, Calumet Township was part of what is now Hyde Park. The township originally had within its limits the villages of Blue Island, Washington Heights, and Morgan Park. Presently comprised of Blue Island (pt.); Calumet Park; Riverdale (pt.); and Chicago (pt.).

CHICAGO–Seat of Cook County

CANFIELD–Maine Township

CENTRAL PARK–Cicero

CHELTENHAM BEACH–Hyde Park

CHICAGO HEIGHTS–Bloom Township; Zip Code 60411; south of Chicago. The city was settled at the junction of the historic Sauk and Old Vincennes trails in the 1830s and has been known respectively as Thorn Grove, Bloom, and Chicago Heights (1892). It developed independently of Chicago's influence and became the area's first steel-producing city.

CHICAGO RIDGE–Worth Township; Zip Code 60415; southwest of Chicago.

CICERO–Cicero Township; Zip Code 60650; east of Chicago. Cicero was founded in 1857 on a swampy lowland. It grew slowly until the Civil War when the rich bottomlands around the settlement were perceived to be agriculturally productive. The community developed steadily as settlers from the East poured into the area. Incorporation came in 1867 as agriculture and the closeness to Chicago spurred industrial growth. Fifty miles of swamplands were drained and put into crops and Cicero eventually became economically independent of its great neighbor. The city gained notoriety in Prohibition days (until 1931), as being the headquarters of gangland leader Al Capone.

CICERO TOWN–Lies immediately west of Chicago. Bounded on the north by Jefferson, on the east by Chicago, on the south by Lake and Lyons and on the west by Proviso. Presently comprised of the town of Cicero.

CLYDE–Town of Cicero

COLEHOUR–Hyde Park

COOK COUNTY—northeast Illinois; Area 954; seat of Chicago. Established in 1830, it is the major population center of the state, cut through by the Illinois and Des Plaines Rivers. The eastern border is formed by Lake Michigan as well as the Indiana state line, and the organization is based on the township and county system, with ten commissioners from Chicago and five from outlying townships serving on the county board.

COUNTRY CLUB HILLS—Bremen and Rich townships; Zip Code 60477; south of Chicago.

COUNTRYSIDE—Lyons Township; Zip Code 60525; west of Chicago.

CRAGIN—Jefferson Park Township

CRESTWOOD—Bremen and Worth townships; Zip Code 60445; southwest of Chicago in an agricultural and industrial region.

CUMMINGS—Hyde Park

DEERFIELD—Northfield Township

DES PLAINES—Elk Grove, Maine and Wheeling townships; Zip Code 60016; northwest of Chicago. Des Plaines was founded in the 1830s as Rand in honor of its first settler, Socrates Rand. It is located on the Des Plaines River, for which it was renamed in 1869. It flourished early as a lumber center whose main mill produced timbers for a plank road between Jefferson Park and Chicago and for ties for the railroad built in 1853.

DIXMOOR—Thornton Township; Zip Code 60406; south of Chicago; incorporated in 1922.

DOLTON—Thornton Township; Zip Code 60419; seventeen miles South of Chicago. Dolton was incorporated in 1892.

DUTCHMAN'S POINT—Niles Township

EAST CHICAGO HEIGHTS—Bloom Township; Zip Code 60411

EAST HAZELCREST—Thornton Township; Zip Code 60429; south of Chicago; incorporated in 1918.

EGANDALE—Hyde Park

ELGIN—Cook-Kane County line; Hanover Township; Zip Code 60120; thirty-six miles W.N.W.; founded in 1835. Land was cleared along the Fox River and a road laid to Belvidere which became part of the Chicago-Galena stage route and was partially responsible for Elgin's rapid settlement. A dam was built to provide power for the grist and sawmills, and the river has since been a link to the city's business. Elgin shipped milk to Chicago as early as 1832, a task which became sufficiently easier when the Galena and Chicago Union Railroad laids its tracks there in 1847. Gail Borden patented the condensed milk process in Elgin in 1856. The Elgin Watch Company, established in 1866, became a great rival to the flourishing dairy industry and essentially initiated Elgin's rise as an industrial center.

ELK GROVE TOWNSHIP—presently comprised of Arlington Heights (pt.); Des Plaines (pt.); Elk Grove Village (pt.); Mount Prospect (pt.); Rolling Meadows (pt.); and Schaumburg (pt.).

ELK GROVE VILLAGE—Elk Grove Township; Zip Code 60007; northwest of Chicago.

ELMWOOD PARK—Leyden Township; Zip Code 60635; west of Chicago; incorporated in 1914.

ENGLEWOOD—Town of Lake

EVANSTON—Evanston Township; Zip Code 60201; north of Chicago. Evanston existed as a settlement as early as 1674 when Pere Marquette and his Indian companions landed in the harbor on Lake Michigan. Temporary encampments came and went until 1826 when the first permanent dwelling was built there. Evanston proper was not platted, however, until 1854, the year before the opening of Northwestern University. The university became the focus of the new town, and Evanston remained small for the next twenty-five years as it channeled all its energies into the development of the school. Cheap transportation eventually made Evanston one of Chicago's leading commuter suburbs. Of historic interest is the Grosse Pointe Lighthouse , built in the 1800s on a high bluff overlooking the lake.

EVANSTON TOWNSHIP—Until Cook County was organized into townships in 1850, the territory now comprising Evanston was included in the "Grosse Point" District, a tract of the county which was of somewhat uncertain dimensions, but was supposed to exist for the convenience of voters. In 1850 when the township of Ridgeville was organized, it included the towns of Evanston and Lake View. Thus it continued until the Township Evanston was formed in 1857, when the Wilmette Reservation was added to the latter. Evanston Township is presently comprised of the City of Evanston.

EVERGREEN PARK—Worth Township; Zip Code 60642; southwest of Chicago; incorporated in 1893.

FLOSSMOOR—Bloom and Rich townships; Zip Code 60422; south of Chicago; incorporated in 1924. The name of the village is of Scottish derivation. It means "gently rolling countryside."

FOREST GLEN—Jefferson Park Township

FOREST PARK—Proviso Township; Zip Code 60130; west of Chicago and on the Des Plaines River. Forest Park was originally the site of an historic Indian burial ground; Founded in 1835. Nearly half of its corporate area is occupied by cemeteries.

FOREST VIEW—Stickney Township; Zip Code 60638; west of Chicago; incorporated in 1924 and is mainly a commuter suburb.

FORESTVILLE—Hyde Park

FRANKLIN PARK—Leyden Township; Zip Code 60131; W.N.W. of Chicago; incorporated in 1892. The area around the village was inhabited in the 1670s after Pere Marquette Louis Joliet declared the Des Plaines River Valley suitable for settlement. Franklin Park is located on the Des Plaines River.

GALEWOOD—Jefferson Township

GARFIELD—Jefferson Township

GLENCOE—New Trier and Northfield townships; Zip Code 60022; twenty-two miles North of Chicago; founded in 1836 and incorporated as a village in

1869. The name is a composite of "glen" suggestive of the site, and "coe" the maiden name of the wife of one of the founders, Walter S. Gurnee.

GLENVIEW—Maine, New Trier, Niles, and Northfield townships; Zip Code 60025; eighteen miles N.N.W. of Chicago; site of a U.S. Naval Air Station.

GLENWOOD—Bloom and Thornton townships; Zip Code 60425; south of Chicago.

GOLF—Niles Township; Zip Code 60029, north of Morton Grove and Chicago.

GRAND CROSSING—Hyde Park

GRAYLAND—Jefferson Township

GROSSDA—See Brookfield

GROSSE POINTE—Point; twenty-five-foot bluff on southwest Lake Michigan at city of Evanston, an early name for that city. Pere Marquette and his Indian companions landed in 1674 at the natural harbor formed by this bluff. In pioneer days, as lake traffic increased, Grosse Point assumed some importance as a port, and as a village grew up around it, it was settled by those who traveled the inland seas.

HANOVER PARK—Hanover and Schaumburg townships; Zip Code 60103; twenty-seven miles W.N.W. of Chicago, near Bartlett; incorporated in 1958.

HANOVER TOWNSHIP—presently comprised of Bartlett (pt.); Elgin (pt.); Hanover Park (pt.); Hoffman Estates (pt.); South Barrington (pt.); Streamwood (pt.).

HARVEY—Bremen and Thornton townships; Zip Code 60426; eighteen miles south of Chicago and six miles west of the Illinois-Indiana line; founded in 1890 by Turlington W. Harvey, a Chicago land developer; incorporated in 1894.

HARWOOD HEIGHTS—Norwood Park Township, Zip Code 60656; northwest suburb of Chicago, three miles east of O'Hare Airport; incorporated in 1947; Name contrived from the "Har" of Harlem and the "wood" of Norwood Park Township.

HAWTHORNE—Town of Cicero

HAZEL CREST—Bremen, Rich and Thornton townships; Zip Code 60429; twenty-three miles south of Chicago Loop; incorporated in 1912.

HAZEL GREEN—(included with Alsip); Zip Code 60482; near Worth.

HEGEWISCH—Hyde Park

HICKORY HILLS—Lyons and Palos townships; Zip Code 60457; fifteen miles southwest of Chicago, near Bridgeview and Justice; incorporated in 1951.

HILLSIDE—Proviso Township; Zip Code 60162; W.S.W. of Oak Park, fourteen miles west of the Chicago Loop; settlement of German farmers in 1837; named by railroad in 1905.

HINSDALE—Lyons Township; Zip Code 60521

HODGKINS—Lyons Township; Zip Code 60525; fifteen miles southwest of the Loop between the Des Plaines River and Joliet Road; Explored by Father Marquette and Louis Joliet (1673), settled by laborers who dug a canal from local tributary of the Mississippi to Lake Michigan, 1836-48; incorporated 1896; major producer of dolomite limestone from a 500-acre quarry.

HOFFMAN ESTATES–Barrington, Hanover and Palatine townships; Zip Code 60172.

HOLBROOK–Zip Code 604ll; near Chicago Heights.

HOMETOWN–Worth Township; Zip Code 60456; S.W. suburb of Chicago; village in the N.W. corner of Oak Lawn between Cicero Avenue and Pulaski Road; developed in 1948 as a subdivision; incorporated in 1953.

HOMEWOOD–Bloom, Bremen, and Rich townships; Zip Code 60430; twenty-two miles southeast of Chicago; settled in 1834 by German, Dutch, and Yankee homesteaders; incorporated 1893.

HUMBOLT PARK–Jefferson Park

HYDE PARK–The act of incorporation approved 20 February 1861 separated the town of Hyde Park (which extended from 39th to 63rd streets and included the settlements of Oakland, Egandale, Forestville, Kenwood, and South Park) from the town of Lake. Lake was the district bounded by 39th Street on the north; by Grand Boulevard or South Park Avenue on the west; by Lake Michigan on the east, and by 87th Street on the south. Under an amended charter of 5 March 1867, the town of Hyde Park embraced all that part of the township which was bounded by Lake Michigan and the State of Indiana on the east; 39th Street on the north; 138th Street and the Indian boundary line on the south; and State Street on the west. By an ordinance approved 1 June 1874, the village of Hyde Park included all that territory bounded by 39th Street on the north; Lake Michigan and the Indiana State line on the east; State Street to the Calumet River, then the Calumet to the center line of 130th Street, then to the eastern line of the Illinois Central Railroad Company's right of way to the Calumet River and then Indiana Avenue to 138th Street, the Calumet River, from Indiana Avenue to the Illinois Central Railroad bridge on the south. The government of Hyde Park was at first merged in that of the town of Lake. In 1889, the village of Hyde Park was annexed to Chicago.

INDIAN HEAD PARK–Lyons township, Zip Code 60525

INVERNESS–Barrington and Palatine townships; Zip Code 60067; exclusive real estate development since 1847; incorporated 1962.

IRVING PARK -Jefferson Park

JEFFERSON TOWNSHIP–bounded by Norwood Park, Niles, and Evanston on the north; by Lake View and Chicago on the east; Chicago and Cicero on the south; and on the west by Leydon and Norwood Park. Jefferson Park was annexed to Chicago in 1889.

JUSTICE–Lyons Township; Zip Code 60458

KENILWORTH–New Trier Township; Zip Code 60043; seventeen miles N.W. of Chicago; founded 1890; incorporated 1896.

KENSINGTON–Hyde Park

KENWOOD–Hyde Park

LA GRANGE – Lyons Township; Zip Code 60525; suburb thirteen miles west of Chicago; settled 1862 when the Burlington Railroad was extended westward across the Des Plaines River; chartered 1879; named for LaGrange, Tennessee.

LA GRANGE PARK – Proviso Township; Zip Code 60525; western suburb of Chicago immediately north of older town of La Grange; founded 1871 from five farms on Salt Creek fifteen miles S.W. of Loop by refugees from the Great Fire; incorporated 1892.

LAKE – See Town of Lake

LAKE VIEW TOWNSHIP – history of early settlement is closely connected to the history of North Chicago.

LANSING – Bloom and Thornton townships; Zip Code 60438; on Indiana border, twenty-four miles south of Chicago; founded 1864 by brothers John and Henry Lansing.

LAKE VIEW TOWNSHIP – The history of the early settlement of North Chicago with that of the southern portion of the town of Lake View is so intimately connected as to form almost the same topic. Lakeview was annexed to Chicago in 1889.

LEMONT – Cook and DuPage counties; Lemont Township; Zip Code 60439; on Illinois River twenty-five miles S.W. of Chicago; name is French word meaning "mountain;" Post Office established 30 May 1850; incorporated 9 June 1873. Lemont is an industrial city served by the Chicago Sanitary and Ship Canal, Calumet Sag Channel, and it has long been known for the limestone quarries.

LEMONT TOWNSHIP – First settled in 1833, the history of Lemont is closely connected to the building of the Illinois and Michigan Canal and the rock quarries. Presently comprised of the village of Lemont.

LEYDON TOWNSHIP – presently comprised of Bensenville (pt.); Elmwood Park; Franklin Park; Melrose Park (pt.); Norridge (pt.); Northlake (pt.); Park Ridge (pt.); River Gorve; Rosemont; and Schiller Park.

LINCOLNWOOD – Niles Township; Zip Code 60645; north of Chicago; incorporated 1911; founded by Germans, farmers, and woodhaulers for the Chicago and Northwestern Railway; once called Tessville.

LITTLEFORT – New Trier Township

LYNWOOD – Bloom Township; Zip Code 60411; near Chicago Heights; incorporated 1959.

LYONS – Lyons and Riverside townships; Zip Code 60534; eight miles west of Chicago; Post Office established 29 February 1848; incorporated 18 July 1888; located at an old portage between the Des Plaines River and the Chicago River, which was used by Marquette and other early French explorers and by the Indians. It is the site of Hofmann Tower, on a dam built in 1908 by George Hofmann to generate electricity for a beer garden.

LYONS TOWNSHIP – bounded on the east by the township of Lake, on the south by those of Worth and Palos, on the west by DuPage County, and on the north by the townships of Proviso and Cicero. Lyons Township is presently comprised of Bedford Park (pt.); Bridgeview (pt.); Brookfield (pt.); Burr Ridge (pt.); Countryside; Hickory Hills (pt.); Hinsdale (pt.); Hodgkins; Indian Head

Park; Justice; La Grange; Lyons (pt.); McCook; Riverside (pt.); Summit; Western Springs (pt.); Willow Springs (pt.).

LYTTLETON'S POINT – Niles Township

MC COOK – Lyons Township; Zip Code 60525

MAINE TOWNSHIP – The first settlement in the township was made in 1832 by Captain Wright. Presently comprised of Des Plaines (pt.); Glenview (pt.); Morton Grove (pt.); Mount Prospect (pt); Niles (pt.); Park Ridge (pt.); and Rosemont (pt.).

MAPLEWOOD – Jefferson Park

MARKHAM – Bremen and Thornton townships; Zip Code 60426; southern suburb of Chicago; incorporated 23 October 1925; named for a former president of the Illinois Central Railroad.

MATTESON – Rich Township; Zip Code 60443; twenty-six miles south of Chicago; founded by German settlers in the 1850s; Post Office established 29 November 1856; incorporated 20 March 1889; named for Governor Joel A. Matteson.

MAYWOOD – Proviso Township; Zip Code 60153; twelve miles west of Chicago on west bank of Des Plaines River; founded in 1860s by a group of New Englanders headed by Col. W. T. Nichols, who named settlement for his daughter, May; Post office established 29 April 1870; incorporated 31 October 1881.

MELROSE PARK – Leyden and Proviso townships; Zip Code 60160; industrial suburb 12 miles west of Chicago with a large Italian population; founded 1860 when road northwest from Chicago toward Galena was cut; Post Office established 28 January 1893; incorporated 13 March 1893.

MERRIONETTE PARK – Worth Township; Zip Code 60655; residential subdivision sixteen miles Southwest of the Loop; incorporated 18 February 1947.

MIDLOTHIAN – Bremen Township; Zip Code 60445; eighteen miles south of Chicago; Named for a golf club built here in 1898 by George R. Thorne, then head of Montgomery Ward, and named for shire in Scotland.

MONT CLARE – Jefferson Township

MONTROSE – Jefferson Township

MORELAND – Town of Cicero

MORGAN PARK – Calumet and Worth

MORTON GROVE – Maine and Niles townships; Zip Code 60053; fifteen miles north of Chicago on north branch of Chicago River; Post Office established 2 July 1874; incorporated 24 September 1895; named for Levi Parsons Morton, an official of the Chicago, Milwaukee, and St. Paul Railroad when it was built in 1872, and later vice-president of the United States under President Benjamin Harrison. First settled in 1831 by immigrant farmers from England, it remained primarily a rural area until after World War II.

Mount Forest – Lyons Township

MOUNT PROSPECT – Elk Grove, Maine and Wheeling townships; Zip Code 60056; twenty-one miles northwest of Chicago; Post Office established 31

December 1885; incorporated 3 February 1917; settled by Busse family, descendants of Friedrich Busse, a German immigrant who came here in 1848.

NEW TRIER TOWNSHIP—In 1829, the United States made a treaty with the Pottawatomie Indians at Prairie du Chien, and 1,280 acres of land on the shore of the lake about fourteen miles from Chicago were ceded to Anton Ouilmette, a Frenchman who had married a Pottawatomie woman of royal blood. After the Black Hawk War most of the Indians removed to Green Bay, but among those who remained on their reservations was Ouilmette, or Wilmette. Presently comprised of Glencoe (pt.); Glenview (pt.); Kenilworth; Northfield (pt.); Wilmette (pt.); and Winnetka.

NILES—Maine Township; Zip Code 60648; fourteen miles north of Chicago; Post Office established 23 May 1850; incorporated 24 August 1899. Once called Dutchman's Point and Lyttleton's Point, it derived its present name from pioneer newspaper owner William Ogden Niles. It was once the site of a Civil War gristmill on the north branch of the Chicago River.

NILES CENTER—Niles Township; settled in the 1850s.

NILES TOWNSHIP—first settled in 1831; presently comprised of Glenview (pt.); Golf; Lincolnwood; Morton Grove (pt.); Niles (pt.); and Skokie.

NORMALVILLE—Town of Lake

NORRIDGE—Leyden, and Norwood Park townships.

NORTHBROOK—Northfield and Wheeling townships; Zip Code 60062; northwest suburb of Chicago; incorporated 8 January 1923; Post Office established 1 February 1923; once called Shermerville. First settlers of Northbrook were French traders and trappers, then Germans.

NORTHFIELD—New Trier and Northfield townships. Zip Code 60093

NORTHFIELD TOWNSHIP—presently comprised of Deerfield (pt); Glencoe (pt.); Glenview (pt.); Northbrook (pt.); Northbrook (pt.); Northfield (pt.); Prospect Heights (pt.); Wilmette (pt.).

NORTHFIELD WOODS—Zip Code 60025; near Glenview.

NORTHLAKE—Leyden and Proviso townships, Zip Code 60164; northeast of Chicago astride North Avenue and Lake Street, west of Mannheim Road.; incorporated 23 April 1949.

NORTH PULLMAN—Hyde Park

NORTH RIVERSIDE—Proviso and Riverside townships; Zip Code 60546.

NORWOOD PARK TOWNSHIP—Located northwest of Jefferson Township and northeast of Leyden Township. When it was organized in 1872 it took from Jefferson, Leyden, Niles and Maine townships. Presently it is comprised of Harwood Heights; Norridge (pt.); and Park Ridge (pt.).

NORWOOD PARK VILLAGE—Norwood Park Township. The first settlement was in 1869 by George Dunlap.

OAK BROOK—DuPage and Cook counties; Proviso Township; Zip Code 60521; sixteen miles west of Chicago; incorporated 21 February 1958.

OAK FOREST—Bremen Township; Zip Code 60452; twenty miles south of Chicago; Post Office established 21 November 1912; incorporated 10 May 1947.

OAKLAND—Hyde Park

OAK LAWN—Worth Township; Zip Code 60453, twelve miles southwest of Chicago, one of the largest suburbs of Chicago in Cook County; settled 1842; Post Office established 22 March 1895; incorporated 1909; bounded by 87th Street on the north, 111th Street on the south, Pulaski on the east, and Harlem Avenue on the west.

OAK PARK—Oak Park Township; Zip Code 60302; ten miles west of Chicago; founded 1833; Post Office established 6 March 1866; incorporated 13 November 1901; initially called Oak Ridge because of a slight, tree-covered rise which has since disappeared due to grading and building. First settler was Joseph Kettlestrings, who came from Maryland in 1833. City is noted for the twenty-five structures, public and private, designed by Frank Lloyd Wright, including his own home and studio and the Unitarian Universalist Church.

OAK PARK—Town of Cicero in Andreas' *History of Cook County.*

OAK PARK TOWNSHIP—presently comprised of the Village of Oak Park.

OAK RIDGE—See Oak Park

OLYMPIA FIELDS—Bloom and Rich townships; Zip Code 60461; south of Chicago; developed 1926; residential community.

ORLAND PARK—Bremen, Orland Park and Palos townships; Zip Code 60462

ORLAND TOWNSHIP—presently comprised of Orland Park (pt.); Tinley Park (pt.); and Westhaven.

PALATINE—Palatine Township; Zip Code 60067; suburb of Chicago; named for a division in Germany by that name.

PALATINE TOWNSHIP—presently comprised of Arlington Heights (pt.); Barrington (pt.); Hoffman Estates (pt.); Hoffman Estates (pt.); Inverness (pt.); Palatine; Rolling Meadows (pt.); Schaumburg (pt.); and South Barrington (pt.).

PALOS HEIGHTS—Palos and Worth townships; Zip Code 60463

PALOS HILLS—Palos Township; Zip Code 60465

PALOS PARK—Palos Township; Zip Code 60464

PALOS TOWNSHIP—situated in the southwestern portion of the county, bounded on the north by Lyons, on the east by Worth, on the south by Orland, on the west by Lemont Township and Downer's Grove in DuPage County. Presently comprised of Bridgeview (pt.); Hickory Hills (pt.); Orland Park (pt.); Palos Heights (pt.); Palos Hills; Palos Park; Willow Springs (pt.); and Worth (pt.).

PARK FOREST—Bloom and Rich townships; Zip Code 60466

PARK FOREST SOUTH—Rich Township

PARK RIDGE—Leyden, Maine and Norwood Park townships; Zip Code 60068

PECK PLACE—New Trier Township

PENNOCK—Jefferson Township

PHOENIX—Thornton Township, 60426

POSEN–Bremen and Thornton townships; Zip Code 60469; twenty miles south of Chicago.

PROSPECT HEIGHTS–Northfield and Wheeling townships

PROVISO TOWNSHIP–town lies in western part of Cook County. bounded on the north by Leyden, on the east by Cicero and Riverside, on the south by Riverside and Lyons, and on the west by DuPage County. It originally contained thirty-six sections, but in 1870 the township of Riverside, consisting of the four southeastern sections, was set off into a separate township. Presently comprised of Bellwood; Berkeley; Broadview; Brookfield (pt.); Forest Park; Hillside; La Grange Park; Maywood; Melrose; Northlake (pt.); North Riverside (pt); Oak Brook (pt.); Stone Park; Westchester; Western Springs (pt.).

PULLMAN–Hyde Park

RAND–See Des Plaines

RICH TOWNSHIP–Presently comprised of Country Club Hills (pt.); Flossmoor (pt.); Hazel Crest (pt.); Homewood (pt.); Matteson; Olympia Fields (pt.); Park Forest (pt.); Park Forest South (pt.); Richton Park; and Tinley Park (pt.).

RICHTON PARK–Rich Township; Zip Code 60471

RIDGEVILLE–Evanston Township

RIVERDALE–Calumet and Thornton townships; Zip Code 60627

RIVER FOREST–River Forest Township; Zip Code 60305

RIVER FOREST TOWNSHIP–presently comprised of River Forest.

RIVERGROVE–Leyden Township; Zip Code 60171; northwest suburb of Chicago.

RIVERSIDE–Lyons and Riverside townships; Zip Code 60546; designed as a Chicago residential suburb, 1866.

RIVERSIDE TOWNSHIP–presently comprised of Brookfield (pt.); Lyons (pt.); North Riverside (pt.). Riverside (pt.).

ROBBINS–Bremen and Worth townships; Zip Code 60472; Chicago suburb near Blue Island.

ROLLING MEADOWS–Elk Grove, Palatine and Wheeling townships; Zip Code 60008

ROSELLE–Schaumburg Township

ROSELAND–Hyde Park

ROSEMONT–Leyden and Maine townships; Zip Code 60018

SAG STATION–Lemont

SAUK VILLAGE–Bloom Township; Zip Code 60411

SCHAUMBURG–Elk Grove, Palatine and Schaumburg townships

SCHAUMBURG TOWNSHIP–presently comprised of Elk Grove Village (pt.); Hanover Park (pt.); Hoffman Estates (pt.); Rolling Meadows (pt.); Roselle (pt.); Schaumburg (pt.); and Streamwood (pt.).

SCHILLER PARK–Leyden Township; Zip Code 60176

SHERMERVILLE—See Northbrook

SKOKIE—Niles Township, Zip Code 60001; fifteen miles north of Chicago. Site of Hebrew Theological Seminary, established 1922.

SOUTH BRIGHTON—Town of Lake

SOUTH CHICAGO—Hyde Park

SOUTH ENGLEWOOD—Town of Lake

SOUTH HOLLAND—Thornton Township; Zip Code 60473; ten miles south of Chicago; settled 1840 by Dutch farmers.

SOUTH LAWN—Thornton Township

SOUTH LYNN—Town of Lake

SOUTH PARK—Hyde Park

STEGER—Bloom Township, Zip Code 60465; thirty miles south of Chicago.

STICKNEY—Stickney Township

STICKNEY TOWNSHIP—Bedford Park (pt.); Bridgeview (pt.); Burbank; Forest View; and Stickney.

STONE PARK—Proviso Township

STREAMWOOD—Hanover and Schaumburg townships; Zip Code 60103.

SUMMIT—Lyons Township; Zip Code 60501; twelve miles southwest of Chicago; on Des Plaines River at crest of watershed between Great Lakes and Mississippi Drainage systems.

TESSVILLE—See Lincolnwood

THORN GROVE—See Chicago Heights

THORNTON—Thornton Township; Zip Code 60476.

THORNTON TOWNSHIP—presently comprised of Blue Island (pt.); Burnham; Calumet City; Dixmoor; Dolton; East Hazel Crest; Glenwood (pt.); Harvey (pt.); Hazel Crest (pt.); Homewood (pt.); Lansing (pt.); Lansing (pt.); Markham (pt.); Phoenix; Posen (pt.); Riverdale (pt.); South Holland and Thornton.

TINLEY PARK—Bremen, Orland and Rich townships; Cook and Will Counties; Zip Code 60477; suburb of Chicago.

TOWN OF LAKE—The township or village of Lake was bounded on the north by 39th Street, on the east by State Street, on the south by 87th and on the west by the township of Lyons. It was incorporated with the above given boundaries in February 1865; but by a subsequent act of the Legislature in 1867, the charter was amended giving enlarged and special powers to village officers to govern the entire territory embraced within the congressional township. The town of Lake was annexed to the city of Chicago in 1889.

UNION STOCK YARDS—Town of Lake

UPWOOD—Calumet and Worth townships

WASHINGTON HEIGHTS—Calumet and Worth townships

WESTCHESTER—Proviso Township; Zip Code 60153

WESTERN SPRINGS—Lyons and Proviso townships; Zip Code 60558; fifteen miles south of Chicago Loop; residential; incorporated by Quakers, 1866; named for local mineral springs believed to be medicinal, which have since dried up.

WEST HAMMOND—See Calumet City

WESTHAVEN—Orland Township; Zip Code 60477

WHEELING—Wheeling Township; Zip Code 60090; twenty miles northwest of Chicago; settled in 1830 as country store.

WHEELING TOWNSHIP—first settled in 1833. Presently comprised of Arlington Heights (pt.); Buffalo Grove (pt.); Des Plaines (pt.); Mount Prospect (pt.); Northbrook (pt.); Prospect Heights (pt.); Rolling Meadows (pt.); and Wheeling (pt.).

WILDWOOD—Hyde Park

WILLOW SPRINGS—Lyons and Palos townships; Area Code 312; Zip Code 60480.

WILMETTE—New Trier and Northfield Townships; Zip Code 60091; suburb of Chicago on Lake Michigan; settled 1829; named for white settler, Antoine Ouilmette, a French Canadian whose Indian wife gained land under a government treaty.

WILMETTE RESERVATION—Evanston Township

WINNETKA—New Trier Township, Zip Code 60093; twenty miles north of Chicago; incorporated 1869; residential village on Lake Michigan.

WORTH—Palos and Worth townships; Zip Code 60482; south of Chicago.

WORTH TOWNSHIP—presently comprised of Alsip; Blue Island (pt.); Bridgeview (pt.); Chicago Ridge; Crestwood (pt.); Evergreen Park; Hometown; Merrionette Park; Oak Lawn; Palos Heights (pt.); Robbins (pt.); and Worth (pt.).

Genealogical Societies

THE AFRO-AMERICAN GENEALOGICAL AND HISTORICAL SOCIETY
OF CHICAGO
P.O. Box A3027
Chicago, IL 60690

Offers genealogy classes and workshops and publishes a monthly newsletter. Meets second Sunday of the month at 1 p.m. at the DuSable Museum of African American History, 740 East 56th Place, Chicago, IL 60637 (312-947-0600).

THE CHICAGO GENEALOGICAL SOCIETY
P.O. Box 1160
Chicago, IL 60690

Publishes a monthly newsletter and the *Chicago Genealogist*, quarterly publication. Sponsors genealogical publications, programs and annual workshops. Meets first Saturday of the month (except Summer months) at 1 p.m. at the Newberry Library, 60 West Walton, Chicago, IL 60610.

CHICAGO IRISH ANCESTRY (C.I.A.),
c/o The Newberry Library
60 West Walton
Chicago, IL 60610

Sponsors occasional meetings and programs.

CHICAGO IRISH INTEREST GROUP
c/o THE CHICAGO GENEALOGICAL SOCIETY
P.O. Box 1160
Chicago, IL 60690

COUNCIL OF NORTHEASTERN ILLINOIS GENEALOGICAL
SOCIETIES
3629 West 147th Place
Midlothian, IL 60445
(312-389-1627)

Coordinates a calendar of events for genealogical societies in northeastern Illinois. Sponsors a clearinghouse, workshops,and meetings for area genealogical society leaders. Cooperates with the Genealogical Society of Utah in preservation and microfilming of records which are of genealogical and historical importance. Works closely with the Illinois State Genealogical Society.

GENEALOGICAL SOCIETY OF DEKALB COUNTY
Box 295
Sycamore, IL 60178

DUNTON GENEALOGICAL SOCIETY
Arlington Heights Public Library
500 North Dunton
Arlington Heights, IL 60004

DU PAGE COUNTY (IL) GENEALOGICAL SOCIETY
P.O. Box 133
Lombard, IL 60148

Publishes *The Review*, a bimonthly newsletter with special Summer and Winter issues. Sponsors projects, publications, and workshops of genealogical and historical interest. Meets on the third Wednesday of September, November, January, March, and May. Maintains a genealogy library collection at the Wheaton Public Library, 225 N. Cross St., Wheaton, IL (for premise use only).

ELGIN GENEALOGICAL SOCIETY
P.O. Box 1418
Elgin, IL 60121-0818

Publishes a newsletter quarterly. Meetings are held at the Gail Borden Public Library, 200 North Grove Avenue, Elgin, IL 60121 on the first Tuesday of every month at 9:30 a.m. and the third Thursday of the month at 7:30. There are no evening meetings in June, July, August, and December. Sponsors projects, publications, and workshops of genealogical and historical interest and works closely with the Gail Borden Public Library.

ELMHURST GENEALOGICAL SOCIETY
120 East Park
Elmhurst, IL 60126

FEDERATION OF GENEALOGICAL SOCIETIES
P.O. Box 220
Davenport, IA 52805

An international genealogical organization sponsoring projects, publications and conferences of genealogical and historical interest. Publishes bimonthly Newsletter. Address correspondence regarding Newsletter to:

FEDERATION OF GENEALOGICAL SOCIETIES
Newsletter Editor
3629 West 147th Place
Midlothian, IL 60445

FOX VALLEY GENEALOGICAL SOCIETY
P.O. Box 459
Naperville, IL 60566

Publishes *Fox Tales*, a quarterly, and special occasional publications of genealogical and historical interest. Meets second Wednesday of the month except December at 7:30 p.m. in lower level of Land of Lincoln Savings and Loan, Mill Street and Ogden Avenue, Naperville, Illinois.

GENEALOGICAL QUESTORS
Des Plaines Historical Society
P.O. Box 225
Des Plaines, IL 60017

GERMAN INTEREST GROUP
c/o CHICAGO GENEALOGICAL SOCIETY
P.O. Box 1160
Chicago, IL 60690

GRAYSLAKE GENEALOGICAL SOCIETY
148 Center Street
Grayslake, IL 60030

GREEN HILLS GENEALOGICAL SOCIETY
Green Hills Library
8611 West 103rd Street
Palos Hills, IL 60465

ILLINOIS STATE GENEALOGICAL SOCIETY
P.O. Box 157
Lincoln, IL 62656

The Illinois State Genealogical Society was established in 1968 as a nonprofit, nonsectarian, educational organization. Individuals, libraries, and societies may apply for membership. Each member receives one volume (four issues) of the quarterly publication and a monthly newsletter. The society holds an annual fall conference with business meetings and a spring conference.

JEWISH GENEALOGICAL SOCIETY OF ILLINOIS
P.O. Box 481022
Niles, IL 60648
(312-564-1025)

Publishes *Search* quarterly and sponsors projects, workshops, and occasional publications of genealogical and historical interest.

ILLIANA JEWISH GENEALOGICAL SOCIETY
Att: Ellen Kahn
3416 Ithaca
Olympia Fields, IL 60461

KANE COUNTY GENEALOGICAL SOCIETY
P.O. Box 504
Geneva, IL 60134
Publishes *Kane County Chronicle* quarterly.

KANKAKEE VALLEY GENEALOGICAL SOCIETY
304 South Indiana Avenue
P.O. Box 1559
Kankakee, IL 60901

LAKE COUNTY GENEALOGICAL SOCIETY
Cook Memorial Library
413 North Milwaukee Avenue
Libertyville, IL 60048

LITHUANIAN GENEALOGICAL SOCIETY
Balzekas Museum of Lithuanian Culture
6500 South Pulaski Road
Chicago, IL 60629

MC HENRY COUNTY GENEALOGICAL SOCIETY
1011 North Green Street
McHenry, IL 60050
(815-385-0036)

NATIONAL GENEALOGICAL SOCIETY
4527 17th Street, North
Arlington, VA 22207
(703-525-0050)

NEW ENGLAND HISTORIC GENEALOGICAL SOCIETY–MIDWEST
　　CHAPTER
c/o The Chicago Genealogical Society
P.O. Box 1160
Chicago, IL 60690

NORTH SUBURBAN GENEALOGICAL SOCIETY
Winnetka Public Library
768 Oak Street
Winnetka, IL 60093

Publishes a Newsletter. Maintains a genealogical reference at the Winnetka Library and sponsors eleven programs throughout the year.

NORTHERN WILL COUNTY GENEALOGICAL SOCIETY
121 Cypress Drive
Bolingbrook, IL 60439

NORTHWEST SUBURBAN COUNCIL OF GENEALOGISTS
P.O. Box AC
Mt. Prospect, IL 60056

Publishes a bimonthly newsletter, *News from the Northwest;* maintains surname and locality files; sponsors projects and programs which are of interest to genealogists.

PALATINES TO AMERICA, ILLINOIS CHAPTER
P.O. Box 3884
Quincy, IL 62301

POLISH GENEALOGICAL SOCIETY
984 North Milwaukee Avenue
Chicago, IL 60622

Publishes a Newsletter and sponsors occasional projects and publications which are of interest to genealogists and historians. Meetings held at the Polish Museum of America. Annual workshop is held in the Fall.

POPLAR CREEK GENEALOGICAL SOCIETY
200 Kosan Circle
Streamwood, IL 60103

SCHAUMBURG GENEALOGICAL SOCIETY
Schaumburg Public Library
32 West Library Lane
Schaumburg, IL 60194

SOUTH SUBURBAN GENEALOGICAL AND HISTORICAL SOCIETY
P.O. Box 96
South Holland, IL 60473
(312-333-9474)

Publishes newsletter monthly, and *Where the Trails Cross,* a quarterly. Meets monthly from September to June on the second Saturday of the month 1:30 p.m. at the Roosevelt Center, 161st Place and Louis Avenue, South Holland, IL. Sponsors projects and occasional publications and an annual workshop of interest to genealogists and historians. Maintains a library of over 2,000 genealogical and historical volumes with an especially good collection of south suburban local histories and a surname index.

WESTERN SPRINGS GENEALOGICAL SOCIETY
Western Springs Historical Society
916 Hillgrove Avenue
Western Springs, IL 60558

WILL/GRUNDY COUNTIES GENEALOGICAL SOCIETY
P.O. Box 24
Wilmington, IL 60481

ZION GENEALOGICAL SOCIETY
Zion Benton Public Library
2400 Gabriel Avenue
Zion, IL 60099
(312-872-4680)

APPENDIX F

Church of Jesus Christ of Latter-day Saints Genealogical Library

T he Genealogical Department of the Church of Jesus Christ of Latter-day Saints (LDS) is engaged in the most active and comprehensive genealogical program in the world. Microfilming is the center of this genealogical operation. Over a million rolls of microfilm have been accumulated thus far and several thousand new rolls are processed each month. These microform records are available for public use at the Genealogical Department Library, 35 North West Temple, Salt Lake City, UT 84150, and through the branch libraries which are located across the country. The International Genealogical Index is organized by country and then by state or province within that country. Each state or province contains an alphabetical list of names and supporting birth and marriage information.

THE COOK COUNTY, ILLINOIS, MICROFILMING PROJECT

Anyone needing Cook County records soon realizes that there are special obstacles to overcome in order to achieve success in researching the metropolitan area. The tremendous volumes of records created by the great population; the limited access to many collections; the destruction of most official county records by the Chicago Fire of 1871; the fact that collections are scattered; and the politics involved can discourage even the most experienced researcher. If the genealogist does not have names, dates, and places confirmed to begin the quest, search and copy fees can make "fishing expeditions" very costly and often nonproductive.

For about the last ten years, the Genealogical Department of the Church of Jesus Christ of Latter-Day Saints (The Genealogical Society of Utah) has been microfilming Cook County official records. "Official records" are those which are created by any government agency. They are now extending the program to include the churches, cemeteries, and other "nonofficial" records. It is estimated that work in this area will continue at least until 1990.

Some of the Cook County records which may be ordered to the branch libraries from Salt Lake City are listed here. Many of these are on indefinite loan, thus eliminating the usual six week wait for films to arrive from Salt Lake City. The Chicago Heights Branch, for example, has a microfiche index of Cook County births, 1871-1922.

Cook County Marriage *Indexes, Males*—1871-1900 (10 reels)
Cook County Marriage *Indexes, Females*—1878-1900 (7 reels)

Cook County Miscellaneous Marriages prior to the Fire (1 reel)
Cook County Marriage Licenses—1871-1920 (chronological, 707 reels)
Cook County Out-of-Town Deaths—1909-19 (11 reels)
Chicago Deaths—1871-1933 (Compiled by the W.P.A., this is an alphabetically
    arranged index of deaths including name, address, and date of death.)
    They are as follow:

Chicago Deaths A-Bou Film #1295943
   "   "   Bou-Cul Film #1295944
   "   "   Cul-Fol Film #1295945
   "   "   Fol-Haw Film #1295946
   "   "   Haw-J Film #1295947
   "   "   K-Lap Film #1295948
   "   "   Lap-McB Film #1295949
   "   "   McC-OB Film #1295971
   "   "   Obr-Rep Film #1295972
   "   "   Rep-Sik Film #1295973
   "   "   Sik-Ste Film #1295974
   "   "   Ste-Wal Film #1295975
   "   "   Wal-Z Film #1295976

Chicago Death Certificates 1878-1915 (692 reels)
Cook County Coroner's Death Records 1879-1904 (27 reels)
Cook County Circuit Court Naturalizations (indexes, 4 reels)
Cook County Circuit Court Naturalizations (Actual records, 62 reels)
Cook County Circuit Court Naturalizations, Declarations of Intentions 1874-1929
    (including indexes, 111 reels).
Cook County Court Naturalizations, Petitions & Indexes 1906-29
    (270 reels)
Cook County Court Naturalizations, Declaration of Intention 1874-
    1906 (25 reels)
Cook County Naturalizations, Naturalization Records 1874-1906 (15 reels)
Cook County Superior Court, Declaration of Intention 1906-29 (163 reels)
Cook County Naturalizations, Petitions & Records of Military Personnel 1904-06
    (1 reel)
Cook County Naturalizations, Superior Court Petition of Aliens under 18-
    1906-08 (13 reels)
Cook County Naturalizations, Superior Court Petitions & Indexes 1906-29 (299
    reels)
Cook County Naturalizations, Superior Court Declarations of Intention
    1871-1906 (7 reels)
Cook County Probate Records 1871-82, vols. 1-12 (6 reels)
Cook County Probate Records 1877-86, vols. 1-23 (12 reels)
Cook County Probate Records 1877-1906, vols. 1-225 (121 reels)
Cook County Probate Records Indexes to Deceased Estates 1912-22
Cook County Birth Records and Indexes 1878-1915 (several hundred reels)

Note: Other official Cook County record groups (such as delayed births) are
in the process of being microfilmed at this time.

Collections which may seem worthy of consideration for the microfilming
project should be brought to the attention of the Council of Northeastern Illinois

Genealogical Societies (CONIGS) or to a local genealogical group. CONIGS was organized in February 1983. As one of its concerns, the council has worked to keep the many genealogical societies in this area informed on the microfilming project. The benefits of participation in this project are several. Preservation of valuable records, of course, is the primary object, but accessibility to the records is still another important consideration.

As record collections which have potential (those containing vital information, family relationships, etc.) come to the attention of the Council, volunteers seek the record custodian's permission to inventory and microfilm the documents. As soon as this is accomplished, listings are submitted to the Genealogical Society of Utah for approval, and microfilming can be scheduled. Donor copies are provided by the Genealogical Society of Utah and additional copies may be purchased (with permission of the original record custodian) at cost. Microfilm copies of most of the "non-official records" will be placed at the Newberry Library, which has designated as the official repository for the collection.

CHURCH OF JESUS CHRIST OF LATTER-DAY SAINTS (MORMON) BRANCH GENEALOGICAL LIBRARIES IN THE CHICAGO AREA

Chicago Heights Branch Genealogical
Library
402 Longwood Drive
Chicago Heights, IL 60411
312-754-2525
Mailing address:
P.O. Box Flossmoor, IL 60422

Naperville Branch Genealogical Library
Ridgeland & Naperville Roads
Naperville, IL 60540
312-357-0211

Schaumburg Branch Genealogical Library
P.O.Box 94205
1320 West Schaumburg Road
Schaumburg, IL 60195
312-882-9889

Wilmette Branch Genealogical Library
2801 Lake Avenue
Wilmette, IL 60091
312-251-9818

All of the branch libraries are staffed by volunteers and have limited research hours during the week. They are open most Saturdays. Hours are subject to change and so it is best to call ahead.

Cook County Libraries

Acorn Public Library
15624 South Central Ave.
Oak Forest, 60452
(312-687-3700)

Alsip-Merrionette Park Public Library
11960 South Pulaski, 60658
(312-371-5666)

Arlington Heights Memorial Library
500 North Dunton Ave., 60004
(312-392-0100)

Barrington Public Library District
505 North Northwest Highway, 60010
(312-382-1300)

Bartlett Public Library District
302 Railroad Ave., 60103
(312-837-2855)

Bedford Park Public Library District
7816 West 65th Place, 60501
(312-458-6826)

Bellwood Public Library
600 Bohland Ave., 60104
(312-547-7393)

Benson, (See Illinois Prairie Public Library)

Berkeley Public Library
1637 Taft Ave., 60163
(312-544-6017)

Berwyn Public Library
3400 South Oak Park Ave., 60402
(312-484-6655)

Blue Island Public Library
2433 York Street, 60406
(312-388-1078)

Bridgeview Public Library
7840 West 79th Street, 60455
(312-458-2880)

Broadview Public Library
2226 South 16th Ave., 60153
(312-345-1325)

Brookfield Free Public Library
3609 Grand Boulevard, 60513
(312-485-6917)

Buffalo Grove, (See Indian Trails Public Library District)

Burbank, (See Prairie Trails Public Library District)

Calumet City Public Library
760 Wentworth Ave., 60409
(312-862-6220)

Calumet Park Public Library
1500 West 127th Street, 60643
(312-385-5768)

Chicago Public Library
425 North Michigan Ave., 60611
(312-269-2900)

Chicago Heights Free Public Library
15th and Chicago Road, 60411
(312-754-0323)

Chicago Ridge Public Library
6301 West Birmingham, 60415
(312-423-7753)

Cicero Public Library
5225 West Cermak Road, 60650
(312-652-8084)

Cook Memorial Public Library District
413 North Milwaukee Ave., 60048
(312-362-2330)

Crestwood Public Library District
13838 South Cicero Ave., 60445
(312-371-4090)

Des Plaines Public Library
841 Graceland Ave., 60016
(312-827-5551)

Des Plaines Valley Public Library District
121 East 8th Street, Lockport, 60441
(815-838-0755)

Dolton Public Library District
14037 Lincoln Ave., 60418
(312-849-2385)

East Chicago Heights Public Library
District
941 East 14th Street, 60411
(312-758-3230)

Eisenhower Public Library District
4652 North Olcott, 60656
(312-867-7828)

Elgin, (See Gail Borden Public Library
District)

Elk Grove Village Public Library
101 Kennedy Boulevard, 60007
(312-439-0447)

Elmwood Park Public Library
4 Conti Parkway, 60635
(312-453-7645)

Evanston Public Library
1703 Orrington Ave., 60201
(312-866-0300)

Evergreen Park Public Library
9400 South Troy Ave., 60642
(312-422-8522)

Flossmoor Public Library
2801 School Street, 60422
(312-798-4006)

Forest Park Public Library
7555 West Jackson Boulevard, 60130
(312-366-7171)

Franklin Park Public Library District
9618 Franklin Ave., 60131
(312-455-6016)

Gail Borden Public Library
200 North Grove Ave., Elgin, 60120
(312-742-2411)

Glencoe Public Library
320 Park Ave., 60022
(312-835-5056)

Glenview Public Library
1930 Glenview Road, 60025
(312-724-5200)

Glenwood-Lynwood Public Library
District
315 Glenwood-Lansing Road, 60425
(312-758-0090)

Grande Prairie Public Library District
3479 West 183rd Street
Hazel Crest, 60429
(312-598-8446)

Green Hills Public Library District
8611 West 103rd Street
Palos Hills, 60465
(312-598-8446)

Hanover Township Library
204 Jefferson Street, 61041
(815-591-3517)

Hanover Park, (See Schaumburg and
Poplar Creek Public Library)

Harvey Public Library
155th and Turlington Ave., 60426
(312-331-0757)

Harwood Heights (See Eisenhower
Public Library District)

Hazel Crest (See Grande Prairie Public
Library District)

Hickory Hills (See Green Hills Public
Library District)

Hillside Public Library
405 North Hillside Ave., 60162
(312-449-7510)

Hodgkins Public Library District
6500 Wenz Ave., 60525
(312-579-1844)

Hoffman Estates (See Schaumburg)

Hometown Public Library
4331 Southwest Highway, 60456
(312-636-0997)

Homewood Public Library
17900 Dixie Highway, 60430
(312-798-0121)

Indian Trails Library District
355 S. Schoenbeck Road, 60090
(312-459-4100)

Justice Public Library District
7641 Oak Grove Ave., 60458
(312-496-1790)

La Grange Public Library
10 West Cossitt Ave., 60525
(312-352-0576)

La Grange Park Public Library District
928 Barnsdale Road, 60525
(312-352-0100)

Lansing Public Library
2750 Indiana Ave., 60438
(312-474-2447)

Lemont Public Library
800 Porter Street, 60439
(312-257-6541)

Lincolnwood Public Library District
4000 West Pratt, 60646
(312-677-5277)

Lynwood (See Glenwood-Lynwood Public
Library District)

Lyons Public Library
4209 Joliet Ave., 60534
(312-447-3577)

McCook Public Library District
50th Street and Glencoe Ave., 60525
(312-447-9030)

Markham Public Library
16640 South Kedzie, 60426
(312-331-0130)

Matteson Public Library
801 South School Ave., 60443
(312-748-4431)

Maywood Public Library
121 South 5th Ave., 60153
(312-343-1847)

Melrose Park Public Library
801 North Broadway, 60160
(312-343-3391)

Merrionette Park (See Alsip-Merrionette
Park)

Midlothian Public Library
14609 South Springfield, 60445
(312-388-4119)

Morton Grove Public Library
6140 Lincoln Ave., 60053
(312-965-4220)

Mt. Prospect Public Library
10 South Emerson, 60056
(312-253-5675)

Niles Public Library District
6960 Oakton Street, 60648
(312-967-8554)

Norridge (See Eisenhower Public Library
District)

North Chicago Public Library
1645 Lincoln Ave., 60064
(312-689-0125)

North Suburban District Library
6340 North Second Street
Loves Park, 61111
(815-633-4247)

Northbrook Public Library
1201 Cedar Land, 60062
(312-272-6224)

Northfield (See Winnetka Public
Library District)

Northlake Public Library District
231 North Wolf Road, 60164
(312-562-2301)

Oak Forest (See Acorn Public Library
District)

Oak Lawn Public Library
9427 South Raymond Ave., 60453
(312-422-4990)

Oak Park Public Library
834 Lake Street, 60301
(312-383-8200)

Orland Park Public Library
14760 Park Lane, 60462
(312-349-8138)

Palatine Public Library District
500 North Benton Street, 60067
(312-358-5881)

Palos Heights Public Library
12501 South 71st Ave., 60463
(312-448-1473)

Palos Hills (See Green Hills Public
Library District)

Palos Park Public Library
8817 West 123rd Street, 60464
(312-448-1530)

Park Forest Public Library
400 Lakewood Boulevard, 60466
(312-748-3731)

Park Forest South Public Library
District
10003 Samson Drive, 60466
(312-534-2580)

Park Ridge Public Library
20 South Prospect Ave., 60068
(312-825-3123)

Poplar Creek Public Library District
1405 South Park Boulevard
Streamwood, 60103
(312-837-6800)

Prospect Heights Public Library District
12 North Elm Street, 60070
(312-259-3500)

Richton Park Public Library District
4045 Sauk Trail, 60471
(312-481-5333)

River Forest Public Library
735 Lathrop Ave., 60305
(312-366-5205)

River Grove Public Library District
8638 West Grand Ave., 60171
(312-453-4484)

Riverdale Public Library District
208 West 144th Street, 60627
(312-841-3311)

Riverside Public Library
1 Burling Road, 60546
(312-442-6366)

Robbins Public Library District
13822 Central Park, 60472
(312-597-2760)

Rolling Meadows Library
3110 Martin Lane, 60008
(312-259-6050)

Sauk Village Public Library District
1909 Sauk Trail, 60411
(312-757-4771)

Schaumburg Township Public Library
32 West Library Lane, 60194
(312-885-3373)

Schiller Park Public Library
4200 Old River Road, 60176
(312-678-0433)

Skokie Public Library
5215 Oakton Street, 60077
(312-673-7774)

South Chicago Heights (See Steger-
   South Chicago Heights)

South Holland Public Library
16250 Wausau Ave., 60473
(312-331-5262)

Steger-South Chicago Heights Public
   Library District
3326 Chicago Road
South Chicago Heights, 60411
(312-755-5040)

Stickeny-Forest View Library District
6800 West 43rd Street
Stickney, 60402

Streamwood (See Poplar Creek)

Summit-Argo Public Library
6209 South Archer Road
Summit, 60501
(312-458-1545)

Thornton Public Library
115 East Margaret Street, 60476
(312-877-2579)

Tinley Park Public Library
17101 South 71st Ave., 60477
(312-532-0160)

Westchester Public Library
10700 Canterbury, 60153
(312-562-3573)

Western Springs-Thomas Ford
   Memorial Library
800 Chestnut Street
Western Springs, 60558
(312-246-0520)

Wheeling (See Indian Trails Public
   Library District)

Wilmette Public Library District
1242 Wilmette Ave., 60091
(312-256-5025)

Winnetka Public Library District
768 Oak Street, 60093
(312-446-7220)

Worth Public Library District
6917 West 111th Street, 60482
(312-448-2855)

FEDERAL DEPOSITORY LIBRARIES IN COOK COUNTY

Chicago Public Library
Government Publications Department
425 North Michigan Ave.
Chicago, 60611
(312-269-3021)

Chicago State University
Paul and Emily Douglas Library
95th Street at King Drive
Chicago, 60628
(312-995-2284)

DePaul University Law Library
25 East Jackson Boulevard
Chicago, 60604
(312-321-7710)

Field Museum of Natural History Library
Roosevelt Road at Lake Shore Drive
Chicago, 60605
(312-992-9410 ext. 281)

Illinois Institute of Technology
Chicago-Kent College of Law Library
77 South Wacker Drive
Chicago, 60606
(312-567-5968)

Illinois Institute of Technology
Kemper Library
3300 South Federal Street
Chicago, 60616
(312-567-6844)

John Crerar Library
Documents Department
35 West 33rd Street
Chicago, 60616
(312-225-2526)

John Marshall Law School Library
315 South Plymouth Court
Chicago, 60604
(312-427-2737 ext. 484)

Loyola University of Chicago
E. M. Cudahy Memorial Library
6525 North Sheridan Road
Chicago, 60626
(312-274-3000 ext. 791)

Loyola University School of Law Library
1 East Pearson Street
Chicago, 60611
(312-670-2950)

Northeastern Illinois University
Documents Department
5500 North St. Louis Ave.
Chicago, 60625
(312-583-4050 ext. 8178)

Northwestern University School of Law
Library
357 East Chicago Ave., 60611
(312-649-7344)

University of Chicago Law Library
1121 East 57th Street
Chicago, 60637
(312-753-3423)

University of Chicago Documents
Section
1100 East 57th Street
Chicago, 60637
(312-753-3423)

University of Illinois at Chicago Circle
Library
Documents Department, Box 8198
Chicago, 60680
(312-996-2738)

Oakton Community College
Learning Resource Center
1600 East Golf Road
Des Plaines, 60016
(312-635-1645)

Northwestern University Library
Government Publications Department
Evanston, 60201
(312-492-5290)

Mount Prospect Public Library
Documents Department
10 South Emerson Street
Mount Prospect, 60056
(312-398-6460)

Oak Park Public Libary
834 Lake Street
Oak Park, 60301
(312-383-8200)

Moraine Valley Community College
Library
10900 South 88th Ave.
Palos Hills, 60465
(312-974-4300 ext. 221)

Governors' State University Library
Park Forest South, 60465
(312-534-5000 ext. 2232)

Rosary College
Rebecca Crown Library
7900 West Division Street
River Forest, 60305
(312-366-2490 ext. 303)

Poplar Creek Public Library
1405 South Park Boulevard
Streamwood, 60103
(312-837-6800)

Municipal Reference Library, Chicago

City Hall-Room 1004
121 North LaSalle Street
Chicago, Illinois 60602
(312-744-4992)

Hours: Monday–Friday, 8:00 a.m. to 5:00 p.m.

The Municipal Library was established in 1900 and was connected with the Bureau of Statistics in early years. The library's purpose is service to city agencies, while also serving as a public reference library. It is a repository for published city documents and has subject strengths in the areas of public administration, sociology, Chicago planning, housing, public employment, criminology, law enforcement, and urban affairs studies. Special collections include city of Chicago published departmental reports, 1871 to date; city council proceedings, 1865 to date; documents from agencies and departments of Cook County, Chicago Board of Education, Metropolitan Sanitary District, Chicago Park District, and the Chicago Transit Authority. Selected State of Illinois departmental reports, house and senate journals, state bills, public laws and statutes are also found in the collection.

Of special interest is an eighty-five drawer file of classified news clippings taken since 1956 from Chicago daily papers and a selection of neighborhood papers. The files are arranged by subject and contain detailed index cards. There are some biographical entries, but it is by no means an every-name index. Personal names must be retrieved by subject in most instances.

Census data is available from early Chicago enumerations to the present in statistical form. The library does not have copies of the actual census schedules. Census data on computer print-outs is available for the 1970 and 1980 census for Chicago. Some items are detailed by census tract, block, group, community area, and ward.

A card file which was compiled from Works Progress Admininstration research gives the origins of Chicago street names, street name changes, and dates when street name changes took effect.

The Municipal Library has Chicago city directories for the years 1839 to 1929, and telephone directories from 1883-1971 on microfilm.

National Archives— Chicago Branch

7358 South Pulaski Road
Chicago, IL 60629
(312-581-7816)

Hours: Monday—Friday 8:00 a.m. to 4:15 p.m. Closed federal holidays.

The National Archives—Chicago Branch is one of eleven field branches of the National Archives and Records Administration. It is responsible for serving the six Great Lakes states—Illinois, Indiana, Michigan, Minnesota, Ohio, and Wisconsin—and has an extensive manuscript collection from the field offices of federal agencies within the region, as well as a microfilm collection pertaining to federal documentation of these states and the nation as a whole.

Genealogists need to consult a variety of records created by different levels of government. Key among federal records are the federal population census schedules. The Chicago branch has these on microfilm for the entire United States from 1790 through 1910, the most recent census available for public research. There is a Soundex index for the 1880, 1900, and 1910 censuses. A special census was taken in 1890 enumerating Union veterans and widows of Union veterans. Printed indexes to the population census schedules are found in numerous repositories, and the Chicago branch has approximately 285 volumes. These cover the period 1790-1880, the core being 1820-50; but they are far from complete.

The Chicago branch has a rather solid microfilm collection of military records. Included are the compiled service records of U.S. Army and U.S. Navy personnel who fought in the Revolutionary War, with indexes to both; Revolutionary War pension and bounty-land warrant application files; Revolutionary War bounty-land warrants in the military district of Ohio; Index to Compiled Service Records of Volunteer Soldiers Who Served During the War of 1812; War of 1812 Military bounty-land warrants; Index to Compiled Service Records of Volunteer Soldiers Who Served During the Mexican War; and Index to Compiled Service Records of Volunteer Union Soldiers who Served in Organizations from the States of Illinois, Indiana, Michigan, Minnesota, Ohio, and Wisconsin.

A third major resource from federal records of interest to genealogists is passenger arrival records. The Chicago branch has the Port of New York lists on microfilm from 1820 to 1902, either by index or the actual lists themselves.

Indexes cover the periods 1820-46 and from 16 June 1897 to 30 June 1902. The lists date from 2 December 1846 to 17 June 1897. In addition, the branch has microfilm copies of Lists of Passengers Arriving at Miscellaneous Ports on the Atlantic and Gulf coasts and at ports on the Great Lakes, 1820-73. They are not indexed.

Rounding out National Archives microfilm publications of potential interest to genealogists are Internal Revenue Assessment Lists for Illinois, 1862-66; Record of Appointment of Postmasters, 1832-1971; and Letters of Application and Recommendation for Appointment to Federal Office, 1797-1869. Genealogists pursuing Indian ancestry may find tribal census rolls helpful. While there were no reservations in Illinois operated by the Bureau of Indian Affairs, the Chicago branch does have those in Michigan and Wisconsin. These include, by reservation: Green Bay (Menominee, Oneida, Stockbridge, and Munsee), 1885-1923; Hayward (Lac Courte Oreilles Chippewa), 1916-33; Keshena (Menominee, Oneida, Stockbridge, and Munsee), 1909-35; Oneida, 1900-20; Sac and Fox (Iowa), 1888-1939; and Winnebago, 1911-13. There are some gaps in the date spans.

The manuscript collection at the National Archives–Chicago Branch is a vast and generally untapped source of information. By far the largest record group is that of the U.S. District and Circuit Courts (RG 21) for Illinois, 1819-1982; Indiana, 1819-1961; Michigan, 1815-1961; Minnesota (Duluth Division) 1890-1957; Ohio, 1803-1961; and Wisconsin, 1839-1961. Of particular interest to genealogists are the naturalization records. Prior to 1906 the naturalization process basically was a function of county government, so researchers are urged to exhaust all local sources first before looking among federal records. After 1906, when naturalizations primarily occurred in federal courts, the records contain significant information, including birthplace and birthdate of the immigrant, date of marriage, birthplace and birthdate of spouse and children, date and port of embarkation, date and port of arrival in the United States, and occupation, among other items. Generally speaking, pre-1906 naturalization records in branch custody contain very little information of genealogical value.

An obstacle to naturalization records is a lack of indexes. However, there are some indexes from federal courts both prior to and after 1906, for example: Detroit, 1837-1916; Toledo, 1875-1940; Cleveland, 1855-1903; Cincinnati, 1852-1906; Peoria, 1905-54; and Springfield, 1906-52. Researchers are welcome to contact the staff of the Chicago Branch for information as to how to proceed with a search for these kinds of records. A special naturalization index that includes Chicago and Cook County is described later as part of another record group.

Apart from naturalizations, court records contain bankruptcy, civil, criminal, and admiralty case files, and dockets. These may be of interest to genealogists if any of their ancestors came in touch with the federal judicial system. Bankruptcy records in particular can be a rich source for family history, for example, listing all the assets and liabilities of the bankrupt. The Chicago branch holds those cases filed under the Federal Bankruptcy Acts of 1841 and 1867, and to a lesser degree, those under the Acts of 1898 and 1946. The court of origin should be contacted for a case number. Court records are arranged by court, type of record, and thereunder numerically by case.

·

The Immigration and Naturalization Service (RG 85) offers a superb Soundex index to all naturalizations, federal and local, occurring in old INS District 9. The district included northern Illinois from the Wisconsin border down through Henderson, Warren, Fulton, Tazewell, McLean, Champaign, and Vermillion Counties; northwest Indiana; southern and eastern Wisconsin; and eastern Iowa. The index spans 110 years, from 1840-1950 (except Cook County, coverage for which begins in 1871 due to the Chicago Fire). The staff of the Chicago branch will conduct searches in this index if provided with name, country of origin, approximate dates, and as much additional information as possible. Duplicates of Cook County naturalizations, 1871-1906, are held by the branch and may be photocopied.

Records of the General Land Office (RG 49) consist of applications to purchase and registers of cash certificates and sales. Volumes for Illinois date from 1814-85; Indiana, 1808-76; and Ohio, 1801-28; and they are arranged by land office, thereunder chronologically. Most are not indexed. There are scattered volumes for Michigan and Wisconsin. A note of caution to genealogists: these records are not donation land entry papers, homestead applications, or other land records one thinks of when land records are discussed in generic terms.

Among the more unusual or less frequently used records are those of the Internal Revenue Service (RG 58). As mentioned earlier, the Chicago branch has microfilm copies of Internal Revenue Service assessment lists for Illinois, 1862-66. This was a special tax levied to support the Union cause during the Civil War. In addition, the branch has bound volumes of tax assessment lists for the periods 1867-73 and 1910-18. The former consists exclusively of business or excise taxes, while the latter includes individual income tax lists. Excise tax lists generally give the name of the proprietor of the business, type of tax or the item subject to tax, assessed value, and amount of tax. Individual income tax lists may contain the name and address of the taxpayer along with amounts assessed and paid. These books are arranged by collection districts within the states for this region and chronologically by tax period. Taxpayers' names are entered alphabetically for each list. There are no name indexes, and the date span for a state may vary somewhat from the periods noted above.

Another unusual source is the Records of the Bureau of Marine Inspection and Navigation (RG 41). These records concern certificates of enrollment and licensing of commercial vessels and yachts; oaths taken by owners and masters, some giving naturalization information; records of mortgages and bills of sale of vessels; and correspondence regarding vessel documentation. Partially indexed by vessel name (not by individual), and arranged by port and thereunder chronologically, the Chicago branch holds records for Illinois, 1865-1952; Indiana, 1865-1968; Iowa, 1865-1939; Kentucky, 1851-1942; Michigan, 1831-1973; Ohio, 1850-1967; and Wisconsin, 1853-1954. These records mention names of owners and masters only, not crew lists.

There are records of genealogical interest among the manuscripts of the Bureau of Indian Affairs (RG 75). Perhaps the best way to describe these records is by subject matter. Census and annuity rolls for Michigan and Wisconsin tribes and reservations date from the 1880s, but mostly cover the early 1900s. They include the Oneida, Winnebago, Chippewa, Stockbridge and Munsee, Brotherton, and Potowatomie. Some are listed by agency, such as Bad River, Lac du Flambeau, and Red Cliff. Early rolls give Indian names only, some with the American equivalent. There are "Birth and Death Lists" for a few of the tribes that are similar to the census and annuity rolls. Reservation school records, primarily for Michigan and Wisconsin, range in date from the 1890s to the 1940s. They include admission cards and lists, attendance lists, and some family cards (names of students, parents, religion, and other data). Information varies with time period and school. In Michigan there is the Mt. Pleasant School; in Wisconsin, the Tomah Industrial School, Stockbridge Day School (1913-14 only), Hayward School, Neopit Day School of the Keshena Agency; and in Iowa, the Sac and Fox (1932-35 only). Among some school records are lists of employees, both Indian and white; faculty; and others. Hospital and health records, generally dating from the 1920s, exist; but access to them is restricted because of content and recent time period.

Some agency records include lists of employees, both Indian and white, giving name and type of job or position. Scattered throughout Bureau of Indian Affairs records are various files containing names but not subject to easy reference, as are census lists. Some examples are Indians employed in the Work Projects Administration and Indians who served during World Wars I and II.

The main problems in working with manuscripts created by federal agencies are the way in which they are arranged, usually by function as opposed to subject matter, and the lack of indexes in many cases. Knowledge of federal agencies and their functions is a definite plus. Yet, these obstacles should not deter genealogists from exploring and examining the records. Should genealogists, individually or by society, wish to assist other genealogists and the Chicago Branch by volunteering to index some of the records, their efforts would be welcome.

The staff does not conduct searches of records on microfilm, but will spend a reasonable amount of time on manuscript records based on the type of information provided by the researcher and the availability of indexes. There are no fees for use of the facility or for searches. Mail requests for photocopies carry a $5.00 minimum charge. Visitors on the premises are charged photocopying fees as posted in the microfilm reading room.

The Chicago branch does not participate in an interlibrary loan program, but certain National Archives microfilm publications are available on a rental basis through libraries and other institutions. Federal population census schedules, the Soundex indexes to the 1880, 1900, and 1910 censuses, and the Revolutionary War pension and bounty-land-warrant application files can be obtained from the Microfilm Rental Program, P.O.Box 2940, Hyattsville, Maryland 20784.

This Appendix was adapted from "Genealogical Resources" by Peter W. Bunce, Director, reprinted with permission *Illinois Libraries* 68, No. 4 (April 1986).

The Newberry Library

THE NEWBERRY LIBRARY
60 West Walton
Chicago, Illinois 60610
(312-943-9090)

Hours: 11:00 a.m. to 7:30 p.m. Tues.–Thurs.
       11:00 a.m. to 5:00 p.m. Friday

The Newberry Library, a landmark on the city's near north side extending along Walton between Dearborn and Clark Streets, is a mecca for scholars, students, and genealogists. Named for Walter Loomis Newberry, pioneer Chicago real estate speculator and philanthropist, its awesome collection consists of roughly 1.4 million volumes and five to six million manuscripts. In general, it is a reference library for history and the humanities. Its areas of specialization include: local and family history, the history of cartography, the American Indian, printing, music, and the Renaissance.

Newberry's treasures are world-famous. Over two thousand of its books were printed before 1500. Its European manuscripts date from the ninth century. Brahms, Mozart, Wagner, and Mendelssohn are among composers whose manuscripts are in the library's possessions, and its music collection is particularly strong in Renaissance items.

Notable, also, are materials collected by Edward E. Ayer on archaeology and ethnology of the North American Indian and the native races of the Philippines, Hawaii, and Mexico. The John M. Wing Foundation provided the library with a comprehensive collection on the history of bookmaking. The Midwest Manuscript Collection is relatively new and includes the personal papers of Sherwood Anderson, Victor Lawson, and Graham Taylor.

At a very early point in the Newberry's history, the library emphasized the acquisition of local and family history materials. This same emphasis in acquisitions continues to this day. The library is, perhaps, best known for this strength and probably fifty to sixty percent of its patrons are genealogical researchers.

The Newberry Library is not affiliated with the Chicago Public Library system, and no fees are charged for the use of the collection, even though the library receives no tax support. In order to receive a library card, one has only to show some form of current identification and fill out a short registration form. This is a noncirculating, closed stack library.

Geographical Scope of the Collection

The geographical scope of the local and family history collection is not limited to Chicago or Illinois or even the Midwest, although it is certainly strong in these areas. The library collects local history (county, town, church, etc.) for the United States and Canada. As for published record transcriptions (vital records, cemetery inscriptions, court abstracts, etc.), the Newberry basically collects such materials for the United States except for the Far West and the Deep South. It also collects them for Ontario, Quebec, and the Maritime Provinces.

The British Isles Collection of printed materials is also strong, consisting primarily of local histories and published county record series, such as the Yorkshire Parish Register series. Basic sources and guides are also available for continental European research. Most of the materials that can be used for continental research are confined to a treatment of nobility and heraldry.

It should be understood that the Newberry is primarily a printed book collection, although many of the newer acquisitions are in microform. The collection does not include original records such as vital statistics or manuscripts found with the county clerk or in state archives. Neither can you expect to find microfilmed copies or original records such as you might find at the L.D.S. branch libraries. What is available at the Newberry generally is a function of what has been printed. If your ancestors came from a county or town which has a publishing genealogical or historical society, there is a good chance that the Newberry Library will have something for you.

Genealogies and Vital Statistics

A collection of fifteen thousand family genealogies comprises an important segment of the local and family holdings. The collection of New England genealogies of the late nineteenth and early twentieth centuries is especially extensive.

In 1902, a Massachusetts law went into effect to promote the publication of Massachusetts town vital records. It provided that the state would purchase the first 500 copies of all such printed volumes. These records were published in a variety of contexts and the Newberry has most, if not all, of them. Much more recently, the Holbrook Institute has begun to reproduce on microfiche the original records of towns whose records had not been published under the old law. The Newberry has been acquiring this set. The Newberry also has other important New England microfilm sets, such as the Corbin Collection covering western and central Massachusetts and the Barbour and Hale Collections covering Connecticut.

Census Records

The Newberry Library does not have all of the microfilmed federal population census schedules for all states or all years. Only the 1810, 1820, and 1850 schedules are complete for all states and territories. However, an excellent representation of census indexes is conveniently located on the open shelf. Only population schedules for Illinois are available as a complete set to 1910. The Library has the 1900 Soundex, but not the 1910 Miracode for Illinois. In connection with Chicago census work, the Newberry has developed its own specialized finding aids. These are in the form of maps and are designed to locate Chicago residents in census schedules based on address alone. The obvious strategy is to obtain the address by consulting the Chicago directory for the corresponding year. The Newberry has a complete set of directories on file. The Local and Family History Section can respond to correspondence requesting information. Such requests are limited to three addresses at a time.

The Newberry Library also has some agricultural and mortality schedules. A few state censuses for Illinois and certain others are available on microfilm. State census schedules at the Newberry are incomplete, but there are substantial holdings for the 1855, 1875, 1905 and 1925 census for New York, the complete 1905 census for Wisconsin and the 1915 census for Iowa. There is also an increasing incidence of genealogical societies transcribing and indexing census schedules for a given year and the Library tries to collect these publications for Illinois.

Local Histories

Probably one of the greatest strengths of the Newberry collection lies in local history. It is still regarded as one of the best in the country. Volumes should be accessed by searching for the name of the county in the card catalogue. For New England, the researcher should also look up the name of the town. City directories are available from all over the United States, mostly from 1870 to 1920.

Biographical Sources

For the last several years, the Newberry's Local and Family History Section has been compiling a card index to all the biographical sketches appearing in a number of selected Chicago, Cook County, and Illinois histories published before 1930. In effect, a single search of the bibliography and industry file eliminates the need to search individually the seventeen titles which have been indexed in this fashion. The project is ongoing and will ultimately treat biographical sketches in at least twenty-five titles. Historical sketches of industries are also included in this file, but the bulk of the entries (over six thousand at present) refer to individuals. Correspondents may ask the staff to consult the file as long as such requests are limited to no more than three subjects per letter. Library patrons are free to consult the file in person. Multivolume biographical and genealogical works such as the *Dictionary of American Biography, Cyclopedia of American Biography,* and the *American Genealogical Index* are also available.

Maps, Atlases and Gazetteers

The Newberry is renowned for its collection of maps, atlases, and gazetteers. Although not a part of the local and family history collection per se, the map collection has great importance to genealogists. A recent development is the completion of the Newberry's collection of maps for Ireland. The Newberry is one of the only libraries in the country to possess a complete set in their original edition. In connection with that set, the library has a complete set of *Griffith's Valuation Lists* on microfiche.

Military Records

Military records of the American Revolution, War of 1812, and the Civil War are available in the form of published roster, pension records, and regimental histories.

Additional Sources

The library has lineage books, rosters, annual reports, periodicals and year books from patriotic and hereditary societies as well as some passenger list information for the years prior to 1820. The Genealogical Index of the Newberry Library, which is available at many libraries, is a massive compilation of family names taken from selected volumes in the Newberry Library. It is not a catalogue of the library's holdings, but is most useful as a clue finder for family history research. It was compiled from 1896 to 1918 and, therefore, contains no reference to any book published after 1918.

Genealogical Society of Utah Microfilmed Records

One of the most recent Newberry acquisitions is the International Genealogical Index (IGI). Formerly known as the Computer File Index, this microfiche lists names found in the computer of the Genealogical Department of the Church of Jesus Christ of Latter-day Saints (Genealogical Society of Utah). It does not include all known information about an individual, but uniquely identifies each person and gives a batch number that can be traced to the original input source.

For about eight years, the Genealogical Society of Utah has been engaged in microfilming records in the Chicago Metropolitan area. Through the efforts of the Council of Northeastern Illinois Genealogical Societies, the Newberry Library was designated the repository for the duplicate GSU microfilms of the nonofficial (those not created by a government agency) records. Genealogists and historians will welcome the news that the Roman Catholic Archdiocese of Chicago has become a participant in this consultation.

CEMETERIES IN METROPOLITAN CHICAGO AREA

AREA	NAME	PHONE	ADDRESS	TOWN	ZIP CODE	TOWNSHIP	COUNTY
North	Acacia Park	625-7800	7800 Irving Park Rd.	CHICAGO	60634	Norwood Pk.	Cook
North	All Saints	298-0450	700 N. DesPlaines River Rd.	DesPlaines	60016	Maine	Cook
North	All Saints Polish Natl. Cath.	825-3701	9201 Higgins Rd.	Chicago	60631	Leyden	Cook
West	Allerton Ridge	627-0070	Highland & Butterfield Rds.	Lombard	60148	York	DuPage
West	Archer Woods Memorial Park	839-8800	Keane Akve & 83rd St	Willow Springs	60480	Lyons	Cook
North	Arlington	832-2599	Euclid Ave.	Arlington Heights	600	Wheeling	Cook
West	Arlington Heights	362-1247	Lake St. & Frontage Rd.	Elmhurst	60126	Addison	DuPage
North	Ascension	758-4774	1920 Buckley Rd.	Libertyville	60048	Libertyville	Lake
South	Assumption	545-0044	19500 So. Cottage Grove	Glenwood	60425	Bloom	Cook
North	B'nai B'rith		6600 Addison St.	Chicago	60634	Jefferson	Cook
South	Bachelor's Grove		Midlothian Turnpike	Crestwood	60445	Bremen	Cook
North	Barrington Center		Old Dundee & Sutton Rds.	Barrington	60010	Barrington	Cook
North	Barrington Union		Algonquin Rd.	Barrington	60010	Barrington	Cook
North	Bartlett		North Ave.	Bartlett	60103	Hanover	Cook
South	Berger		1485 Sibley Blvd.	Dolton	60419	Thortnton	Cook
South	Bethania	458-2270	7701 Archer Ave.	Justice	60458	Lyons	Cook
West	Bethany Lutheran		123rd St.	Lemont	60439	Lemont	Cook
North	Bethel	588-6128	5800 No. Pulaski Rd.	Jefferson	60646	Jefferson	Cook
West	Beverly	385-0750	Kedzie Ave. at 120th St.	Blue Island	60406	Worth	Cook
South	Bloom Evangelical Lutheran		Volmer Rd.	Chicago Heights	60411	Bloom	Cook
South	Blue Island American Legion		127th St. & Highland Ave.	Blue Island	60406	Worth	Cook
North	Bluff City		Wright Ave. & Bluff City Rd.	Elgin	60120	Hanover	Cook
North	Bohemian National	539-8442	5255 No. Pulaski Rd.	Chicago	60630	Jefferson	Cook
West	Bronswood	323-0185	3805 Madison St.	Oak Brook	60521	York	DuPage
West	Brown, M. J. (private)		4400 W. 127th St.	Lemont	60439	Lemont	Cook
South	Burr Oak	233-5676	Between Division & Logan Sts.	Alsip	60658	Worth	Cook
North	Cady		Ela Rd.	Palatine	60067	Palatine	Cook
South	Calumet Park	219-769-8803	2305 W. 73rd Ave.	Merrillville, IN.	46410	Ross	Lake
South	Calvary		Steger Rd.	Steger	60475	Bloom	Cook
North	Calvary	864-3050	301 Chicago Ave.	Evanston	60202	Evanston	Cook
South	Calvary Cemetary & Crematory	219-762-8885	2701 J. Willowdale Rd.	Portage, IN.	46368	Portage	Porter
West	Cass (aka St. Patrick's)	767-4644	Poppelreiter Rd.	Argonne Nat'l Lab.	60439		
— —	Catholic Cemeteries Office	378-7373	1400 So. Wolf Rd.	Hillside	60162	Proviso	Cook
North	Cedar Park	785-8840	12540 So. Halsted St.	Chicago	60643	Calumet	Cook
South	Central Cemetery Co. of Ill.	238-7062	Harrison & Ridge Rds.	Niles	60648	Niles	Cook
South	Chapel Hill Gardens, South		5501 W. 111th St.	Worth	60482	Worth	Cook
West	Chapel Hill Gardens, West	261-1585	Rt. 83 & Roosevelt Rd.	Elmhurst	60126	York	DuPage

CEMETERIES IN METROPOLITAN CHICAGO AREA

AREA	NAME	PHONE	ADDRESS	TOWN	ZIP CODE	TOWNSHIP	COUNTY
South	Chapel Lawn Memorial Gardens	219-322-4441	1/2 mi. S. of US 30 on Cline	Schererville, IN.	46375	St. John	Lake
South	Chicago Burr Oak	233-5676	4400 W. 127th St.	Alsip	60658	Worth	Cook
— — —	Chicago Cemetery Association	445-6429	123rd & Kedzie Ave.	Blue Island	60406	Worth	Cook
South	Christ-Lutheran	349-0431	82nd Ave. & 147th St.	Orland Park	60462	Orland	Cook
North	City Cemetery (aka Lincoln Park)		North Ave. at Clark St.	Chicago	— — —	North	Cook
West	Clarendon Hills	968-6590	6900 So. Cass Rd.	Westmont	60559	Downers Grove	DuPage
South	Con. Kneseth Israel Cem. Fund	219-931-1312	7105 Hohman Ave.	Hammond, IN.	46324	North	Lake
West	Concordia	287-0878	7900 Madison St.	Forest Park	60130	Proviso	Cook
South	Concordia, Hammond	219-932-7437	6551 Calumet Ave.	Hammond, IN.	46324	North	Lake
South	Cong. A.D. Beth Hamedresh Hagadol		71st & Ellis Ave.	Chicago	60619	Hyde Park	Cook
South	Cong. Anshe Sholan (East Jewish)		71st & Ingleside Ave.	Chicago	60619	Hyde Park	Cook
South	Cooper's Grove (aka St. John's)	798-4131	183rd St. &	Tinley Park	60477	Rich	Cook
West	Danish		127th St.	Lemont	60439	Lemont	Cook
North	Dutton		Euclid Ave.	Arlington Heights	600	Wheeling	Cook
South	Ebenezer		162nd & Cicero Ave.	Oak Forest	60452	Bremen	Cook
North	Eden Memorial Park	678-1631	9851 Irving Park Rd.	Schiller Park	60176	Leyden	Cook
West	Elk Grove Cemetery Association		State Rd.	Elk Grove	600	Elk Grove	Cook
West	Elm Lawn	833-9696	401 E. Lake St.	Elmhurst	60126	Addison	DuPage
North	Elmwood	625-1700	2905 Thatcher Rd.	River Grove	60171	Leyden	Cook
South	Elmwood, Hammond	219-844-7077	1413 - 169th St.	Hammond, IN.	46324	North	Lake
North	Evangelical Lutheran		Telegraph Rd.				
North	Evangelical Lutheran (Immanuel)		Schaumburg Rd.			Schaumburg	Cook
South	Evang. Luth. Church of Blue Is.		127th St.	Alsip	60658	Worth	Cook
North	Evangelical Lutheran Immanuel		1850 W. Lake St.			Barrington	Cook
North	Evergreen		Hillside & Dundee Aves.	Glenview	60025	Northfield	Cook
South	Evergreen	776-8434	W. 87th St. & So. Kedzie Ave.	Evergreen Park	60642	Worth	Cook
West	Evergreen	839-8500	9100 So. Archer Ave.	Willow Springs	60480	Palos	Cook
West	Fairmount Hills	455-2714	900 No. Wolf Rd.	Melrose Park	60160	Leyden	Cook
South	Fairview Memorial Park	388-3377	4135 W. 127th St.	Alsip	60658	Worth	Cook
South	First Evangelist Lutheran						
South	First Reformed Church of Lansing		Ridge Rd. & Burnham Ave.	Lansing	60438	Thornton	Cook
West	Forest Home	287-0772	863 Desplaines Ave.	Forest Park	60130	Proviso	Cook
West	Free Sons	366-1190	1600 Desplaines Ave.	Forest Park	60130	Proviso	Cook
South	Gary Oak Hill	219-887-7339	4450 Harrison St.	Gary, IN.	46408	Calumet	Lake
North	German Lutheran	525-4038	3963 N. Clark St.	Chicago	60613	Lakeview	Cook

APPENDIX K

CEMETERIES IN METROPOLITAN CHICAGO AREA

AREA	NAME	PHONE	ADDRESS	TOWN	ZIP CODE	TOWNSHIP	COUNTY
North	Ger. Luth.–St. Paul & Emanuel	344-5600	3963 N. Clark St.	Chicago	60613	Lakeview	Cook
West	Glen Oak	Lake Ave.	Roosevelt & Oakridge Ave.	Hillside	60162	Proviso	Cook
North	Glen View			Glenview	60025	Northfield	Cook
North	Graceland	525-1105	4001 No. Clark Ave.	Chicago	60613	Lakeview	Cook
South	Greenland	219-874-5800	153 Tilden Ave.	Michigan City, IN.	46360	Michigan	LaPorte
West	Haas Park (see Waldheim)	366-1900	863 South DesPlaines Ave.	Forest Park	60130	Proviso	Cook
South	Hazel Green	388-2328	115th St. & 52nd Ave.	Alsip	60658	Worth	Cook
North	Hazelwood		Ridge Rd. & Halsted St.	Homewood	60430	Thornton	Cook
North	Hebrew Benevolent Society	348-6276	3919 N. Clark St.	Chicago	60613	Lakeview	Cook
North	Highland Memorial Park, Inc.	362-5260	Hunt Club Rd. & Rt. 120	Libertyville	60048	Warren	Lake
South	Holy Cross	862-5398	Mich. City Rd. & Burnham Ave.	Calumet City	60409	Thornton	Cook
South	Holy Sepulchre	445-2022	6001 W. 111 th St.	Worth	60482	Worth	Cook
South	Homewood Memorial Gardens	798-0055	600 Ridge Road	Homewood	60430	Thornton	Cook
West	I.O.O.F.		127th St.	Lemont	60439	Lemont	Cook
North	Immanuel Church		Kenilworth Ave.			Northfield	Cook
North	Immanuel Evangelical Lutheran		Schaumburg Rd.	Schaumburg		Hanover	Cook
South	Immanuel Evangelical Lutheran		Saulk Trail & Cicero Ave.	Richton Park	60471	Rich	Cook
West	Immanuel Evangelical Lutheran		22nd St. & Wolf Rd.	Hinsdale	60521	Proviso	Cook
North	Immanuel Lutheran		1850 W. Lake St.	Glenview	60025	Northfield	Cook
North	Independent (Jewish) (Keiger)		Main St. btw. Waukegan & Telegraph Rd.			Niles	Cook
North	Irving Park	625-3500	7777 Irving Park Rd.	Chicago	60634	Leyden	Cook
North	Jewish Graceland	348-6276	3919 No. Clark St.	Chicago	60613	Lakeview	Cook
West	Jewish Waldheim	366-4100	1800 So. Harlem Ave.	Forest Park	60130	Proviso	Cook
West	Jewsih Oakridge	344-5600	Roosevelt & Oak Ridge Avenue	Hillside	60162	Proviso	Cook
West	Joseph Barnett & Son, Inc.	366-2445	1400 So. Desplaines Ave.	Forest Park	60130	Proviso	Cook
South	Kneseth Israel	219-931-5380	5246 Hohman Ave.	Hammond, IN.	46320	North	Lake
West	La Grange	741-4040	Fifth Ave. & 27th St.	La Grange Park	60525	Proviso	Cook
North	Lake Street Memorial Park	366-1008	Rte. 1, Box 121	Elgin	60120	Hanover	Cook
West	Lebovitz Co., Inc.	445-5400	Desplaines & Roosevelt Rd.	Forest Park	60130	Proviso	Cook
South	Lincoln	458-0638	12200 So. Kedzie Ave.	Blue Island	60406	Worth	Cook
West	Lithuanian National	767-4644	Kean Ave. & 82nd St.	Willow Springs	60480	Lyons	Cook
West	Lower Cass (see St. Patrick's)		Poppelreiter Rd.	Argonne Nat'l Lab.	60439		Cook
South	Lutheran (Ebenezer)		165th & Cicero	Oak Forest	60452	Bremen	Cook
North	Lutheran Home for the Aged		Euclid Ave.	Arlington Heights	600	Wheeling	Cook

CEMETERIES IN METROPOLITAN CHICAGO AREA

AREA	NAME	PHONE	ADDRESS	TOWN	ZIP CODE	TOWNSHIP	COUNTY
North	Lyons, M.D.		3652 W. Irving Park Rd.	Chicago	60618	Jefferson	Cook
West	Lyonsville Cong. Church		Joliet & Wolf Rds.			Lyons	Cook
North	Maryhill	823-0982	8600 No. Milwaukee Ave.	Niles	60648	Maine	Cook
South	Matteson		Lincoln Hwy.	Matteson	60443	Rich	Cook
North	Memorial Estates, Inc.	455-2714	Wolf Rd. at Fullerton	Northlake	60164	Leyden	Cook
North	Memorial Park	583-5080	9900 Gross Point Rd.	Skokie	60076	Niles	Cook
West	Memory Gardens	763-8860	2501 E. Euclid Ave.	Arlington Hts.	60004	Wheeling	Cook
North	Menorah Gardens, Inc.	344-1094	2630 So. 17th Ave.	Broadview	60153	Proviso	Cook
North	Montrose	478-5400	5400 No. Pulaski Rd.	Chicago	60630	Jefferson	Cook
North	Mount B'nai B'rith	545-0044	6600 Addison St.	Chicago	60634	Jefferson	Cook
West	Mount Carmel	378-7373	1400 So. Wolf Rd.	Hillside	60162	Proviso	Cook
West	Mount Emblem	626-1332	Grand Ave. & County Line Rd.	Elmhurst	60126	Addison	DuPage
North	Mount Glenwood, South	758-5663	18301 Glenwood-Thornton Rd.	Glenwood	60425	Bloom	Cook
South	Mount Glenwood, West	839-8800	8301 Kean Ave.	Willow Springs	60480	Lyons	Cook
West	Mount Greenwood	233-0136	111th St. & California Ave.	Blue Island	60406	Worth	Cook
South	Mount Greenwood		115th St. & Fairfield Ave.	Chicago	60655	Worth	Cook
North	Mount Hope	371-2818	6600 Addison St.	Chicago	60634	Jefferson	Cook
North	Mount Isaiah Israel	545-0044	6600 Addison St.	Chicago	60634	Jefferson	Cook
North	Mount Jehoshua	545-0044	3600 No. Narragansett Ave.	Chicago	60634	Jefferson	Cook
North	Mount Jehoshua	545-0001	4401 W. Ridge Rd.	Gary, IN.	46408	Calumet	Lake
North	Mount Mayriv	219-980-2750	3800 No. Narragansett Ave.	Chicago	60634	Jefferson	Cook
North	Mount Mercy	545-0044	2755 W. 111th St.	Chicago	60655	Worth	Cook
South	Mount Olive	286-3770		Chicago		Jefferson	Cook
South	Mount Olive	238-4435		Chicago		Jefferson	Cook
South	Mount Olivet			Chicago		Worth	Cook
North	Mount Prospect		Mount Prospect	Mount Prospect		Wheeling	Cook
West	Mt. Auburn Memorial Park	749-0022	4101 Oak Park Ave.	Stickney	60402	Stickney	Cook
North	Mt. Olivet Mem. Park, Ltd.	872-5476	1436 Kenosha Rd.	Zion	60099	Benton	Lake
West	Mt. Vernon Mem. Estates, Inc.	257-7711	119th St. & Archer Ave.	Lemont	60439	Lemont	Cook
South	New Bachelor's Grove		195th St. & Oak Park Ave.			Bremen	Cook
North	New Light	673-1584	6807 E. Prairie Rd.	Lincolnwood	60645	Niles	Cook
North	North Northfield		Dundee Rd.			Northfield	Cook
North	North Side Cemetery		Chicago	Chicago	60631	Northfield	Cook
North	Northfield Union Church	631-3133	Milwaukee Ave.			Northfield	Cook
North	Norwood Park		6505 Northwest Highway	Chicago		Jefferson	Cook
South	Oak Forest (aka Potter's Field)		159th & Cicero Ave.	Oak Forest	60452	Bremen	Cook
South	Oak Hill	445-5401	11900 So. Kedzie Ave.	Chicago	60655	Worth	Cook
South	Oak Hill			Chicago		Worth	Cook
South	Oak Hill, Hammond	219-932-0206	227 Kenwood St.	Hammond, IN.	46324	North	Lake
West	Oak Ridge (Jewish)	344-5600	Roosevelt Rd.	Hillside	60162	Proviso	Cook

APPENDIX K

CEMETERIES IN METROPOLITAN CHICAGO AREA

AREA	NAME	PHONE	ADDRESS	TOWN	ZIP CODE	TOWNSHIP	COUNTY
North	Oak Woods		1035 E. 67th St.	Northfield	60093	Wheeling,	Cook
South	Oak Woods	288-3800	1035 E. 67th St.	Chicago	60637	Hyde Park	Cook
South	Oakglen		Ridge Rd.	Lansing	60438	Thornton	Cook
South	Oakland Memory Lanes	841-5800	15200 Lincoln Ave.	Dolton	60419	Thornton	Cook
South	Oaklawn		Ridge Rd. & Halsted St.	Homewood	60430	Thornton	Cook
West	Oakridge Jewish	344-5600	Roosevelt & Oakridge Ave.	Hillside	60162	Proviso	Cook
West	Oakridge-Glen Oak	626-4200	Roosevelt & Oakridge Ave.	Hillside	60162	Proviso	Cook
West	Old Settlers		St. Charles & Taft Rds.			Proviso	Cook
West	Order of Knights of Joseph		17th & DesPlaines Ave.	Forest Park	60130	Proviso	Cook
South	Orland German M.E. Church		84th Ave. & 171st St.	Tinley Park	60477	Orland	Cook
South	Orland Memorial Park		143rd St.	Orland Park	60462	Orland	Cook
West	Our Lady Of Sorrows	449-6100	1400 So. Wolf Rd.	Hillside	60162	Proviso	Cook
West	Palos Hills Memorial Gardens	257-7711	119th St. & Archer Ave.	Lemont	60439	Lemont	Cook
South	Palos Oak Hill	448-0606	8901 W. 131st St.	Palos Park	60464	Palos	Cook
West	Palos Oak Hills		131st.	Palos Park	60464	Palos	Cook
West	Parkholm	352-4143	2501 No. LaGrange Rd.	LaGrange Park	60525	Proviso	Cook
North	Plum Grove		Plum Grove Rd.			Palatine	Cook
South	Presbyterian		Chicago Rd. at 21st St.	Chicago Heights	60411	Bloom	Cook
West	Progressive Order of the West		16th St. & DesPlaines Ave.	Forest Park	60130	Proviso	Cook
West	Proviso Lutheran		Wolf Rd. & 22nd. St.	La Grange	60525	Proviso	Cook
West	Queen of Heaven	378-7373	1400 So. Wolf Rd.	Hillside	60162	Proviso	Cook
North	Randhill Park	274-2236	Rand Rd.(US 12) & Rt. 53	Palatine	60067	Wheeling	Cook
North	Reformed Church of Northfield		Pfingstan Rd.			Northfield	Cook
South	Restvale	236-4077	115th St. & Laramie Ave.	Worth	60482	Worth	Cook
West	Resurrection	767-4644	7200 So. Archer Ave.	Justice	60458	Lyons	Cook
North	Ridgelawn	824-4145	9900 No. Milwaukee Ave.	DesPlaines	60016	Maine	Cook
North	Ridgelawn Beth El	673-1584	5736 No. Pulaski Rd.	Chicago	60016	Jefferson	Cook
South	Ridgelawn, Gary	219-980-2750	4401 W. Ridge Rd.	Gary, IN.	46408	Calumet	Lake
North	Ridgewood		9900 N. Milwaukee Ave.	Des Plaines	60016	Maine	Cook
North	Rosehill	561-5940	5800 Ravenswood Ave.	Chicago	60660	Lakeview	Cook
North	Rosemont Park	736-2553	6758 W. Addison St.	Chicago	60634	Jefferson	Cook
North	Sacred Heart		905 Burr	Winnetka	60093	New Trier	Cook
South	Sag Bridge (aka St. James)		Archer Rd.			Lemont	Cook
North	Saint Adalbert	545-1508	6800 No. Milwaukee Ave.	Niles	60648	Niles	Cook
South	Saint Benedict	238-4435	4600 W. 135th St.	Crestwood	60446	Worth	Cook
North	Saint Boniface	561-2790	4901 No. Clark St.	Chicago	60640	Lakeview	Cook
South	Saint Casimir Lithuanian	239-4422	4401 W. 111th St.	Chicago	60655	Worth	Cook

CEMETERIES IN METROPOLITAN CHICAGO AREA

AREA	NAME	PHONE	ADDRESS	TOWN	ZIP CODE	TOWNSHIP	COUNTY
North	Saint Henry	561-2790	1929 W. Devon Ave.	Chicago	60660	Lakeview	Cook
West	Saint James at Sag Bridge	257-7000	Rts. 83 & 171	Lemont	60439	Lemont	Cook
South	Saint John, Hammond	219-884-9475	1547 - 167th St.	Hammond, IN.	46324	North	Lake
North	Saint Joseph	625-8416	Cumberland & Belmont Ave.	River Grove	60171	Leyden	Cook
South	Saint Joseph, Hammond	219-844-5762	167th St. & Indianapolis Blvd.	Hammond,IN.	46320	North	Lake
North	Saint Lucas	588-0049	5300 No. Pulaski Rd.	Chicago	60630	Jefferson	Cook
South	Saint Mary	238-3351	W. 87th & So. Hamlin Ave.	Evergreen Park	60642	Worth	Cook
South	Saint Michael	445-2022	159th St. & Will Cook Rd.	Orland Park	60462	Worth	Cook
North	Saint Michael the Archangel	397-3284	Algonquin & Roselle Rds.	Palatine	60067	Palatine	Cook
North	Salem Evang. Church of N. Am.		Plum Grove & Kirchoff Rds.	Rolling Meadows	60008	Palatine	Cook
North	Schaumburg Lutheran		Schaumburg Rd.	Schaumburg		Schaumburg	Cook
West	Schwarzbach's	366-4541	1700 So. Desplaines Ave.	Forest Park	60130	Proviso	Cook
North	Shalom Memorial Park	274-2236	Rand Rd. (US 12) & Rt. 53	Palatine	60067	Wheeling	Cook
West	Silverman & Weiss	378-2838	1303 So. Desplaines Ave.	Forest Park	60130	Proviso	Cook
South	Skyline Memorial Park	534-8256	U.S.54(1/4mi. S. of Junc. 50)	Monee	60449	Monee	Will
South	Sleepy Hollow Memorial Park		111th St. & Central Ave.	Worth	60482	Worth	Cook
West	Solomon C. Kelsy		119th St. & Will-Cook Rds.	Palos	60130	Palos	Cook
West	Sons and Daughters of Joseph	767-4644	Hwy 4A	Forest Park	60130	Proviso	Cook
South	Ss. Cyril & Methodius		1303 S. DesPlaines Ave.	Lemont	60439	Lemont	Cook
South	St. Alphonsus		212 Custer St.	Lemont	60439	Lemont	Cook
North	St. Andrews Ukrainian Orthodox	893-2827	22W347 Army Trail Rd.	Addison	60101	Bloomingdale	DuPage
South	St. Anne's		Sauk Trail & Kedzie Ave.	Richton Park	60471	Rich	Cook
South	St. Gabriel's		165th & Cicero Ave.	Oak Forest	60452	Bremen	Cook
South	St. James (Strassburg)		3430 S. Halsted	Steger	60475	Bloom	Cook
North	St. Johannes Evang. Luth.		Church Rd.			Elk Grove	Cook
North	St. John's Evang. Lutheran		Chicago, Elgin & Ridenberg Rds.			Schaumburg	Cook
West	St. John's Church		La Grange Rd. at 69th St.	Hodkins	60527	Lyons	Cook
North	St. John's Evang. Lutheran		Algonquin & Rosell Rds.	Palatine	60067	Palatine	Cook
North	St. John's Evang. Lutheran		Euclid Rd.	Palatine	60067	Palatine	Cook
North	St. Mary's		Old Buffalo Grove at Lake-Cook R.			Wheeling	Cook
North	St. Mary's Mission		Lee Rd.			Northfield	Cook
North	St. Mary's Training School		Waukegan & Willow Rds.			Northfield	Cook
West	St. Matthew's Evang. Luth.		129th St.	Lemont	60439	Lemont	Cook
North	St. Nicholas Ukrainian Cath.	825-1854	Higgins Rd.(E. of River Rd.)	Chicago	60631	Leyden	Cook
South	St. Paul's "Sedem Prairie"		Volmer Rd.			Rich	Cook
North	St. Paul's Evang. Lutheran		Russel & Henry St.	Mount Prospect	60056	Wheeling	Cook

APPENDIX K

CEMETERIES IN METROPOLITAN CHICAGO AREA

AREA	NAME	PHONE	ADDRESS	TOWN	ZIP CODE	TOWNSHIP	COUNTY
North	St. Paul's Evang. Lutheran		Harms Rd.			Niles	Cook
North	St. Peter's		8116 Niles Center Rd.	Skokie	60076	Niles	Cook
North	St. Peter's Evang. Lutheran		Harris Rd.	Northbrook	60062	Northfield	Cook
North	St. Peter's Evang. Lutheran					Niles	Cook
North	St. Peter's Evang. Lutheran		IrvingPark Blvd.			Schaumburg	Cook
North	St. Peter's Evang. Lutheran		Long Grove Rd.			Schaumburg	Cook
North	St. Peter's Lutheran					Palatine	Cook
North	Stressler					Northfield	Cook
North	Sunset Memorial Lawns	724-0669	3100 Shermer Rd.	Northbrook	60062	Northfield	Cook
South	Swan Lake Memorial Gardens	219-874-7520	5700 East U.S. Rt. 20	Michigan City, IN.	46360	Michigan	La Porte
South	Thorton Township		Ridge Rd.	Thorton	60476	Thorton	Cook
South	Tinley Park (aka Zion Luth.)		167th St.	Tinley Park	60477	Bremen	Cook
South	Tinley Park Memorial		84th Ave. & 171st St.			Orland	Cook
North	Town of Maine	823-3546	Dee Rd. & Touhy Ave.	Park Ridge	60068	Maine	Cook
South	Trinity Evangelical Lutheran		159th St. & Oak Park Ave.			Bremen	Cook
South	Trinity Lutheran		83rd St.			Lyons	Cook
North	Union		Smith St. & Kenilworth Ave.	Palatine	60067	Palatine	Cook
North	Union Ridge	631-0900	6700 Higgins Rd.	Chicago	60656	Jefferson	Cook
West	Waldheim		863 S. DesPlaines Ave.	Forest Park	60130	Proviso	Cook
South	Washington Memory Gardens	798-0645	701 Ridge Rd.	Homewood	60430	Thornton	Cook
North	Westlawn	625-8600	7801 W. Montrose Ave.	Chicago	60634	Norwood Park	Cook
North	Wheeling		W. Dundee Rd.	Wheeling	60090	Wheeling	Cook
North	Whites		Waukegan Rd. & Main St.	Niles	60648	Niles	Cook
West	Wilmer's Old Settlers	442-8500	Bryn Mawr Ave.	Forest Park	60130	Leyden	Cook
West	Woodlawn		7600 W. Cermak Rd.			Proviso	Cook
North	Wunders	525-4038	3963 No. Clark St.	Chicago	60613	Lakeview	Cook
South	Zion Church (aka Evang. Luth.)		Lincoln Hwy.	Matteson	60443	Rich	Cook

Index